# HOME BEFORE THE LEAVES FALL

OSPREY
PUBLISHING

In Memory of Henri-Alban-Fournier, author of *Le Grand Meaulnes* and Lieutenant in the 288 Régiment d'Infanterie. Killed in action in the Fôret de Calonne in the Eparges sector 22 September 1914, aged 27, and buried in the cemetery of St Rémy-la-Calonne.

And also of August Macke, member of the Blaue Reiter group of artists and Feldwebel Leutnant in Reserve-Infanterie-Regiment Nr 60.Killed in action at Perthes-les-Hurlus on 26 September 1914, aged 27, and buried in the military cemetery at Souain.

<blockquote>
As bronze may be much beautified<br>
By lying in the dark damp soil,<br>
So men who fade in dust of warfare fade<br>
Fairer, and sorrow blooms their soul.

*Wilfred Owen*
</blockquote>

# HOME BEFORE THE LEAVES FALL

A New History of the
German Invasion of 1914

IAN SENIOR

First published in Great Britain in 2012 by Osprey Publishing
Midland House, West Way, Botley, Oxford, OX2 0PH
44-02 23rd Street, Suite 219, Long Island City, NY, 11101, USA

E-mail; info@ospreypublishing.com

Osprey Publishing is part of the Osprey Group

A CIP catalogue record for this book is available from the British Library

ISBN: 978 1 84908 843 5
PDF Ebook ISBN: 978-1-78096-865-0
EPUB ISBN: 978-1-78096-866-7

Page layout by Myriam Bell Design, UK
Cartography by Peter Bull Art Studio
Index by Alison Worthington
Cover and plate section originated by PDQ Media, Bungay, UK
Printed in China through Worldprint Ltd

12 13 14 15 16    10 9 8 7 6 5 4 3 2 1

Osprey Publishing is supporting the Woodland Trust, the UK's leading woodland conservation charity,
by funding the dedication of trees.

**www.ospreypublishing.com**

Front cover: The German infantry on the offensive during the First World War. (Corbis)
Back cover: 'En route to Berlin'. These French troops from the administrative sections of XIV Corps,
photographed just prior to the battle of the Marne, would never get anywhere near the German
capital. (Courtesy of Ian Sumner)

# CONTENTS

# LIST OF MAPS

# LIST OF PHOTOGRAPHS

# INTRODUCTION

O
n 18 January 1871, in a lavish and elaborately choreographed ceremony in the Hall of Mirrors at Versailles, Prussia celebrated its victory in the Franco–Prussian War and King Wilhelm I was proclaimed Emperor of a united Germany. After a peaceful interlude which lasted for more than 40 years, in the first week of August 1914 the two adversaries went to war once more in a conflict that this time engulfed the other great European powers. During the intervening period, the parameters that governed warfare were transformed as a consequence of accelerating technological and economic change. Firstly, armies increased more than fivefold in size because of rapid population growth (Germany's population, for example, increased by 17 per cent between 1890 and 1914), they required far greater quantities of equipment, food and ammunition and their deployment necessitated an elaborate and costly rail network (not all of whose lines were suitable for civilian traffic). This put an enormous strain on military budgets, especially in Britain and Germany which towards the end of the period became locked into an enormously expensive naval race. Secondly, new and improved weapons made the battlefield a much more lethal environment, especially during an assault against prepared positions. With the advent of more powerful rifles, the 'zone of death' which separated the attacking infantry from the enemy's lines increased from about 300 metres during the Franco–Prussian War to approximately 1,500 metres in 1914. At the same time, the situation was exacerbated by the appearance of the machine gun, with a range of up to 2,000 metres and a rate of fire greater than 500 rounds a minute. Likewise, the effectiveness of artillery

underwent a steep change in the last years of the 19th century fuelled by developments in metallurgy and chemistry that resulted in more powerful guns, able to hurl their shells over far greater distance than during the Franco–Prussian War, and by the invention of the recoil mechanism during the 1890s which greatly increased the rate and accuracy of fire. (The famous 75mm French field gun, or *soixante-quinze* as it was generally known, could fire at up to 15 rounds a minute and with increased accuracy because it remained completely steady during firing and therefore did not need to be repositioned between each round.) As a result of these changes many well-informed commentators began to suspect that the task of capturing the enemy positions by assault would be too great for even the most highly trained and well-led infantry, despite high morale and excellent artillery support. When these facts received wide attention in the two decades before 1914, the idea took firm hold that wars in the future would have to be short (or might even be impossible altogether) because the human, social and economic costs would be too great to beat.

This point of view was most strongly expressed by the Polish banker and pacifist, Jan Bloch, whose enormous six-volume book, *The Future of War in its Technical, Economic and Political Aspects,* was translated into German in 1899. Although the German military establishment did its best to pick holes in Bloch's arguments, his ideas were well-received and were repeated in a more digestible form in articles in learned journals and in books for a wider audience by authors such as the English Professor, Norman Angell. Although the events of 1914 were to prove Bloch and his adherents wrong, the illusion of the short war permeated all levels of society and all walks of life, from the politicians at the top, to the generals in charge of planning and preparing for the campaign, down to the ordinary man and woman in the street. The plans with which the Germans and the French went to war (the Schlieffen-Moltke Plan and Plan XVII respectively) were therefore based on rapid deployment, on seizing the strategic initiative and on attacking the enemy without delay. The importance of stealing a march on one's opponents and striking the first blow was the paramount factor which governed their strategic thinking.

It is hardly surprising therefore that almost everyone, soldiers and civilians alike, firmly believed that the fighting would be over within a few months and that the troops would be home in time for Christmas. (On the British side, the only important figure to voice his misgivings was the newly appointed Minister for War, Lord Kitchener, who startled his incredulous colleagues by suggesting that the war would last for at least three years and that it was vitally important to recruit a large number of volunteers who would need between one to two years training before they were battle-worthy.) In Berlin, Kaiser Wilhelm II (whose second son, Prince Einzel Friedrich, was in command of the elite 1st Regiment of Foot Guards) said farewell to units of the Prussian Guard as they were about to leave for the front, telling them that they would soon be victorious and would return before the leaves fell. Likewise, officers in the British Expeditionary Force told their loved ones that they would be home before Christmas while those who were left behind pulled all the strings they could in a desperate effort to join their comrades in France before the fighting came to an end. In both France and Germany the troops who enthusiastically chalked *à Berlin* or *nach Paris* on the sides of their troops trains as they set out for the front never thought for one moment that it would last for over four years and that very few of them would be alive and uninjured when it finally came to an end.[1]

To begin with, it must have seemed to many Germans that the Kaiser had been right and that their men folk would indeed return home in time to celebrate Christmas with them. After an initial delay when it took four days longer than expected to seize the strategically important city of Liège (the bottleneck through which the right wing had to pass at the start of the campaign), by the end of August the French armies had been defeated all along the frontier. As far as the German High Command was concerned, the war was as good as won. Less than two weeks later, however, the Germans were defeated in the battle of the Marne and the campaign which had held out so much promise only a short time earlier ended in defeat. Far from being over by December, the war dragged on for another four years, confounding the predictions of Bloch and his supporters but vindicating Lord Kitchener and a few other similarly prescient individuals in Britain and elsewhere. By the end of 1914, the French and German armies had each suffered around three quarters of a million casualties, a substantial proportion of which took place during the approximately three-week-long campaign. To put this into context, German casualties in the five-month-long Franco-Prussian War amounted to approximately 90,000 wounded and 28,000 dead. The aftermath of the five-day long battle of the Marne was described by an anonymous French soldier, who left a vivid description of his part of the battlefield immediately after the fighting was over and before there had been time to clear away the human debris.

On the right bank of the Marne, on the gentle rolling hills beyond, the German resistance had taken on a terrible form. They had built a long row of firing trenches along the edge of the river valley and had constructed numerous covered artillery positions under the protection of the woods. The country in front of their infantry positions was completely open.

We left the valley and reached the edge of the plateau, which was barred by the German trenches. We were presented with a terrible picture, full of horror and yet at the same time impressive. The wide plateau was saturated with corpses. They were French. Hundreds and hundreds of human bodies lay there, as far as the eye could see. Further out, in the hazy distance to the right and left, on the golden stubble of the fields, there extended this mown-down human harvest. Where the plateau ended on either side, the dead appeared only as short, irregular dashes, which formed a long winding line, fading in the distance, diminished and grew blurred. They all lay pointing the same way, like the stalks of mown grass. Death had taken them by surprise during a furious attack. They had fallen in an extended line, all facing the front. Not a single one of them had been inactive at the point when they were overtaken by death. As they lay there, unified in death, they had something great and emotional about them. The corpses were all pointing towards the enemy, their heads facing forwards. One thought, one will, one emotion must have filled them all and given them strength in this final moment. They must have fallen like a hail of swiftly flying arrows, suddenly halted in mid flight.

Almost all of the dead lay there with open mouths, their leaden gaze facing the ground, hit in the forehead or chest. They were stretched out in the unnatural, peculiar and awkward positions which death often gives to the fallen on the field of battle. Several, who had only been wounded at first, had found the time to lie more comfortably as they awaited their end; it seemed as if they were asleep. In front of each corpse lay a rifle which had slipped out of its owner's hand. Their thin bayonets had churned up the earth.

The French attack had begun about seven to eight hundred metres from the German firing line. We could follow its progress exactly enough, more or less as if we had watched it taking place. Notwithstanding their appalling losses, with a wild howling the French masses would have stormed forwards under the hellish fire. Here and there, the German shrapnel had set haystacks on fire, the remains of which were still smoking. However, the German artillery must have stopped their devastating fire just as suddenly as they began it in the first place. From approximately one hundred and fifty metres in front of the trenches there were no more corpses. The enemy had suddenly made off.

When we crossed this area, we came across yet more bodies. This time they were German. On the edge of a wide path their corpses told of a harsh hand-to-hand fight, man against man. A group of German fighters, who had been left behind on their own at an abandoned outpost, had used the road embankment as a breastwork, and had remained there, continuously firing from between the two road ditches. They had been unable to retreat any further and had held out for as long as they could; the last of the fallen French were only three metres in front of them. Then the attack overran them and they were destroyed. The small band of men had fallen, pierced by the enemy bayonets. The many bent bayonets that lay around the place, and the shattered rifle butts, bore witness to the short, violent and desperate struggle which had taken place here. At the front was the NCO who commanded the group; in death, he seemed to be commanding them still.

The Germans had fallen more in concentrated masses, each group of dead was crowded around the corpse of their dead officer. The German retreat had been covered by the sacrifice of this small band of men. In their death, the two sides had become equal; only their uniforms distinguished the one from the other. French and Germans lay stretched out together where they had fallen. The characteristics of each race were no longer apparent from the wild masks of the corpses. So the fallen enemy had been embraced by a sort of brotherhood in death.[2]

There is no doubt that the Marne Campaign of 1914 had a decisive impact on the course of European history. In the early summer of 1940, after a Blitzkrieg offensive by the Germans, France was knocked out of the Second World War and the British were left on their own to lick their wounds and prepare for the long haul; in 1914, however, an equally audacious plan ended in a German defeat and condemned Europe to four years of bloody warfare and a social and economic upheaval which blighted world politics for the next two decades and which led indirectly to the Second World War. Although the French Government in 1914 was much stronger than in 1940, when cabinets came and went with an alarming frequency, and the nation was firmly united and not riven by political strife as it was between the two world wars, it is nevertheless highly likely that a German victory in the late summer of 1914 would have caused the French Government to capitulate. In turn, this would have caused the British to return home and the war might have come to a sudden end.

This book begins with an account of the war plans of the two major protagonists, the Schlieffen–Moltke Plan for the Germans and Plan XVII for the French, and describes their evolution in the two decades before the war. This is followed by a day-to-day account of the campaign from the third week in August, when the two sides clashed for the first time along the French–Belgian border, until 9 September, when the German right wing broke off the fight at the battle of the Marne and retreated to a defensive position along the River Aisne. The narrative focuses on events on the German right wing since it was here that the outcome of the campaign was determined. After the French 5th Army was defeated in the battle of Charleroi between 21 and 23 August it began a fortnight-long retreat, interrupted only by the battle of Guise on 29 August, whose purpose was to take the pressure off the British Army. The battle of the Marne, which began on 5 September and lasted for almost five full days, was in reality two separate but interlinked actions, which took place approximately 50 miles apart. (It was named after the River Marne because this was roughly equidistant between the two battlefields.) In the battle of the Ourcq, which was fought near Meaux to the north-east of Paris, the German 1st Army was attacked by the newly formed French 6th Army which threatened to take them in the flank as they advanced into northern France. At the same time, in the battle of the Petit Morin the German 2nd Army was involved in a vicious fight with the French 5th and 9th Armies along a 60-mile front in the region of Sézanne to the south-east of the French capital. After four days of inconclusive combat on both battlefields, the end came on the evening of 9 September when the British penetrated the imperfectly defended gap between the two German armies, forcing them to retreat before they were attacked in the flank and rear.

The reader will not find a great deal in these pages about the British Army, firstly, because it played only a minor role in the campaign (by early September there were only five British divisions in the field compared to 28 divisions in the three armies of the French left wing), and secondly, because the two major actions in which it took part, the battles of Mons and Le Cateau, have been extensively described elsewhere. While the British contribution was certainly not negligible, the French bore the brunt of the fighting and were almost single-handedly responsible for defeating the Germans. (Of the six battles that took place, four of them – Charleroi, Guise, the Ourcq and the Petit Morin – involved only the French.) The battle of Mons was not, as several British accounts have claimed, a crucially important battle which led to the Allied victory; on the contrary, although it took the German 1st Army by surprise and gave them a nasty shock, it was a small-scale affair compared to the battle of Charleroi which took place at the same time and it only delayed the Germans by a single day. (To put this into perspective, whereas total British casualties at Mons numbered about 1,600, during the battle of Charleroi one regiment alone, the 2nd Zouaves, lost 720 officers and men.) On the other hand, the battle of Le Cateau which took place a few days later was very significant since a defeat here would probably have caused the British Commander-in-Chief, Sir John French, to withdraw his army from the Allied line, thereby preventing the planned counter-offensive from taking place. The fact that the British held on all day despite being outnumbered and then escaped more or less unscathed meant that two weeks later, during the battle of the Marne, they were able to advance into the gap between the German armies on the right wing, thus bringing about their defeat.

The final chapter investigates the reasons that the Germans lost the campaign. Although the German Commander-in-Chief, Moltke the Younger, cannot be completely exonerated, and although serious mistakes were made by Kluck and Bülow who commanded the German 1st and 2nd Armies respectively, it is argued that the plan which Moltke inherited from his distinguished predecessor as Chief of the German General Staff, Alfred von Schlieffen, contained serious and intractable flaws which made defeat inevitable. The plan was extremely audacious but as it was, with a supply system stretched to breaking point, extensive damage to the French and Belgian railways, a lack of motorized infantry and an inadequate signals communication system, it was bound to fail. In short, Schlieffen's strategy, embodied by the eponymous plan that he passed on to Moltke when he retired in 1905, was responsible for losing the campaign and condemned his countrymen to four years of war and eventual defeat.

The ranks of officers and men are given in the original language and so a table of equivalent ranks is given in Appendix 2 to help those readers who are unfamiliar with the foreign names. With the exception of regiments belonging to the Guard Corps, all active German regiments are given the prefix IR (for Infanterie Regiment) *followed* by their number. Each regiment contained three battalions which are given Roman numerals, I, II and III and so II Battalion Infanterie Regiment Nr 66 is written as II/IR66, etc. For historical reasons, some line regiments were designated Grenadier or Füsilier regiments; for the sake of simplicity these are also shown as IR in the text. The Guard Corps (which belonged to 2nd Army) contained the 1st and 2nd Guards Infantry Divisions; the former was composed of four regiments of so-called Foot Guards and the second of four Guard-Grenadier regiments named after rulers or their consorts (Kaiser Franz, Kaiser Alexander, Königin Augusta and Königin Elisabeth). Thus, the I Battalion of the 2nd Guard-Grenadier Regiment Kaiser Franz is abbreviated to I/Franz and so on. Similarly, French regiments are given the letters RI (for Régiment d'Infanterie) *preceded* by their number. As in the German Army, active regiments contained three battalions and which are likewise given Roman numerals. Hence the III Battalion of the 2e (2nd) Régiment d'Infanterie is shown as III/2e RI. All German reserve regiments are referred to as RIR for Reserve Infanterie Regiment. French reserve regiments were not designated as such but were given higher numbers than the active ones. German Jäger infantry were highly trained marksmen formed into battalions that were attached to larger units. German Pioniers were the equivalent of Sappers in the British Army and Engineers in the French Army and their principal tasks during the campaign were building, repairing or blowing up bridges, constructing fortifications and so on. Details of nomenclature are given in Appendix 1 showing orders of battle.

Readers should also note that the German and French Armies operated according to different time zones. The Germans used Central European Time which was one hour in advance of French time. For the sake of consistency French time is used throughout the book except for direct quotations from German sources in which the original is retained. Lastly, it is important to avoid potential confusion due to the fact that the French and British Armies changed direction twice during the campaign (facing north at the start, south during the retreat and north once more during the battle of the Marne). Thus, in these armies the right wing is *always* on the east and the left wing *always* on the west, whatever the direction of march. (The simplest way is perhaps to think of them marching backwards as they retreated.)

My thanks are due to my editors at Osprey Publishing, Marcus Cowper and Emily Holmes, for their help in guiding a novice like myself through the publishing process and to Ian Drury, my agent at Shiel Land Associates, for making several invaluable suggestions for alterations and in particular for deciding on a suitable title. Thanks are also due to my wife, Astrid Senior, for checking my translations from the French and likewise to Mr Mark Stickings for help in translating the German accounts of the fighting and also for his eagle-eyed proofreading. In addition, I am enormously grateful to Mr Ovidiu Precup who gave invaluable assistance in overcoming numerous Word programming problems. Last, but by no means least, I would like to thank my friends in the Common Room at Dulwich College for their support and encouragement and in particular to my colleagues in the Biology Department in which I have been a somewhat semi-detached member during the time it has taken to write this book.

# 1

# THE SCHLIEFFEN-
# MOLTKE PLAN

Metaphorically speaking, the long road that led to the battle of the Marne began in the massive red brick building on the northern side of Berlin's Königsplatz that housed Germany's Great General Staff. It was in this building, adjacent to the Reichstag and facing the famous victory column that commemorated the Wars of Unification, that Alfred von Schlieffen, Chief of the General Staff for almost 14 years, developed the strategy that was used for the invasion of France in the summer of 1914.[1]

Schlieffen was born in 1833 into a family of noble origin, especially on his mother's side. Through his father he inherited a long tradition of military service; from his mother he acquired the seriousness of purpose, the fervent love of order and the life-long habit of hard work that characterized the Hutterite evangelical sect to which she and her mother belonged. As was common practice at the time, his career alternated between regimental and General Staff posts. After graduating from the Prussian War Academy in 1861, he spent the next 14 years in the Great General Staff in Berlin during which time he took part in the wars against Austria and France, although without seeing action. Having gone back to regimental duties in 1875, he served as commanding officer of the prestigious 1st Guard Uhlan Regiment until 1883, when he returned to the General Staff in Berlin. From now on his rise was rapid and culminated in February 1891 in his appointment as Chief of the General Staff in place of Waldersee whom the Kaiser had dismissed for his political intrigues and for openly criticising his performance

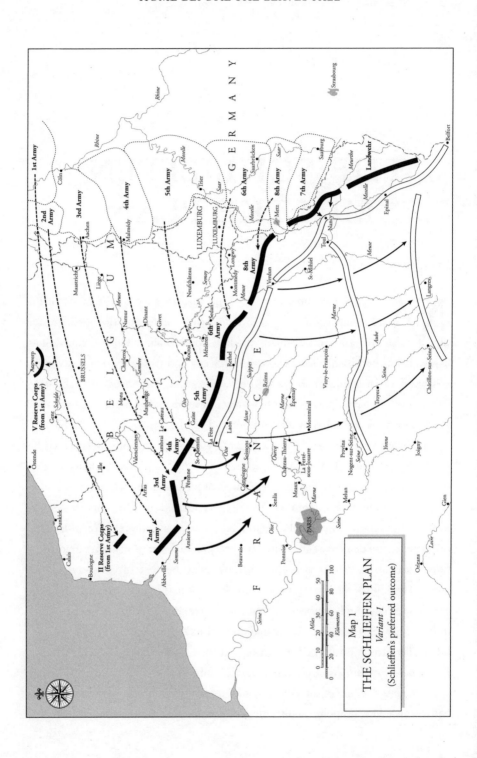

Map 1

THE SCHLIEFFEN PLAN
*Variant 1*
(Schlieffen's preferred outcome)

in the annual manoeuvres. Whereas Schlieffen's severe and unbending character and his unremitting industry and attention to detail inspired tremendous respect in his immediate subordinates, to the more junior officers in the General Staff he was a remote figure, a hard taskmaster whose sarcastic and biting comments were greatly feared by anyone whose work fell short of his exacting standards. Although his word was law within the Königsplatz building, and his pronouncements on strategy were treated almost as holy writ, outside the narrow confines of the General Staff his ability to shape the country's military policy and to prepare the army for war was quite limited. This was because the process for taking military decisions in Wilhelmine Germany involved not only the Chief of the General Staff but also the Prussian Minister for War, the commanding generals of the 23 peacetime army corps and the Kaiser and his Military Cabinet, all of whom had their own agendas to pursue and who tended to operate in a climate of mutual distrust. The Minister for War, for example, was responsible not only for the army's equipment and weapons (including the artillery) but also for setting the annual military budget and presenting it to Parliament for their approval. As a result, he was in a position to deny the funds which were needed to increase the size of the army, to develop new weapons and to modernize and expand fortifications, all of which Schlieffen insisted were necessary to implement his ambitious plans. In some cases Schlieffen got his way, as with the introduction of the mobile heavy howitzers (the so-called foot artillery) and the improvements made to the fortifications at Metz. Even so, the shortage of money delayed the widespread introduction of the heavy artillery and limited the work at Metz to the construction of a few new forts and the updating of several others. Worse still, Schlieffen's repeated demands for the immediate creation of seven new army corps were rejected in favour of a massive expansion of the navy (a project dear to the Kaiser's heart) and the best that he could obtain was a promise to create five new corps on the outbreak of war.[2]

The second power base within the military establishment was occupied by the corps commanders who wielded huge influence within the army and who possessed the enormously valuable right of immediate access to the Kaiser (*Immediatrecht*), which enabled them to put forward their views without the Chief of the General Staff being present. In addition, several of them espoused strategic doctrines which were different from Schlieffen's and which they disseminated by means of articles in military journals and in pamphlets and books. (Bernhardi's book, *War in the Future*, found a wide audience, not only in Germany but also in Britain and in France.) Furthermore, the fact that the corps commanders had sole responsibility for training the men under their command made it very difficult for Schlieffen to impose his tactical doctrines on the army as a whole.

Thirdly, Schlieffen had to contend with the Kaiser and his Military Cabinet. In wartime, the Kaiser was nominally Commander-in-Chief by virtue of his hereditary position as Supreme War Lord (Oberster Kriegsherr), while in peacetime the power of command vested in him as Emperor enabled him to shape the military decisions taken in his name. In addition to appointing and dismissing the Chancellor, the Minister for War and the Chief of the General Staff he could initiate changes in the size and administration of the army, its training and its equipment, providing that the Minister for War approved the necessary expenditure.

However, Wilhelm's mercurial nature and his inability to concentrate on one task for any length of time prevented him from interfering with the day-to-day running of the army, much to the relief of successive Chiefs of Staff and War Ministers. On the other hand, he did have a detrimental effect on the conduct of the annual manoeuvres (the *Kaisermanöver*), which took place in the autumn of each year and which represented Schlieffen's only opportunity to test his tactical doctrines on large bodies of troops. The manoeuvres usually involved a contest between two army corps. Unfortunately, the Kaiser's insistence on taking part turned them into an embarrassing spectacle, completely unsuited to any serious military purpose. Since he was not content with watching passively from the sidelines, it had become his habit to take direct part on the final day of the fighting when he led 'his side' to victory at the head of a staged and completely unrealistic mass cavalry charge. Although in private Schlieffen was scathing about this grotesque interference, he made no attempt to prevent the Kaiser from taking part, even though he was condemned by his fellow generals for what they regarded as his supine acceptance of the situation. (No doubt he was mindful that his predecessor had been dismissed for speaking out about it.)

In his involvement in military affairs, the Kaiser was advised by his Military Cabinet, which acted as a channel to the other military agencies, including the

War Ministry and the General Staff, and which had a stranglehold over the promotion of senior officers. At a time when a close personal relationship with the Emperor was the key to acquiring influence, the Chief of the Military Cabinet was a tremendously powerful figure, answerable not to Parliament but directly to the Kaiser with whom he was in close and daily contact. (In addition to his own one-to-one meetings, he had the right to be present at meetings between the Kaiser and other holders of this privilege, including the Chief of the General Staff.) Since the Kaiser and his Military Cabinet were in a position to control the appointment and promotion of all officers within the Prussian Army, including those at the very highest level, neither Schlieffen nor his successor, Moltke the Younger, were able to choose the generals who would execute their plans once war had broken out. Furthermore, this system occasionally led to the promotion of generals whose strategic doctrines differed from Schlieffen's, such as Karl von Bülow, who firmly believed that there was still a place for the frontal attack on the modern battlefield and whose 2nd Army was to play a pivotal role in the campaign.

Despite these limitations to his power, the Chief of the General Staff was a figure of very great consequence within the military hierarchy of Wilhelmine Germany. In wartime he would become the Commander-in-Chief not only of the Prussian Army but also of the Bavarian, Saxon and Württemberg contingents, each of which had its own General Staff, and several of his section heads would serve as his senior staff officers. In peacetime his principal task was to formulate strategy and to oversee the production of the annual war plan (the *Aufmarschweisungen* or deployment directives) which came into effect on 1 April each year and which gave detailed instructions for the mobilization, deployment and initial movements of the army. In addition to war planning, he was also responsible for the selection and training of staff officers, running the War Academy, organizing annual manoeuvres and overseeing work on military history.[3] Having expanded considerably during Schlieffen's time in office, when he retired at the end of 1905 the General Staff consisted of approximately 600 officers of whom about two thirds belonged to the Great General Staff, which was housed in the building on the Königsplatz, and one third to the Troop General Staff which consisted of officers who were seconded to divisional and corps headquarters. Every few years, officers rotated between the two branches so that they would obtain experience at all levels, both in the field and at the office desk.

Within the Königsplatz building the Great General Staff operated like a hugely efficient and well-oiled machine. (So much so that according to some commentators it was one of only five perfect European institutions, along with the French Opera, the Russian Ballet, the Papal Curia and the British Parliament.) It was organized around several semi-autonomous sections (15 on the outbreak of the war) of which the most important by far was the 2nd Section, responsible for the development of the annual mobilization and deployment plan. Together with the attached Railways Department (which had the mammoth task of planning the troop movements during mobilization) this was the largest section and its head reported to the Chief of the General Staff several times a week rather than just once a week like all the others. Furthermore, on the outbreak of war its head would accompany the Chief of Staff to Supreme Headquarters and act as his Operations Officer. The work of the 2nd Section, and to a lesser extent that of the so-called Language Sections which gathered non-covert intelligence about foreign armies, revolved around the mobilization year (*Mobilmachungsjahr*) that ended on 1 April when the new war plans were issued. When this enormous task was over, workflow rapidly declined and the spring and summer months (the summer half) were a relatively quiet time during which new staff officers began their probationary period and war games and staff rides were carried out.

Each year, usually once in late springtime and once in early autumn, Schlieffen chose approximately 30 senior and middle-ranking staff officers to accompany him on an extended staff ride through a carefully selected area adjacent to the border with either France or Russia. At the start of the ride they were divided into two sides and given the initial strength and disposition of their own force together with a limited amount of information about the enemy. When each side had analysed the situation and developed a strategic plan, the game was played out over the next fortnight or so during which time they spent many hours in the saddle, moving along the border and pausing only to be brought up to date with the situation and to issue new orders. At the end of the ride, Schlieffen held a conference in which he passed judgment on the plans and their execution in the form of a written exercise critique. The purpose of the staff rides was twofold;

firstly, they enabled Schlieffen to test his strategy by seeing how well it would stand up to a variety of operational stresses and strains and secondly, they played an important role in the training of the more junior participants by testing their operational skills in the field and by subjecting their decisions to the judgment of their peers and to the Chief of Staff himself. Although the rides took place on German territory and the psychological pressure of battle was missing, they got as close as possible to the reality of war since decisions were taken after a long and exhausting day in the saddle and in real time extended over several weeks.[4]

In the winter half, which ran from late autumn until the end of the following March, activity picked up rapidly as work began in earnest on next year's war plan. In mid-November, by which time he had an accurate picture of the army's man-power, Schlieffen decided on the broad outlines of the deployment and informed the head of the Railways Department whose task it was to develop the enormously complicated transport plan. From now on, until the end of the mobilization year the following April, the 2nd Section was a hive of activity as it absorbed a wealth of information from the Language Sections, supplemented by covert intelligence from Oberst Nikolai's Section 3B, and worked out the details of the deployment in conjunction with the Railways Department. Everything possible was done to keep the whole process secure; documents were classified according to levels of secrecy and were issued on a need-to-know basis in order to prevent all but the most senior officers gaining an overview of the plan. In particular, once the new plans had been issued on 1 April all copies of the previous ones were burnt in the ovens of the state bakery, together with all of the associated paperwork. Sensitive documents were locked away when not in use, the two entrances to the building were guarded around the clock and sentries kept a 24-hour watch at the entrance to the 2nd Section because of fears that foreign agents might have infiltrated the building. Outsiders were few and far between; there were no secretaries (since there were very few typewriters in the building all documents were written out, longhand) and apart from the cleaners it was an exclusively male world. Although there were very few telephones in the building, instantaneous contact with the outside world was maintained by the central communications office adjacent to the main entrance, which was connected to the networks of the Berlin Post Office and the Main Telegraph Office. It was from this office, which was manned 24 hours a day, 365 days a year, that the message would be sent to district commands telling them that war had been declared and that mobilization was to take place immediately.

When Schlieffen became Chief of the General Staff in 1891 he inherited a deployment plan that had undergone almost no modifications since it had been developed by Moltke the Elder in the years following the Franco–Prussian War. According to this, the army would be split in two, approximately one third on the Eastern Front facing Russia and two thirds in the West against France, and used to fight simultaneous campaigns. Instead of seeking a rapid and decisive victory on either front, which he thought would not be possible, Moltke hoped to achieve limited territorial gains that would act as a powerful bargaining counter when the enemy was sooner or later forced to come to the negotiating table. In the East, the army would mount a surprise attack from the East Prussian salient, crossing the Narew and Niemen rivers so as to catch the Russians while they were still assembling and forcing them to retreat in order to avoid being encircled. In the West, however, an immediate offensive was ruled out by the great belt of fortresses that the French had constructed soon after the Franco–Prussian War along the common border from Verdun in the north to Belfort in the south. Here, the plan was for the army to remain initially on the defensive behind the River Saar, with its flanks supported by the fortifications of Metz and Strasbourg, where it could safely await a French attack. When the force of the blow had been absorbed, if necessary by falling back as far as the Rhine, they would mount a powerful counter-attack and throw the French back across the border and then further still, behind the line of their fortresses.

Unlike Waldersee, who did not make any significant changes to the plan during his brief time in office, Schlieffen decided that radical alterations were necessary and in place of a long drawn-out fight with limited objectives he advocated a rapid campaign aimed at achieving a decisive victory in as short a time as possible. In particular, Moltke's counter-offensive strategy was anathema to Schlieffen since it would hand over the initiative to the French at the beginning of the campaign and prevent the Germans from dictating events. In his opinion, the war would be won by the generals in the field and not by the politicians at the negotiating table. In order to win the war as rapidly as possible Schlieffen decided that, instead of dividing up the army as Moltke had done, he would deploy almost all the available strength against the stronger of the two enemies even though this would leave only a skeleton force to hold off the weaker adversary. When the first enemy had been defeated, Germany's excellent rail network would be used to transfer the armies to the other front where they would bring about a second victory. In this way Germany's inner position would be turned to her advantage instead of being seen as a sign of weakness leading to a war on two fronts.

In the summer of 1892, when he had been Chief of Staff for less than two years, Schlieffen began to reshape Germany's strategy along these lines. Firstly, he decided to remain on the defensive against Russia because they had recently strengthened their defences along the Narew and Niemen, which made it less likely that an attack from East Prussia would take them by surprise.

> We will therefore not succeed in fighting a decisive battle and destroying the Russian Army but rather engage in frontal battles against an enemy who could withdraw into the interior of an immense Empire, while our lines of communication would be the least favourable that we could imagine and endangered to the highest degree.[5]

On the other hand, he proposed to launch an immediate offensive against France on the grounds that they were the stronger of the two enemies, even though this meant that the Germans would run up against their fortresses. For the next few years Schlieffen wrestled unconvincingly with how to achieve a rapid breakthrough of the fortress belt by first of all using the new heavy howitzers to capture Nancy, which was in an exposed position well ahead of the main French line and therefore vulnerable to attack. Frustrated by this problem, in 1894 he briefly toyed with the idea of outflanking the fortress belt to the north of Verdun while at the same time pinning down the French centre by means of an attack on Nancy, but reluctantly came to the conclusion that he did not have enough men for both tasks. Three years later, in 1897, he returned to the theme, exploring it in more detail. In a phrase which was uncannily prescient of events in the summer of 1914, he wrote:

The circumstances north of Verdun are the most favourable. The Meuse will certainly be occupied, but not with considerable strength. Here, at least, the right wing is free and there is the possibility of crossing the river by means of an envelopment. If this is successful, one can direct one's march against the rearward communications of the enemy and thus force the French Army away from Paris.[6]

However, several difficulties stood in his way. Firstly, as we have seen, the Minister for War turned down his repeated requests for the immediate creation of the seven new army corps that were needed to carry out the plan. Secondly, there were not enough roads in the area between Verdun and the Belgian border for the movement of all of the troops involved in the manoeuvre. The way round this particular problem, he concluded, was simple, logical and compelling: 'an offensive which must swing to the north of Verdun must not be shy of violating the neutrality of Belgium in addition to that of Luxembourg.'[7] Thirdly, while the German right wing was enveloping the northern end of the enemy's line, it might be attacked from the direction of Verdun, cut off from the centre and defeated. For this reason, in the second half of the 1890s, Schlieffen pushed hard for the fortress of Metz to be strengthened in order to cover against a French offensive out of Verdun and at the same time to act as a solid fixed point around which the right wing could pivot as it carried out the envelopment. After a protracted argument with the Minister for War, who as usual was concerned to limit the cost, in 1899 Schlieffen received approval for the construction of a small number of new forts and the updating of a few others.

The 1899 deployment plan was the first to involve outflanking the northern end of the fortress line. In a memorandum written at the time, Schlieffen explained that there were two variants depending on whether the enemy attacked or defended. A French offensive into Lorraine (the most likely option according to the latest intelligence) would be resisted by the three armies of the German centre and then enveloped on both wings in a giant pincer movement, which would throw them back beyond the fortresses. On the other hand, if they remained on the defensive it was imperative to defeat them quickly before the Russians could intervene.

Each day and week that follows after the first day of mobilization, the Russians can come closer to our borders, perhaps even approaching the Vistula. With each day the situation in the East becomes more dangerous and the necessity to deploy stronger forces there more pressing, and therefore we weaken our forces in the West.[8]

In this situation, two armies would pass through Luxembourg and the eastern tip of Belgium, pivoting on Metz, and would envelop the fortress line to the north of Verdun. Their right flank would be protected by an army composed of six reserve divisions, and their left flank by 3rd Army opposite Verdun, which would follow them across the Meuse if the manoeuvre was successful. In the centre, 4th and 5th Armies were to attack Nancy, and having captured the town and its surrounding forts, would advance through the gap in the fortress line between Toul and Epinal, thereby remaining in contact with the right wing. On the left wing, 6th Army would remain on the defensive, guarding against a French incursion into Alsace or Lorraine. At the same time, the small force allocated to the Eastern Front would fight a delaying action against the Russians, if necessary falling back behind the Vistula in order to buy time for a victory in the West.[9]

This plan remained in force with only minor modifications for the next five years. However, in the spring of 1904, following the outbreak of war between Russia and Japan and after intelligence revealed that the French left wing had been extended considerably to the west, Schlieffen began a fundamental reassessment, which was to lead, less than two years later, to his eponymous plan. In the western staff ride in the spring of 1904 the movement of the right wing took on much greater amplitude than before. On the German side, a strong right wing (15 active and 6 reserve corps, approximately half the total strength) carried out a wide outflanking movement in which for the first time a large force (two armies strong) advanced west of the Meuse. On the extreme right wing, 1st Army passed through Dutch territory before advancing towards Brussels while its neighbour, 2nd Army, advanced through the Ardennes and then crossed the Meuse to the north of Mézières. Although the French were defeated in Lorraine where they had carried out a massive and impetuous attack, in his exercise critique Schlieffen argued that he was nevertheless in favour of strengthening the right wing and sending it on an even wider sweep through Belgium.

> Another possibility is to completely go around the French position and march around Verdun with the entire German Army or at least with the larger portion of it. In other words, one does not attack the front Verdun–Belfort [ie the fortress belt] but rather the front Verdun–Lille, for it will be necessary to extend the flank this far in order to gain enough space for free manoeuvre. There are fortifications on this new front, but not so strong or so difficult to overcome as on the front facing us. Many of the smaller forts would be taken without difficulty and the fortresses can be by-passed. The lines of communication would not be unfavourable. The [railway] line Meuse–Sambre is on the direct line between Berlin and Paris. If it is possible at any point to establish a connection between the French and German rail networks then it is through the use of the Belgian rail system.[10]

However, this audacious plan had several disadvantages. Not only would it be necessary to violate Dutch as well as Belgian territory in order to gain space for the manoeuvre, but also the time taken to complete the wheeling movement would remove the element of surprise and give the enemy time to respond before the right wing reached the French border. Despite these problems, by the autumn of 1904 Schlieffen had become sufficiently convinced of the soundness of this strategy that he decided to use it as the basis for the following year's deployment plan. In *Aufmarsch I (West)* of 1905 (for a war against France alone), seven out of the eight armies were to deploy between Wesel (opposite Dutch territory) and Metz and carry out the wheeling movement, pivoting on Metz. The cavalry was to reconnoitre ahead of the right wing (as far as Antwerp on the extreme right), seize the crucial railway line between Aachen and Liège and, if the Dutch refused to allow free transit of German troops through their territory, capture the bridges across the Dutch sector of the Meuse. This left only one army to cover Lorraine and Alsace in the case of an enemy attack. From now on, this strategy formed the basic framework for all German deployment plans up to and including the one in force when the War began.

However, several questions needed to be answered before Schlieffen could be absolutely certain about this. Was the fortified camp of Metz strong enough to act as an unshakeable pivot for the right wing and to serve as a base from which to repel an enemy offensive into Lorraine? If the French attacked in strength into Alsace and Lorraine should the right wing send reinforcements to support the threatened left wing? If so, how large a force should be sent? In the spring of 1905 Schlieffen used the last general staff ride before his retirement to subject the new strategy to a more stringent test in order to answer these questions.[11] Before the ride began, he took the unprecedented step of asking all of his deputies and section heads to produce a plan for the French side, assuming that they had become aware of a wide envelopment movement through Dutch and Belgian territory. Of the four solutions to survive the initial screening, Schlieffen chose three to be played out during the ride and rejected the fourth (by Oberst Matthias) on grounds that are no longer clear. In another highly unusual decision which testifies to the exceptionally high importance he gave to these war games, Schlieffen commanded the German side in all of the exercises, pitting himself in turn against each of his three subordinates. Oberst von Steuben launched a massive attack into Lorraine leaving only a weak force of mainly reserve divisions to oppose the German right wing. When the German counter-attack proved too weak Schlieffen was forced to transfer two armies and part of a third from the right wing to retrieve the situation. With their help the front was stabilized and the French offensive gradually petered out. In the meantime, the German right wing (reduced to half its original size) enveloped the fortress line from the west, forcing the French into a general retreat and bringing the campaign to an end. In contrast, Oberstleutnant Freiherr von Freytag-Loringhoven countered the German move by extending his line westwards as far as Lille and then advanced his strong centre in the direction of Brussels–Namur in order to sever the German right wing from its pivot at Metz. However, this offensive failed after being hit in the flank by a German counter-attack from Metz, after which his now isolated left wing was thrown back in disorder on to the reserve divisions and encircled. Acting on the assumption that the German left wing must be weak, Major von Kuhl, the future Chief of Staff of 1st Army, launched simultaneous attacks in a northerly direction, either side of Metz. On the left, the offensive failed almost immediately after it ran up against a superior German force; on the right, where the advance took place into Lorraine, progress was initially good but came to an abrupt end when the Germans counter-attacked from the direction of the Upper Rhine with units which Schlieffen had transferred from the right wing.[12]

After delivering his exercise critique as usual, Schlieffen made the extraordinary decision to replay the rides after he had allowed each of the three officers to modify their plans. In Steuben's case, the second ride differed very little from the first and Schlieffen had no difficulties in winning the contest. However, although he also defeated Kuhl and Freytag-Loringhoven for a second time, he was forced to modify his operational plan after both of them strengthened their left wing and extended it to the west. In response, he pushed his right wing even further to the west, enveloped the French left wing and threw it back to the south-east. In Freytag-Loringhoven's case (Freytag II), he forced the French away from Paris and, after advancing down the eastern side of the capital, forced them back across the Marne and the upper Seine until eventually, on the 34th day after mobilization, they approached the Swiss border. In Kuhl's case (Kuhl II), the French retreated to the Seine to the east of Paris before the German envelopment could be completed. With the French left wing now resting on the fortified camp of Paris, Schlieffen marched his right wing around the western side of the city, and having crossed the Seine between Paris and Rouen on the 34th day after mobilization, outflanked the enemy once more, causing them to resume their retreat towards the Langres plateau to the south-east.

In this way, the new strategy had been put to the test. Six different scenarios had been tried out and in each case the German side had been victorious. As a result, Schlieffen was now convinced that the plan was sufficiently flexible and robust to withstand whatever the French might throw at it, either by attacking the German right wing or by advancing in strength into Lorraine. Although in two of the scenarios (Steuben I and Kuhl I) he had been forced to send troops to Lorraine to oppose the enemy's offensive, in both cases the right wing was still strong enough to envelop the weak opposition. Nevertheless, the Belgians and the Dutch would probably refuse entry to German troops and would declare war when their territory was violated, Antwerp would have to be covered during the advance through Belgium, Metz required strengthening in order to act as a secure pivot for the right wing and lastly, as the staff ride had shown, the transfer of troops from one front to another to counter a French attack into Lorraine was likely to encounter considerable frictions.

After almost 14 years as Chief of the General Staff, Schlieffen retired on 31 December 1905 and handed over to Helmuth von Moltke the Younger, his deputy and the nephew of Moltke the Elder, the famous victor of the Wars of Unification. Several months before he retired Schlieffen began work on a detailed explanation of his strategy for Moltke's benefit which, when its existence came to light after the war, became known as the Great Memorandum (*Grosse Denkschrift*) but which later achieved notoriety as the Schlieffen Plan. Night after night, accompanied by his devoted adjutant and son-in-law, Major von Hahnke, who acted as his secretary, Schlieffen worked his way through many drafts, elaborating and clarifying his ideas as he went along. At the end of January 1906, by which time he had been retired for several weeks, the work was finished and several copies were made, one of which was handed over to Moltke and another remained in Schlieffen's possession.[13]

The first point to make about the Great Memorandum is that it was very closely related to the 1906 Deployment Plan for a war against France alone (*Aufmarsch I West*). Firstly, with the exception of eight additional (*ersatz*) corps which would be raised on the outbreak of war and which would, if necessary, be used to besiege Paris, the size of the army was almost exactly the same in both cases. (There are 81 divisions in the Memorandum and 79 in the 1906 Plan.) Secondly, the two plans are remarkably similar with regard to the initial deployment, the distribution of forces between the two wings (approximately 7:1 in both cases) and the enormous wheeling movement through the Netherlands and Belgium west of the Meuse. However, whereas the 1906 plan said very little about the course of events after deployment was complete, the Memorandum went into considerable detail about what might happen when contact was made with the enemy either in Belgium or in northern France.[14]

The Memorandum begins with a prediction that was unmistakably based on the poor condition of the Russian Army in the aftermath of their war with Japan. 'In a war with Germany, France will probably at first restrict herself to defence, particularly as long as she cannot count on effective Russian support.'[15] In the next few pages Schlieffen rehearses the argument against making a frontal attack on the French fortress line which would be a costly and time-consuming affair and unlikely to lead to rapid victory. An envelopment of the western end of the main fortress belt was much more promising but the French would probably respond by extending their line westwards along the river Aisne and possibly even further, along the high ground on which were located the minor fortresses of Rheims, Laon and La Fère. In order to be certain of success, the right wing would therefore have to be pushed out more to the west so that it could mount:

> … an attack from the north-west, directed on the flanks at Mézières, Rethel, La Fère, and across the Oise on the rear of the position.* To make this possible, the Franco–Belgian frontier left [ie west] of the Meuse must be taken, together with the fortified towns of Mézières, Hirson and Maubeuge, three small barrier forts, Lille and Dunkirk, and to reach thus far the neutrality of Belgium and the Netherlands will have to be violated.[16]

The Belgian Army, he suggested, would retreat to Antwerp, where it would have to be contained whereas observation would probably suffice for the forts of Liège and Namur, which were only weakly garrisoned.

Of the 81 available divisions, 71 were to take part in the envelopment manoeuvre, leaving a mere ten to the east of Metz to cover the left wing. After they had deployed between Metz and Wesel, the seven armies of the right wing (23 active corps and 12 and a half reserve corps) would gradually wheel left against the line Lille–Verdun, pivoting on Metz and preceded by eight cavalry divisions which would reconnoitre and seize the Belgian rail network and rolling stock before they could be destroyed. Meanwhile, an army of three and a half active corps, one and a half reserve corps and three and a half cavalry divisions would remain on the right (eastern) bank of the Moselle to cover the left wing and attack Nancy in order to draw in the enemy's reserves and prevent him from transferring forces to his threatened left wing.

---

\* One of the maps which accompanies the 1906 Deployment Plan shows the western end of the main French line at Rethel, on the Aisne, with a few small units, mainly cavalry, a short distance to the west in the vicinity of Laon.

The cutting edge of the attack was on the right wing where two front-line armies, the 2nd and 3rd (a total of nine corps), would cross the Meuse between Maastricht and Namur before setting out across the Belgian plain in the direction of the French border. They would be accompanied on their left by 4th Army (six and a half corps) which would cross the Meuse between Namur and Givet and then continue in a strongly south-westerly direction. If the French remained on the defensive in Lorraine, these 15 and a half corps would be joined by a further two corps transported by rail from the right bank of the Moselle, bringing the total number of corps on the right wing to 17 and a half. In the centre, two more armies (5th and 6th, amounting in all to eight corps) would link the right wing to Metz and join in the wheeling movement by advancing through the Ardennes forest in Luxembourg and the eastern part of Belgium and then crossing the Meuse to the north-west of Verdun. The right flank of the wheel would be covered by 1st Army composed of seven reserve corps (five of which would be detached to screen Antwerp) and the left flank by an army of five reserve corps which would counter a French offensive from the direction of Verdun intended to sever the link between the German right wing and its pivot at Metz.

It was vitally important for 2nd and 3rd Armies to have passed through the narrow gap between Brussels and Namur before encountering the enemy so that they could deploy to their full extent prior to wheeling left towards the French frontier. For this reason the march of the right wing would have to be accelerated as much as possible. If the French came out into the open and sought battle along the border with Belgium, Schlieffen was confident that he could easily defeat them. However, he expected that their left wing would be more likely to remain on the defensive behind the Aisne and along the high ground between Rheims and La Fère. In this case, when the Germans reached French territory along the line Mézières–Maubeuge–Dunkirk the task of 2nd, 3rd and 4th Armies was:

... to push the enemy's left wing southwards and thus away from Paris, at the same time using the right wing to envelop the rear position Rheims–La Fère and causing the fall of the fortresses of La Fère, Laon and Rheims, which are not very strong on their western fronts.[17]

In what was very much his preferred outcome, the French would be pushed away from Paris towards the south-east and forced to abandon the fortress belt. (This was the scenario which had been played out in Case Freytag II in the 1905 western staff ride.)

As Schlieffen put it:

> … the whole hill position [La Fère–Laon–Rheims] designed against an attack from the north-east will be taken and the Aisne position will have to be evacuated. With this the Meuse forts between Verdun and Toul, which can offer only insignificant attack from the west, will be exposed. Verdun and Toul will become isolated fortresses. The whole French fortress system directed against Germany will threaten to collapse.[18]

How would the French respond if this defensive position came under serious threat? The worst-case scenario would be if they extended their line westwards along the Oise between La Fère and Paris to prevent the Germans from getting round their open flank. In this situation, while 4th Army and part of 3rd (ten corps in all) mounted a frontal attack against the line of the Oise, 2nd Army and the rest of 3rd (a total of seven corps) would outflank the French position by marching all the way around the western side of Paris before advancing once more in a south-easterly direction.

Even if the French abandoned the line of the Oise and retreated behind the Marne and then the upper Seine (which Schlieffen thought highly unlikely since it would involve giving up a great deal of territory, several fortresses and the northern part of Paris), their left flank would still rest on Paris leaving the Germans with the same problem.

> The position behind the Oise may not be very strong in front, but on the left it rests on the colossal fortress of Paris. Even if it is mastered in front, even if the defender retreats behind the Marne or Seine, the victor must still submit to the necessity of investing Paris, first on the northern and then on the other fronts and is obliged with considerably weakened forces to continue the attack against a more numerous enemy. To dislodge the latter from his new position, he will by-pass the

left flank resting on Paris and will thus again have to use strong forces for the investment of the western and southern fronts of this gigantic fortress... We shall be therefore well advised to prepare in good time for a crossing of the Seine below its junction with the Oise [approximately 12 miles to the west of Paris] and for the investment of Paris.[19]

As we have seen, this was the scenario played out during the staff ride of 1905 in Case Kuhl II and so Schlieffen was familiar with the problem. However, bringing it to a successful conclusion in a war game was one thing; to succeed in a wartime situation was another thing altogether, especially since, as Schlieffen acknowledged, the army was simply not strong enough for the task. In order to invest Paris, and at the same time have a sufficient number of active corps with which to continue the outflanking manoeuvre, it would be necessary to raise eight *ersatz* corps on the outbreak of war by taking up the slack in the mobilization system. (In the Memorandum, he indicated that six of the eight *ersatz* corps would be needed to invest Paris, leaving the remainder to be employed elsewhere, possibly on the left wing.)

We have as many reserve battalions as infantry regiments. From these and the available reservists, and if need be from the Landwehr as well, fourth battalions must be formed as in 1866 [during the war with Austria]; and from these and *ersatz* batteries, again as in 1866, divisions and army corps must be formed. Eight army corps can be created in this way. We shall not wait until the need becomes painfully obvious, until operations are brought to a standstill, before undertaking these re-formations, but do it immediately after the mobilization of the other troops.[20]

In addition to these units and to the reserve corps, it would be necessary to employ a large number of Landwehr brigades in secondary roles in order to free the active corps for the business of fighting; six brigades would be used to strengthen the garrison at Metz, 15 would mask the minor fortresses in Belgium and northern France and several would cover the extreme left wing between Belfort and the Swiss frontier. Lastly, the Landsturm would be used to guard the lines of communication, particularly behind the right wing in Belgium and the Netherlands, and to occupy and secure the towns and cities.

Only towards the end of the Memorandum does Schlieffen discuss the situation on the German left wing where a small force, one army strong (7th Army), remained to the east of the Moselle. Their initial task was to attack Nancy to draw in as many enemy troops as possible and hold them down with the help of an enlarged Metz so that they could not be transferred at short notice to the French left wing. If the French did not counter-attack, two corps would be sent as soon as possible to reinforce the right wing, leaving behind only a skeleton force consisting of one active corps, one and a half reserve corps and several Landwehr brigades. On the whole, Schlieffen felt that the French would be wary of launching a large-scale attack into Lorraine once they were aware of the threat to their left wing since, as he put it, this would be equivalent to a garrison leaving their fortress just as the siege was about to begin. If they were foolish enough to do so, it would make the envelopment of their left wing that much easier.

The problem was how to parry the blow if the French attacked Lorraine in force. During the 1905 staff ride, Schlieffen had responded to a French offensive between Metz and Strasbourg by transferring troops from the right wing to the left. (This involved two and a half corps in the case of the massive attack in Steuben I and an unspecified number to meet the smaller offensive in Kuhl I.) This concept of a sliding scale of reinforcements, carefully calibrated to the strength of the French offensive in Lorraine, appeared in the first draft of the Memorandum.[21] However, in the final version he concluded that it would not be necessary to reinforce the left wing under these circumstances. Instead, it would absorb the initial impact by falling back towards the Saar, and, if needs be, further still to the Rhine. The enemy offensive would peter out because of the threat to their flanks from the direction of Metz and Strasbourg (as several staff rides had demonstrated) and because they realized that their left wing was about to be enveloped. In short, everything must be done to keep the right wing as strong as possible since it was here that the decisive battle would take place.

On 31 December 1905 Schlieffen handed over to Moltke and went into retirement. Moltke's selection by the Kaiser was completely unexpected within the High Command and greatly dismayed his fellow generals, most of whom favoured either Karl von Bülow, former Generalquartermeister in the General Staff and commander of III Corps, Hans von Beseler, Oberquartermeister in the General Staff (he was also Schlieffen's preferred candidate) or Colmar von der Goltz, commander of I Corps and a prolific writer on military affairs. In their opinion Moltke was unsuitable because he had relatively little experience as a staff officer and because he had not held one of the all-important corps commands. Unlike them, his career had not followed the traditional route of troop commands alternating with postings within the Great General Staff. On the contrary, after serving for almost a decade as personal adjutant to his famous uncle, in 1891 he became the Kaiser's aide-de-camp, a highly prestigious position that involved daily attendance on the latter, not only at court but also during his numerous travels. Even when between 1896 and 1904 he occupied a succession of troop commands including that of Regiment Kaiser Alexander, the 1st Guards Infantry Brigade and the 1st Guards Infantry Division, he continued in this role. In 1904 his appointment as Schlieffen's deputy was met with incredulity in several quarters; for example one of his former teachers at the War Academy predicted that he would be a disaster and the Austrian Military Plenipotentiary wrote that 'His military knowledge, his expertise, do not exceed those of an average officer and are, according to my Russian colleague here, supposed to be so shallow that for that reason alone his suitability for this high, responsible post must be completely denied. He is a complete stranger to the activities within the Great General Staff.'[22] Further, many of those who knew him well harboured doubts about his strength of character and looked askance at his unsoldierly interests. Whereas Schlieffen devoted almost every available hour to his professional duties to the exclusion of all forms of pleasure except for his daily horse ride (he regularly worked late every evening and on many weekends), Moltke was a highly cultured man with a wide range of interests including music (he was an accomplished cellist), painting and reading. While this was sufficient on its own to make him slightly suspect in the eyes of his fellow generals, what really worried them was his interest in spiritualism and the occult which he had developed under the influence of his wife, Eliza, who was a disciple of Rudolf Steiner, the founder of the spiritual cult of Anthroposophy. (She dominated her husband to the extent that when war broke out she accompanied him to the Kaiser's Military

Headquarters so that she could keep a close eye on him.) For example, Dietrich von Hülsen-Haeseler, the Chief of the Military Cabinet was appalled at the Kaiser's decision to appoint Moltke because 'above all, he was a religious dreamer [who] believed in guardian angels, faith-healing and similar nonsense.'[23]

The Kaiser ignored Hülsen-Haeseler's advice and chose Moltke because of the close personal friendship which had developed between them during the latter's long service as his aide-de-camp and which transcended the purely military aspects of the post. (The Kaiser habitually called him by his nickname, Julius, and used the familiar '*du*' in conversation.) To the Kaiser, Moltke's affable nature and extensive cultural interests weighed more heavily in the balance than his ability as a strategist and military thinker. (Moltke did, however, tell the Kaiser that he would only accept the post if the latter stopped taking part in the annual manoeuvres.) Having had to put up with the prickly and taciturn Schlieffen for several years, the Kaiser longed for someone whom he trusted and with whom he could discuss matters with an easy familiarity. As he explained to Moltke when he offered him the post: 'General von der Goltz has also been recommended to me, whom I don't want, and also General von Beseler, whom I don't know. I know you, and I trust you.'[24]

Schlieffen's concerns that his successor would radically alter his war planning turned out to be unfounded. In a memorandum probably composed in 1911 during the second Moroccan crisis, Moltke made it clear that he was in broad agreement with Schlieffen's strategy though he believed that a war on two fronts was more likely now that the Russian Army had recovered from the conflict with Japan.

It may safely be assumed that the next war will be a war on two fronts. Of our enemies, France is the most dangerous and can prepare the most quickly. Accounts must be settled with her very soon after deployment. Should the defeat of the French be achieved quickly and decisively, it will also be possible to make forces available against Russia. I agree with the basic idea of opening the war with a strong offensive against France while initially remaining on the defensive with weak forces against Russia. If a quick decision is sought against France, the attack should not be exclusively directed against the strongly fortified Eastern Front of that country… If one wants to meet the enemy in the open, the fortified frontier line must be outflanked … an advance through Belgium would force the French back into their interior.[25]

However, although Moltke accepted the basic framework of the plan, he disagreed with Schlieffen on several points. First of all he cast doubts on Schlieffen's decision to violate Dutch territory. In his opinion, the Dutch would not stand idly by when the Germans invaded their territory but would declare war on them. (In the Great Memorandum Schlieffen had optimistically suggested that they would come to an agreement because they saw Britain as their true enemy and not Germany.) In particular, Moltke was concerned that if the Dutch declared war on them it would provide the British Army with an advanced base from where they could attack the Germans in the rear.

> A hostile Holland at our back could have disastrous consequences for the advance of the German army to the west, particularly if England should use the violation of Belgian neutrality as a pretext for entering the war against us. A neutral Holland secures our rear, because if England declares war on us for violating Belgian territory she cannot herself violate Dutch neutrality.[26]

In addition, in a phrase which suggests that he did not completely share the widely held view that the war would be of short duration, he went on to say:

> Furthermore, it will be very important to have in Holland a country whose neutrality allows us to have imports and supplies. She must be a windpipe that enables us to breathe… If we turn Holland into our enemy then we block our last windpipe through which we are able to breathe.[27]

However, avoiding Dutch territory would present the Germans with a complicated logistical problem. In order to make sufficient space for the enormous wheeling manoeuvre, 1st Army would have to deploy along a 50-mile stretch of the German–Dutch border to the north of Aachen. On their left, 2nd Army would deploy along the Belgian border opposite the narrow gap between the Maastricht

Appendix (the southernmost part of the Netherlands) and the heavily wooded Ardennes Plateau. Thus, if 1st Army was denied the use of the Dutch road and rail network, not only 2nd Army but also 1st (a total of about 600,000 men together with horses, equipment and supplies) would have to squeeze through the 12-mile gap with the minimum of delay. This meant that the fortress of Liège, which stood in their way, would have to be overcome within the first few days of the campaign, otherwise the great wheeling movement by the right wing would be strangled at birth and the plan would fail.

> However awkward it may be, the advance through Belgium must therefore take place without the violation of Dutch territory. This will hardly be possible unless Liège is in our hands. The fortress must therefore be taken at once. I think it is possible to take it by a *coup de main* (*Handstreich*). Its salient forts are so unfavourably sited that they do not overlook the intervening country and cannot dominate it. I have had a reconnaissance made of all roads running through them into the centre of the town, which has no ramparts. An advance with several columns is possible without their being observed from the forts. Once our troops have entered the town I believe that the forts will not bombard it but will probably capitulate. Everything depends on meticulous preparation and surprise. The enterprise is only possible if the attack is made at once, before the areas between the forts are fortified. It must therefore be undertaken by standing troops immediately war is declared.[28]

The 1908 Deployment Plan was the first one to avoid violating Dutch territory though this was retained as an option in case the attack on Liège was unsuccessful. In order to take the Belgians by surprise and capture the city and its fortifications before 1st Army arrived, five reinforced infantry brigades (later increased to six) were to be kept on permanent standby near Aachen, ready to cross the border immediately war was declared and to capture the forts by the 10th or 11th mobilization day at the latest. This was subsequently brought forward to the fifth mobilization day, following intelligence that the Russians would be able to mobilize considerably faster than had previously been expected. According to this new timetable, if the initial *coup de main* failed and the forts had not been captured by the eighth day, a second attempt was to be made with increased strength. If this also failed, the town and its fortifications would be besieged and, on receipt of a direct command from Moltke, 1st Army would enter Dutch territory and cross the Maastricht Appendix.

The second significant departure from Schlieffen's strategy was an increase in the strength of the left wing, doubling it in size from one to two armies. This probably stemmed from a desire to introduce greater flexibility into what would otherwise be a very rigid plan. (According to Ludendorff, who was the head of the 2nd Section in the years immediately preceding the war, Moltke questioned Schlieffen's willingness to risk everything on the wheeling manoeuvre.) By increasing the size of the left wing while at the same time keeping the right wing strong, victory could be sought in either location, depending on the course of events. If the French remained on the defensive in Alsace and Lorraine, the powerful right wing would bring about victory as Schlieffen had intended. If, however, they launched a massive attack into Lorraine, and also possibly into Alsace, they would first of all be held up by the newly strengthened left wing and then defeated with the help of reinforcements transferred from the right. (As mentioned above, this scenario had been played out in several staff rides but had been rejected by Schlieffen in the final version of the Great Memorandum.)

The strengthening of the left wing began in a relatively small way in the 1908 Deployment Plan in which for the first time an army corps was located on the Upper Rhine to oppose a French incursion into Alsace from the direction of Belfort. This had previously been the task of a handful of Landwehr brigades. If the French attempted to penetrate the Vosges into Alsace they were to fall back as far as the line Fortress Kaiser Wilhelm II–Strasbourg, taking with them anything that might be of use to the enemy, including stocks of food, rolling stock etc. Alternatively, if the French remained on the defensive opposite Alsace this force would be transferred by train to Lorraine where they would take part in the operations of 7th Army. In the following year, the task of protecting Alsace was given to the whole of 7th Army (four corps strong) rather than a single corps. The preamble to the deployment plan referred to this as a fundamental alteration. If Alsace was not threatened with invasion this would be transferred by rail either to Lorraine or to some other, unspecified part of the front. The task of 6th Army in Lorraine also depended on the enemy's movements. If it was attacked in force, it was to fall back to the north-west in conjunction with the newly arrived 7th Army and prevent the enemy from outflanking the German left wing in the region of Metz; if, however, the French remained on the defensive it was to advance against the Moselle to fix them in place and to prevent them from transferring troops to their left wing. Since it was important to determine the enemy's intentions as soon as possible after mobilization was complete, 6th Army was reinforced by 3rd Cavalry Corps, which was transferred for this purpose from the Meuse sector between Sedan and Verdun. From now on, Moltke made only two minor modifications to the left wing. Firstly, in order to co-ordinate their activities as closely as possible, 6th and 7th Armies and 3rd Cavalry Corps were formed into a unified force, whose commander would be chosen when hostilities began. Secondly, the provision for transferring parts of 7th Army to another part of the battle front disappears from the plans; instead of being used to reinforce the right wing, as Schlieffen had indicated, it would remain on the left wing.[29]

This, then, was the plan that was used for the invasion of Belgium and France in the summer of 1914. For over a decade, Schlieffen had developed the new strategy step by step, testing it out in numerous war games and staff rides until he was convinced that it would lead to a rapid and decisive victory in the west, leaving sufficient time to transfer the armies to the east to stop the Russian steamroller before it could enter German territory. Not only was the plan audacious in the extreme but French intelligence completely failed to get wind of it and it was not until the war had been going for approximately two weeks that it gradually dawned on the French High Command what was in store for them. On the other hand, the strategy was inflexible and could not be altered if circumstances did not turn out as expected. In particular, it did not take into account how the French might respond once they became aware of the massive threat to their left wing. In short, victory would depend on only one throw of the die; if this failed, there would be no second chance.

# 2

# PLAN XVII

For almost two decades, from the Dreyfus Affair in the 1890s until the second Moroccan crisis in 1911, the process for taking military decisions was as fragmented in France as it was in Germany. In the first years of the new century, the radical republicans who had seized power in the aftermath of the Dreyfus affair began a root and branch reform of the army in an attempt to bring it more closely under civilian control. Unfortunately, these measures had a disastrous effect on the army's morale, its efficiency and its preparedness for war.[1] The Supreme Command was divided up between the Chief of Staff and the Vice-President of the Conseil Supérieure de Guerre (Supreme War Council), an advisory body that kept the Minister for War informed about military planning and the state of the army. In addition to the Vice-President, the Supreme War Council consisted of 12 senior generals who had been designated as army or corps commanders on the outbreak of war and the Minister for War who acted as chairman. In peacetime, the principal responsibility of the Vice-President was military planning; in wartime, he would take over command of the north-eastern front, facing the Germans, and in effect would become the Commander-in-Chief. The Chief of Staff, on the other hand, was in charge of the day-to-day administration of the army and was responsible for setting the military budget. This post was purely bureaucratic and was occupied by relatively minor functionaries drawn from the ranks of the most junior major generals. When hostilities began, he would remain at his desk in the War Ministry from where he reported directly to the Minister of War. The third strand in the decision-taking process consisted of 14 departments within the War Ministry (the *services et directions*), which were responsible for developing the army's equipment and weaponry (including artillery), and for overseeing the transport, supply and medical services. Their civilian directors were powerful and independent figures, entrenched within their own narrow little world, answerable only to the Minister for War and able, if they so wished, to thwart the wishes of the Vice-President of the Supreme War Council and, on some occasions, the Minister himself. Even when they were not actively opposed to new developments, changes invariably took place at a snail's pace as they took time to digest the advice they received from a bewildering array of technical and advisory committees.

At the head of this unwieldy and inefficient system stood the Minister for War, through whom the Government's control of the army was exerted and who was, in theory at least, in a position to co-ordinate the activities of his subordinates. In practice, however, governments fell at such frequent intervals during the Third Republic that ministers were not in the post long enough to see through a coherent set of reforms. Between the end of the Franco–Prussian War and the beginning of the First World War the average term in office was only about one year and on numerous occasions the turnover was greater still. (On eight occasions there were three Ministers in the space of one year, on two occasions there were four and on one occasion there were five.) Another reason why it was difficult to push through much-needed reforms was that, apart from a few notable exceptions such as Millerand and Messimy, the great majority of Ministers of War were weak and insignificant figures who lacked the drive and the determination needed to get things done. In an age when the position was traditionally occupied by a soldier, very few officers of high ability wanted a job in which they would have to spend their time either desk-bound or rubbing shoulders with politicians and which would not serve as a stepping stone to a much sought-after appointment as a corps or army commander. In consequence, the post was filled by officers of relatively modest rank, such as divisional commanders, who were unable to impose their will on their fractious or prevaricating subordinates.[2]

At about the same time as the radical republicans began to reform the army, French strategy also underwent a significant transition. Previously, the plan had been to remain strictly on the defensive behind the great belt of fortresses that had been constructed after the defeat by Prussia and which, with the exception

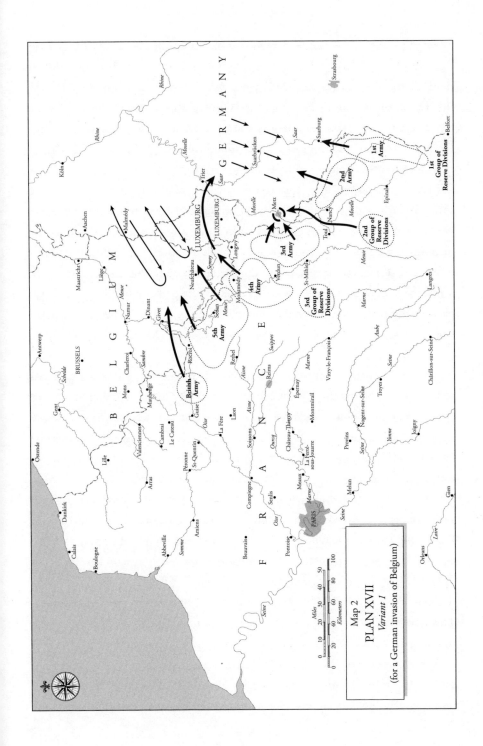

Map 2

PLAN XVII

*Variant 1*

(for a German invasion of Belgium)

of a narrow gap in the centre, extended from Verdun in the north to Belfort in the south. Towards the end of the century, however, as the war became a distant memory this strategy was replaced by one which corresponded more closely to the new spirit of confidence within the High Command and which at the same time acknowledged France's inferiority in numbers and slower mobilization than Germany. According to this new counter-offensive strategy, which was developed by Général Henri Bonnal of the Ecole Supérieure de Guerre, when war broke out the main body of the army would remain behind the fortress line while a strong covering force was sent ahead to monitor the enemy's movements and work out the direction of their attack. When this was known with certainty, the main force would manoeuvre into a favourable position, wait until the enemy's offensive had run out of steam and then counter-attack and throw them back across the border. From 1898, when the new strategy was embodied in the war plan for the first time (Plan XIV), until the autumn of 1911 when Joffre began work on Plan XVII, Bonnal's concept formed the basic framework for almost all French war plans.[3]

Plan XV, which was introduced by Général Brugère in 1903 and which was still in force in 1905 when Schlieffen composed his Great Memorandum, was a typical example of this strategy. Of the four front-line armies, three were massed opposite the lost provinces of Alsace and Lorraine, leaving only one to cover the left wing along the Meuse heights to the north-west of Toul. Three groups of reserve divisions, each four divisions strong, supported the front line, one behind the centre and one behind each wing. Since Brugère was convinced, like his predecessors, that the German offensive would be confined to the border with France, the left wing extended only as far as the midway point between Verdun and Sedan, opposite the extreme south-eastern tip of Belgium. In late 1903 and early 1904, however, new intelligence suggested that the Germans intended to outflank the fortress line via Luxembourg and the eastern part of Belgium. This information was contained in documents passed to an agent by someone claiming to be a disaffected German staff officer (code name Vengeur) who melodramatically concealed his identity by swathing his head in bandages from which, according to his handler, there poked out a severe looking Prussian moustache. In the light of this information, in the spring of 1904 the Deuxième

Bureau (the Intelligence Section of the General Staff) carried out a detailed appraisal of all recent intelligence on German deployment, including not only the Vengeur documents (whose credibility was doubted in some quarters) but also accounts of recent German rail construction along the borders with both France and Belgium. In the report which they prepared for a meeting of the Supreme War Council, they concluded that on balance the evidence indicated that the Germans would violate Belgian territory in an attempt to outflank the fortress line but that their main offensive would probably take place in Lorraine. Evidence from rail construction was ambiguous. On the one hand, new lines and lengthened platforms in the Eiffel region suggested that the German right wing would move through Luxembourg and Belgium east of the Meuse; on the other hand, the massive building programme which had been observed around Metz–Thionville pointed towards an offensive by their centre and left wing in Lorraine. When the Supreme War Council met that summer to discuss the matter, the report met with a varied response. Some, including Brugère, disagreed with its conclusions and insisted that Plan XV did not require alteration, others suggested that the left wing should remain where it was but should be strengthened by more reserve divisions and a few wanted to remove front-line units from Lorraine and use them to extend the line westwards to cover the left flank. After a great deal of wrangling, Brugère won the argument and the decision was taken to leave the plan unchanged.[4]

During the next few years, however, as the Germans increased their rail building activity in the Eiffel region and in the vicinity of Aachen, double-tracking lines, widening bridges and extending platforms (one agent reported that the whole area was ablaze with activity), the doubters on the Supreme War Council were gradually won over to the views expressed by the Deuxième Bureau. Unfortunately, the flow of intelligence had dried up since the Vengeur coup, and in the absence of further information it was impossible to predict the timing and relative strength of the two offensives. By 1907 a German advance through Luxembourg and the eastern part of Belgium was regarded as a certainty within the High Command, even though at the time the Deuxième Bureau complained that they possessed no definite information concerning the German plan of operations. Beginning with Général Hagron's Plan XV *bis* in 1907, in which the newly created 5th Army was located behind the Meuse heights to the north-west of Verdun, the left wing was gradually strengthened and extended to the west. The greatest strength remained in Alsace and Lorraine, however, since it was here that the principal German offensive was confidently expected to take place. In Plan XVI, which came into operation in March 1909, Hagron's successor, Lacroix, strengthened the left wing slightly by adding two more reserve divisions to the force covering the rear of 5th Army and also created a new army (6th), which he placed in the second line, behind the centre. Referred to as the Army of Manoeuvre, its purpose was to increase operational flexibility by using the well-developed rail network to transport it rapidly to where it was most needed, depending on the direction of the enemy's offensive.

Until now the French High Command had been content to make incremental adjustments to the plan, modestly extending the left wing to oppose the anticipated enemy movement through the Ardennes. From 1910 onwards however, a small number of senior officers, including the Assistant Chief of the General Staff, Général Regnault, and more importantly Général Michel, who in July of that year replaced Lacroix as Vice-President of the Supreme War Council, began to suspect that the Germans intended to make a much wider sweep through Belgium towards the huge unguarded gap between the left wing and the Channel coast. They were led to this disturbing conclusion by the Deuxième Bureau's latest appraisal of how the Germans intended to use their reserves. Seeing the question through the lens of their own experience (the poor quality of the French reserves, their lack of training – especially since the introduction of the Two Year Law in 1905 – and the scarcity of officers and NCOs), most senior generals were convinced that the Germans would not use reserve units in the front line alongside active ones but would employ then on secondary duties such as guarding lines of communication and masking fortresses. Even when in 1911 the Deuxième Bureau obtained a copy of the highly secret handbook for officers in the German General Staff, which conclusively established the formation of reserve corps, they did not change their minds.

> The proportion of reserve formations [in the German field army] will depend
> without doubt on the role given to each army. The armies that have the most

arduous task will probably consist only of active corps; reserve corps will, however, enter in a certain number into the composition of armies having a less taxing mission, such as operating round a fortified area or besieging an entrenched camp.[5]

Other indications that the Germans intended using reserves in the front line came from Russian intelligence analysts who pointed out that that they could easily get round the lack of officers by using retired ones, former NCOs and one-year volunteers, and also from General Henry Wilson (from 1910 the Director of Military Operations) who seems to have based his conclusions on the fact that the German right wing would be able to deploy more fully west of the Meuse and have greater freedom of movement than in the difficult Ardennes territory.

Within a few months of taking office, Michel was sufficiently convinced that the Germans would make a wide sweep through Belgium that he decided to replace Plan XVI with something radically different. On the left, instead of an empty gap between Mézières and the sea, there were to be almost 500,000 troops whose task was to oppose the German right wing and then throw it back across the Belgian border by means of a vigorous counter-offensive. In the centre, an approximately 300,000 strong force was to be located to the north-west of Verdun to counter an enemy advance through the Ardennes. On the right, Alsace and Lorraine would no longer be covered by three armies as in Plan XVI but by a smaller force whose task was purely defensive. Lastly, a strategic reserve, approximately 200,000 strong, would be established in the vicinity of Paris to strengthen either the left wing or the centre, as necessary.[6] Unfortunately, for the plan to work it would be necessary to double the size of the army, increasing the number of corps from 20 to at least 40. (Michel calculated that the Germans would be able to put a total of 42 active and reserve corps in their front line.) The way in which he intended to obtain this increase in numbers was as radical as the plan itself and, as we shall see, subsequently brought down the wrath of his fellow generals on his head and led to his dismissal. In place of the present system, in which one reserve brigade was attached to each corps, he proposed that each active regiment should be accompanied in the front line by a reserve regiment, the two of them forming a so-called demi-brigade under the command of a regular colonel. This would result in the doubling in size of each regiment, each brigade and each division and would reduce the ratio of active to reserve units from 4:1 to parity.

However, the gods were not on Michel's side. Général Lebrun, the Minister for War to whom he submitted the new plan for approval, died a few days later without having seen it. His successor was struck down by a mortal illness a few weeks after taking office and Général Goiran, who took over from him, was ousted only 20 days later when he proved incapable of dealing with the tensions engendered by the second Moroccan crisis.[7] His lamentable performance in the Chamber of Deputies, where he was unable to explain the army's poor state of readiness, led to the fall of the Government and its replacement by one under Joseph Caillaux. Worse still, the new minister, Adolphe Messimy, a former captain on the General Staff, told Michel in their first meeting that he lacked the support of his fellow generals and that he, Messimy, had little faith in his abilities.

On 19 July 1911, with the Moroccan crisis rumbling on in the background and with war getting closer and closer, Michel presented his scheme for doubling the size of the army to a meeting of the Supreme War Council. Intent on taking things one step at a time and not providing the opposition with too much ammunition, he prudently left the new war plan off the agenda, hoping to introduce it at a later stage after agreement had been reached over the reserves. However, as he later said, its contents had already become common knowledge within the High Command. Although he was aware that the meeting would be difficult, the savage response meted out to his proposals must have come as a nasty shock. With hardly any exception, and with the approval of Messimy who was in the chair, France's most senior generals condemned his proposals outright. Several of them gave their reasons (poor training, insufficient reserve officers, delays to mobilization, decreased efficiency of the active regiments to which they were twinned), while others limited themselves to making terse and wholly negative comments, including one officer at the back of the room who growled that Michel had gone loony (*maboul*). That evening Michel left for Belfort on a tour of the eastern fortifications. The next morning, he was appalled to find that the results of the meeting had been leaked to a national newspaper, *Le Matin*, which had printed an extensive account under the heading 'One against all'. A few hours later, a telegram arrived from Messimy asking for his resignation on the grounds that he no longer had his confidence or that of his fellow members on the Supreme War Council.[8]

With Michel gone, Messimy set about looking for his successor. His first choice was Galliéni, a distinguished veteran of the colonial wars and one of Michel's many critics, but he rejected the offer on the grounds that he had not long to go before retirement. Next, Messimy turned to the highly respected Général Pau, but changed his mind after Pau insisted on being given control of senior appointments, which would have reduced civilian control of the army and was too much to stomach even for a reformist minister such as Messimy. In addition, the fact that Pau was fervently Catholic did little to recommend his cause at a time when the Church was still regarded with considerable suspicion by the strongly anti-clericalist republican Government. The mantle of command therefore fell by default on Messimy's third choice, the 59-year-old Joseph Jacques Césaire Joffre. An undistinguished though competent officer and an engineer by training, Joffre had doggedly worked his way up the military hierarchy in a series of overseas postings in south-east Asia and Africa until he returned to France for good in 1904 and was made Director of Engineers. After a succession of troop commands he was raised to the rank of general in 1910, promoted to Director of Support Services for Metropolitan France and became the youngest member of the Supreme War Council. Although a proficient engineer and well-versed in logistics, including the use of railways, his limited command experience (he had spent only a short time in charge of a corps) was hardly adequate preparation for the role of Commander-in-Chief. In addition, unlike the great majority of his fellow generals he had not attended the Ecole Supérieure de Guerre, and so his knowledge of strategy, operations and staff work was unusually deficient in someone who would be responsible for devising the nation's war plans.

On the other hand, as far as Messimy was concerned, Joffre's inexperience was more than compensated for by his positive qualities, in particular his ability to work well with politicians, which was a tremendous asset at a time when civil-military relations were still strained. One look at him was enough to show that this was not the sort of man who would rock the political boat; he was extremely corpulent (his occasional attempts at riding a horse were a cause of great merriment), easy-going and self-effacing and unlike many of his contemporaries he was comfortable dealing with politicians, never putting them under undue pressure but always remaining acutely sensitive to their wishes. In short, although he appeared rather stolid and unimaginative and his track record as a soldier was not particularly distinguished, he would at least be a safe pair of hands. Only later, during the first weeks of the war, when he summarily dismissed numerous incompetent generals, did his political masters suddenly realize that this placid and almost somnolent exterior concealed an iron will.

If Joffre had filled exactly the same role as his predecessors his relative inexperience and narrow military background would not have mattered quite so much. However, as the Moroccan crisis refused to go away, and with the chances of conflict increasing with every month that passed, the Caillaux Government hastily instituted a series of military reforms (the so-called nationalist revival) which were designed to sweep away the decade-long changes of the André era and to prepare the army for war. ('In the wake of the Moroccan crisis, Parliament concluded that the German Army was a bigger threat to the future of the French Republic than was their own.'[9]) Although most of these reforms had only a limited impact in the short time that remained before the war began, they did bring about a radical change at the very top of the army. Under two successive Ministers of War, first Messimy and then Millerand, the divided command structure was dismantled, leaving power concentrated in the hands of one undisputed Head of the Army who was answerable in all matters only to the Minister himself. The functions of the Chief of Staff were abolished and his place was taken by a Deputy Chief of the General Staff who worked directly under the Head of the Army rather than within the War Ministry. As Joffre later said:

In this way, all of the powers of the military establishment finally became concentrated in my hands. It was the first time that any such authority had been confided to a single man. My action embraced the training of the Army, its doctrine, its regulations, its mobilization, its concentration. As to the matter of the promotion of officers, the new Minister informed me that it was his intention to ask my advice. We had at last arrived at the logical conception that the man who would have the responsibility of commanding the army in time of war, should in time of peace, have in his own hands, all the organs of preparation.[10]

Joffre's appointment on 28 July 1911 happened at a highly inauspicious time, as the Moroccan crisis was intensifying and the country appeared to be sliding inexorably towards war. In France, the final measures were put in place for mobilization and the cabinet discussed whether or not to send troops to Agadir; in Britain, Lloyd George gave a characteristically belligerent speech and the stock market fell very sharply. Since there was not enough time to produce a new war plan, Joffre made stop-gap changes to Plan XVI to remedy what he saw as its main deficiencies. In the new version which came into effect in September (Plan XVI *bis*) the left wing was strengthened by the addition of three cavalry divisions and a North African corps and was moved closer to the border with Belgium, the Army of Manoeuvre was moved into the front line to support the centre, and the mass of armies on the right wing were moved to a forward position in preparation for an immediate offensive into Lorraine.

In the autumn of 1911, as the threat of war receded, Joffre began work on a new war plan (Plan XVII). In his memoirs, he summarized the basic principles that guided his thinking at the time.

> Starting out from this idea that the war would be short, everything possible had to be done to concentrate all the nation's strength into that decisive battle which … would be the beginning and end of the war. If the idea could be contested that the first great encounter could end the war, there would be no doubt that general actions would closely follow the completion of detraining and that by no trick of manoeuvre would it be possible to delay these early combats… Therefore every mobilized unit belonging to the first line should be sent to the scene of action so that all could simultaneously participate in the first encounters. There could no longer be any idea of transporting distant reserves to those points where the turn of events rendered them most useful. Therefore the essential principle that guided me was the following: assemble every available man for battle. The second basic idea that guided me thus was this: seize the initiative. In the first place, this attitude would prevent French territory from being invaded and becoming the theatre of the first battles; it would permit us to preserve our freedom of action and prevent our manoeuvre from being dominated from the start by the enemy's decisions; moreover, the attitude conformed to the military conventions entered into between the French and Russian General Staffs.[11]

In a clean break with the counter-offensive doctrine that had held sway since the late 1890s, the new plan focused exclusively on the offensive. Instead of massing far back from the border and waiting for the enemy to show his hand, the armies would take up a forward position and begin the offensive as soon as possible after mobilization was complete. This shift towards an offensive strategy was due to a variety of causes, some of which were common to other countries and some of which were peculiar to France. Firstly, as previously mentioned, in Europe in general there was the widespread belief not only in military circles but also among politicians, economists and many ordinary citizens that a long drawn-out war of attrition was impossible in modern, highly industrialized society because of the intolerable human and economic damage that it would cause. Secondly, in France the offensive was seen by many people, civilians and soldiers alike, as the way in which the army could compensate for its obvious inferiority to the Germans in numbers, training and equipment. To many Frenchmen, the answer to these defects, which had surfaced during the recent crisis, was to be found in the past, in the victories of the Wars of Revolution and the Napoleonic era. Admittedly, so the argument went, the Germans might possess more and better trained troops and have plentiful heavy artillery but they lacked the natural fighting spirit or *élan vital* which was the birthright of the French soldier and which had led to the victories at Valmy, Austerlitz and elsewhere. Ever since the Franco–Prussian War, the army had adopted a timid, wait-and-see strategy; now, four decades later, with the trauma of that defeat fading into history, the time had come for the army to go on the offensive once more and seize the initiative instead of cravenly hiding behind the great fortress belt and waiting to see what the enemy would do. Thirdly, the change was also a response to the new *tactical* doctrines which were being developed at this time by the so-called 'Young Turks', a small group of youngish middle-ranking staff officers of whom Ferdinand Foch and Loyzeaux de Grandmaison were the best known. At the time of Joffre's appointment in 1911, tactical doctrines were in a state of flux following the misguided reforms which had divided the high command and had denied corps commanders the power to train and inspect the troops whom they would lead in battle. In the absence of a single guiding hand it had not been possible to impose a uniform set of tactical doctrines on the army as a whole and instead regimental commanders were left free to train their men according to whatever tactical system they themselves preferred. In addition, the lack of control from the top opened the way for Foch, Grandmaison and others to call for the adoption throughout the army of a purely offensive doctrine, known as the *offensive à l'outrance*. Although their ideas were in the ascendant by the summer of 1911, they were competing with several other doctrines and there was no certainty that they would prevail. What decisively tipped the scales in their favour and led to their views receiving official acceptance was the enthusiastic support they received from Joffre. As a result, in October 1913 their doctrines became enshrined in the *Regulations for the Conduct of Large Units* (which began with the notorious phrase 'The French Army, returning to its traditions accepts no law in the conduct of operations other than the offensive') and two months later in the *Regulations for the Conduct of Small Units*.

However, it is simplistic to believe that these doctrines were single-handedly responsible for the horrendous loss of life which took place in the opening battles when French infantry charged the German lines in thick masses, drums sounding, bugles blaring and with little or no artillery support. For a start, as Joffre later explained, there was not enough time between the publication of the new regulations and the opening of hostilities for the new doctrines to make much of an impact. 'Unfortunately [the new infantry regulations] were still being studied by the troops when war broke out. It takes a long time for a doctrine to reach the lower grades, above all after a period of moral inertia such as our Army had experienced.'[12] Secondly, there was the pernicious effect of the Two Year Service Law of 1905, which increased the proportion of relatively untrained men (first year conscripts and reservists recalled for annual training) to approximately 70 per cent in most companies. This caused many regimental commanders to train their men in close-order tactics so they could keep them firmly under control on the battlefield and prevent them from going to ground when they came under fire or, worse still, from breaking and fleeing to the rear. (In 1908 for example – well before Foch and Grandmaison came on the scene – the Minister for War criticized infantry units for too often seeking cohesion in rigid deployments instead of acting in autonomous groups orientated towards a common end and freely using the terrain to attain that end.)

Likewise, it is arguable that the poor performance of the artillery in the opening battles, and in particular the inadequate co-operation with the infantry, owed as much to inter-service rivalry and technical deficiencies as it did to misguided theory. (Even the most ardent supporters of *offensive à l'outrance* conceded that fire superiority was essential if the troops were to reach the jumping off position for the final assault without incurring an excessive number of casualties.) In particular, artillery officers appear to have thought of themselves as an elite and were disdainful of their infantry colleagues, from whom they were separated by both background and training. (Whereas most artillery officers passed through the prestigious Ecole Polytechnique where they received a highly technical training, infantry and cavalry officers attended the military academy of St Cyr where the curriculum was much less rigorous and intellectual in tone.)

A final factor in favour of an immediate offensive was that when combined with a simultaneous attack by the Russians it would throw the Germans off balance and force them to divide their strength between the two fronts. Following the signing of a military convention between France and Russia in 1892, high level staff talks took place almost annually between the two countries in an attempt to co-ordinate their actions when war began. In the years immediately after the Russo–Japan War, when the Russian Army was in a parlous condition and it looked as if Russian promises of support could not be trusted very far, the French stepped up their efforts to achieve a binding agreement. By 1910, for example, they were promising to mount an all-out and immediate offensive when war began and one participant smoothed the way for Russian co-operation by suggesting that 'even if beaten, the French Army will have opened the way for the Russian offensive and assured the final success [of the two allies].'[13] In the autumn of 1911 Général Dubail elicited a grudging promise from the Russian Chief of Staff that the Russian Army would open its offensive on the 16th day of mobilization, several days earlier than had previously been the case. In order to strengthen the ties between the two armies still further, and to ensure even closer co-operation, Joffre himself took part in the talks that were held in 1912 and 1913. On the second occasion, he agreed with his counterpart that:

With regard to the conduct of operations, it is especially necessary that the allied armies obtain a decisive success as rapidly as possible. A check of the French armies at the beginning of the war will permit Germany to transfer to the Eastern Front a part of its forces which already have fought against France. If, on the contrary, French armies obtain a success rapidly against the forces concentrated by Germany before them, this success will equally facilitate operations by the Russian armies since the forces concentrated by Germany on the Western Front cannot possibly be transferred towards the East. Thus, it is essential that the French armies have numerical superiority over German forces in the West. This condition will be realized easily if Germany has to guard its eastern frontier with large forces. The military value of the alliance resides above all in the possibility of obtaining simultaneous attacks in the East and the West.[14]

To honour their side of the bargain, the Russian Chief of Staff promised that 800,000 Russian soldiers would be deployed along the border with East Prussia, ready to attack from the 15th day of mobilization onwards.

Having come to the conclusion that an early offensive was necessary, Joffre now had to work out where it should take place. Despite all his grand talk about seizing the initiative, he decided that he needed to know how the Germans were deploying before choosing where to attack them. Unfortunately, the picture was far from clear on this point. In a memorandum produced at the end of 1911 the Operations Bureau of the General Staff said that although an enemy offensive through the eastern part of Belgium appeared highly likely, they could not be absolutely certain because of difficulties in interpreting recent reports of rail construction in the Aachen area, where the Germans continued to lengthen platforms and build new stations. The troops that detrained here could either spearhead an advance through Belgium and Luxembourg or could take a south-easterly route, and having skirted around the eastern side of Metz, act as flank guard to a major offensive directed against Lorraine. Renewed suggestions that the Germans might be planning a wide envelopment west of the Meuse were rejected on the usual ground, as were indications that they intended using reserve units for front line duties.[15]

Confirmation that the enemy would probably move through Belgium left Joffre with a dilemma. If he waited for the Germans to exit the Ardennes and cross the border before attacking them, he would lose the initiative and the first battles would take place on French soil. On the other hand, if he sent troops across the border as soon as war broke out in order to ascertain German movements, he ran the risk of alienating not only the Belgians, whose neutrality would be violated, but also the British, who were the principal guarantors of the 1839 neutrality treaty. Unless the Belgians could be talked into allowing free access to French troops on the outbreak of the war, the French left wing would, initially at least, have to remain on the defensive. Unfortunately, the Belgians were determined to cling on to their neutrality at all costs since they believed that the incursion into their country of *any* foreign power might precipitate a widespread conflict in which they would be the losers. Previous attempts to get round the problem had failed ignominiously, as the British had found to their cost in staff talks held in April 1911 when they informed the Belgian Chief of Staff that they would send troops to support them if they were attacked by the Germans. When the Belgian Minister for War got to hear of this he said that if British troops set foot on Belgian soil he would personally order his men to fire on them. As diplomatic relationships continued to be strained, both France and Britain must have begun to wonder which side the Belgians were on. For example, more Belgian troops were deployed on the French border than on the German one and in late 1912 the Belgian Minister for War claimed that British troops (with or without the French) would be the first to violate Belgian neutrality and not the Germans, as the British were claiming.

On 12 January 1912 Joffre brought the Belgian question before the Council of National Defence, a consultative body that included the President of the Republic, the Minister of Foreign Affairs, the Minister for War and the Head of the Army. Although he came away empty-handed after being told by the President that a pre-emptive advance into Belgium was out of the question, the fall of the Caillaux Government only a few days later opened the way for a renewed attempt. Thus, less than one month later, on 21 February 1912, in a late night meeting in the Foreign Office which had been called by the new President, Raymond Poincaré, Joffre once more presented the case for entering Belgium as soon as war broke out. During this meeting he explained why he preferred Belgium to Alsace–Lorraine as the location for the principal offensive:

In case of war with Germany, the plan which would be most fruitful in decisive results consists in taking from the very start a vigorous offensive in order to crush by a single blow the organized forces of the enemy. The existence close to the Franco–German frontier of natural obstacles and fortified barriers restricts our offensive to narrowly limited regions. Alsace is closed on the north by the system of Strasbourg–Molsheim; it is bordered on the east by the Rhine, where our adversaries have fortified the bridgeheads. An offensive against Strasbourg, opposed in front and menaced on the flank, could not lead to other than the most limited results. In Lorraine, the frontier is closed north of Metz by the fortified system of Metz–Thionville: it is cut up towards Dieuze by the Lake Region and closed to the east of Sarrebourg by the Vosges.

Between the entrenched camp of Metz and Dieuze on the one side, and the Vosges on the other, there exist two wide passages, the first being twenty miles and the second only twelve. It is clear that we could not operate in these corridors except with relatively restricted forces. Supposing that our attacks there should make progress, they would soon come up against organized positions in front, while being threatened in the flank by counter-offensives from the direction of Metz and Strasbourg. [This what the Germans had repeatedly demonstrated in war games.]

Therefore, neither in Alsace nor in Lorraine do we find ground favourable for an offensive having in view immediate decisive results. The situation would be infinitely more advantageous if it were permissible for us to extend our left [wing] beyond our frontier into the Grand Duchy of Luxembourg. In this region we could develop all our means of action, and we would be passing far to the north of all the fortified systems constructed at great cost by our adversaries. In case of success, our armies would throw the German masses back towards southern Germany and directly menace their principal line of retreat as well as their communications with Berlin. Moreover, a movement through Belgium would make it possible for the British Army to participate more efficaciously in our operations, and the assistance of this army would bring us a marked superiority as compared with our adversaries.[16]

Once again, however, the politicians were not swayed by his arguments and although he received support from the new Minister for War, Millerand, and the

Minister for the Navy, Delcassé, his proposal for diplomatic overtures to the Belgians were turned down on the grounds that it risked alienating the British on whose support the French Government was relying. (Although high level staff talks had regularly taken place during the last few years, Britain had as yet consistently refused to make any binding agreement with them.)

Now that the broad parameters were in place, Joffre and his staff began work on the new plan, a brief outline of which was submitted to a meeting of the Supreme War Council on 18 April 1913 when it was approved after the bare minimum of discussion. Detailed work then took place and the plan was completed in the spring of 1914.[17] The text of Plan XVII was divided into seven sections, the basis for the plan, the mobilization plan, the transport plan, intelligence on foreign armies (the largest section), the concentration plan, the cover plan (for guarding the borders during mobilization) and the intelligence gathering plan (to establish German deployment in the first weeks of the war). Unusually, the concentration plan, which was the only part to deal with operations, was not only one of the shortest sections but was also hedged about with uncertainties and ambiguities which were only resolved after the war had been in progress for several weeks.

Since Joffre's strategy was essentially reactive, several pages of the plan were devoted to an assessment of the enemy's numerical strength and the direction of their deployment. According to the Deuxième Bureau, by the 13th day of mobilization the Germans would have ready for action against France 20 active corps, ten reserve corps, eight reserve divisions and eight cavalry divisions. Knowledge of how they intended to employ their reserve corps came from a German mobilization plan, which had recently fallen into French hands. This up-to-date document (it carried the date 9 October 1913 and its provisions were due to come into operation on 1 April the following year) stated unambiguously that the Germans would use their reserve corps in exactly the same way as their active corps. The Deuxième Bureau ended its report as follows:

> In conclusion, the reserve corps, destined to be employed on active operations like the active corps, have become, according to this new mobilization plan, a more homogeneous and better officered tool than previously, while remaining lighter than an active army corps.[18]

Unfortunately, it contained no information about their deployment and so the French were still as much in the dark about this as they had been for the last few years. While an offensive in Lorraine appeared a foregone conclusion, a simultaneous advance into Belgium, although very likely, was far from certain since the little evidence available could be interpreted in different ways. ('There can be no certainty in this respect and one can only make hypotheses concerning the amplitude of the enveloping movement by the German right wing.'[19]) A wide envelopment (through Belgium to the west of the Meuse) was thought to be out of the question since the number of platforms and detraining sites which had recently been constructed to the north of Trier were only sufficient for 11 army corps at the most. Furthermore, an attempt to strengthen their right wing by shifting troops from Alsace would take several days and risk losing the initiative.

> In summary, despite the possibilities of an attack in force via Belgium, it is estimated that an important role will be given to the group of armies which will assemble behind the position Metz–Thionville and that for political and moral reasons the Lorraine plateau still exercises an attraction for the Germans.[20]

To oppose the Germans, the French had available 21 corps, three autonomous divisions (two of them from North Africa) and 25 reserve divisions, making a total of 71 divisions in all. However, as Joffre explained to his fellow generals when he presented an outline of the plan to the Supreme War Council, he did not intend using the reserve divisions for front line duties even though they accounted for almost one third of the available force. In addition, the total strength of the reserve divisions was reduced from 396 battalions in Plan XVI (22 divisions, each of 18 battalions) to 300 in Plan XVII (25 divisions, each of 12 battalions). The usual reasons were trotted out for these changes, with the proviso that the situation might change at some indeterminate time.

> It is to the [active units] that the high command entrusts the offensive manoeuvres on which depend the success of operations, counting on their better instruction, their superior training, and the solidity of their tactical links, which unite all their elements. If better organized, better officered, better commanded, the reserve

divisions in Plan XVII would become capable of fulfilling certain missions of a special character alongside active troops.[21]

By his unwillingness to match the Germans in using reserve units in the front line, Joffre had therefore placed his army at a numerical disadvantage (46 active French divisions opposed to 71 German active and reserve divisions), making it all the more important for the British Army to contribute their four to six infantry divisions to the struggle.

In February 1914 designated army commanders each received a dossier that contained the general directive for the concentration (common to all of the armies) together with specific instructions (*directives particulières*) for their own army. Although the general directive began with a very positive statement of intent ('Whatever the situation, it is the Commander-in-Chief's intention to advance with all forces united and attack the German armies'), it was clear from what followed that actions would be governed by the enemy's opening moves. Until these could be worked out with a fair degree of certainty, Joffre was not prepared to make any firm commitments about the direction and strength of his own offensives. Thus, the armies were to 'prepare' for an attack, 5th Army would advance 'either northwards into Belgium or north-eastwards into German territory', and 4th Army was to support an offensive into 'either Belgium or Lorraine'.

Although the exact dispositions could only be determined after the start of the conflict, there were to be twin offensives, either side of Metz.

> The intervention of the French armies will be manifested in the form of two principal actions which will develop; the one on the right, in the terrain between the wooded massif of the Vosges and the Moselle downstream of Toul, the one on the left, to the north of the line Verdun–Metz. These two actions will be narrowly linked together by forces acting against the Meuse heights and in Woëvre.[22]

Four of the five armies were placed in the front line from Epinal in the south to Mézières in the north, leaving a gap between the left wing and the sea, which was filled by several weak territorial units and by the British Army (if it arrived at all).

In a reversion to Lacroix's Army of Manoeuvre, the remaining army (4th) was located in the second line, behind the centre, to allow strategic flexibility. The four groups of reserve divisions were located to the rear where they would be employed on secondary duties and also act as flank guard to the active troops in the front line. The right-hand offensive, into Lorraine, was the responsibility of 1st and 2nd Armies. 1st Army was to prepare for an attack in the general direction Baccarat–Sarrebourg–Sarregemuines with its right supported by the crest of the Vosges. On its left, 2nd Army was instructed to prepare an offensive in the general direction of Château Salins–Sarrebruck, after having established an advanced base at Nancy to serve as a jumping off point for the attack. One group of reserve divisions was to cover 2nd Army's left flank against an enemy counter-attack from the direction of Metz and another group was to cover the right wing of 1st Army from an outflanking move by the Germans between Belfort and the Swiss frontier. In the centre, the task of 3rd Army was to act as a link between the two principal offensives, one in Lorraine and the other to the west of Verdun, holding itself ready to reject German troops debouching from the area of Metz–Thionville or alternatively to invest Metz on its western and north-western sides. Meanwhile, the movement of 5th Army on the far left depended on the deployment of the German right wing. If the latter violated Belgian neutrality, on receipt of a direct order from Joffre 5th Army was to advance through Luxembourg and the eastern part of Belgium in the general direction of Neufchâteau, strongly echeloned back on its left and meet the Germans head on. If, however, the German right wing did not enter Belgium but instead skirted down the eastern side of Luxembourg (along the right bank of the Moselle towards Lorraine), it was to advance in a north-easterly direction (avoiding Belgian territory), and, having passed round the fortified area Metz–Thionville, envelop the enemy's right wing and throw it back to the north. A strong part of its force would be used to cover the left flank along the Meuse heights to the west of Verdun in case the Germans attempted a wider envelopment than had at first been anticipated. Similarly, the movements of 4th Army depended on what the Germans were doing. If the latter's main offensive took place in Lorraine, 4th Army would debouch between 2nd and 3rd Armies and add their weight to a French offensive in this direction. On the other hand, if the German right wing advanced in strength through Belgium, 4th Army was to slot into place between 3rd and 5th Armies (the latter was to close up to the west to make room for it) and support the offensive into Belgium by advancing into the Ardennes in the general direction of Arlon. Arrangements for the British Army (referred to obliquely as 'Army W') were made in a secret Annexe to the plan, rather than in the main text. If they arrived in time, the British force (from four to six infantry divisions and several cavalry divisions in strength) was to assemble in the area Hirson–Maubeuge from where it would cover the left flank of 5th Army as it advanced to meet the German right wing.

Not only was there very little mention of strategy in the plan, but Joffre also refused to divulge his thoughts on the matter either to his political masters or to his fellow generals, principally because his actions were conditional on those of the enemy. This astonishing lack of candour (both the Supreme War Council and the Minister for War approved the plan after hardly any discussion at all) continued into the first few days of the war and only terminated on 8 August when Joffre hinted at his plans in General Instruction No 1. According to Lanrezac, who commanded 5th Army, in the first meeting Joffre had with his army commanders after the outbreak of the war, he restricted himself to banalities, much to the consternation of his generals, some of whom wanted to know exactly what was expected of them. When Dubail, in charge of 1st Army, requested reinforcements on the assumption that his troops would carry out the principal offensive in Lorraine, Joffre equivocally replied, 'That may be your plan, it isn't mine.'[23]

# 3

## OPENING MOVES

On the evening of 20 August, Captain Edward Spears was sitting with a French colleague on the high ground that overlooked the great iron and steel town of Charleroi in southern Belgium. Although so far there had been very little for him to do as liaison officer between British General Headquarters (GHQ) and the French 5th Army, this was about to change and before long he would have a ring-side seat in the campaign which determined the fate of France.

A French officer was sitting beside me on a hill from which we could see the great industrial area of Charleroi with the Sambre flowing below. Northwards, the vast plain of Belgium spread as far as the eye could see. Mining villages dovetailed endlessly into each other until in the grey distance they all seemed to merge into a vast, low, squatting town of smoke and mist, miles away, miles in extent. Much further than the horizon, far beyond the murky skyline, was the North Sea. To the right was more open country, possible country from a soldier's point of view, and beyond the villas and villages, invisible behind woods and copses lay Namur. Further still lay Liège and Germany.

The evening was still and wonderfully peaceful. The ominous rumble of guns from the direction of Namur, which had been going on all the afternoon, had ceased. A dog was barking at some sheep. A girl was singing as she walked down the lane behind us. From a little farm away on the right came the voices and laughter of some soldiers cooking their evening meal. Darkness grew in the far distance as the light began to fail.

Then, without a moment's warning, with a suddenness that made us start and strain our eyes to see what our minds could not realize, we saw the whole horizon burst into flames. To the north, outlined against the sky, countless fires were burning. It was [as] if hordes of fiends had suddenly been released, and dropping on the distant plain, were burning every town and village. A chill of horror came over us. War seemed suddenly to have assumed a merciless, ruthless aspect that we had not realized till then. It was quite dark now. The distant fires glowed red against a violet black sky.[1]

The conflict for which the armies of the major European powers had been preparing for the last two decades began on 1 August when Germany declared war on Russia. Two days later, on the evening of the 3rd, they also declared war on France and the day after that on the Belgians and on Great Britain. On the morning of the 4th, German cavalry entered Belgian territory to the north of Liège, followed a short while later by the heads of several infantry columns, and when this became known to the Belgian Government they immediately appealed for help to the British and the French. This enabled Joffre to set in motion his ambitious intelligence-gathering plan whose principal purpose was to establish whether the German right wing would be used to support a major offensive in Lorraine or whether it would advance through Luxembourg and the eastern part of Belgium. Four days later, on 8 August, he issued General Instruction No 1 according to which the main enemy mass appeared to be located in the centre, around Metz and Thionville, and also in Luxembourg, from where they could debouch either to the south or to the west. It seemed probable that a maximum of six German corps opposed 1st and 2nd Armies in Lorraine and that one army, approximately five corps strong, was in action against the Belgians. Although Joffre explained that he would wait until the situation became clearer before deciding what to do, less than a week later, on 14 August, he committed himself to a large-scale offensive in Lorraine, timed to coincide with an invasion of East Prussia by the Russians. (The other premature decision, which involved inserting 4th Army between 3rd and 5th Armies, was made the day *before* hostilities began when he had no idea in which direction the Germans were deploying.) At first the offensive went well and the news was greeted with elation at Joffre's headquarters (Grand Quartier Général,

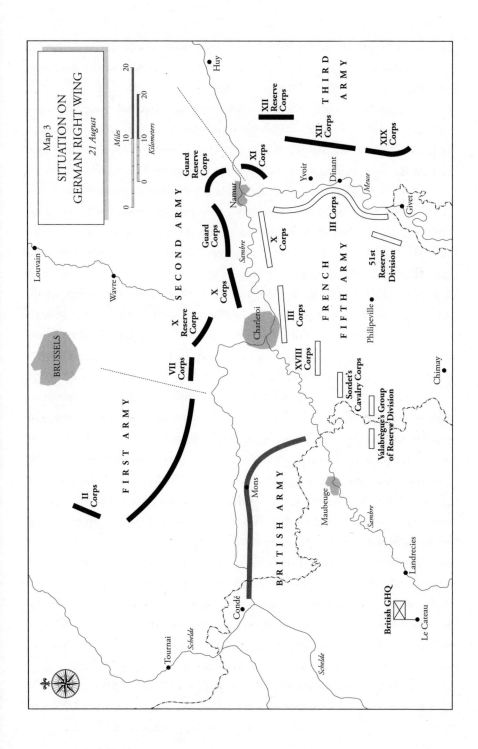

Map 3

SITUATION ON
GERMAN RIGHT WING

*21 August*

henceforth GQG) and in the French press, but on the morning of the 20th the Germans counter-attacked (the battles of Sarrebourg and Morhange) and threw 1st and 2nd Armies back with heavy casualties.

By this time the task of gathering intelligence had been under way for several days. In particular, on 7 August Joffre had ordered Général Sordet's Cavalry Corps to advance through the Belgian Ardennes and reconnoitre the area around Liège to determine the strength and direction of the German right wing. Unfortunately Sordet's mission failed because he arrived there too early, several days before the Germans had begun to bombard the forts and when almost half a million of their infantry were still behind the border, backed up along the roads leading into the city from the north-east. Therefore, when the French cavalry reached the area (they halted when they were about 8 miles south of the city) they encountered only a few small detachments of German cavalry and hardly any infantry at all. After retracing their steps through the Ardennes forest in stifling heat and with very little water, by the nightfall of the 10th they were back where they had started having accomplished very little but with their horses in a desperately poor condition after the 100-mile round trip.

Meanwhile the Germans were finding it more difficult than expected to capture Liège. The initial *coup de main*, which took place during the night of 5–6 August, failed with considerable loss of life and although the city itself and its ancient citadel were captured without a fight, the forts remained intact and fully garrisoned. Instead of repeating the attack, General von Emmich decided to hand over the task to the formidable siege artillery, even though it would set back the very tight timetable by several days. The enormous 42cm howitzers were in place on the 12th and began a bombardment that lasted until the 16th, when the two remaining forts capitulated. The following day, approximately four days behind schedule, Kluck's 1st Army passed through the city, crossed over to the north bank of the Meuse, and set off in the direction of Brussels, accompanied on its left by 2nd Army commanded by Bülow. At the same time, 3rd Army under General Max Freiherr von Hausen was also making good progress through the heavily wooded Ardennes as it advanced towards the Meuse valley to the south of Namur.

When Joffre issued General Instruction No 1 on 8 August he was completely unaware that three German armies were bearing down on his left wing. However, as an increasing number of reports confirmed that large numbers of German troops had crossed to the north bank of the Meuse to the west of Liège, he gradually began to suspect that the German right wing was stronger than anticipated and that it might be necessary to alter his initial dispositions. The principal catalyst for change came on the 14th when Richthofen's I Cavalry Corps, which was advancing ahead of the German 3rd Army, attempted to capture the strategically important town of Dinant, halfway between Namur and Givet and a major crossing point over the Meuse. If the Germans had arrived a few days earlier they would have found the town unoccupied by French troops and could easily have overpowered the weak Belgian garrison; however, after repeated complaints from Lanrezac, the commander of 5th Army, that his left flank would be exposed if he advanced into the Ardennes, Joffre had allowed him to move his I Corps westwards to guard the Meuse between Namur and Givet. As a result, they arrived just in time to prevent the Germans from capturing the town.[2] A few days later, as a precautionary measure Joffre allowed Lanrezac to move the rest of 5th Army north-westwards into the Sambre–Meuse Salient, the area between the Sambre and Meuse rivers which at this point flow at right angles to one another.

By now French intelligence had built up a more accurate picture of the German right wing although its exact direction was still uncertain. According to an intelligence bulletin issued at this time, this 'northern group of armies' was seven to eight corps strong rather than five as previously believed and most of them were advancing to the west of the Meuse. Far from being dismayed by this news, Joffre believed that in order to make their right wing strong while at the same time advancing in force into Lorraine the Germans must have denuded their centre. He therefore decided to use 5th Army and Sordet's Cavalry Corps, supported by the British Army if this arrived on time, to envelop the German right wing, while 4th Army advanced through the Ardennes and attacked the German centre as it passed across their front. If the plan succeeded, the German right wing would be cut off from their centre and defeated.[3] Since 4th Army faced the greatest challenge, Joffre strengthened it by transferring one corps from each of its neighbours, 3rd and 5th Armies. The next day, he instructed its commander, Général de Langle de Cary, to prepare for the attack by crossing the river Semois, but to delay the advance until the German right wing had left the area to the north of the Ardennes. However, late on the 20th, after receiving further reports that the German right wing was crossing the Meuse in force (the Belgian garrison at Namur reported that large bodies of troops had crossed to the west side of the river between Huy and Liège) Joffre changed his mind and ordered 3rd Army to advance the following day in the direction of Arlon, accompanied on the left by 4th Army which was to head towards Neufchâteau, taking as its immediate objective the enemy forces in Luxembourg.

On the evening of 20 August the situation of the two sides was as follows. In Lorraine, the French 1st and 2nd Armies had suffered a severe setback and had been forced to go over to the defensive against the German 6th Army. In the centre, the French 3rd and 4th Armies had crossed the border with Belgium and Luxembourg and were advancing into the difficult and heavily wooded Ardennes, unaware that the next day they would encounter two German armies, 4th and 5th, and not the weak enemy force Joffre had indicated. Meanwhile, the three armies of the German right wing had spent the last four days on the march across the Belgian plain and by the evening of the 20th had reached a south-west facing line between Brussels and Ciergnon (to the east of Givet, on the Meuse above Namur) in the south. Although 1st and 2nd Armies were in close contact with one another at Wavre (close to the battlefield of Waterloo), there was a considerable gap between 2nd and 3rd Armies because of the fortress of Namur. On the right wing, IV Reserve Corps and III Reserve Corps, both of which belonged to 1st Army, were in the vicinity of Louvain, several days' march to the rear after having set off in the second line behind the active corps. When they were level with Brussels, the former was to leave Lepel's Brigade behind to occupy the city while the latter screened the Belgian Army in the fortified camp of Antwerp. (It was due to be joined by IX Reserve Corps, which had been kept back in Schleswig-Holstein to guard against a surprise attack on Germany's northern coast.) The point had now been reached in the campaign when 1st and 2nd Armies would have to pass through the narrow gap between Brussels and Namur and wheel to their left, pivoting on Namur, so as to change course to the south. The task of capturing Namur, which was surrounded by a ring of powerful, modern forts, was given to XI Corps from 3rd Army and the Guard Reserve Corps from 2nd Army. By the evening of the 20th these had closed in on the town from the north-west and had cleared away the weak enemy forces from outside the fortified area, thus cutting off the garrison (the Belgian 4th Division) from the rest of the Belgian Army in Antwerp. Rather than try and rush the forts as had happened at Liège, General von Gallwitz decided to wait for the siege artillery to destroy them.

On 20 August, the Intelligence Section of German Supreme Headquarters (Oberste Heeresleitung, henceforth OHL) produced a report of the enemy strength and positions, which was sent to all of the armies the next day.[4] As far as the French left wing was concerned, this indicated that the French 5th Army was assembling in the angle between the Sambre and the Meuse; between one and two corps were already close to the Sambre to the west of Namur, three more were believed to be along the Meuse between Namur and Givet and a further three, thought to contain several reserve divisions, were approximately two days' march to the south. The British Army, it claimed, had not yet disembarked in strength but would shortly do so, probably at Boulogne, after which it would advance in a north-easterly direction towards Lille from where they would be able to reinforce the Belgians at Antwerp. However, this information met with considerable scepticism at 1st Army Headquarters, where it was firmly believed that the British had already disembarked and were concentrating prior to starting their advance. In addition, neither Kluck nor his Chief of Staff, Kuhl, accepted that the British aimed to link up with the Belgians; instead, they strongly maintained that they were intending to join up with the French 5th Army, though exactly where it was impossible to say.[5] As it happened, Kluck and Kuhl were correct since the British Army had already been on French soil for several days, having landed at Le Havre, Rouen and Boulogne between the 12th and the 17th, and rather than moving northwards towards Lille had already completed their concentration in the area between Maubeuge and Le Cateau, where they extended the French left wing. On the other hand, the report correctly identified the presence of two French corps along the Sambre to the west of Charleroi (III and X Corps) and others advancing into the Sambre–Meuse Salient from the south (XVIII Corps and Valabrègue's Group of Reserve Divisions, which was equivalent in size to a corps). However, it overestimated 5th Army's strength by suggesting that the Meuse sector Namur–Givet was held by three corps, whereas in reality it was only occupied by I Corps.

On the evening of the 20th, Kluck, Bülow and Hausen received a message from Moltke which spelt out his intentions for the next phase of the campaign and which were clearly based on the recent intelligence summary.

The 1st and 2nd Armies will close up on the line reached on August 20th, covering themselves against Antwerp. The attack on Namur is to begin as soon as possible. The imminent attack on the enemy forces which are to the west of Namur [ie the French 5th Army] will be combined with an attack by 3rd Army on the line of the Meuse between Namur and Givet by agreement with the commanders of the two armies. In the course of further operations on the right wing, the movement of a strong force of cavalry west of the Meuse is desirable. Therefore I Cavalry Corps will clear away from the front of 3rd and 4th Armies and begin moving around the northern side of Namur. Once it has arrived on the right [ie western] bank of the Meuse it will pass under orders of 2nd Army.[6]

In other words, the French 5th Army would be subjected to a pincer movement; while the German 2nd Army crossed the Sambre and engaged them frontally, fixing them in place, 3rd Army would cross the Meuse to the south of Namur and attack them in the flank and rear, trapping them in the Salient and cutting off their retreat. It was a bold plan, which, if successful, would allow them to roll up the French left wing before it could withdraw to the defensive position along the high ground at La Fère–Rheims–Laon and behind the Aisne. By the time the British arrived to give them support the campaign would be over. On the other hand, if the trap were to spring shut on Lanrezac's troops, trapping them in the Salient and preventing their retreat, 3rd Army would have to cross the Meuse at exactly the same time as 2nd Army advanced over the Sambre. Without the most careful co-ordination, the French would be able to escape before the jaws of the pincers snapped shut.

# 4

# THE BATTLE OF CHARLEROI

## 21 AUGUST: THE GERMAN 2ND ARMY ESTABLISHES BRIDGEHEADS OVER THE SAMBRE

At dawn, the advance guards of the French 5th Army and the German 2nd Army were less than 12 miles apart and separated from each other by the Sambre valley. Despite being urged on by Joffre to advance, Lanrezac decided to wait for several days to allow time for his neighbours to reach his level and cover his flanks (the British on the left and 4th Army on the right) and for all of his units to arrive. (Valabrègue's Group of Reserve Divisions, XVIII Corps and the 51st Reserve Division were at least one day's march away from the Sambre.) In the meantime, since he was uncertain about the strength of the German right wing he took precautions against a possible surprise attack. Because of its highly industrialized nature, the Sambre Valley to the west of Namur was completely unsuited to defence. Flanked on both sides by steep slopes, the heavily polluted river meandered along, frequently turning back on itself in large loops each of which enclosed a village. The valley floor was occupied by a dense and confused mass of factories, warehouses and dwellings whose brick walls were blackened by the accumulated residue of smoke and dust. It would be impossible to defend the line of the river against a determined attack because of the restricted fields of fire, the numerous covered approaches and the large number of bridges, rail viaducts and locks, not all of which could be guarded in strength. (There were over 60 bridges in the 12-mile sector between Charleroi and Namur, eight of them in the village of Auvelais alone.) Furthermore, artillery support would be difficult from the edge of the plateau since the flat trajectory of the French field guns (the famous *soixante-quinzes* or 75mm guns) would prevent them from hitting targets at the bottom of the valley, unlike the German heavy howitzers with their plunging fire. In the instructions he gave to his corps commanders, Lanrezac explained how they should respond if the Germans attacked:

> Do not at any price allow the troops to rush forwards to meet the enemy in the bottom of the valley. Wait for the attack at the top of the slopes, in open country, where our 75mm guns can be at their most effective. Only go over to local counter-attacks after deliberation, having clearly broken the attacks... As to the advance posts on the Sambre bridges, they are simply there to sound the alarm.[1]

Thus, when III and X Corps arrived in the area during the evening of 20 August they pushed forward strong advance guards to the wooded heights overlooking the river and sent weak outposts into the valley to occupy the bridges and keep watch for the enemy.

By now, the German right wing had almost completed the wheeling movement that would bring it facing south, parallel to the Sambre and on a collision course with the French. On the right, 1st Army was approaching the industrial area around Mons, unaware that the British were only a few miles away to the south and heading in their direction.[2] On the left, Hausen's 3rd Army was not expected to reach the Meuse to the south of Namur until the evening of the 22nd at the very earliest and so Bülow decided to mark time until they were in place and also to allow time for the 14th Infantry Division and X Reserve Corps to catch up with the rest of his own army. (They had the furthest to go because they were on the outside of the wheeling movement.) Thus, on the morning of the 21st he ordered General von Winkler and General von Emmich, the commanders of the 2nd Guards Infantry Division and X Corps respectively, to halt before they reached the Sambre and send cavalry and cyclist patrols to reconnoitre the valley and the area to the south. However, when they

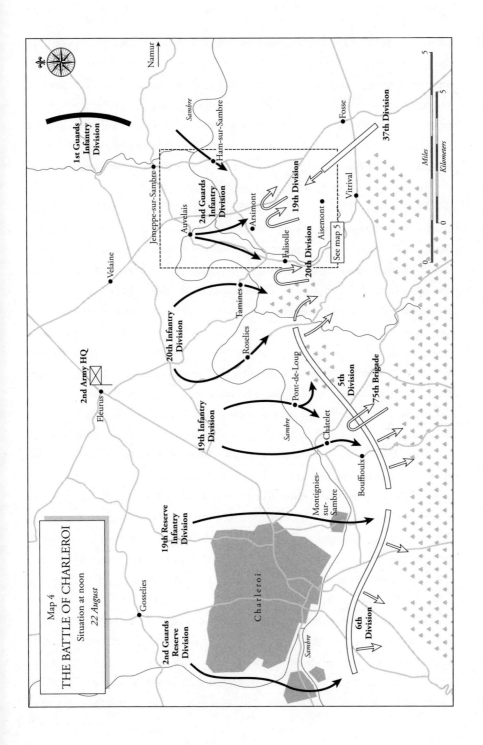

Map 4

THE BATTLE OF CHARLEROI

Situation at noon

22 August

became aware that the bridges were only weakly held by enemy outposts they independently decided to capture them before they were reinforced. In the early afternoon, therefore, their advance guards set off towards the river, X Corps on the right towards the sector Tamines–Charleroi and 2nd Guards Infantry Division on the left towards the sector Auvelais–Ham-sur-Sambre. The 1st Guards Infantry Division on the extreme left was echeloned back to cover against an attack from the direction of Namur and therefore took no part in the subsequent fighting.

By early evening X Corps had crossed the river at two points. On the right, the 19th Infantry Division drove the French out of Roselies and established a shallow bridgehead while on the left the 20th Infantry Division captured the bridge at Tamines but was then pinned down by rifle and machine-gun fire despite using civilian hostages as human shields. At nightfall they gave up the attempt and vented their anger and frustration on the inhabitants, some of whom they shot or bayoneted in a display of barbarity that was a foretaste of the massacre that took place the next day.[3] Meanwhile, Winkler's advance guard, Regiment Königin Augusta, ran into strong opposition at Auvelais and was reinforced by Regiment Kaiser Franz, its sister regiment in the 4th Guards Infantry Brigade. At the same time Winkler handed over command of all of the troops in Auvelais to the brigade commander, General von Gontard, and ordered him to establish a bridgehead in the peninsula formed by the large loop in the river around Auvelais. After an increasingly unequal struggle, the defenders were forced to retreat to avoid being cut off by units from Regiment Franz which crossed the river over the undefended railway viaduct to the west of the village. While the German Pioneers began to repair the damaged road bridge and to construct a nearby pontoon bridge, Gontard reorganized the badly mixed up units into two battle groups under Oberst von Roeder, the commander of Regiment Franz, and Oberstleutnant von Walther, the commander of Regiment Augusta, and gave the order for the advance to begin at 5.00pm.

From the southern outskirts of Auvelais the land rose steeply for several hundred yards to the village of Arsimont and the neighbouring hamlet of Haut-Batys on the high ground near the edge of the plateau. Although it was open countryside there were numerous signs of industry to the east of Haut-Batys including several large spoil heaps and isolated groups of pit buildings with names such as Fosse St Albert, Fosse No 1 and Fosse No 2. Although Roeder's group met with very little resistance and reached their objectives within an hour of setting off, Walther's group, on the left, was struck by two violent attacks in rapid succession, which inflicted a large number of casualties.[4] The first of these, which was carried out by a battalion from the 70e RI (the other two had formed the outposts at Tamines and Auvelais) was overcome with relative ease, but the second one which took place about half an hour later, as the light was beginning to fade, was a much more serious affair, carried out by the whole of the 71e RI. According to the latter's orders, II Battalion on the left was to capture Tamines, I Battalion in the centre Arsimont and III Battalion on the right Haut-Batys and Fosse No 2. When Arsimont and Haut-Batys had been taken, I and III Battalions were to continue down the hill, capture Auvelais and throw the Germans back across the river. The attack was to begin at 7.30pm and would be signalled by the first cannon shot.

When patrols alerted Walther to the enemy's approach, he decided to forestall their attack by going over to the offensive himself. On the left, II/Augusta advanced in the direction of Fosse No 2 while on the right I/Franz hastily occupied Haut-Batys and Arsimont. The brunt of the attack was borne by I/Franz, which was approaching the edge of the plateau when the French skirmishing line came into view and opened fire on them. With little time to spare before the main enemy mass reached them, Major Fircks immediately deployed his 1st and 2nd Companies and gave the order to attack. The left wing was directed on a red villa at the eastern end of Haut-Batys and the right wing on the tower of Arsimont church.

I found Fircks sitting in an armchair behind a low wall, leaning forwards and directing the battle, and a little further down Oertzen [the commander of the 1st Company], somewhat nervous and reluctant because his men had gone into the fight without sufficient ammunition since in their hurry they had only put on a few belts from the ammunition wagons, which had got stuck. This didn't seem so serious to me because it was already getting dark. My thoughts were much more focused on whether he had enough men and so I made [Marwitz's section] available to him. As I was returning, I saw that the whole firing line was bunching together on the left where a few isolated houses provided cover and much further back where they were drawn towards a high mound with a chimney. As a result, I reported this to Fircks as I passed him and suggested that I should deploy my remaining sections more to the right in order to prevent an outflanking movement from the village of Arsimont, which lay in this direction. It was already getting dark as I dived into the field of oats to follow the firing line. My overall view was now completely lost; I could see only what was nearest to me and felt that it was a great risk to send forwards such a weak force into uncertain darkness. Also they were still all pulling away to the left and on the right the line was getting thinner and thinner. From Pagenstecher and Oertzen the signal now rang out, 'Fix bayonets' and soon afterwards, 'attack'.[5]

They were only just in time. No sooner had they fixed bayonets and set off at the double than the French front line was upon them. In a repeat of the earlier attack, Commandant Jeanpierre's I Battalion got as far as the centre of Arsimont before it was halted by fire from the Germans who had hastily concealed themselves in the houses and farm buildings. Unable to go forwards and unwilling to retreat, some of the French sought refuge behind walls and within houses while others worked their way round the quieter western side of the village in an attempt to outflank the German position. For a short while the German right wing was in a difficult situation because it was bent back at a sharp angle to the main firing line but the timely arrival of several sections from Hauptmann von Rieben's 4th Company abruptly turned the tide in their favour, though not before they had suffered some nervous moments.

While our troops on the left were already breaking through a long way ahead of us, the counter-attack from Arsimont fell on our wing. The thin line of the 2nd Company began to slip back and I made those who were near me wheel round to the right and fire at the running French. There weren't in reality very many of them but in the darkness they seemed tremendously numerous. They were bowled over like rabbits before the muzzles of our rifles. After the firing was over I halted the men in the position which we had reached and ran to the right wing, roaring the whole time at them 'get back into position' and cursing terribly

I pointed my pistol at the heads of the section leaders. Thus we managed to form a continuous line, which for the moment could repel the enemy. There now appeared my last section, Eckardt's, and Malsburg's from [Regiment] Augusta with which I strengthened the right flank [at the same time as] the advance of the other companies continued to go forwards. Every few moments we could hear shouts of 'Hurrah'; they seemed to be a long way ahead of us. Thus, the centre and the right wing began to advance once more.[6]

A short distance to the east meanwhile, Commandant Michon's III Battalion suffered dreadful losses as it was swept by rifle and machine-gun fire as it crossed the open fields leading to Haut-Batys and Fosse No 2. Even so, the German line came under severe pressure and had to be reinforced in the moments leading up to the impact.

'Second section up. March, March!' As if we were on a visit to [the training ground at] Döberitz we charged forward once more through potato fields and finally over fields of stubble on which we could run much better. We couldn't fire since the 2nd Company was somewhere ahead of us. As we entered the firing line it began to get dark. Off we go, first clean our spectacles, wipe away the sweat, then open our eyes, finger on the trigger. Directly ahead of us at the edge of the village we could see [the enemy], they were moving back. Then, what's this? They were coming out of a group of houses. We were forced to bend our firing line back a little. I didn't hear anything more from my section leader but the Hauptmann sent an order to swing the right hand groups back since the enemy appeared to be coming from this flank. We hit them with incredible fire the moment they arrived and all of them fell. Only two Frenchmen managed to reach our firing line where they too were brought down by our fire.[7]

Despite the ferocious fire, several of the attackers got as far as the entrance to the hamlet where they were overcome in a desperate hand-to-hand struggle which left most of them killed or wounded, including Michon, who died of a stomach wound soon after the fighting was over. Apart from on the extreme right where one company reached the river because they were concealed from view by a ravine, it had been an unmitigated disaster. (The promised artillery support never materialised because the observers were unable to locate the German positions in the gathering gloom.) In just over an hour the two battalions had been decimated, losing more than 600 men and 14 of their 46 officers. General von Gontard, who visited the scene of the attack the following afternoon, described the results of the bitter fighting:

> In front of the firing trenches occupied by I/Franz lay numerous corpses from the French line Regiments 70 and 71 in their colourful peacetime uniforms – steel blue tunics, bright red trousers, képis and white puttees. They had fallen during the counter-attacks on the 21st. A row of brave men had got as far as the edge of the German trenches. Life had been taken away from them in the blink of an eye by the German bullets. They lay on the ground in their attack positions, their legs apart as if running, their rifles firmly clasped to their hips, and their mouths open, as if they were shouting 'en avant' or 'vive la France'. They were all stocky, sinewy men with reddish-blond hair and sharp features, all from Brittany.[8]

Later that evening, Général Bonnier ordered his 19th Division to fall back to a defensive position on the plateau. After a difficult withdrawal due to darkness and the lack of officers, it was almost midnight before they set off towards Vitrival, which they reached shortly before dawn. In his report to Defforges, X Corps commander, Bonnier said that he had been attacked by a superior force and that he would only be able to maintain his position the next day if he received support from the 20th Division.

In the late afternoon, Lanrezac issued orders for the next day. Since he was unaware that his troops had been attacked he merely repeated his orders to remain on the defensive, adding that the main bodies should close up on the advance guards in readiness for crossing the river. On the other hand, three battalions from I Corps were sent to reinforce the Belgian garrison at Namur, which was about to be besieged. After an uneventful journey, they arrived as dawn was breaking with their standards unfurled and the bands playing the Sambre–Meuse March.

THE BATTLE OF CHARLEROI

When news of the day's events reached Bülow he briefly toyed with the idea of ordering a general advance the next morning even though 3rd Army was still at least a day's march away from the Meuse. However, he changed his mind after receiving an intelligence report from OHL according to which an enemy force, approximately three divisions strong, had been spotted on the march towards the Sambre. (It was probably XVIII Corps and Valabrègue's Reserve Divisions.) Since he lacked the cavalry with which to reconnoitre the area (Richthofen's Cavalry Corps, which had been assigned to him from 3rd Army had not yet arrived because it had been forced to make a long detour around Namur), and since there was no guarantee that the X Reserve Corps and 14th Infantry Division would reach the battlefield the next day, he decided to delay crossing the Sambre until 23 August by which time Hausen's troops would be in position. In the late evening, therefore, he gave orders for the main bodies to close up on the river on the 22nd while the advance guards expanded the bridgeheads in preparation for the breakout the day after that. At the same time a message was sent to 1st Army asking them to swing inwards to the south-east so as to menace the French left flank and thereby ease 2nd Army's passage over the Sambre on the 23rd.

## 22 AUGUST: THE FRENCH MAKE DESPERATE ATTEMPTS TO ELIMINATE THE BRIDGEHEADS

When Spears returned to Lanrezac's headquarters at dawn after visiting British GHQ, he was surprised to find that news of the fighting had been greeted with equanimity.

> The fighting on the front of III and X Corps had, it seemed, been far more severe than was at first thought. There appeared to be no doubt that the enemy had got across the Sambre and pushed well beyond it … The staff did not appear unduly concerned at this news from the Sambre front. It was pointed out that General Lanrezac had not wished to fight in the valley. The general impression seemed to be that the enemy was doing little more than feel the front of the Army and there was absolute confidence that he could be thrown back into the river with the greatest of ease whenever this was desired.[9]

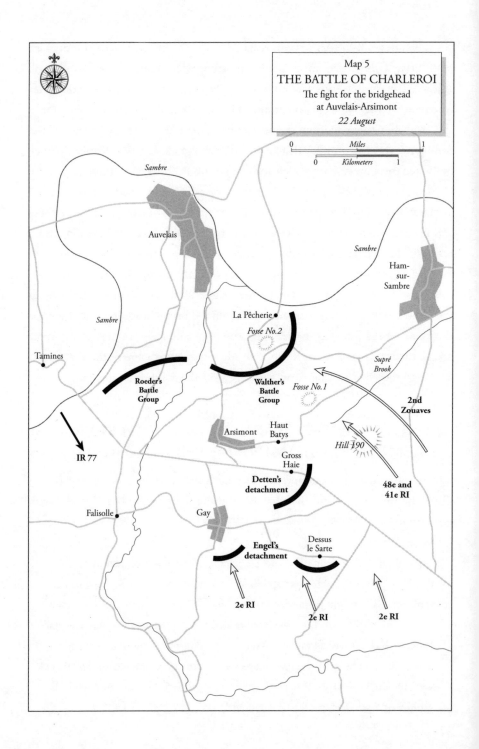

Map 5
THE BATTLE OF CHARLEROI
The fight for the bridgehead
at Auvelais-Arsimont
*22 August*

Miles

Kilometers

Sambre

Auvelais

Sambre

Ham-
sur-
Sambre

Sambre

La Pêcherie

*Fosse No.2*

Tamines

Roeder's
Battle
Group

Walther's
Battle
Group

*Fosse No.1*

Supré
Brook

2nd
Zouaves

IR 77

Arsimont

Haut
Batys

Gross
Haie

*Hill 190*

Detten's
detachment

48e and
41e RI

Falisolle

Gay

Engel's
detachment

Dessus
le Sarte

2e RI

2e RI

2e RI

In addition, he was told that Lanrezac had not altered his orders for the day; as before, the army was to remain on the defensive and only attack the Germans if they advanced out of the valley and on to the plateau.

During the night, the Germans took measures to consolidate the Auvelais bridgehead. Gontard was told that his advance guard would be reinforced by Regiment Kaiser Alexander and that his left flank would be covered by Regiment Königin Elisabeth, which would cross the Sambre during the morning. With their help, and with the support of the Guard Corps heavy artillery which would target the French batteries on the high ground to the south of the river, he was to hold on to the captured territory whatever the cost. In the early hours of the morning Regiment Alexander crossed the river, passed through the shattered and burning remains of Auvelais, and began the ascent towards Arsimont. Oberstleutnant Graf von Finckenstein, in command of II Battalion, described the unearthly scene from the north bank as his men waited impatiently to cross the damaged road bridge:

> From here [there was a] gripping picture of the first battle. The whole valley was transformed into a bubbling, howling, chattering hell. In the light from the burning villages the coal heaps raised themselves up in peculiar pyramid-like formations. News about how the fighting was progressing in the valley was very sparse.[10]

When they arrived at Arsimont they were met with great relief by Walther, whose men had spent a cold, miserable and sleepless night in the shallow trenches they had laboriously hacked out of the stony soil, hardened by several weeks of scorching hot weather. Losses had been great, especially in I/Franz, and it had therefore been impossible to form a continuous line. As a result, Regiment Alexander was used in a piecemeal fashion to fill the gaps; one part remained at Arsimont where it replaced the three most badly damaged companies of I/Franz and another was inserted on either side of Fosse No 2. The machine gun company was also split up, one section remaining at Fosse No 2 while the other two sections, under the command of Hauptmann von Engel, were sent to the right wing where they reinforced the 4th Company/Franz to the north-west of Arsimont. When they were all in place Walther's front line extended for just over a mile from La Pêcherie, where the left wing was firmly anchored on the river, to the north-west of Arsimont where the right flank was in the air because it had not been able to make contact with Roeder's Battle Group.

It was at this point, just as dawn was breaking, that the rumble of gunfire was heard towards the west, where X Corps was trying to break out of the bridgehead at Tamines. When several junior officers heard the noise they disregarded Gontard's orders to remain on the defensive and pushed their men forward to a position from where they could give support. Although most of the infantry were quickly brought back into line by staff officers, Engel's two machine gun sections had disappeared from view in the dense early morning mist by the time they arrived. One section, accompanied by an infantry detachment under Hauptmann von Detten, occupied the large farm of La Grosse Haie, at a bend in the high road that led towards the battlefield while the other section, together with a strong detachment from 4/Franz, all under Engel's command, occupied the farm of Dessus les Sarts and the nearby hamlet of Gay, from where they covered the approaches to Arsimont. As a result of Engel's impetuous decision, the two machine gun sections were now in a terribly exposed position, out of contact with the main firing line which was more than a mile to the rear, and shrouded by the dense early morning mist which restricted visibility to as little as 50 yards in some places. Having set up their guns and knocked loopholes in the thick walls of the farm buildings and outhouses, they settled down to wait for the enemy to appear. On their right, they could hear the distant noise of the fighting at Tamines; ahead of them, however, in the direction from which the French would come, there was not a sound to be heard.

It did not take long for the French to arrive. During the night, following Bonnier's appeal for help, Defforges had ordered both of his divisions to renew the attack at dawn even though this was contrary to Lanrezac's instructions to engage the enemy on the plateau and not in the valley. The 20th Division, which was on the left, was to drive the Germans out of Tamines while Bonnier's 19th Division eliminated the bridgehead at Auvelais. The principal effort was to be made by the 48e RI which was ordered to head directly for Auvelais, passing to the east of Arsimont and supported on its right by two battalions from the 41e RI. Before the attack began, however, it was vitally important to occupy Arsimont to cover the left flank as it skirted down the eastern side of the village.

Since Bonnier had no fresh troops of his own available, he was forced to borrow the 2e RI from the 20th Division. They were to begin their attack at dawn so that Arsimont would be in their hands by 8.30am when the main offensive was due to begin. No problems were expected, since a report that arrived at Corps Headquarters during the night stated that the village was unoccupied and that the Germans were nowhere to be seen. In reality, however, the 2e RI was heading directly towards the German machine guns whose positions were concealed from them by the dense mist. As a result, they immediately became pinned down in front of Dessus les Sarts and La Grosse Haie and were forced out of Gay after a violent hand-to-hand fight. As the pressure of French numbers began to tell, Engel's small force skilfully fell back in short bounds, halting from time to time to pour fire into the steadily diminishing French ranks. In the late morning they were back where they had started in the firing line of 4/Franz, much to the relief of the company commander, Hauptmann von Rieben, half of whose men had gone with them.

By holding up the enemy for almost three hours Engel ensured that the Germans were still in possession of Arsimont when the French launched their main attack. At 8.00am, the leading units of the 48e RI reached the high ground at Hill 190, the last but one crest before they came into view of the Germans. On their left, on the far side of the high road, they could hear the sound of rifle and machine-gun fire coming from the farm at La Grosse Haie, which was still under attack by the 2e RI. (Detten's detachment had remained in place when Engel's men fell back from Dessus les Sarts.) In front of them and to their right all was quiet except for the regular drone of passing shells from the German heavy artillery on the high ground to the north of the river. When they reached the valley of the Supré brook they halted and shook out into attack formation while Colonel de Flotte went ahead to reconnoitre from the top of a spoil heap at Fosse No 1. From here the land sloped gently down to the pit buildings and the spoil heaps of Fosse No 2, which were faintly visible through the thin veils of lingering mist. However, de Flotte was unable to distinguish the enemy's firing line and there was no sign of the promised artillery support, even though he had sent a liaison officer to the batteries only a short distance away on the edge of Ham Wood to let them know that the attack was about to take place. (Some of them had been silenced by the German heavy artillery and the rest held their fire because they too had been unable to locate the German trenches.) Weighed down with apprehension, de Flotte returned to his troops, gathered his officers around him and gave orders for the I Battalion on the left to capture Haut-Batys and II Battalion on the right to advance in the general direction of Fosse No 2.

A short while later, the buglers sounded the charge and the two battalions crossed the ridge and set off across the open fields towards the German positions. As soon as they came into view they were caught in a devastating crossfire from ahead (the pit buildings at Fosse No 2) and from the left flank (Haut-Batys and Arsimont). Colonel de Flotte was one of the first to be hit, falling mortally wounded in the opening minutes of the attack, quickly followed by many of the other officers, all of whom were easily distinguishable to the Germans by their white gloves. In addition to the colonel, the casualties included six company commanders, nine out of the 16 lieutenants and over one third of the rank and file. Their only success was on the left where they reached the southern edge of Arsimont and almost cut off Detten's detachment at La Grosse Haie. To make matters worse, the 41e RI, which was meant to support the attack, became disorientated in the dense mist and was also overwhelmed by the hail of fire.

Bonnier had watched the 48e RI march past his headquarters on their way to the battlefield. Convinced that the attack would succeed, he decided to throw more troops into the battle while the Germans were off balance and before they had time to bring up reinforcements. Since he had no fresh troops of his own and had already borrowed a regiment from the 20th Division, he made a direct appeal for help to Général Comby, whose 37th (North African) Division was approaching the front line. Comby was at first reluctant to lend his support, but after being told (erroneously) that Auvelais was only weakly held by the enemy he agreed to the request and placed the 2nd Regiment of Zouaves and an artillery group at Bonnier's disposal. Since their commander, Lieutenant-Colonel Trousselle, knew very little about the situation (the division had only arrived in France a few days earlier and had not even been issued with maps) he rode on ahead of the march-column to find out what he could about the enemy's strength and position. Although he was warned by survivors from the 48e RI that the Germans were dug in and had plenty of machine guns, he nevertheless decided to launch an immediate attack in the general direction of Fosse No 2 despite the fact that there was no time in which to organize artillery support. In the meantime, his men were marching in perfect order past Hill 190, their baggy white trousers and dark tunics standing out against the golden stubble and with the battalion and regimental standards flapping in the gentle early morning breeze at the head of the column. When they arrived at the valley of the Supré brook where Trousselle was waiting for them, they deployed into attack formation and fixed their highly polished bayonets, which scintillated in the sunlight. At about 9.30am, the buglers sounded the charge and they launched themselves over the crest and ran full tilt towards the firing line of II/Augusta about 800 yards away.

The Zouaves descended to the right of the farm [the Farm of the Four Laurels near the head of the Supré valley] not very anxious about the bullets for they were still two kilometres from the enemy. They crossed the Supré brook and before arriving at the crest they were brought to a halt by whistles blown by their section leaders. They were kneeling on the ground, ahead of them their officers, white-gloved, pipes in their mouths and canes in their hands, impatient to charge the Prussian Guard which they knew lay in front of them. On their left, the debris of the 48e, galvanised by their example, recrossed the Supré and arrived level with them.

The Zouaves' buglers sounded the charge. In front of them there wasn't the least cover until they reached Fosse No 2 and Haut-Batys but the terrain of the attack was open to view from the heights of the Bois de Curé on the far side of the river. Then from all of the buildings in Haut-Batys and Fosse No 2 there burst out rifle and machine gun bullets which swept the crest; and almost immediately afterwards there arrived from the heights of the Bois de Curé the 'gros noirs' [the 150mm Howitzer shells which exploded with a great spurt of dense black smoke] and which burst on the crest.

Large gaps were produced in the ranks. The Zouaves continued their march; the officers rushed forwards and fell, Lieutenant-Colonel Trousselle was among the first of them. The soldiers continued onwards past those who had fallen and in a magnificent charge reached the Pêcherie brook [about halfway to the German firing line]. About 50 of them from Decherp's Battalion got as far as Fosse No 2. In a rapid hand-to-hand fight they took possession of the factory. We could see some of them climbing up the spoil heap, outlined for a little while on the top, then a moment after descending any old how and falling back into the neighbouring copse of trees. In this woodland, a bugler, turning back, sounded the charge once more. A new group of Zouaves left the brook and entered the factory but couldn't hold on to it. They clung on in the woodland to the right of Fosse No 2 and at a bend in the brook. The 2nd Zouaves had been brought to a definite halt.[11]

Within half an hour they had lost their colonel, 20 other officers and more than 700 men, approximately one third of their strength. Once more the German machine gunners had proved themselves masters of the battlefield, leaving the fields around the village of Arsimont strewn with the corpses of yet another French regiment, the sixth in the space of the last 24 hours.

From his headquarters, Bonnier looked on as the wounded men arrived on foot and on carts, seeking the town's field hospital. A further appeal to Comby for help was not surprisingly turned down, although he agreed to deploy the 2e Tirailleurs to cover the retreat. For the next few hours the debris of the Zouaves and the 48e and 41e RI slowly fell back through the covering lines of the Tirailleurs without coming under pressure from the Germans. After a while they halted in the fields to rest and eat a little and then trudged down the high road leading to the centre of the plateau. By midday the French had pulled out completely, leaving the exhausted Germans in possession of the battlefield. On the right, Roeder's Battle Group made contact with units from X Corps which had forced their way on to the high ground overlooking Tamines and on the left Walther's Battle Group linked up with Regiment Elisabeth, which had crossed the river in the late morning. With the bridgehead now secure, the men settled down to rest in the hot afternoon sunshine.

Events in the other bridgehead, at Roselies, took a roughly similar course to those at Auvelais–Arsimont. When the first attempt to recapture the village failed, GénéralVerrier, the commander of the 5th Division, upped the stakes by ordering it to be repeated in much greater strength. Unfortunately, by the time the attack took place the Germans had moved fresh troops into the village and had prepared it defensively, barricading the streets and hauling machine guns to the tops of the nearby spoil heaps. In addition, they brought forward an artillery battery to the north bank of the river from where it could bring short-range fire to bear on the approaches to the village. As a result, the French regiment involved was struck so violently that they lost almost a quarter of their men before they got as far as the first houses. Driving forwards into the interior, the survivors became easy prey for the German machine gunners and retreated in great disorder, covered by the fire from one of their artillery batteries.[12] Following this, the outposts which were defending the bridges at Châtelet and Pont de Loup were forced to fall back to avoid being cut off, thereby allowing the 19th Infantry Division to cross the river unopposed and ascend the long slopes towards the Bouffioulx Ridge which overlooked the valley at this point. To begin with the French held on tenaciously in trenches they had dug the previous day with the help of local civilians, but in the late morning they were forced to fall back when the Germans penetrated the gap at Roselies and threatened to envelop their right flank.

By midday, the French 5th Division was in a very difficult situation; in the centre, the defensive position on the Bouffioulx Ridge was about to collapse and the right wing was in the air after Général Boë's 20th Division (X Corps) had retreated from Tamines. Since Verrier had no reserves left, the corps commander, Sauret, ordered the 75th (North African) Brigade to retake Châtelet and eliminate the bridgehead. After leaving the security of Châtelet woods, they deployed and prepared to cross the ridge and attack.

> They filed past us with their bronzed faces, their shining teeth and eyes, their wide mouths grinning. An unstoppable flow, in excellent order; their baggy linen trousers, their cloaks, their massive packs resting on their spines, on their sides, two litre water bottles. At the head of each section marched an officer in khaki … cane in their hand. They were going to charge, they were going to die.[13]

Pausing only to fix bayonets, the 1e Tirailleurs swept over the final crest and advanced down the long bare slope, completely devoid of cover, in the direction of the village more than half a mile away. Their sudden appearance came as a complete shock to the German infantry who were just about to capture the ridge after several hours of painfully slow progress and who were overwhelmed and thrown back in the direction of the village. However, the attack began to lose impetus as the Tirailleurs came under rifle and machine-gun fire from the German trenches at the southern exits of Châtelet and from the batteries firing at close range from the far side of the river. Nevertheless, in a magnificent though futile display of elan, they surged forwards through the hail of fire and got as far as the first houses before most of them were either mown down or captured. The few survivors retreated over the corpse-strewn slopes and were reassembled with difficulty under the cover of the woods at the edge of the plateau. Losses were enormous and the regimental standard had changed hands five times as successive standard bearers had fallen; in the laconic words of the Tirailleur's war diary: 'The standard bearer was killed five times.'[14] When Verrier became aware that they had failed to retake Châtelet he gave up the attempt to eliminate the bridgehead and ordered the 5th Division to fall back to a defensive position on the plateau. At the same time the 6th Division on their left also retreated to protect their flank and because the German 19th Reserve Infantry Division (from X Reserve Corps) had crossed the river at Montigny-sur-Sambre on the outskirts of Charleroi.

By early evening, therefore, III and X Corps had retreated on to the plateau, leaving the Germans in undisputed control of the bridgeheads at Auvelais and Roselies. The first reports about the fighting to reach Lanrezac's command post at Mettet in the early afternoon were fragmentary and inconclusive. However, as the dismal procession of wounded and stragglers passed through the town's streets in ever-increasing numbers, it rapidly became clear that things were far from well. During the afternoon further reports arrived telling of the failure of successive counter-attacks, of heavy losses and of ground given up. Men spoke of the terrible machine-gun fire and the devastation wrought by the German heavy artillery, whose huge shells they described as *marmites* (cauldrons). In the middle of the afternoon a car drew up in front of the command post carrying Général Boë who had been badly wounded in the stomach while organising the withdrawal of his men from Tamines. According to Spears, Hély d'Oissel, 5th Army Chief of Staff:

> ... almost ran to the car, and clasped Boë's hand. He did not speak. Boë was silent for a moment, looking towards Lanrezac. Then he whispered, 'Tell him,' he gasped,

then speaking louder as he realized Hély d'Oissel could hardly hear him, he repeated, 'tell the General that we held on as long as we could.' His head fell back, his eyes were very sad. Hély d'Oissel grasped his hand again and said nothing. The car grated into gear, and drove slowly on.[15]

In the late afternoon, Lanrezac ordered III and X Corps to occupy defensive positions in the centre of the plateau, supported on their left by de Mas Latrie's XVIII Corps and on the right by Franchet d'Esperey's I Corps when it was relieved from guarding the Meuse by the 51st Reserve Division. Since there was no reply to his message to 4th Army, asking them how their attack into the Ardennes was progressing, he ordered the Meuse bridges to be destroyed except for the ones at Givet, Hastière and Dinant, which were to be blown up on the approach of the enemy. He was also concerned about the situation at the other end of the battlefield where a gap of about 8 miles had opened up between XVIII Corps and the British Army, which had advanced during the day to the area of Mons. Unfortunately, Valabrègue's Group of Reserve Divisions, which was responsible for covering the army's left flank, had been delayed and was not expected to arrive for at least another 24 hours. In the meantime, the job of sealing the gap would have to be temporarily carried out by Sordet's Cavalry Corps until in compliance with Joffre's orders it moved westwards to cover the left wing of the British Army. A request to the British for help was turned down by Sir John French, on the grounds that he expected to be attacked the next day by a large German force (the German 1st Army) which had been detected on the march towards his left wing along the Mons–Condé canal. All that he could promise was to remain in his present position for a further 24 hours in the hope that this would give Lanrezac some support.

As far as Bülow was concerned, the day had been a complete success; the bridgeheads had been consolidated and in some cases expanded, the enemy driven back on to the plateau in considerable disarray and with the exception of the 14th Infantry Division which was due to arrive early the next day, the army was up to full strength. Thus, in his orders for the 23rd, 2nd Army would cross the Sambre except for VII Corps on the right, which was to screen Maubeuge, and VII Reserve Corps on the left, which was to cover the left wing against Namur.

Once again 1st Army was requested to swing inwards to put pressure on the French left wing and at the same time to detach troops to invest Maubeuge. All being well, the French would be caught in the trap that had been laid for them and heavily defeated within the next couple of days.[16]

## 23 AUGUST: THE FAILED PINCER MOVEMENT BY THE GERMAN 2ND AND 3RD ARMIES

The task that faced Hausen on the morning of the 23rd was extremely difficult. At this point in its course, the swiftly flowing Meuse was enclosed between very steep limestone cliffs and the few narrow roads which approached the valley from the east, in the direction of their advance, were not only completely devoid of cover but were overlooked by the French batteries on the high ground on the far side of the river. Even if the German infantry safely reached the bottom of the valley they would then have to cross the river under fire, using either the three intact bridges or hastily constructed pontoon bridges. Since neither XII Reserve Corps nor XI Corps was available (the former was at least half a day's march to the rear and the latter was taking part in the siege of Namur), Hausen divided the sector in two, assigning the northern half (Dinant inclusive to Yvoir) to General d'Elsa's XII Corps and the southern half (Dinant exclusive to Hastière) to General von Laffert's XIX Corps. When XII Reserve Corps arrived in the late afternoon it would be used to reinforce the right wing in the vicinity of Yvoir. On the far left the line was echeloned back to guard against an attack by the French 4th Army, which was thought to be in the area.

On the stroke of 5.00am the German artillery opened fire in the general direction of the enemy batteries on the far side of the river and advance guards were sent into the valley to test the strength of the defences. (The French troops belonged to Boutegourd's 51st Reserve Division, which had relieved I Corps during the night, earlier than expected.) The Germans made much better progress in the southern sector, which was less strongly defended than the northern side. After an attempt to capture the bridge at Hastière failed with heavy losses, they quickly identified several suitable crossing points and started to build pontoon bridges. By the early afternoon four bridges had been completed and a small

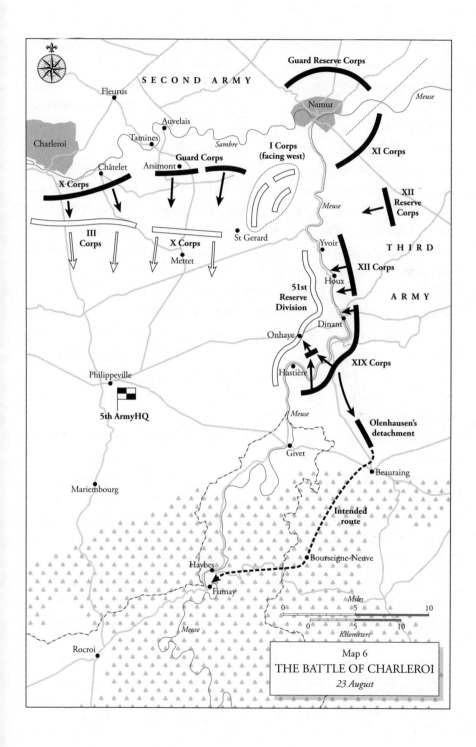

Map 6
**THE BATTLE OF CHARLEROI**
*23 August*

number of infantry and an artillery group had crossed to the other side. In the middle of the morning, however, Hausen received a radio message from OHL that contained new orders. 'The line of the Meuse between Namur and Givet will be opened today by the left wing of 2nd Army. It is recommended that all available parts of 3rd Army move across the Meuse to the south of Givet to delay the retreat of the opposing enemy forces.'[17] In other words, all the units that could be spared were to be diverted to the south, down the *eastern* side of the river and were only to cross over to the western bank once they had passed Givet. In this way, they would be able to cut off the rapidly retreating French instead of striking them in the flank or allowing them to escape. Hausen therefore instructed Laffert to send the largest force possible down the eastern side of the river under the command of one of his divisional generals, Götz von Olenhausen, with the immediate objective of Fumay, approximately 15 miles south of Hastière. A short while later, after aerial reconnaissance confirmed that the French were falling back rapidly in front of 2nd Army, Hausen decided to divert not only Olenhausen's detachment to Givet but all of XIX Corps except for those units which had already crossed the river. The latter were ordered to advance to the south-west and capture the village of Onhaye, an important road junction at the centre of the plateau.

In comparison, resistance was much stronger in the northern sector. Repeated efforts to build pontoon bridges failed with heavy casualties, as did several attempts to seize the intact bridges at Dinant and Bouvignes. Although the partially damaged bridge at Houx was captured in the early afternoon, the French continued to resist stubbornly and it was not until early evening that they gave up the fight and abandoned their positions. After pausing to regroup, the Germans set off westwards and at nightfall went over to rest in the centre of the plateau. Likewise, at Leffe, to the north of Dinant, the pioneers were only able to begin building a bridge in the late afternoon after the French had gone and this was not completed until midnight, when a few troops crossed the river and went into bivouac on the west bank.

The heaviest fighting of the day took place at Dinant, which was defended by only one French regiment, the 273e RI. In 1914 the town had approximately 7,000 inhabitants and was enclosed within a narrow 2-mile-long strip of land sandwiched between the eastern bank of the river on one side and almost vertical cliffs on the other. In the centre, where the town was at its widest, the narrow winding streets were intersected by several small squares, open to the river on their western side. At both ends of the town the buildings gradually petered out until they reached the outer suburbs of Leffe and Bouvignes to the north and Les Rivages to the south. The fact that the town had two bridges, and that several roads radiated out from here on to the plateau to the west, made it the linchpin of the Meuse position and one that the French could not afford to lose.

Early in the morning, the first German troops descended the steep roads leading into Dinant. In the north, units from the 32nd Infantry Division entered Leffe while at the same time two columns from the 23rd Infantry Division arrived in the town centre. From the moment they entered the deserted streets the Germans appeared to be expecting trouble from the inhabitants, most of whom had taken refuge in their cellars when the bombardment began.

> They marched in two columns down the deserted street, those on the right aiming their rifles at the houses on the left, and vice-versa, all with their fingers on the trigger and ready to fire. At each door a group stopped and riddled the houses, especially the windows, with bullets ... I know that the soldiers threw many bombs into the cellars.[18]

Throughout the morning the townsfolk were forced out of their houses, assembled into groups and led away into captivity in the town prison, the Bouille iron foundry or the cloth factory and the abbey church at Leffe. Men, women and children were taken away with no consideration for age or infirmity and those who were either too old or too ill to walk were carried out on chairs or on people's backs. When the houses had been cleared of their occupants, grenades were thrown into them or they were set on fire. As soon as the leading troops came into view of the French on the opposite bank they came under fire and were forced to seek cover. Unable to pass safely through the Place d'Armes they rounded up about one hundred people, both men and women, and used them as human shields, making them stand in the square to screen their movements. A short while later, a similar event took place at Les Rivages, where the German infantry were working their way southwards to where the pioneers were preparing to construct a pontoon bridge.

By the middle of the afternoon the six German battalions had made very little progress. Two attempts to rush the bridge in the centre of the town were easily repelled and the construction of the pontoon bridge at Les Rivages was abandoned when it was only about 40 yards long because of enemy fire. With the nerves of his men stretched to the limit and their tempers boiling over, the commander of I/IR 100, Oberstleutnant Graf Kielmannsegg, ordered the prisoners in the Bouille iron foundry to be taken out and shot in retaliation, so he said, for having fired on wounded soldiers in a nearby field hospital. As the hostages were being escorted into the town centre they were passed by part of a German bridging train which was carrying pontoons towards the river and were made to shout 'Long live Germany'. A few of the soldiers menaced them with their rifles and abused them with calls of 'cowardly Belgian pigs'. At that moment several soldiers passed by carrying a mattress on which there was a wounded officer with a white moustache, his head swathed in bandages. 'He was in a rage, foaming at the mouth, he insulted us and spat at us, "dirty Belgian dogs," he said, and shook his fist at us.'[19]

When they reached the street that ran past the house of State Prosecutor Tschoffen they were halted and the men were separated from the women in preparation for the execution. Many harrowing scenes took place as loved ones bid each other a hasty and final farewell. Madame Firmin had already lost her father and her husband that morning, the former shot in the head by the Germans and the latter dying from loss of blood after his arm had been slashed by a sabre. Now, she was also about to lose her three sons.

> When they were separating the men from the women, one of the soldiers put the infant of Henri Georges into my arms. My eldest son then came to say goodbye and to give me encouragement by saying that they were going to find their father in heaven. He had asked his brothers not to leave him and they departed from me, holding on to one another by their elbows. I then saw my three sons fall from the bullets and I fled holding my hands to my head! When the next day, at six o'clock in the morning, I returned to the pile of corpses, I found my three sons still in the same embrace.[20]

One of the officers however, (possibly Major von Loeben who was in charge of the execution squad), allowed several of the older men and those with young families to return to the group of women and children. In some cases a ghastly tug of war broke out as some of the men were allowed to leave the condemned group only to be immediately forced to return by other, less compassionate, soldiers. Mademoiselle Binamé, the governess of the children of M Wasseige (himself one of the condemned), described what happened to two of the children in her care as the men in the family were about to be shot:

> M [Wasseige] gave me his money and placed the children in my care … I shall see
> him in my thoughts for a long time, that pale and resigned figure! Pierre had just
> time to say to me, 'you will pray for us, won't you?' As for Jacques, he didn't say a
> word. I moved away with the other children when a soldier came to take André
> and Etienne, aged 17 and 15 respectively, and put them in the group of men. An
> officer separated them but three times the soldier took them back. At last, the two
> children were able to rejoin me.[21]

After the women and children had been taken away, the condemned men were lined up in four rows in front of the long wall that separated the street from the garden of Tschoffen's house. As they awaited their end, some silent as if resigned to their fate, others quietly praying for salvation or making desperate appeals for mercy, they were harangued in poor French by Kielmannsegg, who explained why they were being executed. One of the condemned, M Drion, described what happened next:

> We were arranged in a depth of three or four men, except for one spot where there
> were up to six; within moments there would have been a pile of bodies more than
> a metre high here. The execution squad wasn't big enough so the officer called for
> other men to join them, placing them on the side just opposite me. I heard him
> shout, *'Noch zwölf, noch sechs'*, ['twelve more, six more'] and the soldiers rushed
> forwards as if they were going to the fair! There must have been approximately 125
> soldiers altogether. Suddenly, I heard someone blow a whistle and immediately a
> volley rang out accompanied by cries of horror and fright coming from the groups
> of women and children who witnessed this terrible scene.

All of the men along the wall fell. It was about 6 o'clock. One corpse fell on top of me, three others were on my legs. I pretended to be dead. I didn't have a scratch. Hardly had we hit the ground when a second salvo rang out… At that moment I was hit by two bullets which had ricocheted; one of them wounded me in the region of my ear and the other hit me in the back of the head near the nape of my neck. A few moments afterwards there was a third, fairly long burst of firing from the right and the left but not in a salvo. I then heard steps … it was the officers and soldiers who were going about from one end to the other finishing off the wounded.[22]

Only about a dozen men survived the execution, some, like M Drion, because they were protected from the bullets by the men in front of them, others because members of the execution squad took pity on them and deliberately aimed too high. According to one of the Belgians, 'The corporal who was opposite me made a sign that he wouldn't fire at me,' while the retired Colonel Roulin, who had been reprieved on account of his age, said 'Certain soldiers carried out their orders badly and fired too high. Traces of the bullets were left on the parapet of the garden wall and on the gables of Drion's house, 50 metres from the wall.'[23] Despite this, 137 civilians had been killed in what became known as the Tschoffen Wall Massacre, the worst crime against non-combatants on the Western Front in the whole of the war. Seven of the victims were over 60 years old, the oldest being Julien Disy, shopkeeper, aged 68, and 11 were less than 20 years old, the youngest of whom were Jules Vinstock, student, and Vital Sorée, factory worker, both aged 15. This was not the only execution to have been carried out; others took place at Leffe and at Les Rivages where the dead included 38 women and 15 children below the age of 14. By the end of this ghastly day, a total of 674 inhabitants were dead, almost 10 per cent of Dinant's population, and numerous others were awaiting deportation to Germany.

Resistance came to an end in the late afternoon when the French blew up the bridges at Dinant and Bouvignes and retreated up the hill to the plateau, covered by a weak rearguard along the river. With the enemy gone, the pioneers resumed their work on the pontoon bridge at Les Rivages, which was completed in the late evening allowing the first troops to cross the river. The division went over to rest at nightfall with one brigade in the town and the other in bivouac on the west bank, a long way short of the day's objectives.

While the German 3rd Army had been attempting to force its way across the Meuse, 2nd Army had experienced mixed fortunes. On the left wing, the Guard Corps and X Corps cautiously followed the French as they retreated to a new defensive position in the early morning and apart from a few minor rearguard actions there was no contact between them. On the right wing, however, the 14th Infantry Division and the X Reserve Corps were involved in a prolonged and violent fight when they attempted to set foot on the plateau to the south of the river. In the early afternoon, the 14th Infantry Division crossed the river near Lobbes without difficulty but became caught up in a bitter and inconclusive contest with part of the French XVIII Corps for possession of the Heuleu plateau to the south of the village. As more and more reinforcements arrived on both sides, the fighting surged this way and that across the large clearing around Philemon Farm until nightfall when the French retreated and the Germans recrossed the river with most of their troops, leaving only a small force to guard the bridges in and around Lobbes.

A short distance to the east, meanwhile, the 2nd Guards Reserve Division was severely mauled by the rest of XVIII Corps when it attempted to break out of the shallow bridgehead which it had established the previous evening. Accurate French rifle and machine-gun fire from well-prepared positions tore huge gaps in the German lines as they tried to capture the villages of Marbaix and Gozée and in the late afternoon the troops at Gozée panicked and fled when they were hit by a massive artillery bombardment and then violently counter-attacked. Although the Germans captured the two villages during the evening, after they had been strongly reinforced, in his situation report the corps commander said that if they were attacked the next morning they would probably not be able to hold on to their positions.

Early that morning Bülow had been confident that a decisive victory was within his grasp; during the evening, however, when he was informed of the problems on the right wing (in particular the losses in the 2nd Guards Reserve Division) he veered round completely and began to worry that he faced defeat the next day unless he obtained help from his neighbours. He therefore sent a message to Kluck asking for his nearest available unit, IX Corps, to attack the French near Maubeuge to take the pressure off his right wing and at the same time requested Hausen to come to his aid by advancing westwards with the whole of 3rd Army the following morning instead of to the south-west as Moltke had requested.

As it happened, Lanrezac had no intentions of mounting an attack. Having pulled his forces back on to the middle of the plateau his immediate intention was to stay where he was for the moment and wait for 4th Army to come to his support. However, as the hours passed without any news from them his confidence began to waver and for the first time he began to think that it might be necessary to retreat still further.[24] In addition, he gradually realized that after two days of hard fighting his troops were in a worse condition than he had first thought. As the morning wore on, the endless procession of refugees which crawled through the narrow main street of Philippeville, past his command post, contained an increasing number of stragglers and walking wounded, intent on putting as much distance as possible between themselves and the enemy. Spears, who witnessed this, left a vivid account of the tragic scene on this cold and misty Sunday morning:

[Lanrezac] was one of those who stood on the place [the main square] and watched; he was there nearly the whole morning. In his black tunic and red breeches, black-gaitered legs apart, hands behind his back, he stared. The heavy folds of his face seemed to droop more than usual. He made no comment, but I have heard it said that what he saw that morning made a deep impression on him, as indeed it did upon us all. It was whispered that the sight of those people driven forward by the wind of defeat did much to shake his confidence. Once he was startled out of his contemplation by some gendarmes who came up, bringing a couple of Zouaves they had in charge. Although I remember well the gendarmes saying they had found these men without arms behind the lines, and the Zouaves' explanation that they had been cut off and had dropped their rifles in escaping over a wall they had climbed, I have entirely forgotten General Lanrezac's decision. I can see him shake his head, then speak looking away and over the heads of the prisoners and their escort, and I remember the Zouaves being led away, that is all.

The main street, a continuation of the great chaussée up which Napoleon's IV Corps had marched to Waterloo, led into Philippeville from the north. It ran along one side of the place, and was packed with people, all going in one direction, their backs to the north. A grey mob, grey because the black clothes most of them wore were covered with dust, was filing endlessly by; they occupied the whole width of the road, pouring past like a crowd returning from a race meeting, but in absolute silence, the only sound being that of very tired feet dragging on the *pavé* [the cobblestones]. Each individual in that slowly moving mass looked the embodiment of a personal tragedy; men and women with set staring faces, carrying heavy bundles, moving on they knew not where, formed a background of grim despair to this or that group of individuals whose more vivid suffering seemed to illuminate that drab flow of desolation.

I can still see a couple of young girls, sisters perhaps, helping each other, hardly able to drag themselves along, the blood from their torn feet oozing through their low silk shoes; a very sick woman, who looked as if she were dying, balanced somehow on a perambulator; a paralytic old man in a wheelbarrow, pushed by his sturdy daughter; a very old, very respectable couple, who for years had probably done no more than walk arm in arm round a small garden, now, still arm in arm, were helping each other in utter bewilderment of mind and exhaustion of body down the long meaningless road.[25]

In the early afternoon, Lanrezac's worst fears were confirmed by news that the Germans were across the Meuse in force and were advancing towards Onhaye, to the rear of 5th Army's right wing. This news, which originated from Général Boutegourd, was a gross exaggeration. As we have seen, at this time only a few German battalions had crossed the river to the north of Hastière. A German advance from this direction posed enormous problems for I Corps in particular, which was facing westwards as it prepared to attack the German 2nd Guards Infantry Division as it passed their front. Although Lanrezac had turned down Franchet d'Esperey's request to execute the attack, his troops had manoeuvred into position and were now threatened with being taken in the rear from the direction of Onhaye. At about 2.00pm, therefore, Lanrezac ordered him to reinforce the 51st Reserve Division immediately and with their help throw the Germans back across the Meuse.[26]

By late evening, Lanrezac had a fairly clear picture of the overall situation. He was aware that XVIII Corps had been involved in heavy fighting and had sustained considerable losses and that III Corps was in a poor condition and had been forced to retreat rapidly after being attacked in the middle of the afternoon. In addition, although Franchet d'Esperey reported that the enemy force which had crossed the Meuse was smaller than expected and had been forced back towards the river, there was no guarantee that the Germans would not repeat the attempt in greater force the next day. Lastly, the fall of Namur was confirmed by the arrival of a group of Belgian officers who had escaped from the city just before the last of the forts had capitulated. In the absence of news from 4th Army, Lanrezac was increasingly worried about the security of his right flank along the Meuse and began to have second thoughts about waiting for them to arrive. He was also unaware that the British had been in action all day at Mons against the German 1st Army and after having brought the enemy to a sudden halt were about to retreat the next day.[27] At 9.00pm he made up his mind to retreat in order to prevent his troops from being trapped in the Sambre–Meuse Salient. Orders were issued for the retreat to begin the next morning, starting at 3.00am and to continue until they reached the base of the Salient.

# 5

# THE RETREAT BEGINS

## 24 AUGUST: THE FRENCH ESCAPE FROM THE BATTLEFIELD

Several hours before dawn 5th Army began a retreat which was to last for almost a fortnight, only coming to an end on 5 September, the eve of the battle of the Marne. After an uneventful march they ended the day along the northern outskirts of the heavily wooded area at the base of the Sambre–Meuse Salient. On the left, XVIII Corps was strongly angled back to the north-west to keep in touch with the British Army, which was retreating after the battle of Mons the previous day.

Their escape from the battlefield was made possible by Bülow's hesitancy and because Hausen's troops wasted the early morning by marching westwards to come to his aid. By the time Hausen discovered that this was unnecessary, and that the French were retreating as rapidly as possible, it was too late to cut them off. Except for the small force which was advancing towards Onhaye, XII Corps recrossed the Meuse and set off down the eastern bank of the river but the heavily wooded terrain prevented them from getting very far before nightfall intervened. Likewise, Olenhausen's detachment which had left for Fumay the previous afternoon was held back by weak French rearguards in the great woods to the east of the town and was unable to cross the river because they did not possess bridging trains.[1] In the meantime, 2nd Army spent all morning in its overnight positions because Bülow believed that he was about to be attacked, and so when he became aware that the French had slipped away during the night he was unable to catch up with them. The previous evening he had been so worried about his safety that he had asked both Hausen and Kluck for help; now, however, with the enemy in full retreat, he decided that victory was his for the taking. In the early afternoon, the good news was sent to OHL: 'Enemy right wing decisively defeated. 3rd Army moves over the Meuse near Philippeville. His Majesty the Kaiser to be informed. All remains in attack.'[2]

Although neither the French nor the British came under serious pressure on the 24th, the stress of keeping at least one step ahead of the Germans had an increasingly harmful effect on the already fragile relationship between Lanrezac and Sir John French. Firstly, soon after dawn Spears brought news from the British that if their left (western) flank was threatened with envelopment they would fall back in a south-westerly direction, along their lines of communication, even though this would uncover the French left wing and open up a gap between the two armies. Secondly, in the middle of the afternoon Lanrezac instructed XVIII Corps and Valabrègue's Reserve Divisions to halt temporarily to support the British right wing, which he erroneously believed was about to make a counter-attack near Maubeuge. When Spears passed on the good news to Murray, the British Chief of Staff, it was not received with the expected show of gratitude.

> [Murray] pointed out that XVIII Corps was 10 miles in the rear of the British right; Lanrezac's condition that he would only attack if the British did so also, was absurd. An attack by Lanrezac with his left might be a great advantage and help us out, but to make it a condition that we should advance if he did was tantamount to offering to have a whack at the lion if we first put our head into its mouth.[3]

By now, Joffre was acutely aware that his carefully prepared plans were in disarray. On the right, 1st and 2nd Armies had been violently counter-attacked and forced to retreat, in the centre 4th Army had been decisively defeated in the Ardennes and on the left 5th Army had suffered heavy casualties and was threatened with envelopment. Towards noon he alerted the Minister for War to the perilous state of affairs and outlined the measures he intended taking to stabilize the situation. Firstly, no time would be lost in weeding out incompetent generals whose names would be passed on to the War Ministry with a recommendation either of employment on secondary duties, well away from the front line, or retirement

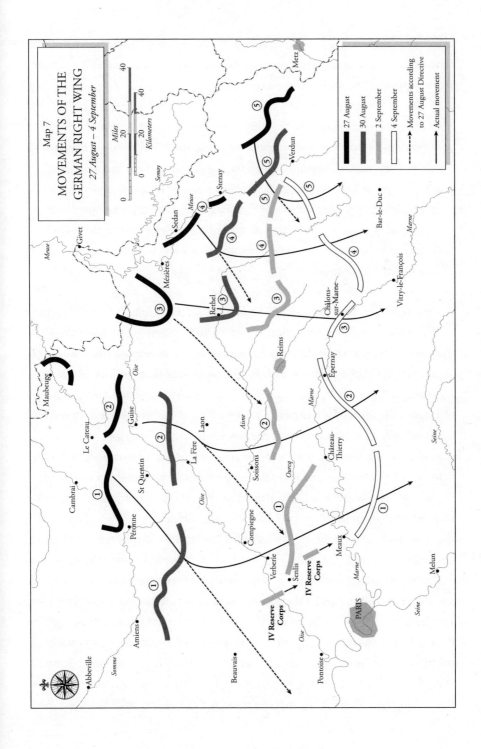

Map 7

MOVEMENTS OF THE
GERMAN RIGHT WING

*27 August – 4 September*

27 August
30 August
2 September
4 September
Movements according
to 27 August Directive
Actual movement

from active service. (Millerand went even further by suggesting that any officer found guilty of cowardice should be court-martialed and then shot.) Secondly, Joffre explained his immediate strategy:

> We are forced to conclude from the evidence that, despite the numerical superiority which is assured to them, our corps have not shown in the open country the offensive qualities which we had hoped for following the partial successes in the early fighting in the mountains. We are therefore condemned to a defensive attitude resting upon our fortified places and on the great obstacles of the terrain, giving up as little territory as possible. Our aim must be to hold out as long as possible, trying to wear down the enemy and to retake the offensive when the moment comes.[4]

For the next few days 4th and 5th Armies would pass through heavily wooded terrain, which would prevent effective use of their 75mm guns. However, when they were out of this area they would be in open country where they would be able to go over to the offensive with the full support of their artillery. In the early morning, Joffre therefore ordered Lanrezac to manoeuvre in retreat, taking as points of support the fortress of Maubeuge to the west and the wooded hills to the east while keeping in close touch with the British on the one side and 4th Army on the other. At the same time he sent a message to Sir John French asking him to delay the Germans along the line Maubeuge–Valenciennes; 'in other words along the prolongation of the line Givet–Beaumont, where I hope to see 5th Army make its stand.'[5] In the meantime it was necessary to strengthen the left wing, which was threatened with envelopment. Unfortunately, neither the British nor the Belgians could provide help; the two divisions which had remained behind in Britain on the outbreak of the war could not be dispatched for several weeks and the Belgians needed all of their troops for the defence of Antwerp. In the absence of help from France's allies, the only solution was to withdraw troops from less sensitive parts of the front and transfer them to the threatened sector. As a start, Joffre sent a telegram to the Army of Alsace to say that the greater part of VII Corps would be taken from them and transported to the left wing. In addition, to give extra support to the British he ordered two reserve divisions to be withdrawn from the Paris garrison and used to reinforce d'Amade's weak territorials who were guarding the gap between the British Army and the coast. At the same time Joffre took Sordet's Cavalry Corps under his direct control and ordered it to move westwards to cover the British left wing against a possible outflanking movement by the Germans.

## 25 AUGUST: THE GERMAN HIGH COMMAND SENSES VICTORY

For the German 2nd and 3rd Armies, the day was once again spent in vain pursuit of the enemy; the former was unable to catch up with them and Hausen's men had slowed to a crawl in the difficult terrain either side of the Meuse. Bülow suffered a final blow to his hopes in the late evening when he received a message from Hausen saying that he would change course to the south-east the next day to help 4th Army overcome resistance in the Sedan area. Although the pincer movement had failed, Bülow ordered the pursuit to continue the next day in a south-westerly direction, despite the fact that this would open up a gap with 3rd Army. At the same time, Maubeuge would be besieged by a composite force consisting of IX Corps from 1st Army and the 13th Infantry Division and 14th Reserve Infantry Division, both of which belonged to 2nd Army.

For the second day in a row 1st Army also failed to catch up with the British main force because Kluck did not know in which direction they were retreating. Even so, during the late evening and in the night the German advance guards made contact with the rearguards of Haig's I Corps in the villages to the south of the Forest of Mormal and several brief skirmishes took place in the darkness. At Landrecies, for example, the 4th (Guards) Brigade came under attack from the advance guards of the German IV Corps, which had also been allocated the village as their billets. Although the Guards quickly got the situation under control (they only lost about 100 men, most of them wounded), when news of the attack reached I Corps Headquarters late that night it caused considerable alarm. Not knowing the enemy's strength, and worried that they might penetrate the gap between the two corps, Haig informed Sir John French that the situation was critical and that he needed II Corps to come to his aid. When this message arrived at British GHQ in the early hours of the morning it brought about a minor panic during which French warned Smith-Dorrien, in command of II Corps, that 'the enemy appears to be working round to the south of Landrecies. GOC [General Officer Commanding] 4th Brigade doubts if he can move south.'[6] An hour or so later he appealed for help to Generals d'Amade, Sordet and Lanrezac, explaining to the latter that I Corps 'is retreating if it can, on Guise southwards, if not, south-eastwards in the direction of La Capelle... In these circumstances, Field Marshal French asks you to help him by receiving I Corps until it can rejoin the main body of the British forces.'[7] To make matters worse, at about 5.00am an urgent message arrived at GHQ from Smith-Dorrien saying that his men would be forced to stand and fight the next morning because the Germans were too close for them to retreat from their positions at Le Cateau. A short time later, Smith-Dorrien and Wilson, the Deputy Chief of Staff, were able to speak to one another by means of a railway telegraph line that had been connected up to II Corps Headquarters at Bertry. After Smith-Dorrien had described the situation in more detail, Wilson explained the measures taken by Sir John French and warned him that 'if you stand and fight there will be another Sedan.' Smith-Dorrien replied that 'it was impossible to break away now, as the action had already begun, and that he could hear the guns firing as he spoke.'[8]

At GQG meanwhile, Joffre spent most of the day discussing a possible plan of action with his senior staff officers. After considering several proposals, he finally settled on a manoeuvre that would ultimately lead to the victory of the Marne. According to this plan, a new army (6th) commanded by Général Maunoury would be created on the extreme left wing, to the north of Amiens, from where it could take the German 1st Army in the flank. The troops required would be removed from the centre and the right wing and transported to the Paris region by rail. When the time came, they would attack in a north-easterly direction, supported on the right by the British and by the left wing of 5th Army whose right wing would remain firmly anchored along the high ground from La Fère to Laon and Craonne. In order to gain sufficient time in which to assemble the new force, everything possible would have to be done to slow down the German advance by means of rearguard actions and partial offensives. During the evening, Joffre's staff prepared General Instruction No 2, which contained an outline of the plan, and copies were sent out during the night to all of the armies, including the British.[9]

Although this plan appeared attractive on paper, Joffre was not without misgivings. Would Lanrezac carry out his promise to engage the enemy strongly once 5th Army had reached the open terrain where the 75mm guns would be at their most effective? Would the German 1st Army reach Amiens before 6th Army's concentration was complete and it was ready to attack? (On the night of the 25th they were less than 60 miles or about four to five days' march away.) Would Sir John French put aside his grievances with Lanrezac and lend his full support? If the plan was to have any chance of success it was necessary to get the participants together to hammer out the details and to try and improve the relationship between Lanrezac and Sir John French. Thus, before he retired for the night, Joffre sent a message to Huguet, his liaison officer with the British, asking him to arrange a meeting the next day at St Quentin between himself, Lanrezac, Sir John French and the senior staff officers on both sides.

There were no such worries at German Supreme Headquarters, however, where the war on the Western Front was felt to be as good as won. The mood at the time was described by General von Plessen, who was in charge of the Kaiser's Military Headquarters:

> I regularly attended the daily presentation which the Chief of Staff made to the Kaiser and can definitely assert that after the arrival of the detailed report from 2nd Army Headquarters on the course of the battle in the area of the Sambre and Meuse the view of the Chief of Staff was extraordinarily optimistic. The Chief of Staff, as well as the Chief of the Operations Section, Oberstleutnant Tappen, was of the opinion that the battles along the border had completely brought about the decision in the West to a very favourable conclusion for the Germans... On the 25th, Oberstleutnant Tappen expressed himself to me with the words, 'In six weeks the whole affair has been finished'.[10]

Until quite recently, all the good news had been confined to the left wing where the French had been badly defeated in Lorraine and forced to retreat; however, in the last few days similar reports had arrived from the centre and, more importantly, from the right wing. Thus, 4th Army's situation report for 23 August spoke of a complete victory in the fighting in the Ardennes and 5th Army said that to the north of Verdun they had thrown the enemy back in a westerly direction and forced them to use their last mobile reserves from the Verdun forts to cover their withdrawal across the Meuse. (On the morning of the 25th the Crown Prince wrote to his father with the news that 'yesterday's victory to the south of Longwy is complete.'[11])

As Plessen mentioned, it was Bülow's situation report for 24 August that confirmed that the campaign was approaching a victorious conclusion. According to this paean of victory:

> On the 24th, the second day of the battle of Namur [the name given to the battle of Charleroi in many German accounts], 2nd Army has decisively defeated the opposing enemy in heavy fighting in spite of stubborn, and in parts offensive, resistance. Numerous cannon have been captured. I took the decision to attack the superior enemy force across the Sambre in order to open the way over the Meuse for 3rd Army. 1st Army is in a fight with the British to the west of Maubeuge and has begun envelopment. According to [Marwitz's Cavalry Corps] two shattered English brigades, a divisional commander and numerous officers have been captured.
>
> [Richthofen's 1st Cavalry Corps] reports that the English are retreating in flight from their positions. Parts of the 3rd and 6th English Divisions have been identified. The attack against Namur has ended in victory. The town and up to four forts are in our hands. Several thousand prisoners and ten field guns have been taken. Beside the Belgian garrison were French Regiments 45 and 148 from their II Corps… Up to half a division of the besieging force is now free for other purposes. The attack against Maubeuge is being prepared. On the evening of the 24th 2nd Army is on the line Beaumont–Hemptinne; on the 25th, further advance in a south-westerly direction to free up the front of 3rd Army…[12]

Although Kluck's situation report was more muted (he said that they had forced back two to three English divisions and that their main body was believed to be a short distance away to the south), it seemed that it was only a matter of time before the British would also be defeated. On the other hand, just as the war in the West appeared to be coming to an end, the situation on the Eastern Front had taken a decisive turn for the worse. The first sign of this was contained in a report from General von Prittwitz, according to which he had ordered his 8th Army to break off the fighting at Gumbinnen in order to avoid being outflanked and was retreating to the Vistula. When Moltke spoke to him over the telephone a short while later, Prittwitz said that unless he received urgent reinforcements he would be compelled to retreat further still, as far as the border with East Prussia. The following day, Moltke dismissed Prittwitz and his Chief of Staff, Waldersee, and replaced them with Hindenburg, who was called out of retirement, and Ludendorff, whose star was greatly in the ascendant after his prominent role in the capture of Liège just over a week earlier. Moltke's thoughts now turned to how he could reinforce 8th Army to prevent the invasion of German territory. In the absence of a general army reserve the only first-line unit which was immediately available was IX Reserve Corps, which had until now remained behind in Schleswig-Holstein to guard against a surprise landing by the British. News that the latter had begun disembarking in France, which had reached OHL on 22 August, sparked an argument between Moltke and Tappen about whether to use IX Corps to screen the Belgian troops in Antwerp as originally intended (alongside III Reserve Corp) or to use it to reinforce 8th Army. In the end, Moltke insisted that it should be sent to Antwerp as planned and that they should look elsewhere for reinforcements for the Eastern Front. As Tappen later explained, the good news from the Western Front could not have arrived at a better time.

> The French, as expected, had offered battle to prevent us from penetrating into France. The highly favourable reports which came in as late as 25 August, in conjunction with the great victory of 6th and 7th Armies in Lorraine on the 20th and 25th, aroused in Supreme Headquarters the belief that the great decisive battle in the West had been fought and concluded in our favour. Under the impression that there had been a 'decisive victory', the Chief of the General Staff resolved on the 25th, in spite of arguments to the contrary, to detach forces to the East. He believed the moment had come when, in conformity with the great operations plan, a decisive victory in the West having been won, considerable forces could be sent to the East to obtain a decision there also.[13]

On the evening of the 25th Moltke therefore decided to transfer six corps to the East, two each from the right wing, the centre and the left wing. (This would more than double the size of 8th Army.) Of these, only the Guard Reserve Corps and XI Corps (belonging to 2nd and 3rd Armies respectively) were immediately available because they had been taking part in the recently completed siege of Namur and had not yet returned to the front line; the other four corps were still in action and it would be several days before it was safe for them to disengage and leave for the East. However, in the late evening 5th Army's situation report arrived with the news that the enemy on their front had been 'shattered'. As a result, Moltke decided to withdraw V Corps from the Crown Prince's army immediately and send it to the East at the same time as the other two corps. Excluding III Reserve Corps which was screening Antwerp, there had until now been 33 corps on the Western Front; once all the designated corps had been sent to the East this would fall by almost a fifth to 27 corps, more than enough, so Moltke thought, to put the final touches to a victory which had already been won.

## 26 AUGUST: JOFFRE MAKES PLANS FOR A COUNTER-OFFENSIVE AND THE BRITISH COME UNDER ATTACK

The meeting at GHQ at St Quentin to discuss Joffre's plans for a counter-offensive took place in a dimly lit and oppressively humid billiards room whose windows were closed and shuttered against the harsh glare of the late morning sun. The French were represented by Joffre and his Deputy Chief of Staff, Berthelot, and the British by Sir John French and Sir Henry Wilson. After waiting in vain for Lanrezac and Hély d'Oissel to arrive, the meeting began with a situation report on the British Army by Wilson and one on the French Army by Capitaine Fagalde from 5th Army's Intelligence Section. Before the latter had finished, however, he handed over to Hély d'Oissel who had just arrived with Lanrezac after a difficult journey through the rear area of XVIII Corps along roads full of baggage trains and clogged by masses of fleeing refugees. According to an officer who spoke to him at the time, 5th Army's commander was not in the best of moods:

He seemed to be extremely displeased and expressed himself in violent language. He did not mince words in his criticism of GQG and of the allies. He was much irritated against the former and the British. The gist of what he was saying was that all he required was to be left alone, that he would retire as far as was necessary, that he would choose his own time and then he would boot the enemy back whence he came.[14]

When Hély d'Oissel finished speaking, Sir John French intervened and in an excitable state, and doing his best to express himself in French, said that his men had been violently attacked and that his two corps were in danger of being pulled apart. At Guise, I Corps had been forced to fall back into 5th Army's area and as he spoke II Corps was in combat with a greatly superior force at Le Cateau. He then launched into a diatribe against 5th Army, comparing Lanrezac's actions unfavourably with his own, declaring that the French had had a much easier time than his own troops who were facing a much stronger enemy, and that they had broken off the fight and had fallen back without warning, leaving his army exposed to encirclement. Part way through this tirade, as his thoughts raced ahead of his tongue, Wilson began to translate for him and at the same time tried to smooth over some of his wilder and more inflammatory statements. In the face of this outpouring of feeling, Joffre had the good sense to remain silent while a clearly irritated and resentful Lanrezac merely shrugged his shoulders from time to time and said very little in his own defence. After a while Joffre intervened and, speaking in a steady and even tone, attempted to mollify his opposite number. He said that they should not lose sight of the fact that all of the left wing armies, French as well as British, had been under intense pressure during the last few days and that they had both fought bravely and lost many good men. However, although the initial campaign had gone against them victory was still possible providing that the British Army took part in the new manoeuvre directed against the Germans' exposed right flank. After a slight delay a look of incomprehension fell across French's face, betraying the fact that this was the first time he had heard of the plan. The arrival of General Instruction No 2 during the night apparently went unnoticed in the general turmoil surrounding the fighting at Landrecies. Dismayed by this unexpected turn of events, Joffre now wearily outlined the plan for the benefit of his British audience, paying particular attention to the role he hoped they would play. This was not, however, greeted with any show of enthusiasm by Sir John French who seemed more concerned with how quickly his force could retreat in the direction of St Quentin than with turning about at some point soon and engaging the enemy. Gradually, the conversation faded away leaving a heavy and embarrassing silence that heralded the end of the meeting. In a token spirit of amity, Sir John invited Joffre and his fellow officers to a late lunch but although Joffre accepted, perhaps in the forlorn hope of coming to a better understanding during the meal, Lanrezac claimed that he had pressing business elsewhere and immediately took his leave. As Joffre later said, the outcome of the meeting did not bode well for the success of his plan:

> I carried away with me a serious impression as to the fragility of our extreme left, and I anxiously asked myself if it could hold out long enough to enable me to effect the new grouping of our forces. I was impressed, moreover, by the lack of mutual comprehension between Field Marshal French and the commander of our Fifth Army. The temperaments of the two men, their mentalities, were so wholly different, that they seemed quite unable to work together under the hard strain of battle.[15]

At the same time as Sir John French was venting his feelings on his allies, his II Corps was fighting for its life less than 20 miles away at Le Cateau. According to Kluck's own account of the situation, he was attempting to carry out a double encirclement by first of all pinning down the British frontally with IV Corps and Marwitz's Cavalry Corps and then enveloping both their wings with the rest of the army. Smith-Dorrien's troops were now in an extremely perilous situation; they were outnumbered, several units had arrived only shortly before dawn in an exhausted state, including the 19th Brigade which had hardly cleared Le Cateau when the first Germans appeared in the northern suburbs, and the Suffolks and the King's Own Yorkshire Light Infantry on the extreme right wing were exposed to enfilade fire from the high ground on the far side of the valley of the River Selle. I Corps should have been holding this position but had followed French's order to retreat.

Two factors saved the British from destruction. First of all there was the superb marksmanship and tenacity of Smith-Dorrien's infantry and the enormous courage of the gunners who gave them exceptional support from almost suicidal positions immediately behind the firing line. Secondly, the Germans failed to push home their advantage because the two envelopment wings arrived on the battlefield late in the day after a somewhat leisurely march, by which time the British had gone. If the German centre had prevented the British from withdrawing in the early afternoon, and the right and left wings had shown more urgency, then the trap would have closed on them. By holding off a superior enemy for almost nine hours, under extremely difficult circumstances, and then breaking off the fight and making an orderly retreat, II Corps had performed an incalculable service to the allied cause, ensuring that the army remained whole and able to take part in the battle of the Marne just over a week later.[16]

Although the British escaped, Kluck seems to have believed that they had been heavily defeated and would therefore retreat in a westerly direction towards the coast along their line of communications. (His judgment may have been clouded by the destruction of the King's Own Yorkshire Light Infantry, the Gordons and other units which did not receive the order to withdraw and which fought on courageously, holding the Germans at bay, until they were finally overwhelmed in the late afternoon.) During the evening, he therefore issued orders for an advance the next day in a south-westerly direction towards the Somme bend at Péronne. The army was to have captured the Somme crossings in the neighbourhood of the town by the 28th at the latest, at which point 'there would be an attractive prospect of throwing back the enemy's left wing on to the French forces retreating southwards in front of 2nd Army'.[17]

News that II Corps had not only survived but was also retreating in good order was slow to reach GHQ, which was convinved that they had been badly defeated. The extremely pessimistic mood at the time was reflected in a telegram from Huguet to Joffre in which he painted a very bleak picture of the situation. 'Battle lost by British Army, which seems to have lost all cohesion. It will demand considerable protection to enable it to reconstitute. GHQ tonight Noyon. Fuller details will follow.'[18] As if this was not bad enough, further disturbing news soon arrived which cast doubts on the success of the coming counter-offensive.

Firstly, 4th Army was said to be in full retreat behind the Meuse having blown up the bridges behind it and secondly, the Governor of Maubeuge reported that the fortress was incapable of lasting out for more than a few days at most, after which the besieging force would be free to rejoin the field army. The only glimmer of hope was that 5th Army was continuing to outdistance its pursuers and having left the heavily wooded terrain of the last few days would soon enter more open country where they could bring their field artillery into play. On the other hand, having sensed Lanrezac's pessimism, and having seen at first hand his animosity towards Sir John French, Joffre now began to consider removing him from command of 5th Army. In the meantime, to make sure that he took delaying action against his pursuers, he sent Colonel Alexandre to 5th Army Headquarters at Marle to keep an eye on things. From now on, as Alexandre rather tactlessly put it, there would no drifting back without any attempt at dealing a blow to the enemy.

## 27 AUGUST: THE GERMANS EXPOSE THEMSELVES TO ATTACK

Once again, Lanrezac's troops never came under serious threat all day and having crossed the Oise to the east of Guise went over to rest a short distance to the south of the river. Likewise, the only problems experienced by the British were due to exhaustion brought on by the difficult terrain and not from Kluck's army, which wasted the day on a wild goose chase to the south-west. After an exhausting night march, broken by only a few hours' rest, Smith-Dorrien's II Corps began to reach St Quentin soon after dawn on the 27th. As successive units arrived, they were fed, and having rested for a while, continued to retreat in good order and crossed the Somme in the late afternoon. To the east meanwhile, the scarcity of good roads forced the whole of I Corps to use the main road south through Guise with the result that infantry and vehicles were double-banked, with staff officers located at critical points to sort out the unavoidable congestion. Although the right wing of the German 2nd Army was close behind them, they managed to stay out of trouble except for a battalion of the Münster Regiment, which was acting as rearguard and was overwhelmed after it had failed to receive the order to retreat. At nightfall, the corps reached the high ground to the south-west of

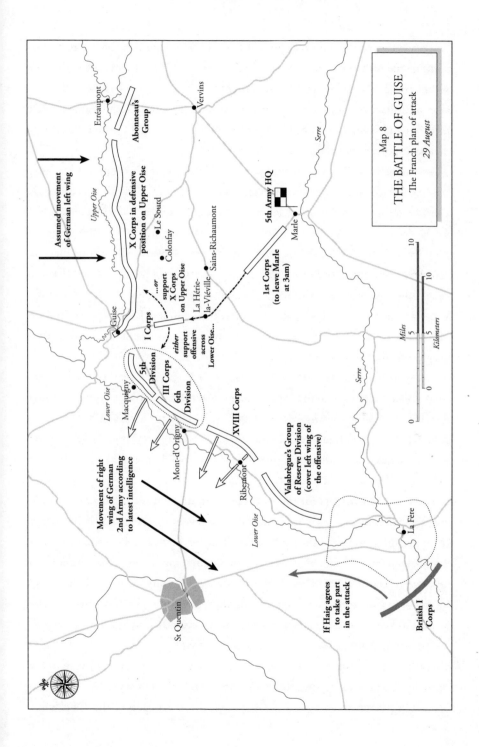

Erteaupont

Guise

Abonneau's Group

Vervins

Serre

Assumed movement of German left wing

Upper Oise

X Corps in defensive position on Upper Oise

Le Sourd

Colonfay

Sains-Richaumont

5th Army HQ

Marle

...or support X Corps on Upper Oise

1st Corps (to leave Marle at 3am)

I Corps

La Hérie-la-Viéville

either support offensive across Lower Oise...

Macquigny

Lower Oise

5th Division

III Corps

6th Division

XVIII Corps

Mont-d'Origny

Ribemont

Valabrègue's Group of Reserve Division (cover left wing of the offensive)

Movement of right wing of German 2nd Army according to latest intelligence

Serre

Lower Oise

La Fère

St Quentin

If Haig agrees to take part in the attack

British I Corps

10

10

Miles

5

5

Kilometers

0

0

Map 8

THE BATTLE OF GUISE

The French plan of attack

*29 August*

117

Guise where they bivouacked. At 8.00pm GHQ gave orders for the retreat to continue the following morning to a line south of La Fère (I Corps) and the area of Noyon (II Corps). In a desperate attempt to keep ahead of the enemy, they were told that, 'All ammunition on wagons not absolutely required and other impedimenta will be unloaded and officers and men carried to the full capacity of all transport, both horse and mechanical.'[19]

In contrast to the uneventful course of events at the front, tensions were building between the senior commanders on both sides. On the German side Kluck's simmering resentment at having to remain under Bülow's control had boiled over the previous evening over the arrangements for the siege of Maubeuge. Whereas Bülow decided that the two divisions allotted to the task from his own army should be augmented by IX Corps, Kluck insisted that the place posed no risk since its fortifications were obsolete and its garrison weak. As far as he was concerned, all of 1st Army, including IX Corps, should be pushed forwards across the Somme without delay to prevent the British from escaping to the coast. In the late evening, after his objections had been turned down by Bülow, he sent a radio message to OHL complaining about the situation and asking once more to be given his independence. On the morning of the 27th the reply came back saying that he was no longer subordinate to Bülow and that Maubeuge would be invested by 2nd Army alone. The decision to grant Kluck his freedom was one that Moltke would come to regret bitterly only a few days later.

For Kluck, the orders for the next day were straightforward; his men would cross the Somme and once more attempt to prevent the defeated British Army from escaping towards the coast. For Bülow, however, the situation was complicated by the fact that the two neighbouring armies were pulling in opposite directions, 1st Army to the south-west in pursuit of the British and 3rd Army to the south-east in support of 4th Army. After a brief deliberation, he decided to keep in touch with Kluck's left wing, even though this would increase the gap that had already opened up with 3rd Army. He therefore ordered his right wing (the 14th Infantry Division and X Reserve Corps) to change course to the south-west, and advance towards St Quentin, while the left wing (X Corps and Guard Corps) remained on the defensive on the north side of the Oise while reconnaissance was carried out on the other side of the river. Richthofen's I Cavalry Corps was to skirt round the south side of St Quentin and either attack the British in the flank or, in conjunction with Marwitz's Cavalry Corps, cut off their retreat altogether.

At Joffre's headquarters the day was dominated by his efforts to support the British Army so that it would be able take part in the planned counter-offensive in a few days' time. Since d'Amade's weak territorials and Sordet's worn out cavalry were not strong enough for the task, he decided that the only way to take the pressure off the British was for 5th Army to turn around and attack the Germans as they crossed the Oise. At 6.30am therefore, the following order was transmitted over the telephone to Lanrezac's headquarters at Marle:

> You have expressed your intention, once you have left the wooded terrain where the use of your artillery is difficult, to throw back the troops that are following you by a counter-offensive, well supported by artillery. Not only do I authorise this, but I believe that this attack is indispensable. The state of your troops is good, their morale is excellent. It is necessary to profit from this. To act otherwise would diminish the morale and perhaps put the outcome of the whole campaign at risk. The area of Vervins, into which you are moving, lends itself well to this operation. There is no need to take into account what the English are doing on your left.[20]

Needless to say, Lanrezac was not pleased at being made to delay his retreat in order to get the British out of trouble. Although he was forced to give way, he successfully insisted that the attack could not take place until the 29th because the army would have to spend a day side-stepping to the west in order to get into position. Concerned with Lanrezac's obvious reluctance, Joffre sent Alexandre back to 5th Army Headquarters to see that his orders were carried out. By now Lanrezac was in a thoroughly bad temper and 'the atmosphere, already charged with electricity, became dangerously tense'.[21] After informing Hély d'Oissel of the new march boundaries with the British I Corps, Alexandre went on to discuss the preparations for the attack. This led to an acrimonious exchange between Lanrezac and Hély d'Oissel on one side and Alexandre on the other. Acting as Joffre's mouthpiece, Alexandre accused Lanrezac of being too concerned with putting as much space as possible between his army and its pursuers rather than attempting to delay the Germans by means of vigorous counter-attacks. Lanrezac insisted that this was unnecessary and wasteful and that the best time to attack would be when they reached the strong defensive position at Laon–Rheims. There was also the considerable danger that both his flanks would be exposed if the retreat were delayed; there was already a gap on the right with 4th Army and if the British continued to retreat precipitately his left flank would also be uncovered.

While Alexandre was doing his best to deal with Lanrezac, Joffre had sent a telegram to Sir John French telling him about the attack and asking him to delay his retreat for a short while to cover Lanrezac's left wing. The reply, which came back via Huguet a short while later, contained a mixture of good and bad news. On the one hand, French had agreed to the request and had ordered II Corps to halt at St Quentin and I Corps to the south-west of Guise; on the other hand he reiterated that his troops were in a very poor condition and would only be able to survive further attacks if they received immediate and substantial support, especially from Sordet's Cavalry Corps.

From this point onwards things started to go badly wrong for Joffre. In the early afternoon, news arrived that the British had not cut short their retreat as promised but had evacuated St Quentin and were once more on the march south. Worse still, just as Joffre was about to host a dinner for the Minister for War, Millerand, and his predecessor Messimy, Major Brécard arrived from GHQ with the appalling news that Sir John French was threatening to pull his troops out of the line altogether. According to Brécard, the mood when he left was extremely depressed. In particular, II Corps was believed to be in a critical condition after its losses at Le Cateau; several units were thought to have been more or less destroyed and a large number of guns and much equipment lost. There were serious doubts as to whether it would be able to offer even the slightest resistance if it was attacked. According to Wilson, the army would only be fit enough to rejoin the campaign after at least three of the five divisions had undergone a long rest and complete reorganization. This would mean a delay of several days or even a few weeks but in view of the uncertain conditions it was impossible to be more precise.[22]

At about the same time as this bombshell arrived, Joffre also received a detailed report which shed new light on the recent movements of the German right wing. In addition to giving for the first time a fairly accurate assessment of the German order of battle, it said that they appeared to be sliding obliquely across the front of 5th Army in an attempt to catch up with the British. This was just the opportunity he had been waiting for. In the early evening he modified the orders that had been sent to Lanrezac only a few hours earlier. Instead of facing north and attacking the Germans as they crossed the upper Oise, Lanrezac was now told to make the principal attack in a north-westerly direction, towards St Quentin, against the flank of the enemy force which was in pursuit of the British. At the same time, his right wing would act defensively to prevent the German 2nd Army from crossing the Oise to the east of Guise. It was a risky manoeuvre, since if things went badly wrong 5th Army might be split in two and defeated; on the other hand it was an opportunity to strike a decisive blow against the enemy rather than merely delaying them for several days.

When Lanrezac received this message he predictably flew into a furious temper which was raised to a dangerous level a short while later when Alexandre appeared once more, hotfoot from GQG with the unenviable task of making sure that he complied with the new instructions. No sooner had Alexandre arrived than he became involved in a rancorous argument with Schneider, the Chief of the Operations Bureau, who was responsible for drafting the complex orders needed to get the troops into position for the attack. (The orders for the northward attack across Oise had only just been sent out.) Schneider argued with Alexandre, pointing to the map and vehemently claiming that GQG completely underestimated the difficulties involved in the new manoeuvre. In reply, Alexandre expressed amazement that Schneider was being so unco-operative; placing his hand on the map with his fingers extended and pointing northwards, he rotated his palm so that they were now facing north-west. It was as easy as that! At this point the conversation degenerated into a slanging match with Schneider shouting at Alexandre not to be so stupid and the latter defending himself by claiming that 5th Army had never done anything to help slow down the German advance. Lanrezac now leapt to Schneider's defence, telling Joffre's mouthpiece in no uncertain terms just what he thought of GQG's attempts at strategy. Shaken by this verbal assault, Alexandre telephoned GQG to warn them of Lanrezac's intransigence and was told to pass on the message that Joffre himself would visit 5th Army Headquarters the next morning to see that his orders were carried out to the letter.[23]

At OHL meanwhile, Moltke was beginning to have second thoughts about sending six corps to reinforce the front in East Prussia. In the two days that had elapsed since he had given the order for the Guard Reserve Corps, XI Corps and V Corps to transfer to the East, the situation had altered significantly on both fronts. On 25 August, it had seemed to Moltke and Tappen that the war in the West was as good as won; however, when they reviewed matters on the evening of the 27th the situation was less certain. On the one hand, Kluck's latest report claimed a significant victory over the British. 'In four days of fighting from Mons to Solesmes [ie Le Cateau] the English Army with three French territorial divisions, two of them from Paris, has been defeated. Retreat to the west has been prevented. Several thousand English prisoners, seven English field batteries and a heavy battery have been captured.'[24] On the other hand, in his situation report for the 26th Bülow rowed back from the extravagant claims he had made two days previously, saying that although victory had been achieved it was not decisive and that the enemy was retreating in good order. Similarly, Hausen said that on the 25th his army had been delayed by numerous encounters with French rearguards and the Crown Prince summed up the recent fighting on the front of 5th Army by concluding, 'My army has spent the last four days in heavy fighting against an enemy which has fallen back from one position to another.'[25] In contrast, the situation on the Eastern Front had greatly improved since Hindenburg and Ludendorff had taken over the command. In a message that arrived during the evening, Ludendorff said that 8th Army had defeated between two to three Russian corps and that in his opinion reinforcements were no longer necessary. Moltke now had to decide whether to allow the three corps to continue to the East or to keep them in the West where they could be used either as a general reserve or to fill the gaps that had opened up between the armies on the right wing. Fortunately, there was still time to recall them since V Corps was at Diedenhofen where it was about to entrain, while the other two were on the march towards their embarkation points of Aachen (Guard Reserve Corps) and Malmédy–St Vith (XI Corps).[26]

As Tappen later explained, events on the right wing had so far taken place more or less according to plan. 'At this date the maps which had been established in peacetime to indicate the projected movements of the right wing still corresponded almost exactly with the maps bearing the movements effectively executed by the armies.'[27] However, now that the armies had reached the furthest limits of the deployment plan the time had come to issue instructions for the final stage in the campaign. After he had evaluated all of the latest information, on the evening of the 27th Moltke issued a long document entitled *Allgemeine Anweisungen an die 1. bis 7. Armee für den Fortgang der Operationen* (General Directions for the 1st to the 7th Armies for the Further Conduct of Operations).[28] After a long preamble, which summarized the overall situation, he stressed the need to land a knockout blow before the French could strengthen their left wing and before the Russians renewed their offensive:

> The French, or at least their northern and central groups, are in full retreat towards the west and south-west, ie in the direction of Paris. It is likely that in the course of this retreat they will put up a new and fierce resistance. All the news coming from France confirms that the French Army will fight to gain time and to tie down the majority of the German forces on their front in order to facilitate the Russian offensive. The Franco-English groups in the north and centre may, after the loss of the line of the Meuse, offer new resistance behind the Aisne with the extreme left being perhaps pushed as far as St Quentin, La Fère and Laon and with the right wing established to the west of the Argonne, fairly close to Ste-Menéhould. The next line of resistance will very likely be the Marne with the left wing leaning on Paris. It is equally possible that forces will be concentrated on the lower Seine [ie downstream from Paris].[29]

If they caught up with the French before they were level with Paris, it would be possible to envelop their left wing, forcing it away from the capital. ('The strong resistance which may be expected on the Aisne, and later on the Marne, may necessitate a wheel of the armies from a south-westerly to a southerly direction.') The pursuit was to take place as quickly as possible 'in order to leave the French no time to reorganize and offer serious resistance'. The right wing was therefore to advance to the south-west, in the general direction of Paris, not with the intention of investing the capital but because the French were retreating in this direction. ('It is therefore most important by a rapid march of the German forces on Paris to prevent the French Army from coming to rest, to stop the assembly of fresh bodies of troops and to take from the country as much as possible of its means of defence.') Nowhere is there any mention of making preparations for besieging the city. 1st Army was to advance down the western side of Paris in the direction of the lower Seine, 2nd Army was directed towards the city itself and 3rd Army was to advance through Laon towards Château-Thierry. The 4th and 5th Armies were also to advance towards the south-west, the former in the direction of Rheims–Epernay and the latter to Châlons-sur-Marne–Vitry-le-François. 5th Army would initially continue to be responsible for protecting the flank of the four right wing armies and in addition would invest Verdun. The situation on the German left wing in Lorraine and Alsace was uncertain and everything depended on whether the French renewed their failed offensive. If they retreated, 6th Army would cross the Moselle and advance in a westerly direction towards Neufchâteau, reinforced by two corps taken from 7th Army. Then becoming independent, 7th Army would guard against an enemy breakthrough between Epinal and the Swiss frontier. If all went according to plan, the enemy would be caught in a huge trap with their left wing enveloped and thrown back to the south-east of Paris towards the Langres plateau to the east of Troyes, where they would be taken in the rear by 6th Army advancing in a westerly direction from Neufchâteau.[30]

## 28 AUGUST: FINAL PREPARATIONS FOR THE FRENCH ATTACK

During the early morning, 5th Army began side-stepping westwards in preparation for the offensive, screened from the north by Valabrègue's Reserve Divisions which occupied the Oise crossings in and to the east of Guise. When this movement was complete the latter would be relieved by X Corps and go into reserve behind the left wing. The attack was to take place in a north-westerly direction towards St Quentin and would be carried out by XVIII and III Corps, supported by the 37th (North African) Division, which had been transferred from

X Corps. Meanwhile, the rest of X Corps was to remain on the defensive behind the Oise between Guise and Etréaupont. Valabrègue's Reserve Divisions and I Corps would be held back in reserve, the former behind the left wing and the latter behind the centre. Cavalry reconnaissance was ordered in the area of Guise and St Quentin and a staff officer, Capitaine Helbronner, was sent to GHQ with a copy of the orders and a request for the support of their I Corps, which was in the neighbourhood of La Fère.

As the headquarters staff were hurriedly packing up for the move to Laon, Joffre appeared with Colonel Gamelin and began discussions with Lanrezac and Hély d'Oissel. These did not go well. When Lanrezac once more prevaricated by claiming that X Corps was not strong enough for its task and that the gap with 4th Army was too large and inadequately defended, Joffre's habitual imperturbability gave way and he flew into a violent temper, shouting that this was all an excuse and that the plan stood every chance of success if only it was properly executed. With the unspoken threat of dismissal hanging in the air, Lanrezac gave way in the face of the onslaught though only after insisting on having Joffre's orders in writing in case things went badly wrong and he became a scapegoat. Before leaving for GQG, Joffre took the opportunity to meet briefly with de Mas Latrie and Hache, the commanders of XVIII and III Corps respectively, whose troops would spearhead the offensive. Unfortunately, neither of them created a favourable impression; the former complained that his troops were exhausted because of the retreat and the latter weakly explained that he had not sought promotion and would much prefer to be back at Verdun in command of his old division. (According to Joffre's later account, de Mas Latrie was in poor health, suffering from dysentery and appeared to be in a partial state of collapse.) Still angry from his contretemps with Lanrezac, Joffre swept aside their doubts and hesitations and impressed on them the vital importance of their task. Having announced that he would return the next morning to make sure that the battle was conducted according to his orders, he set off for GQG leaving Lanrezac and his staff to breathe a collective sigh of relief.

During the afternoon, Lanrezac held a conference for the Corps Chiefs of Staff, during which he raised the question of how to strengthen the attack. Ideally, he would have used I Corps for this purpose since it was the strongest corps and

Franchet d'Esperey was a dynamic and forceful commander, but its position well to the rear of the right wing meant that it was too far away to take part. However, during the meeting he came up with the idea of transporting it to the left wing by rail during the night, in time to take the offensive at dawn. This remarkable suggestion was received with astonishment by Général de Lardemelle, I Corps' Chief of Staff, who pointed out that it would be entirely dislocated (due to lack of capacity, the baggage trains would have to move by road) and that there would be insufficient time to reconstitute it before the attack was due to begin. Instead, he suggested that if they set off at 3.00am and marched non-stop down the great high road to Guise they would arrive behind the centre of the battlefield in the middle of the afternoon, in time either to support the offensive or to reinforce X Corps along the upper Oise. In order to check de Lardemelle's calculation, Lanrezac placed his hand on the map and, having extended his fingers, used it as a makeshift set of dividers. De Lardemelle was right; if they left at 3.00am they would be level with the village of Le Hérie-la-Viéville by the middle of the afternoon, at the hinge between the two wings of the army. He therefore decided to follow the suggestion with the slight modification that part of the corps would be detached and used to support the 51st Reserve Division and Abonneau's 4th Cavalry Division, which were covering the right wing. Not long after the conference was over Helbronner returned with better than expected news about the British. Although II Corps was worn out after two days of forced marches, its morale was intact and its overall condition was not as bad as Lanrezac had been told. Better still, the condition of I Corps was remarkably good, with the men in excellent fighting order and with high morale, albeit suffering from the long marches through difficult terrain. Most important of all, Haig had said that he would do everything in his power to support the French offensive the next day by advancing along the La Fère–St Quentin high road against German columns which had been seen to the south-west of St Quentin.

These columns belonged to Bülow's right wing, which had been pushed forwards to keep in touch with 1st Army. Originally, they were only meant to advance a short distance on the 28th, coming to a halt when they were level with St Quentin, but when Bülow learnt that the British were retreating faster than expected he ordered them to extend their march along a course parallel to the lower Oise. The X Reserve Corps on the right was to advance along the western side of the river and send strong detachments to seize the bridges over the Somme at Ham and the Crozat Canal at St Simon by nightfall. At the same time, X Corps on the left was to cross the Oise between Guise and Flavigny-le-Grand and advance down the eastern bank, keeping level with them. As a result, by the end of the day the army should have been spread out along an arc from Ham-sur-Somme in the west (where the right wing would attack the British in conjunction with 1st Army) to Etréaupont in the east (where the Guard Corps would temporarily remain on the defensive along the upper Oise).

Events did not work out as expected, however. Whereas X Reserve Corps reached its billets in the villages to the south-west of St Quentin late at night after an exhausting 22-mile march in torrid heat, X Corps encountered strong resistance when it attempted to cross the Oise at Guise and Flavigny-le-Grand. After a delayed start, it was already early afternoon by the time that the 19th Infantry Division reached the Oise at Guise and the 20th at Flavigny-le-Grand. Despite being hugely outnumbered, the defenders (from the 53rd Reserve Division) hung on tenaciously until late afternoon when the Germans finally forced them back and set foot on the high ground to the south. However, by this time the noise of the gunfire had attracted the attention of the French 35th Division (XVIII Corps), which was on the march towards the left wing where it was due to take part in the offensive the next morning. One brigade supported by the whole of the divisional artillery was diverted to Guise where they arrived just in time to prevent the Germans from debouching from the newly established bridgeheads. When the fighting ended at dusk, the French left to rejoin the rest of their division and the Germans bivouacked on the battlefield, a short distance to the south of the river and a good 12 miles short of their objectives. As we will see, their failure was to have near fatal consequences the next day for their right hand neighbour, the 19th Reserve Infantry Division.[31] Meanwhile, on the left wing, after aerial reconnaissance had shown that there were no enemy forces immediately south of the river, the Guard Corps crossed the Oise in the late morning and went over to rest on the southern bank, oblivious to the fact that the French X Corps was less than 8 miles away from them, hidden from view by the undulating terrain.

Yet again, the German 1st Army spent a fruitless day in pursuit of the British, who were retreating in a southerly direction and not towards the coast as Kluck still persisted in believing. However, II Corps and Marwitz's Cavalry Corps, both of which had been pushed out wide on the right wing to prevent the British from escaping, saw action during the afternoon near Péronne against units belonging to the nascent 6th Army. According to Joffre's orders, the new army, under Maunoury's command, was to have assembled in the neighbourhood of Amiens by 2 September at the latest, ready to go over to the offensive. (It was to consist of VII Corps, one of whose two divisions was left behind in Alsace and replaced by the 63rd Reserve Division, the 61st and 62nd Reserve Divisions under Général Ebener, the 55th and 56th Reserve Divisions commanded by Général de Lamaze and Ditte's Moroccan Brigade.[32]) By the morning of 26 August the only units close to the assembly area were the five Moroccan battalions which had arrived at Bordeaux from North Africa on the 19th and had been transported by train to Amiens, where they guarded the station against a surprise attack while waiting for the rest of the army to arrive. Later that day the 61st and 62nd Reserve Divisions detrained at Arras and set off towards the Somme bend at Péronne where they were to cover the army while it assembled in the area behind the river. On the morning of the 28th they advanced towards the Somme accompanied by part of Sordet's Cavalry Corps and a battalion of chasseurs, which was transported to the front in vehicles. However, Kluck's right wing had already reached the area. In the early morning the reserve divisions were violently attacked by units from II Corps and from Marwitz's Cavalry Corps and thrown back in disorder. The 61st Reserve Division fell apart and ended the day in scattered groups as far afield as Albert, Amiens and Bapaume while the 62nd Reserve Division was forced to make a fighting retreat in the direction of Arras where the majority of its units arrived between 9.00pm and midnight in a poor condition. (The two divisions fled so quickly that at midnight neither Maunoury nor Ebener, who was yet to take command, had the faintest idea where they were.) In the meantime, the weight of German numbers had caused Sordet's cavalry to fall back behind the Somme and the chasseurs to abandon the bridges they had been guarding and to evacuate Péronne. As a result, during the afternoon and evening the German II Corps arrived at the Somme in and around Péronne and pushed their advance guards over to the western side of the river.

Since the German 1st Army spent the day sliding southwestwards across the British rear, the only action between the two sides involved minor skirmishes between the British cavalry rearguards and units from Richthofen's Cavalry Corps which were moving round the southern side of St Quentin. (The German cavalry were held back by a shortage of fodder and of new horseshoes with which to replace the existing ones, which had almost worn through.) At midday, when it became clear that the British had once more escaped, Kluck began to consider changing direction and cutting in behind the French 5th Army before it could reach the defensive position at Rheims–Laon–La Fère. Although this would let the British off the hook, he was convinced that they had been badly beaten at Le Cateau and presented no further threat. In the early afternoon a staff officer was sent to 2nd Army Headquarters with this new appreciation of the situation and a request for Bülow's assistance. According to Kluck's plan, the two armies would make an inward wheel against the lower Oise to envelop the French left wing, 1st Army (on the outside of the wheel) advancing against the river section Compiègne–Noyon and 2nd Army (on the inside) against Quierzy–Chauny (downstream from La Fère).

# 6

# THE BATTLE OF GUISE

## 29 AUGUST: THE ENCOUNTER BATTLES ON THE GERMAN LEFT WING

Unaware of each other's presence, the German Guard Corps and the French X Corps spent the night in bivouac to the south of the Oise, less than 8 miles apart and concealed by the darkness and the low hills which separated them. On the French side, they had orders to set off at dawn and complete the western side-step which they had begun the previous day. When the head of the column was level with Guise, all units were to turn 90 degrees to the right and occupy defensive positions along the Oise.[1] On the German side, a short advance was due to take place in a southerly direction, beginning with the 1st Guards Infantry Division on the right and extending eastwards to the 2nd Division which was echeloned back on the left to cover the army's open flank. Since the two sides were moving at right angles to each other, the fighting took the form of a series of encounters that began in the west and spread progressively eastwards.[1]

The immediate objectives of General von Hutier's 1st Guards Infantry Division were the villages of Colonfay and Le Sourd, less than an hour's march away across the rolling countryside. By the time that the 1st Regiment of Foot Guards, commanded by the Kaiser's second son, Prinz Eitel Friedrich, was approaching Colonfay, the nearest French unit (the 48e RI) had been alerted to their presence by the sounds of gunfire further to the west where the 39th Brigade was already in action against the 3rd Guards Regiment. Thus, when the prince's II Battalion entered Colonfay, the French were ready and waiting for

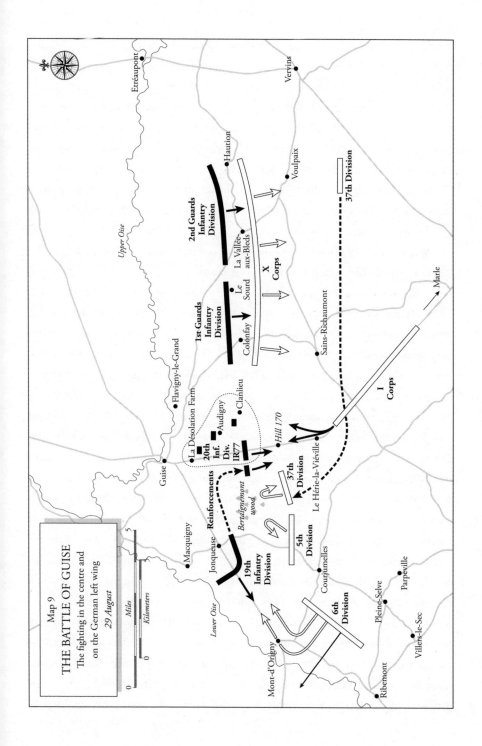

Map 9

THE BATTLE OF GUISE

The fighting in the centre and
on the German left wing

29 August

them, concealed in the houses and outbuildings. To begin with, all appeared peaceful to the Germans as they advanced unsuspectingly along the main street with the battalion standard at their head. Suddenly, however, when they arrived at the open area adjacent to the church they were met with a hail of rifle fire from the nearby houses and outbuildings. Although they deployed their reserves and gradually drove the French out of the village, moments afterwards they were hit by a violent bombardment and forced to flee for their lives, scattering in all directions. After suffering heavy losses, the battalion was completely dislocated, its units widely dispersed and out of touch with one another and with both battalion and regimental headquarters.

When Eitel Friedrich became aware of this disaster, he ordered the III Battalion to halt when it reached the country road between Colonfay and Le Sourd and wait for artillery support. In the meantime, Major von Bismarck (the youngest son of the former Chancellor), who was the battalion commander, went forwards to a point about 500 yards to the east of Colonfay to reconnoitre the enemy positions. Looking southwards he saw a long, gentle, downward slope, covered with fields of sugar beet and harvested oats and beyond this a hollow, the bottom of which was out of sight. From here the fields gradually ascended to a shallow ridge on whose summit he could see enemy infantry who had opened long-range rifle fire. To his right, he could hear the sounds of gunfire from the direction of Colonfay; to his left, however, there was no sign of the 2nd Regiment which should have been level with them by now as it advanced towards Le Sourd. At this point, events were taken out of his hands by several of his subordinates who were frustrated at having to lie still under the steady bombardment and independently decided to assault the ridge. Hauptmann von Schütz's 12th Company was the first to attack; when the buglers sounded the charge, his men ran at full tilt down the slope until they reached the hollow at the base of the hill where they threw themselves down to catch their breath. After a brief pause, during which the French gunners adjusted the range and were hitting them once more, Schütz called for another forward rush. Suffering badly as the enemy bullets whipped through the crops of sugar beet and caused terrible wounds as they ricocheted off the hard earth, they went to ground again when they were about 300 yards from the crest. Schütz noticed a French officer, the gold braid of his képi glinting in the bright sunshine, who seemed to be preparing his men for a counter-attack. Meanwhile, they had been joined on their left by Freiherr von Hornstein's 10th Company and on their right by a section from the 5th Company. In addition, two sections of the regimental machine gun company were brought forwards through the heavy bombardment and opened fire on the western end of the ridge, causing the French to fall back from the crest.

Interpreting this movement as a sign that the enemy line was on the verge of collapse, Hornstein and Schütz gave the order for the assault. However, as they charged, a large mass of enemy infantry crossed the ridge on their right front and swept down upon them with fixed bayonets:

> At no moment did the brave group waver. As if by command, the left half of our front stood firm and repelled the French. The right half, where I was, ran a little to the right under the leadership of Freiherr von Hornstein and Leutnant Brümmerstädt. As soon as we had deployed, we stood without support and opened an incredible fire on the enemy. Their column came to a halt.* Only 50 steps separated them from us. The enemy absolutely showered us with a rain of bullets. Oberleutnant Freiherr von Hornstein, who was very close to me on my left, fell with two shots to the chest, in the next moment Vizefeldwebel Bode also went down. Soon afterwards all were laid low. Füsilier Dostatni was still standing to my right. I received a shot through my right knee, but I could still support myself on my left leg. I fired desperately into the thick mass of the French. I didn't need to load my rifle because the mortally wounded Leutnant Brümmerstädt and Drummer Rosinski continually passed loaded rifles to me. Unteroffizier Bochert and some other badly wounded men raised themselves up and also fired. We would all have fallen victim to the enemy's superior strength if a machine gun had not intervened, firing from our right rear. I was hit again, in my upper arm and shortly afterwards through my left shoulder. I just saw the French running away before I fell over. The courageous Dostatni was also mortally wounded. Unteroffizier Bochert, Füsilier Hommery and I remained alive on the right wing. The 10th Company had suffered very badly. The victory had cost us 42 dead and 106 wounded.[2]

---

* According to another report, the French were in two ranks, the first one kneeling.

The French also suffered terrible losses, in particular from the fire of the German machine guns.

> The lieutenant gave the command 'forwards!' The company surged forwards in a single mass. But the enemy fire redoubled. In the blink of an eye, almost everyone was wounded and thrown back, including the lieutenant who, hit by eight bullets, still had the strength to cross the crest to collapse and die a few metres beyond. Those wounded at the same time as him included a young sous-lieutenant, newly out of St Cyr, Adjudant Vincent, Sergent-Major Boie and the Adjudant Chef Dieusel. I had three bullets in the legs and shoulder. There were no more officers remaining nor section leaders. The walking wounded flowed back to the rear. The few unhurt men then stopped halfway down the rear slope and returned over the crest to look for those who had been seriously wounded. Among these brave men I recall a soldier called Lebas; he was a navvy by profession, fairly mediocre in peacetime and often punished by Adjudant Vincent for lapses in conduct. When the adjudant had been wounded for the first time and lay on the crest, Lebas searched for him under the flying bullets and then carried him back on his shoulders until the moment when a second bullet hit the adjudant, killing him.[3]

The Germans quickly deployed their last reserves, allowing the counter-attack to be beaten off and the position stabilized. Even so, the French were left in possession of the ridge whereas the Germans remained pinned down by accurate rifle fire a few hundred yards away on the stubble and the fields of sugar beet in the blazing heat. At about noon, however, after the 2nd Regiment had captured Le Sourd the French abandoned the ridge to avoid being outflanked and retreated to a new defensive position on the high ground to the north of Richaumont. The carnage had been truly dreadful. On the French side, the 48e RI, which had already suffered severely at Arsimont a week earlier, lost 18 out of its 26 remaining officers and about half of its rank and file. On the German side the losses in the 1st Regiment of Foot Guards exceeded the 1,056 casualties suffered by the Prussian Guard in its epic encounter at St Privat in the Franco–Prussian War. In the three days of fighting, from 28–30 August, the regiment lost 26 of its 58 officers and approximately 1,200 other ranks from a total of 2,900, almost all of whom fell in the action at Colonfay. The casualty rate in the 5th, 10th and 12th Companies, which were the first to attack the French positions along the crest, exceeded 80 per cent, most of them dead.[4]

To the east of Colonfay, the 2nd Regiment, which was commanded by Oberst Graf zu Rantzau, had the task of occupying Le Sourd. Although the dense mist had reduced visibility to less than 100 yards, the advance began on time so as not to expose the flank of the 1st Regiment on their right. After a delay because the lead battalion became lost in the mist (the officers had neglected to use their compasses), the advance restarted with the I Battalion heading towards the village, the 1st and 3rd Companies in the first line followed by the 2nd and the 4th Companies. Major von Schönstadt, the battalion commander, together with Rantzau and their respective staffs, rode in the interval between the two rear companies. As the head of the march-column approached the village, it deployed into half sections and descended the steep hill leading to the first houses. At this point the road crossed a narrow brook and a light railway line, and then, having passed the church on a raised knoll, ascended to the centre from where it was possible to see the high ground to the south. At this time of year the place was a picturesque scene in which the houses were half-hidden by a profusion of orchards, bushes and gardens. Appearances were deceptive however, since the French 71e RI had already occupied the far end of the village and the ridge, which overlooked it from the south. When the two leading companies reached the dip in the road, they split off to either side and slowly began to work their way through the gardens and the numerous small cattle enclosures, surrounded by barbed wire, which filled the edges of the village. The 2nd and 4th Companies had just entered the main street when a staff officer arrived from brigade headquarters with news that the 1st Regiment was in difficulties at Colonfay and that they were to go to its aid. Since there was no sign of the enemy, Rantzau decided to save time by recalling the 1st and 3rd Companies and then pushing the whole battalion through the village along the main street. While they waited for them to return, the other two companies halted opposite the church where they formed a dense mass, more than 400 strong, clustered around the battalion and regimental staffs. For some time now shells had been passing low overhead in both directions, howling as they went, as the French and German batteries exchanged shots. Suddenly, without warning, a shell burst with devastating violence directly in the middle of the 2nd Company and the regimental staff. As further shells followed and as the survivors rushed for whatever cover they could find, the point sections, which had advanced a short distance beyond the church, came under fire from windows and roofs in the centre of the village. The officers, including the regimental and battalion commanders, immediately leapt off their horses, grabbed the rifles of fallen soldiers and entered the fray. The encounter now degenerated into a confusing fight among the buildings and the surrounding gardens and orchards in which small groups of men, often without officers, their views obstructed by the buildings and the thick hedges, fought it out at close quarters with bayonets and rifle butts.

While this was taking place, the 1st Company, commanded by Hauptmann von Oesterreich, had also come under fire in the hamlet of Rue des Fontaines into which they had strayed by mistake after taking a wrong turning.

I was alone with my 80 men. On the other side of the railway embankment we climbed over several fences and crept carefully through the gardens closer to the first houses. They were empty. The road in front of them seemed equally deserted. In the meantime the shooting had increased. We couldn't make out where it was coming from or who was being shot at. In between these noises we could hear the enemy artillery. Since nothing suspicious appeared, we slowly climbed the steep village street, keeping close up against the walls of the houses, in order to reach its upper end. Suddenly, about 200 metres away, as if by magic, there stood five horsemen. I clearly recognized them by their képis. Unfortunately, in the same moment they disappeared. Shortly afterwards about six infantrymen appeared on the road. They appeared not to have any weapons and put their hands up as if they wanted to surrender. At that time in the war we still trusted people and we went on without firing. Then suddenly all hell broke loose; from hedges and houses which had seemed so dead, from all sides there came bangs and hisses and whistles. Steel splinters sprayed around and ricochets hummed through the air like enormous bumblebees. In no time at all, half a dozen of my men were swept away. Bristling with anger, the others wanted to rush forward but I considered for a moment. Where would we go? The enemy was well hidden; they were nowhere to be seen. The narrow street meant certain death. 'Back to the nearest corner.' The few moments it took to get there were dreadful. Bullets swept along the street like hailstones, knocking down whatever was in their way. Then we found cover, terribly reduced in numbers. Despite all of this I wanted to try once more; perhaps we would succeed in pushing through the village. My men immediately agreed with me. We ran off again up the street. The French fired everything they had at us. With the men we had left I reached our old position. Not far from there lay Hauptmann von Oesterreich with the section commanded by Leutnant Halledt. He had reached the road from the other side. What now? Hauptmann von Oesterreich sent us back to the railway embankment. Standard Bearer Mauff and another soldier were carrying the mortally wounded Vizefeldwebel Torberg who had implored us not to leave him behind alive. He bled to death three days later. The embankment gave us little cover from the salvo.[5]

By now, the Germans in the centre of the village had gradually got the situation under control and worked forwards from house to house, clearing the enemy out as they went, until they arrived at the southern exits. They were now, however, in view of the French machine gunners on the ridge a few hundred yards away, who brought the advance to an abrupt halt. For the next two hours, they spent an uncomfortable time sheltering in the houses and behind the orchard walls, reluctant to make the slightest movement lest it attract a deadly burst of fire. Their ordeal came to an end in the early afternoon when the brigade artillery commander, Oberstleutnant Winzer, brought his guns forwards until they were immediately behind the firing line and opened fire on the French positions. Soon after, they were joined by two batteries of heavy artillery which unleashed a devastating bombardment, after which the German infantry fixed bayonets and swept forwards towards the ridge, causing the defenders to flee in disorder. At the same time, the 4th Guards Infantry Regiment, which was on the left of the 2nd, attacked the rest of the French 71e RI which also broke and ran, firstly as far as Lemé and then further south.

By mid-afternoon the fighting was over on the front of the 1st Guards Infantry Division. As the exhausted victors halted to rest and reorganize, the remnants of the French 37th and 39th Brigades retreated to Sains-Richaumont, covered by the 38th Brigade which had been held back as corps reserve. In a message to X Corps Headquarters at 1.00pm, Bonnier claimed that he had less than 400 men available, almost no officers and very little ammunition. He added that he would attempt to hold on to the high ground at Sains-Richaumont for as long as possible.

While the 1st Guards Infantry Division was overcoming enemy resistance at Colonfay and Le Sourd, the 2nd Division had been in action a short distance to the east at La Valleé aux Bleds and Voulpaix. Their orders were to cover the army's left wing in case the enemy attempted to penetrate the gap that separated it from 3rd Army. Opposing them was a makeshift group under Général Abonneau consisting of the 4th Cavalry Division, the 51st Reserve Division and a few units from I Corps. Given the weakness of this mixed force (the majority of the 51st Reserve Division had not yet arrived in the area) the Germans should have made short work of them but instead they advanced very cautiously because of concerns for their open flank and also perhaps because of their traumatic experience at Arsimont a week earlier. At La Valleé aux Bleds, for example, two reserve battalions held up Regiment Franz for several hours until the latter was reinforced, at which point they retreated before they could be attacked. When the noise of the artillery bombardment reached the 3rd Guards Infantry Brigade, which was approaching nearby Voulpaix, several battalion commanders ordered their men to join in the fighting. Since other units continued along the road, the brigade became completely dislocated with units facing in different directions. At the same time the march-column was hit by artillery fire from the east (a battery belonging to the 4th Cavalry Division) giving rise to a short-lived panic and causing the combat train of Regiment Elisabeth to break loose and gallop riderless to the rear. Although the small French force was beaten off, causing Abonneau's group to retreat, the damage had been done and it was not until well into the afternoon that General von Petersdorff managed to reassemble his by now widely dispersed brigade. By the early afternoon the fighting had ceased along the front of the Guard Corps. In the late afternoon Plettenberg gave the order for the advance to restart after aerial reconnaissance showed that the French were still retreating, but it could not be carried out because of the heavy losses, exhaustion and disorganization, especially in the 1st Division which had suffered the worst of the fighting.

# THE GERMAN RIGHT WING:
# THE 19TH RESERVE INFANTRY DIVISION
# FIGHTS FOR ITS SURVIVAL

After an enormously long march, the 19th Reserve Infantry Division reached their billets in the villages to the south and south-east of St Quentin at about midnight on the 28th/29th. Oberstleutnant Riebensahm's 39th Reserve Infantry Brigade occupied Neuville-St Amand and Essigny le Grand and Oberst von Winterfeldt's 37th Reserve Infantry Brigade, Homblières and Mesnil-St Laurent. Their orders for 29 August were to assemble at Essigny-le-Grand (the most southerly of the four villages) in the late morning and then make a short advance towards La Fère along the western side of the lower Oise. The next day, or possibly the one after that depending on the arrival of the heavy artillery, they would take part in the siege of La Fère along with the 19th Infantry Division on their left.

Since there was no urgency, the men were allowed an extra couple of hours sleep to help them recover from their exertions the previous day. The earliest unit to rise was Major von Hochwächter's RIR73, which had the furthest to go from its billets in Homblières. Their route would take them through Mesnil-St Laurent, which was occupied by Oberstleutnant Bauer's RIR78 whom they were to follow to the assembly point at Essigny-le-Grand. However, when they arrived at Mesnil they found that Bauer's men had overslept and were swarming through the narrow village streets as they made last-minute preparations for the march. As they tried to force their way through, they became tangled up not only with Bauer's infantry but also with horsemen, with the vehicles of the medical services and with a heavy field howitzer battery which was on its way to the siege of La Fère. Another battery stood stranded at the northern edge of the main street, unable to move. As a result of this congestion, RIR73 became split in two with the front half (one and a half battalions and the regimental staff) just squeezing through and escaping in the direction of Itancourt, leaving behind the rear half (the other one and a half battalions) which was trapped in the impassable streets. It was at this point, as Bauer was watching the first of his units leave the village, that his attention was drawn to a group of riders in a stand of trees near Lorival Farm, on a ridge a few hundred metres to the east. At first, he mistook them for Germans, possibly a patrol from the 19th Infantry Division on the other side of

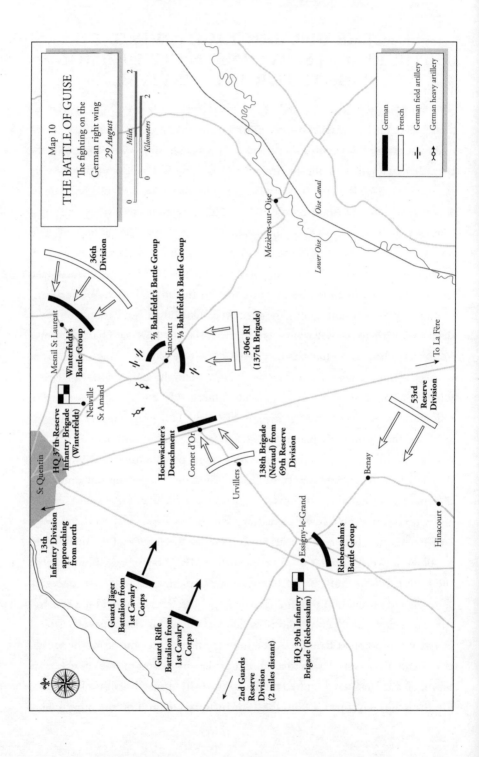

Map 10

THE BATTLE OF GUISE

The fighting on the
German right wing
29 August

the river, but this assumption was rudely shattered a few moments later when shells began to fall in rapid succession on to the crowded village streets.

The French troops who had opened fire belonged to Général Jouannic's 36th Division (XVIII Corps), which formed the spearhead for the attack across the lower Oise in the direction of St Quentin. Their orders were to cross the bridges between Mézières and Ribemont at dawn, advance as far as the first line of hills and wait for the 75th (North African) Brigade to arrive. When the attack was under way, it would be supported on the right by III Corps and, it was hoped, on the left by the British I Corps advancing down the La Fère–St Quentin high road. However, while the 36th Division was pausing as instructed, de Mas Latrie received a message saying that Haig's offer of help had been overruled by Sir John French and that in their absence Valabrègue's Reserve Divisions would cross the river and advance in the direction of Urvillers to support his left wing. Jouannic's troops then set off again, screened from German outposts by the mist which was slow to clear, until at about 8.00am they reached the ridge overlooking Mesnil-St Laurent and saw the streets teeming with the enemy.

The 5,000 or so German infantry in the village were outnumbered by almost three to one, overlooked from the high ground and out of touch with both brigade headquarters and with the brigade artillery which was approaching Itancourt, several miles away. As the shells rained down on them, the officers rounded up the nearest men and led them to the eastern edge of the village where they formed a firing line in the houses and gardens at the bottom of the slope. At the same time the two howitzer batteries took up position to the south-east of the village from where they opened fire on the area around Lorival Farm. Soon afterwards Bauer handed over command to the brigade commander, Oberst von Winterfeldt, who had turned back on hearing the gunfire when he and his staff were halfway between Itancourt and Urvillers.

The 19th Reserve Infantry Division was now in an extremely perilous situation, split into three parts that were widely dispersed across the battlefield and out of touch with one another. Firstly, in the north, at Mesnil-St Laurent, the main portion of Winterfeldt's Brigade (about five battalions strong) was heavily outnumbered and fighting for its life. Secondly, about 8 miles to the south of Mesnil, at the assembly point of Essigny-le-Grand, Oberst von Riebensahm had with him four battalions belonging to his 39th Brigade, two of which had spent the night there and two of which had arrived on time from their billets at Neuville-St Amand. There was, however, no sign of the other two battalions from Neuville-St Amand, or of his brigade artillery and Winterfeldt's Brigade, all of which should have arrived at Essigny long ago. Several patrols were sent out to look for them but they all returned empty-handed. Thirdly, at Itancourt, between Essigny and Mesnil-St Laurent, there was a mixed group of approximately three and a half battalions together with the 37th Brigade artillery, under the command of the divisional commander, General von Bahrfeldt. This ad hoc force consisted of the front half of Hochwächter's RIR73, which we last saw escaping from the traffic jam at Mesnil just before the village came under fire, together with Riebensahm's two missing battalions which were en route from Neuville-St Amand to Essigny. As the two groups arrived in succession at Itancourt and heard the gunfire from Mesnil, they halted and organized defensively, facing northwards in the direction of the noise. By chance Bahrfeldt and the divisional staff were passing through the area at the time so he took over from Hochwächter and set up a command post in an old mill at the edge of the village from where there was an excellent view of the surrounding countryside.

In the late morning, the situation became critical when the French reserve divisions launched their attack. According to Valabrègue's orders the principal effort was to be made in the direction of Itancourt by Général Néraud's 138th Infantry Brigade (69th Reserve Division) supported by the whole of the divisional artillery. They were to be reinforced on their right by the 137th Infantry Brigade and on their left by the 53rd Reserve Division, which was to advance towards Benay and Essigny-le-Grand. If Néraud's Brigade succeeded in capturing Itancourt the 19th Reserve Infantry Division would be irretrievably split in two, leaving the forces at Mesnil-St Laurent and Essigny-le-Grand isolated and exposed to defeat. Shortly before noon, Bahrfeldt's small force at Itancourt was alerted by patrols to the presence of a large enemy force which was heading in their direction and soon afterwards shells began to strike the village, causing the men to duck down for cover against the walls, and the baggage trains and field dressing station to be hurriedly evacuated. At about the same time, at Bahrfeldt's command post in the old mill, an artillery officer arrived at the gallop on a foaming and sweat-covered horse and dramatically announced that while passing through woodland to the south of Urvillers he had seen the enemy gun line and also a large mass of infantry which was moving towards them. As the noise of the gunfire intensified Bahrfeldt quickly reorganized his scanty force to meet this threat. Firstly, he sent a battalion through the village to reinforce the lone company standing guard at the southern exit. Two companies entrenched across the road down which the attack was expected to come, and a third was pushed out on the right to form a flank guard in a sunken lane that ran alongside the railway track. Another company was sent out to reconnoitre to the north-east but failed to return after it was taken by surprise and overwhelmed. Secondly, in an attempt to disrupt the enemy's advance, a battle group of one and a half battalions and a machine gun company, under Hochwächter's command, was pushed forwards to the hamlet of Cornet d'Or where the La Fère–St Quentin high road crossed the country road from Itancourt to Urvillers. By 12.30pm Hochwächter's men had barricaded the Urvillers road down which the French would come and had formed a firing line in the scattered buildings around the crossroads.

On its own, this small group of about 1,000 men would have been easily swept away by a French force more than five times its size, leaving the troops at Mesnil open to envelopment. What saved them from destruction, however, was the enormously powerful artillery support which they received. First of all, the two heavy howitzer batteries which until now had been supporting the troops at Mesnil were moved at the trot to the northern outskirts of Itancourt, from where they opened fire on Néraud's positions in front of Urvillers. Secondly, Bahrfeldt ordered one of the three field artillery batteries adjacent to Itancourt Station to switch their fire from Lorival Farm to Urvillers in anticipation of the French attack. In the sweltering heat, the gunners manhandled their guns over the rough ground near the station until they found a suitable position near the railway embankment from where they had a clear view towards Urvillers. A little later they were reinforced by three batteries from Riebensahm's Brigade artillery, which instead of continuing to the assembly point at Essigny had turned back to Itancourt when they heard the sounds of cannon fire. Lastly, four heavy howitzer batteries which were passing through the area on the way to the siege of La Fère were intercepted to the west of Itancourt by General von Kirchbach, the commander of X Reserve Corps, and ordered to intervene in the fighting. At approximately 1.30pm, after stepping up their own bombardment, Néraud's Brigade left Urvillers and advanced across the open fields towards the crossroads at Cornet d'Or. When they came into view of the German observers, the fields they had to cross to reach Hochwächter's firing line were targeted by no less than 24 field guns and 20 heavy howitzers. To begin with, the French batteries continued to provide the infantry with support, but they were soon silenced by the heavy artillery, which was out of their range. Having achieved complete fire supremacy, the German artillery, their howitzers in particular, wrought dreadful destruction among the advancing French infantry. Despite the deluge of fire (in less than an hour the two heavy batteries at Itancourt alone fired the astonishing number of 1,000 shells) the brave French reservists, urged forwards by officers on horseback, ploughed forwards, closing up to fill the gaps torn in their ranks. When they were within rifle range (the Germans could heard shouts of 'en avant' from the French officers), Hochwächter's men opened rapid fire on the seemingly irresistible waves that threatened to submerge them. Very soon, however, the French first faltered under the effect of the German machine guns and then turned tail and streamed back across the corpse-strewn fields, once again running the gauntlet of the appalling shellfire. After the survivors had been assembled with great difficulty behind Urvillers, the whole of the 69th Reserve Division was pulled back during the afternoon to a defensive position halfway to the Oise.

By repelling the attack on Itancourt, the Germans had gained precious time in which to bring up reinforcements. In addition, their position at Mesnil was now more secure than it had been all morning because Lanrezac had called off the offensive when he learnt that X Corps was under attack. From now on XVIII Corps and Valabrègue's Reserve Divisions were to remain on the defensive and mask St Quentin while the rest of the army attempted to drive the German left wing back across the river to the east of Guise. If Jouannic's infantry had attacked Mesnil-St Laurent in strength early in the morning when Bauer's men were completely isolated, there is no doubt that the Germans would have been overwhelmed; by early afternoon, however, this golden opportunity had gone. Even so, the 19th Reserve Infantry Division was not yet completely out of trouble. In the early afternoon, Riebensahm's four battalions at Essigny-le-Grand came under fire from the French 105th Brigade (53rd Reserve Division) which advanced as far as Benay and Hinacourt, before halting and digging in. Since they showed no sign of aggression, Riebensahm decided after a while to seize the initiative and drive them off, even though he was outnumbered and lacked artillery support. In the fierce midday heat, his two lead battalions advanced in extended order up the long slopes leading towards Benay, across the stubble and between the he recently harvested wheat. When they got within rifle range, the attack slowed, causing Riebensahm to deploy another battalion. Although they were struggling to achieve fire supremacy, their hopes were lifted when they saw, in the distance behind them, long lines of grey uniforms crossing the road to the south of Essigny-le-Grand. The 2nd Guards Reserve Division had arrived.[6] As shells from the newly arrived German artillery fell on the village, Riebensahm's lead battalions attacked it from the front while the other two worked round to the south. At about 3.00pm the flanking battalions fixed bayonets and then, at the charge, swept the defenders off the high ground around the village cemetery, causing their position to collapse. A short while later the French abandoned Hinacourt when the right wing of the 2nd Guards Reserve Infantry Division caught them off guard and threw them back in disorder towards the Oise. When Valabrègue became aware of events at Urvillers and Benay, he gave the order for all of his troops still on the western bank to recross the river under cover of the rearguards and the fire of the heavy artillery. By nightfall they reached the eastern side without further incident and bivouacked in the same positions as the previous evening.

At Mesnil-St Laurent meanwhile, the afternoon was spent in stalemate; the French remained on the defensive after Lanrezac had called off the attack and the Germans were unable to advance up the hillside towards them. However, when reconnaissance revealed that the enemy's left wing was in the air at Lorival Farm, Winterfeldt ordered an artillery section (two guns and four ammunition wagons, each drawn by a six-horse team) to gallop along a country lane which ended at a patch of woodland 300 yards to the east of the farm. Although one of the guns was overturned and several men killed when they were detected at the last moment, the remaining gun team reached the end of the road intact and unlimbered next to a patch of woodland. Firing at more than six rounds a minute, and plentifully supplied with ammunition, they took the end of the French line in enfilade, causing huge losses.

When the French defence around the farm began to crumble as a consequence of this unexpected onslaught, the German right wing advanced towards the crest, whereupon the enemy suddenly gave way and the survivors fled down the road to the rear. A similar attack at the opposite end of the line, near Cambrie Farm, ended in disaster, however, after the French counter-attacked, taking the Germans by surprise as they were relaxing after their victory and completely routing them. However, at this critical moment when it seemed as if the German line would be rolled up from the north, the French suddenly turned back and disappeared over the hill. The reason for this sudden reversal in fortune was the sight of the long march columns of the German 13th Infantry Division approaching the battlefield from the direction of Homblières, to the north-west. They had left Maubeuge at dawn (where they had taken part in the siege) and set off to rejoin the 14th Infantry Division, which had reached the Crozat Canal, two days' march ahead of them. At noon, by which time they had covered more than 22 miles and were looking forward to halting for the day at St Quentin, they received an order from Bülow to come to Winterfeldt's aid at Mesnil-St Laurent. With their help the French were driven away and in the late afternoon the latter retreated under cover of their artillery and recrossed the Oise, leaving the Germans in undisputed control of the battlefield for the first time since eight o'clock that morning.

## THE FRENCH I CORPS COUNTER-ATTACKS IN THE CENTRE

After the German X Corps failed to break out of the bridgeheads at Guise and Flavigny-le-Grand the previous day, it spent the night in bivouacs to the south of the Oise, several miles short of its objectives. Their orders for the 29th were to advance down the eastern side of the Oise until they were level once more with the 19th Reserve Infantry Division on the other side of the river. At the point where the main road south from Guise ran through the centre of the corps' front it branched in two, the right fork leading to the Oise at Mont-d'Origny and the left one to Le Hérie-la-Viéville where it turned sharply to the left and continued along the route nationale to Marle. Initially, the 19th Infantry Division was to advance down the right-hand fork and the 20th down the left-hand one. By advancing in the direction of Mont d'Origny, the former was guaranteed sooner or later to run into the French III Corps which was moving at right angles across their front on the way to the Oise to support the attack by XVIII Corps; likewise, by advancing towards Le Hérie-la-Viéville the latter was set on a collision course with the French I Corps which had left Marle before dawn and was marching up the high road towards the centre of the battlefield.

To begin with, events were dominated by the exceedingly dense and persistent mist, which made navigation difficult and prevented the two sides from seeing each other. Thus, the advance guard of the 19th Infantry Division captured Jonqueuse without a fight after it took the French completely by surprise as they were gathered round their bivouac fires, eating breakfast. A short while later, the divisional artillery struck the French 9th Brigade (at the head of the 5th Division) with devastating fire as it crossed the hills near Bertaignemont Wood, causing them to flee a long way to the south. Their defeat placed Hache in a dilemma, because the 37th (North African) Division was only just arriving after a nine-hour forced march from Marle and there was no sign of I Corps which was due to cover his right wing. If the 6th Division crossed the river as planned they might be taken in the flank as the Germans advanced down the road towards Mont-d'Origny; on the other hand, if they remained on the eastern side and turned to face the threat, they would be unable to take part in the offensive. In the late morning, by which time only a few units had crossed the river, Hache prudently ordered the 6th Division to suspend all further crossings and wait for the 37th Division to arrive. When the latter appeared in the early afternoon, it carried out an attack towards Bertaignemont Wood and the nearby farm, supported by those units from the 5th Division that had not been involved in the earlier fighting. Progress was good at first but the situation was transformed by the intervention on the German side of several heavy howitzer batteries, which had only just reached the front after worming their way through the immense traffic jam at the bridge in Guise and which inflicted huge damage on the unfortunate Zouaves and Tirailleurs, bringing the attack to an abrupt end.[7] Now that his flank was secure, the divisional commander, General Hofmann, gave the order for a general advance along the high road in the direction of Mont d'Origny, unaware that the French 6th Division was moving in the opposite direction. When the two sides met in the late afternoon, an inconclusive fight took place for possession of the high ground to the east of the village, which ended at nightfall when the French retreated leaving the Germans to occupy the battlefield.

Although the 19th Infantry Division had not advanced very far, they had at least prevented Hache from taking part in the offensive. In comparison, General Schmundt's 20th Division had nothing to show for the day's fighting other than heavy losses. Their advance was slow to start, partly because of the thick mist and partly because most of the division, including all of the artillery, had spent the night on the north bank of the river as a precaution against a surprise attack. After they had forced their way through the mass of vehicles cramming the streets of Guise, the infantry were already two hours behind schedule by the time they reached the assembly point at La Désolation Farm (close to the fork in the high road). Further delays then took place after they discovered that Audigny, on their left flank, had been occupied by the enemy (the head of X Corps column). After a thoroughly confusing fight in a blanket of almost impenetrable mist, the French were eventually driven out, leaving the place in German hands. Emboldened by their success, several company commanders then ordered their men to capture the nearby village of Clanlieu, which was taken without a fight a short while later. In the meantime, Schmundt had ordered his division to advance down the main road in the direction of Le Hérie-la-Viéville. Unfortunately, since two of the four regiments were still occupying Audigny and Clanlieu, and a third was in divisional reserve, only one regiment, IR77, followed his orders. For the rest of the day, while the other three regiments remained completely inactive only a few miles away, IR77 was involved in a desperate fight against units from the French I Corps.[8]

After leaving Marle well before dawn, the latter set off down the dead straight route nationale towards the front in one enormous 15-mile-long march column. On their way they were passed by large numbers of refugees accompanied by a variety of carts and other vehicles which occasionally threatened to block the route altogether. Since I Corps was from the Pas de Calais region, which had been overrun by the enemy, many of the refugees came from the same towns and cities as the soldiers, particularly those from the 2nd Brigade whose regiments were garrisoned at Cambrai and Avesnes. In a few touching cases, soldiers recognized friends and relatives among the dense crowds and left the ranks to catch a few fleeting words with them before being ordered back into the column.

At 7.00am, after five hours of non-stop marching, the advance guard reached the bend in the road at Le Hérie-la-Viéville from where they had a panoramic view of the battlefield. Ahead of them, in the far distance, they could make out the Oise at Guise and Flavigny; closer by, on their right, they saw the distinctive white shrapnel bursts around Audigny. When the 1st Brigade arrived a short while later, its commander, Général Marjoulet, ordered it to occupy a defensive position on the northern outskirts of Le Hérie, facing in the direction of the gunfire, and to wait for the other brigades to come level with them. Two battalions from the 43e RI were pushed forwards along the road to Guise to act as an advance guard, one to La Bretagne Farm and the other (the II Battalion), a little further on, to a shallow ridge marked on the map as Hill 150. By chance, as they reached these positions the Germans (IR77) were advancing down the road towards them.

IR77 now began an ordeal which, with the exception of a brief pause in the late afternoon, was to continue until nightfall; they were on their own, the divisional artillery was still held up by the congestion in Guise, and the terrain was completely unfavourable. Ahead of them, fields covered in sugar beet or stubble sloped gently downwards into a shallow depression and then ascended gradually for about a mile to Hill 150. At no point was there the slightest cover from enemy fire, or from the blazing sun, and with the ground very hard after several weeks without rain it was exceedingly difficult to dig trenches in which to seek shelter. When the artillery did arrive several hours later, it was completely ineffective; several batteries fired on the wrong targets, including two heavy howitzer batteries that aimed at Le Hérie, too far to the rear, and a light howitzer battery which for a while bombarded Audigny under the mistaken impression that it was still occupied by the enemy. The only batteries that targeted the enemy position on Hill 150 were very weak, because most of their guns had been destroyed at Flavigny-le-Grand the previous day when they had been caught in the open by the French artillery. In addition, it was difficult for the German artillery observers to get an accurate fix on the French positions because of the strong heat haze from the scorched ground and because they were looking directly into the sun.

For the next few hours the Germans inched forwards towards Hill 150, advancing in short rushes separated by long periods spent hugging the ground in an attempt to shelter from the incessant shellfire. Unable to escape from the burning heat of the sun, they soon emptied their water bottles and were forced to chew the leaves of the sugar beet in a vain attempt to quench their thirst. When they got to within about 1,000 yards of the French position Major Bode, the regimental commander, was forced to deploy two companies from his reserve to fill the numerous gaps in the firing line. In the early afternoon, however, they were unexpectedly reinforced by two detachments from the 19th Infantry Division; one of them, three companies strong, commanded by Hauptmann Graf von Büdingen and the other, four companies strong, under Oberst Winkelhausen. (When Schmundt asked the 19th Infantry Division for help it seems to have completely slipped his mind that his own IR164 was waiting in reserve at La Désolation, only a short distance from his command post.) After the reinforcements had extended the line of IR77 on the right, the advance restarted and they slowly ground their way forwards until they were forced to halt about 400 yards from the enemy's line. It was about 1.30pm and their situation was extremely precarious. Most worrying of all, several units were starting to run out of ammunition.

I was worried about how to replace our cartridges and about the progress of the battle since we only had the ammunition we were carrying. I repeatedly gave the order to fire only a little in order to save the cartridges and I received constant reports from the firing line as to how many had been fired. From time to time the fire stopped altogether and I heard how the morale of the men was good and how they joked to one another. Losses took place, sometimes light, sometimes heavy. I was worried whether the nerves of my men would hold out against the terrible ordeal but this is eventually what happened, as the enemy infantry began to ease off their fire and some of them fled from their trenches. My men then began to dig in. As a result of the heat and the earlier marching, their thirst had become very great but it was not possible to get water from anywhere because the artillery fire was so strong. It fell partly on us and partly over us but the men always stood firm and at no time was communication lost between the companies. There were always runners available to deliver orders and reports very bravely, sometimes even walking calmly and upright. Written reports too arrived from the front line. We were firmly convinced that only slight reinforcements would have been needed to break out of the hell in which we found ourselves, to move forward and launch an attack against the French, which we strongly believed would have been successful. It was clear to me that my task was to defend to the last man the position which we had achieved since a French breakthrough at this point would have torn the battlefront apart.[9]

While Oberst Winkelhausen went up to the front line to judge the situation, his adjutant, Oberleutnant Vogelen, bravely rode back through the fire and returned with sacks of bullets, which volunteers distributed among the most hard-pressed units. In spite of this, some companies ran out of ammunition altogether and received the order to fix bayonets in case they were attacked. In the middle of the afternoon, Bode finally gave up the attempt to take Hill 150 and ordered his front line to fall back a short distance, covered by Winkelhausen's and Büdingen's detachments which were echeloned back on the right in the direction of Bertaignemont Farm. Losses had been enormous, not only in IR77 but also in the reinforcements from the 19th Division. IR78, for example, suffered more than 50 per cent casualties in what was its worst day in the whole of the war. Relative peace now descended on the battlefield as the exhausted, decimated and leaderless companies lay scattered among the fields of stubble and sugar beet, desperately hoping that they would not be called on to do any more fighting that day.

Meanwhile, at Le Hérie-la-Viéville Franchet d'Esperey had been waiting all afternoon for the last of his units to arrive before he launched his attack. At about 5.00pm all was ready; Pétain's Brigade, which was at the tail of the march column, had arrived and the batteries of the divisional and corps artillery were all in place and given objectives. Franchet d'Esperey gave the order to open fire to his artillery commander, Général Bro, and moments later the horizon was lit up with the muzzle flashes of over a hundred guns. From the high ground, the spectacle of the troops advancing across the plateau towards Guise was unforgettable.

On all sides, towards the horizon lit up by the rays of the setting sun, French columns went into the attack like a rising tide. To the north-west, the huge Bertaignemont Farm was once more in flames under an avalanche of shells; to the north, some haystacks had just been set on fire; to the east, Clanlieu and Audigny were beginning to burn; immense plumes of smoke twisted themselves into luminous shapes. Everywhere the French troops infiltrated without pause. All we could see were their blue jackets and the scintillating bayonets, in a tumultuous atmosphere.[10]

On the right, Marjoulet's 1st Brigade made two unsuccessful attempts to capture Audigny and Clanlieu in order to support X Corps but was only able to occupy the villages at nightfall after the Germans had left. In the centre, Sauret's 2nd Brigade was to pass through the line of the 43e RI at La Bretagne Farm and Hill 150 and then continue along the main road and recapture Guise. However, just as the advance was getting under way, the Germans renewed their attack in response to an order from the corps commander, Emmich, who was dissatisfied with the lack of progress. Thus, in the early evening, as IR 77 set off once more towards Hill 150, the advance guard of the French 2nd Brigade was approaching it from the other direction (one battalion from the 1e RI, supported on the left by two battalions from the 84e RI). The first attempt by the French to cross the ridge ended in failure when the Germans opened fire on them at close range, causing them to flee back down the hill to La Bretagne Farm. As the leaderless debris milled around the farm (they had lost 13 of their 15 officers), Colonel Lamotte ordered the regimental standard to be unfurled and his bugler to sound the assembly. When the men had been reorganized, the standard was paraded up and down the road to rally them and they then returned to the attack, led by Général Sauret himself, sword in hand. To begin with, they were no more successful than before, since they were an easy target as they crossed the crest, illuminated by the rays of the setting sun but the Germans were soon forced to withdraw when they were threatened with being outflanked. By nightfall, Hill 150 was firmly in the hands of the 1e RI while the 84e RI was scattered among the rolling hills and shallow valleys to the south of Louvry Farm.

For the exhausted, hungry and thirsty survivors in IR 77 there remained one final act in this day-long drama. When darkness fell, Bode organized his men in a defensive position supported by the machine gun company from Winkelhausen's Detachment. Before long they heard bugle calls in the near distance and saw a dense column of men approaching them rapidly, silhouetted against the light of the burning buildings in Le Hérie:

> As we too sent off a bugle call in their direction, the advancing column answered it with the self-same call but which sounded strange to us.* As soon as the troops approached to within calling distance, we shouted to them, asking to which regiment they belonged and received only the reply 'Comrades'. At the same time we heard loud groans and cries of pain so we supposed that they were German wounded dragging each other back. When their head was only 15 metres away, a nearby machine gun manned by a one-year volunteer suddenly, without an order, began to fire into the mass of men. More machine guns and the firing line then joined in. A few minutes later the whole mass of them had been shot to pieces. After the firing and whistling had fallen quiet, a breathless stillness prevailed. None of us knew if they had been friend or foe. A few of us crept forward to the nearest dead; it had been a French company sent forwards on a strong reconnaissance mission, which had been completely shot down.** The machine gunner had heard a soft '*en avant*' and as a result had opened fire. In this way we were able to recognize enemy troops who were following this column at a distance and we now opened fire on them as well.[11]

As the French recoiled from the encounter, they came under attack from Winkelhausen's detachment and in the confused fighting which took place IR78 lost its adjutant, who was killed, and its commanding officer, Major Lockeman, who was mortally wounded. The regiment had no more officers left. At the end of a ghastly day's fighting, which had gone on almost without a break from the early hours of the morning until after nightfall, IR77 was also in a terrible condition. In the three days from 28–30 August, they lost 725 men, most of them on the 29th, more than any other any other regiment except for the 1st Guards Infantry Regiment at Colonfay.

---

*  The pitch of the French bugles was higher than that of the German's.

** They belonged to Pétain's Brigade and had strayed into the sector from the west after losing their way in the dark.

Pétain's 4th Brigade, which was on the left wing of the attack, had orders to capture the high ground around Bertaignemont Farm and make contact with III Corps in the vicinity of Jonqueuse. Having been the last to arrive at Le Hérie, the light was already starting to fade as they began their advance and there were further delays when they had to cut their way through the numerous barbed-wire cattle enclosures. Because of this it was dark by the time they approached Bertaignemont and they either lost their way in the gloom or navigated as best they could by the light of burning buildings and haystacks. When they were quite close to the still strongly burning farm they encountered large numbers of Zouaves and Tirailleurs who had been wounded or killed in the earlier attack.

We arrived at Bertaignemont Farm. Everywhere were ruins, fires, wounded and dead. Many of the wounded were groaning, laid on beds of straw, up against the great wall of the farm. The straw was reddened with blood; in places smoked and burnt … the flames reached some neighbouring haystacks. We rushed to put out the fires, which threatened the wounded with the most cruel agonies. Who had been so careless as to put so many wounded in such an exposed spot? Almost all were from the 33rd Infantry Regiment but there were also Algerian Tirailleurs. We went to look for water … men fought around a pump; the heat was atrocious, the cries of the wounded were heartbreaking.

Worn out, I sat down but then jumped up again with horror; I was next to the burnt and blackened trunk of a man whose melted fat had broken through his skin. There was no longer any trace of uniform on this corpse. Without turning towards him, I shouted to my neighbour to see this wreck, but he didn't reply. I turned to him. Impassive, Général Pétain eyed me with a glacial look. I tried to strike up a conversation but he didn't hear me, he was as silent as a sphinx, he put on a small cap without stripes or stars and leather slippers, which a staff officer gave him. This pale old man impressed me with his distant attitude, concerned and concentrated, and I couldn't meet his gaze as he was observing the measures which had been taken to extinguish the fires.

My section went off as an advance guard. It was in a sunken road about 200 metres from the farm, to the right of it; this small track was filled with the corpses of Tirailleurs, probably killed by our own guns, for they had no traces of wounds on them and had been cut down while they were in column. Some of them had clung to some railings as they died, their faces were pulled into a frightful grimace. We were forced to separate the bodies and block the path by overturning an old farm cart.

Behind this feeble obstacle I was on sentry duty during this sinister night. Shots were heard, everywhere. Where was the enemy? No one knew exactly. On the path my comrades slept, worn out with tiredness, mixed with the dead, a hundred of them between the farm and the guard post. But suddenly, on the path a tall silhouette stood out against the flames in the background. I shouted 'Halt, who goes there?' It was Général Pétain himself who replied, 'France, Général commanding the brigade.' He advanced towards me with firm steps and after having looked at our barricade, he said, 'I am going to see if the 84e are over there', and alone, he went off into the night … at midnight, I was relieved from my watch. I wasn't able to sleep.[12]

The fires in the ruins were extinguished with difficulty, after which outposts were placed and the others went over to rest.

## THE END OF THE BATTLE

Except for the occupation of Bertaignemont Farm by Pétain's Brigade and isolated incidents such as the final attack on IR77, the fighting ended at nightfall. From Benay in the west to Voulpaix in the east the exhausted troops went over to rest leaving the stretcher-bearers to their melancholy task of retrieving the dead and wounded. In a touching little ceremony, which must have been repeated with numerous variations on both sides that evening, the surviving members of Leutnant Artur Kutscher's company buried their dead in the sunken track to the south-west of Itancourt which they had occupied for most of the day.

We buried our dead under a pear tree which stood next to the path. We dug a grave for our comrades in the stony ground; I had known one of them as a kind young student of Philology and Theology. [Kutscher was a University Professor.] He now lies there almost unknown, and none of his family knows that we dug a grave for him. We carried their bloodied corpses in a tent cloth and laid them down with the cloth over their faces. We stood and removed our helmets and then quietly moved away. The moon and the stars shone down over the path. Everywhere there were burning villages. All was still.[13]

While most soldiers fell into a deep sleep, others remained awake, turning over the events of the day in their minds, dwelling perhaps on the loss of close friends and colleagues or on their own lucky escape from what had seemed like certain death. One soldier spent the night wandering about the battlefield in search of a fellow officer, calling first at the bivouacs of the 1st Guards Infantry Regiment and then, having been unsuccessful, moving on to the nearby field hospital. General von Plettenberg, the commander of the Guard Corps, was searching in vain for his son, a junior officer in the 1st Guards Infantry Regiment, who had been killed in the attack at Colonfay together with 25 other officers and more than 1,100 men.

Neither side had achieved victory in what had been a desperately hard fight, though the survival of the German 19th Reserve Division had been a near miracle and the Guard Corps had suffered very badly at Colonfay and Le Sourd. Despite this, Bülow decided to go over to the offensive the next day, emboldened perhaps by the successful intervention of the 13th Infantry Division for which he had been personally responsible. In what was essentially a mirror image of the French attack that morning, the German right wing would cross the Oise below Guise, take the French in the flank and cut off their retreat. In order to pack as large a punch as possible, the 14th Infantry Division was ordered to fall back from the Crozat Canal and reinforce the 13th Infantry Division and X Corps, slotting into place to the right of the latter. In addition, Bülow asked Kluck for the loan of IX Corps, which was known to be to the west of St Quentin. If Kluck agreed to this, it could come into the line at Origny-Ste-Benoite, to the north of the 13th Division, leaving the 18th Division at St Quentin as army reserve. The X Corps and the Guard Corps were also ordered to attack although Plettenberg was given permission to retreat to the north side of the river if his open flank was threatened with envelopment.

Joffre had spent a difficult day trying to keep alive his plans for the counter-offensive. Early in the morning he drove to 5th Army Headquarters at Laon, where he watched as Lanrezac and his staff conducted the battle.

At 9.00am, General Joffre, flanked by Gamelin and de Galbert, appeared, clad in his long black overcoat. He spent all the morning at the school, a great deal of the time in Lanrezac's room, occasionally walking up and down the recreation ground accompanied by one or other of his orderly officers, the smooth Gamelin or the impulsive Galbert, but never a word did he utter; he watched.[14]

After a break to take lunch at the nearby station buffet, he returned for a short time and then drove off to see Sir John French at Compiègne. Joffre began the meeting by giving them news about Lanrezac's attack together with the latest information about 6th Army and followed this with a plea for them to remain in the line and take part in the planned counter-offensive. As far as the next day was concerned, he reminded French and Murray that they were a day's march to the rear of 5th Army and asked them to delay their retreat for one day so that Lanrezac's troops could catch up with them. With this in mind, he helpfully pointed out that the Crozat Canal offered an excellent defensive position behind which their troops could safely wait. However, his arguments fell on deaf ears.

> My arguments seemed to produce no effect upon French. Moreover, while I was talking, I distinctly saw his Chief of Staff, Sir Archibald Murray, pulling the skirts of the Field Marshal's tunic, as if to prevent him from yielding to my insistence. Thus all I could obtain from him was the reply, 'No, no; my troops need forty-eight hours of absolute rest. When they have had this I shall be ready to participate in anything you want to do; but not any sooner.'[15]

At this point Murray was called away from the room, leaving the two men to negotiate a period of brief but awkward silence until he returned with news that strong enemy forces had been detected in front of the army. In light of this, there was no way that Joffre could convince them to remain in position for at least one more day to provide support for Lanrezac's left wing. Since there was clearly nothing more to be said about the matter, he said goodbye and set off on the long drive back to GQG.

During his absence, worrying news had arrived from Maunoury about 6th Army. Neither of Général de Lamaze's two reserve divisions had arrived at the front because the 55th was only just beginning to disembark and the 56th had not yet reached Paris. Secondly, it would take considerable time to reconstitute the 61st and 62nd Reserve Divisions, which had fled after the debacle the previous day on the Somme bend near Péronne. Thirdly, Sordet's Cavalry Corps, which was meant to fill the gap with the British, was in a parlous condition with men and horses so exhausted that their fighting strength was reduced to that of a single division. Maunoury ended by saying that it was necessary to fall back behind the River Avre, trading space for time, in order to allow the new units to assemble in safety, even though this meant that the counter-attack would have to take place from further back than had been intended. The other message waiting for him was from Lanrezac, giving an account of the day's events and seeking permission to retreat to the defensive position at Laon. Since 4th Army was falling back on their left and the British were refusing to halt to allow 5th Army to catch up with them, Joffre had no option but to give in to the request.

# 7

# THE RETREAT CONTINUES

## 30 AUGUST: THE BRITISH THREATEN TO PULL OUT OF THE LINE

Due to an error in transmission, Joffre's order to retreat did not reach Lanrezac's headquarters until about 7.00am, by which time the fighting had already resumed. In spite of this they were able to make an orderly withdrawal thanks to the bravery of the 38th (North African) Division, which prevented the Germans from crossing the Lower Oise until the late afternoon. As a result, by nightfall the army was safely behind the River Serre, ready to continue the next day towards the Aisne. Likewise, the British II Corps and the newly formed III Corps reached the Aisne as planned but I Corps ended the day to the north of the river after making slow progress through the heavily wooded terrain, intersected by numerous steep-sided valleys. Even so, they were still about a day's march ahead of Lanrezac's left wing and separated from it by a gap of more than 12 miles.

In the early hours of the morning Lanrezac sent Spears and Commandant Duruy on an urgent mission to GHQ to ask Sir John French to delay his retreat so that 5th Army could catch up with them. After a hair-raising drive at tremendous speed along the Aisne valley, they arrived at Compiègne just as dawn was breaking and were immediately ushered in to see French and Murray. After Spears had been questioned about the previous day's fighting, Duruy described the difficult situation of 5th Army and passed on Lanrezac's request. Although the British refused to commit themselves, when Spears and Duruy arrived back at Laon several hours later they were told that their journey had not been in vain since GQG had received a telegram from Huguet containing good news:

> Marshal French has just given orders to stop the retrograde movement of his Army. As regards the eastern column, I Corps is, by its rearguards, to maintain contact with the left of Fifth Army at La Fère. The main body is to halt as soon as the order reaches it, and in any event not to go beyond Coucy-le-Château. To the west, the 3rd, 4th and 5th Divisions are for the moment to remain within ten kilometres of the Oise. It is not possible to hope that these three divisions will be able to participate in the general action, but I think I can obtain that the 1st and 2nd Divisions [ie I Corps] will receive a little later orders to turn about and to attack. It is important in this connection that any turn for the better in the situation should be immediately made known here so that the Field Marshal may be informed at once.[1]

Joffre immediately sent French a message of thanks in which he suggested that everything possible should be done to delay the German advance until the time was ripe for the counter-offensive to take place. Now that this little difficulty was out of the way, he decided to visit the headquarters of 3rd and 4th Armies to see how affairs were progressing in the centre. Arriving first of all at 3rd Army Headquarters, he came to the conclusion from his interview with the army commander, Général Ruffy, that recent rumours of his inadequacy were true and sacked him on the spot, ordering him to hand over command to Général Sarrail. He then drove on to 4th Army Headquarters where he found that its dynamic commander, Général de Langle, not only had the situation well under control but was keen to go over to the offensive as soon as possible. Impressed by his enthusiasm, Joffre gave permission for a limited action in conjunction with the left wing of 3rd Army so as to take the pressure off Foch's detachment.[2] When he got back to Vitry-le-François in the late afternoon, however, he found that bad news was waiting for him; Sir John French had changed his mind about delaying his retreat and, worse still, had decided to pull his army out of the line altogether to allow time for new drafts to arrive from England. The message read as follows:

Colonel Huguet has just explained to me your new plan of retirement. I feel it very necessary to impress upon you that the British Army cannot under any circumstances take up a position in the front line for at least ten days. I require men and guns to make good casualties which have not been properly estimated owing to the continual retirement behind the fighting rearguards. You will thus understand that I cannot meet your wishes to fill the gap between the Fifth and Sixth Armies, namely the line Compiègne–Soissons.[3]

This was appalling news. It would open up an almost 20-mile gap between 5th and 6th Armies, wreck the plans for the counter-attack and disrupt 6th Army's lines of communication. Only that morning he had offered to delay his retreat and, if necessary, to attack with I Corps; now, however, he intended to pull the whole of his army out of the line to refit. This sudden about turn may have been prompted by Joffre's suggestion that it might be necessary to inflict on the enemy a severe lesson like the one given yesterday. In French's opinion, fighting the occasional rearguard action was one thing (hence his offer for I Corps to turn about and attack), but mounting a counter-attack on the scale of the previous day's battle was entirely another, given the state of his army in general and of II Corps in particular. From what he had seen of his troops on his way to his new headquarters at Compiègne, and from anecdotal evidence, he firmly believed that II Corps was in no condition to fight, let alone take part in another full-scale battle. Many years later, this experience was still fresh in his memory. 'It was distressing, indeed, to look at some battalions which I had seen near Mons only some three or four days earlier in all their fresh glory and strength, now brought down to a handful of men and two or three officers.'[4] Secondly, as he made clear in a letter he wrote to Lord Kitchener at the time, he no longer believed that the French High Command had what it took to win the campaign:

I cannot say that I am happy in the outlook as to the further progress of the campaign in France. My confidence in the ability of the leaders of the French Army to carry this campaign to a successful conclusion is fast waning, and this is my real reason for the decision I have taken to move the British forces so far back.[5]

Although he remained on cordial terms with Joffre (mainly due, it has to be said, to the latter's sensitive handling), his relationship with Lanrezac, which had been poor from the start, had by now deteriorated to the point where they no longer trusted one another. As he saw it, Lanrezac had left him in the lurch by retreating without warning on 23 August when the British had been faced with a superior enemy at Mons and there was no guarantee against his doing so again. This was a risk he was not willing to take, even though pulling out of the line would compromise Joffre's strategy. Instead, a new base would have to be established at Le Mans for the army to rest, reorganize and incorporate the replacement drafts, which were expected to arrive very soon from England.

Once again, the German 1st Army was unable to catch up with the enemy. On the left there was no contact with the British and on the right II Corps said that the French force which they had decisively beaten the previous day at Proyart was in a wild flight to the south and south-west. In the late morning, a radio message arrived from Bülow announcing a victory and asking Kluck to wheel inwards the next day so as to take the French in the flank as they retreated:

> The enemy has been decisively defeated today. Strong forces are retreating towards La Fère… In order to exploit this success fully, a wheel of 1st Army is urgently desired against La Fère–Laon, pivoting on Chauny. The 17th Division [which had been lent to him by Kluck] is this evening on the Origny–St Quentin road. Thank you for your support.[6]

Kluck now had to decide whether to swing the whole of 1st Army inwards the next day and ignore the French forces in the neighbourhood of Paris, or to continue on his present path and possibly throw away a golden opportunity of defeating the French 5th Army. Having weighed up all the facts, he decided to co-operate with Bülow, though with one important modification; instead of advancing due east towards the line La Fère–Laon, as requested, he would advance in a south-easterly direction and, having crossing the Oise below La Fère, cut off the enemy's retreat before they could reach the Aisne. With the exception of IV Reserve Corps and II Corps, which were to cover the right flank, the army would wheel to the left, cross the Oise between Chauny and Compiègne and advance as far as the line Coucy-le-Château–Bailly–Compiègne. Marwitz's Cavalry Corps was ordered to advance in the general direction of Soissons and act against the French rear, while Richthofen's Cavalry Corps (which was attached to 2nd Army) was requested to seize the Oise bridges and to co-operate the next day by advancing through Noyon ahead of the infantry.

During the previous night, the Kaiser's Military Headquarters had moved from Koblenz to Luxembourg. At noon on the 30th Moltke and his senior staff officers used their regular midday conference to take stock of the overall situation on both fronts. Everywhere they looked, the news was good. In the East, 8th Army had decisively defeated the Russians at Tannenberg even though the Guard Reserve and XI Corps had not yet arrived; in the West, 1st and 2nd Armies had reported victories against the French on the Somme bend and in the battle of Guise respectively, and were in rapid pursuit of the enemy. On the other hand, 5th Army had got into difficulties as it attempted to cross the Meuse to the north of Verdun, and the armies of the right wing and centre were having problems in keeping in touch with one another as they marched to the south-west according to 27 August Directive. In the afternoon, when Moltke was grappling with these problems, the OHL radio operators overheard Bülow's request to Kluck for 1st Army to wheel inwards the following morning. In the Directive Moltke had speculated that the time might come when it would be necessary for the right wing armies to alter course from the south-west to the south, or even to the south-east, in order to envelop the enemy's left wing. In light of Bülow's victory at Guise, together with the need to support 5th Army as it attempted to cross the Meuse, Moltke decided that the right wing should now change direction. To lend its weight to the attack by 5th Army, 4th Army would incline to the south-east, and the three right wing armies would conform to this movement to prevent gaps from opening up between them and at the same time to envelop the French left wing. What had been a short-term tactical manoeuvre on Kluck's part had been translated by Moltke into a change in strategy. At 9.00pm Kluck and Bülow were informed that their intended change of direction met with his approval.

Third Army has wheeled south to the Aisne, attacks south via Rethel-Semuy and will follow a direction to the south. The movements begun by First and Second

Armies respond to the intentions of OHL. Co-operate with Third Army. Left wing of Second Army in the approximate direction of Rheims.[7]

At a stroke, the march directions of the 27 August Directive had been abandoned; from now onwards, the five armies which formed the great wheeling movement into northern France were no longer travelling towards the south-west but had turned on a southerly, and in the case of 1st and 2nd Armies a south-easterly course, taking them away from Paris. They were playing into Joffre's hands.

## 31 AUGUST: THE FRENCH 5TH ARMY IS ALMOST CUT OFF AT THE AISNE

At dawn, Richthofen's cavalry crossed the Oise in single file over the precariously swaying suspension bridge at Bailly and set off to the south-east in the direction of Soissons. In the absence of any fighting, their only hindrance was the difficult and waterless country, the burning heat and the wafer-thin horseshoes they were unable to replace. News that they were on the move reached Lanrezac's headquarters at 8.30am in the form of an intercepted radio message from Kluck to Richthofen, which asked him to advance towards Vauxaillon (6 miles to the north of Soissons), approximately halfway between the Oise and the Aisne and on the line of retreat of the reserve divisions. After the fighting at Benay and Cornet d'Or on the 29th, followed by the retreat through very difficult terrain, the latter were in an extremely fragile condition and might fall apart at the slightest blow, leaving the Germans to move along the Aisne valley, destroying the bridges and cutting off the rest of the army. Next to them, XVIII Corps had not yet recovered from the attack against the German right wing on the 29th, and an attempt to get help from the British failed because their headquarters were moving to a new location and could not be found. As Lanrezac and his staff desperately cast about for ideas, Colonel Daydrein, the Deputy Chief of Staff, pointed out that Vauxaillon lay on the Laon–Soissons railway line and that there were several empty supply trains standing empty at Laon station which could be used to transport reinforcements to the threatened area. Gratefully seizing on this idea, Lanrezac ordered III Corps to assemble a mixed detachment at Laon station by noon, consisting of the 75th (North African) Brigade, an artillery

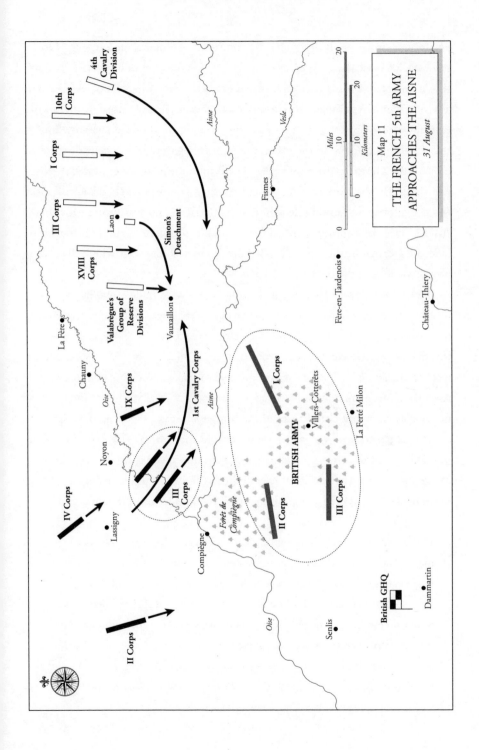

Map 11

THE FRENCH 5th ARMY
APPROACHES THE AISNE

31 August

group and a troop of cavalry, under the command of Colonel Simon of the North Africans. Secondly, he ordered the 4th Cavalry Division to move westwards along the Aisne as far as Soissons from where it could threaten the flank of the German advance. Thirdly, Valabrègue was instructed to shift his line of retreat further to the east, away from Soissons, even though this would lead to severe overcrowding at the remaining bridges. In the event, these measures were more than adequate to prevent the Germans from interfering with the retreat, although it was a close-run thing. By the time that the Guard Cavalry Division reached Vauxaillon in the late afternoon, Simon's detachment had arrived and was waiting for them. After a series of confusing encounters which took place as the light began to fade, the German cavalry retreated a short distance to the west where they went into bivouac at nightfall.

Meanwhile, Kluck's left wing had crossed the Oise at midday and had followed in the steps of the cavalry, several hours' march to their rear. In the early afternoon, he gave orders for the advance to accelerate when aerial reconnaissance revealed that the British had cleared away from their front but that the French had not yet reached the Aisne. The left wing was ordered to make a forced march in order to reach the Aisne by nightfall and mixed detachments of cavalry, artillery and infantry in vehicles were sent ahead to seize the bridges ahead of the French. Despite an enormous effort, however (some units covered more than 30 miles), they were unable to reach the river by nightfall and went into bivouac on the high ground to the north-west. After the great heat of the day it was a beautiful balmy night and the exhausted troops fell asleep in the open fields underneath the cloudless sky.

> In the dusk we marched through the picturesque village of Tracy-le-Mont, and thence through the northern part of the Forest of Compiègne on to a bare plateau, where late in the evening we bivouacked near a lonely farm, called La Falaise. After a day of such burning heat the night was so mild that the men did not trouble to put up their bivouac tents, and simply spread out the unthreshed straw from the farm over the ground to sleep on. It was a beautiful, though melancholy picture, this bivouac on the bare lonely hill in the brightest starlight with burning flames reaching skyward to the south, the first we had seen since leaving Belgium. I slept with the battalion staff on straw in a small shed.[8]

In the late evening, Kluck decided that it would after all be impossible to prevent the French from escaping over the Aisne the next day, partly because his left wing had not yet reached the river and partly because, according to Bülow, 2nd Army was about to have yet another rest day, the second in a row, while preparations were made for the siege of La Fère. On the other hand, according to a pilot the British right wing had retreated only a short distance and was spending the night to the north of Villers-Cotterêts, well within striking range. He therefore gave orders for the left wing to cross the Aisne by 7.00am the next morning and then swing southwards and attack the British, leaving 2nd Army to deal with the French. On the right wing, II Corps was to continue in a southerly direction and cross the Oise near Verberie and IV Reserve Corps was to remain echeloned back to cover the exposed flank in the direction of Paris. The 17th Infantry Division, which had been loaned to Bülow on 30 August, was ordered to rejoin the 18th Division by means of a forced march.

When Lanrezac became aware in the afternoon that the German cavalry were being followed by a large mass of infantry, he gave the order for the retreat to continue through the night and into the following day, at any cost and whatever the consequences, only stopping when they were behind the Aisne. Capitaine Lucien Grard, from the 33e RI, left a vivid description of the march in his diary:

On the next day, the 31st, we continued to retreat to the south at a breathtaking pace. Stages of 45 to 50 kilometres; the heat was overwhelming, we were unable to sleep any more since we marched through the night and because the enemy artillery did not cease pursuing us day and night with their shells until 4 September. The food was bad, consisting of rabbits, hens, biscuits and water. We understood the difficulties which the quartermasters must have encountered in bringing forwards food to troops who were fleeing with such rapidity. The men were so tired that it was necessary to requisition huge carts to carry the sick and the knapsacks. Around these vehicles there were incredible scenes regarding who was going to climb on to them. The bad characters and the lazy ones hid themselves in the road ditches. In order to make them obey, it was necessary to be rough with them and yet several stayed there, exhausted, with neither strength nor will power and who would, an hour later, be taken prisoner by the Germans.

Vehicles as well, some belonging to the army, others not, were also abandoned, broken down. They had been filled up too much without taking into account that they were only constructed for a limited load. The small munitions wagons and those for the baggage (infantry) could not resist the weight. The first were too fragile for war service, the others (former company vehicles which had been modified) were too old, their wheels and stretchers rotten. We had a struggle on our hands to prevent those men who were still carrying their packs (many were in the vehicles) from jettisoning them. In the daytime, one could keep watch but it was difficult during the night. The men easily threw away their packs, entrenching tools and even their cartridges. This is a state of mind during a retreat but it was necessary to make examples in order to stop or at least reduce the number of these serious faults, whose consequences were extremely grave.[9]

The mood at GQG on the 31st was sombre. Lanrezac's troops were in danger of being attacked, several of Maunoury's units had been already been defeated before his army was fully assembled and the British were threatening to pull out of the line to refit. The only slight ray of hope was that Sir John French had promised that he would only make a short retreat the next day to the line Nanteuil-le-Haudouin–Betz and would remain there for a short while providing that 5th and 6th Armies did not fall back any further. However, he repeated that his army would not be able to take offensive action until it had reorganized and refitted. Although Joffre was unaware of it, Sir John French was already under pressure to change his mind from the British Government. When the letter containing his decision to fall out of the line to refit reached Lord Kitchener, the Minister for War, early that morning, it initiated an exchange of telegrams between the War Office and GHQ at Dammartin. On one side, an increasingly alarmed Kitchener passed on the Cabinet's concerns that it would threaten the security of the French Army and might possibly even lead to the loss of the war; on the other, French attempted rather petulantly to justify his decision by unfairly denigrating the French High Command.

If the French go on with their present tactics, which are practically to fall back to the left and right of me, usually without notice, and to abandon all idea of offensive operations, of course then the gap in the French line will remain, and the consequences must be borne by them. I can only state that it will be difficult for the force under my command to withstand successfully in its present condition a strong attack by even one German Army Corps, and in the event of a pause in my retirement I must expect at least two Army Corps at least, if not three. If owing to the Russian pressure, the withdrawal of the Germans turns out to be true, it will be easy for me to refit to the north of Paris; but this I cannot do while my rearguard is still engaged, as it was up to last night. An effective offensive movement now appears to be open to the French, which will probably close the gap by uniting their inner flanks. But as they will not take such an opportunity I do not see why I should be called upon to run the risk of absolute disaster a second time to save them. I do not think you understand the shattered condition of the Second Army Corps and how it paralyses the powers of offence.[10]

Since French seemed to be completely impervious to their arguments, the Cabinet decided that Kitchener would have to go over to France the next day and make him see reason. After a further exchange of telegrams, the British Embassy in Paris was chosen as the location for a meeting that was to have far-reaching consequences for the outcome of the campaign.

At OHL's new headquarters in Luxembourg the day was dominated by the difficult situation of 5th Army's left wing which was struggling to hold on to its bridgehead across the Meuse to the west of Verdun. During the afternoon a liaison officer arrived from the Crown Prince's headquarters with the news that their right wing had also been violently attacked and that they could not be certain of maintaining their foothold on the west bank. An enemy breakthrough either side of the city would have potentially catastrophic consequences since it could lead to the German forces on the Western Front being cut in two, leaving the two wings exposed to encirclement and defeat. From a letter which Moltke wrote to his wife on this day it is clear that he expected the outcome of the campaign to be decided here, in the centre, and not on the right wing. 'Our armies in the centre are fighting today and will fight again tomorrow. This will be a decisive combat, whose issue will have considerable consequences.'[11]

# 1 SEPTEMBER: THE WORST DAY
# OF THE RETREAT

For Lanrezac's troops, the march to the Aisne was the low point in the whole fortnight-long retreat. Men fell asleep on the march, others dropped out, collapsing with exhaustion into the roadside ditches, oblivious to commands to keep moving and past caring that they might be taken prisoner. Some of them took advantage of the darkness to reduce their load by throwing away their entrenching tools, then their knapsacks and in many cases also their spare cartridges. The roads were few and bad and often obstructed by abandoned carts and the bodies of dead and dying horses, which had to be dragged out of the way to clear a path. Every so often their way was completely blocked as vehicle columns crossed one another and became entangled with the infantry and artillery, forcing the exhausted officers to sort out the congestion by the dim light of torches. Morale was poor in some units, especially those which had been roughly handled in the recent battle, and in spite of draconian punishments if caught there were many instances of groups of men leaving the line to pillage or desert. In some cases men panicked, thinking that the enemy was about to catch up with them, and fled without heeding the cries of their officers.

> Duruy fell in with a stream of men running away. He stood in the road, huge and stern, shouting to them to stop. It was to no avail. The stream of unharmed men pressed on unheeding, open mouthed and with glazed eyes. Duruy, seeing that fear rode on these men's shoulders and panic reigned in their hearts, drew his revolver and fired; but the men merely stumbled over the prostrate ones and went on, hardly attempting even to dodge the levelled weapon.[12]

Général Mangin, who had just been promoted to the command of the 5th Division, spent part of the night with one of his staff officers, Brzumienski, watching his troops pass by. He was not impressed by what he saw:

> Their aspect was lamentable. The men slept while marching, the cavalry on their horses, the artillery on their ammunition limbers. Soon the 6th Division doubled the column of the 5th and ... quarrels began in the march... I sent officers ahead

and to the rear in an attempt to remove the blockage. They told me that it had been like this for the last eight days and nights. As for the artillery, of which I only saw one or two batteries, the colonel answered casually that he didn't know where his regiment was and that he would rejoin it where and as he could. I ordered him to send one of the numerous officers who accompanied him to look for his artillery groups. When the parade had gone by, Brzumienski said to me, 'you've been given a pretty present!'[13]

With the exception of the rearguard units, some of which did not arrive until the late evening, they all crossed the Aisne by noon and halted on the far side, after which the bridges were prepared for demolition.

If Richthofen's Cavalry Corps had advanced in an easterly direction along the valley of the Aillette, as originally intended, they would probably have cut off the reserve divisions and XVIII Corps. (His original objective was Chavignon, directly in the path of the latter.) However, following Kluck's decision to pursue the British rather than the French, they turned due south and advanced through Soissons in order to reconnoitre ahead of 1st Army's left wing. When the Guard Cavalry Division was on the point of capturing Soissons it was recalled to reinforce the rearguard, which was under attack under by Simon's detachment and by units from the 4th Cavalry Division. After a disorganized fight among the broken and hilly ground to the north of Soissons, the German cavalry went over to rest on the north side of the Aisne, more or less where they had started the day and too far away to menace the French retreat.

To the west of Soissons, meanwhile, 1st Army had mixed success in its attempt to overhaul the British. III Corps almost caught up with Haig's I Corps but the latter escaped thanks to a skilful, though costly, rearguard action by the 4th (Guards) Brigade in the forest to the north of Villers-Cotterêts. In the German centre, IV Corps made no contact at all despite an enormous forced march of more than 30 miles which ended well after midnight. Further to the west, however, at Néry on the southern outskirts of the great Forest of Compiègne, a British rearguard consisting of the 1st Cavalry Brigade together with L Battery Royal Horse Artillery was taken by surprise in the thick early morning mist by General von Garnier's 4th Cavalry Division. After L Battery lost all but one of its guns (in an action that led to the award of three Victoria Crosses), and after the cavalry suffered considerable losses as the enemy shells fell without warning on to the narrow village streets, the British called in reinforcements and quickly gained the upper hand. The fighting ended in the middle of the morning when the Germans fled from the scene leaving behind approximately 180 dead and wounded men, the bodies of over 200 horses and the shattered remains of eight of their 12 guns. For the next 24 hours they wandered around in a hopeless attempt to locate the other two cavalry divisions and finally bivouacked in the Forest of Ermenonville where they remained all the next day, only emerging when the British had gone. When they left, they abandoned their four remaining guns because they had left most of their ammunition behind the previous day in an attempt to speed up their advance.[14] Lastly, on the extreme right the 9th Cavalry Division saw action at Verberie (to the south-west of Compiègne) against a French rearguard consisting of the Provisional Cavalry Division (formed on 29 August from the most battle-worthy units in Sordet's Cavalry Corps), and four battalions of reserve Chasseurs Alpins. Since the French had destroyed both bridges in the sector and since cavalry divisions did not possess bridging trains, the Germans were forced to wait for II Corps infantry to arrive. When the latter reached the river in the early afternoon, however, they were pinned down by the French artillery and it was only during the night, by which time the French had gone, that the first infantry began crossing the river on a pontoon bridge which had been constructed upstream of the town.

In the afternoon Kluck realized that he was unlikely to overhaul the British and so he decided to give his troops a rest day on 2 September, the first since the start of the campaign. A message was sent to OHL letting Moltke know that they had failed to catch up with the French, that they had been in action at Verberie against the English and that the army would stand by the next day on the line Verberie–La Ferté Milon and await orders. A few hours later, however, he changed his mind after receiving a captured British billeting order which showed that their right wing had cut short its retreat and would spend the night only a short distance to the south of Villers-Cotterêts. With all thoughts of a rest day now gone, orders were issued for the pursuit to be resumed in the morning. While the three central corps (II, IV and III) engaged the British frontally, the 18th Infantry

Division on the left and IV Reserve Corps on the right would envelop their flanks after making a long approach march.

Moltke's attention on 1 September was once more focused on the centre where 5th Army was still having a difficult time holding on to the bridgehead over the Meuse to the west of Verdun. In the afternoon, however, a message arrived from the Crown Prince saying that they had not only weathered the French attack but had gone over to the offensive in conjunction with 4th Army. The news that the enemy was now in flight could not have come at a better time for Moltke, firstly because it was the anniversary of his uncle's famous victory at Sedan in the Franco–Prussian War and secondly, because the Kaiser had fortuitously chosen the day to visit his son's headquarters.

Ironically, at the very time when Moltke was concentrating on events in the centre, Joffre was once more making plans to attack the German right wing. After the rapid advance of the German 1st Army had prevented the planned counter-offensive from taking place near Amiens, he briefly toyed with the idea of replacing it with an offensive in the centre in order to sever the German right wing from its pivot at Metz. However, he reverted to his original strategy after British pilots reported that the German right wing had changed direction the previous afternoon and was now advancing to the south-east, taking them away from Paris. His mind was now made up. The attack would begin as soon as 6th Army was complete and 5th Army had reached a strong defensive position, either along the Aube and the Seine or, if the conditions were favourable, to the north of the two rivers. In the meantime, 3rd Army, around which the left wing would pivot during the offensive, would be strengthened by units transferred from Alsace and Lorraine. In addition, a new cavalry corps commanded by Général Conneau would be formed from the 6th and 8th Cavalry Divisions (then in the region of Epernay) with orders to protect Lanrezac's left wing if the British pulled out of the line. The new plan was summarized in General Instruction No 4, copies of which were sent to 3rd, 4th, 5th and 6th Armies as well as to Galliéni (the Military Governor of Paris) and, in a significantly amended form, to Sir John French. The version handed to the British dwelt more on the need for an orderly withdrawal than it did on the subsequent offensive.[15] In a telegram he sent to the Minister for War during the morning, Joffre explained that he had more or less written the British out of his plans.

… it would be very advantageous if the English troops equally accepted to co-operate in a battle on a front to the north of Paris. But, because he had received nothing from them but successive opposition to propositions of this nature, he could no longer ask anything of them.[16]

As it happened, however, his pessimism was premature. After leaving London at 2.00am and crossing the Channel in a destroyer, Kitchener met Sir John French in the British Embassy in Paris early that afternoon. Although no record was kept of their three-hour conversation, the outcome was brutally clear from the telegram that Kitchener sent to the Cabinet:

French's troops are now engaged in the fighting line, where he will remain conforming to the movements of the French Army, though at the same time acting with caution to being in any way unsupported on his flanks.[17]

To remove any lingering uncertainty, French was given a copy of the telegram as a record of what had been agreed, together with a letter that included the following:

I feel sure that you will agree that the above represents the conclusions we came to; but, in any case, until I can communicate with you further in answer to anything you may wish to tell me, please consider it as an instruction. By being in 'the fighting line' you of course understand I mean dispositions of your troops in contact with, though possibly behind, the French as they were today; of course, you will judge as regards their position in this respect.

To which the chastised, if not completely repentant, Field Marshal replied 'I fully understand your instruction; I am in full accord with Joffre and the French.'[18]

In the evening, not long after Joffre received a letter from Messimy containing the good news about the British, a telegram arrived from Lanrezac containing information of the highest importance. In a dramatic intelligence coup, a French patrol had fired on a German car in the vicinity of Coucy-le-Château, killing its occupants, one of whom was an officer belonging to the Guard Cavalry Division. When the bloodstained contents of the man's bag were examined at 5th Army

Headquarters, among the food and clothing was a map on which was marked the line of march of each corps in 1st Army, together with a list showing their billeting areas for the day. At a stroke this confirmed the results of yesterday's aerial reconnaissance and demonstrated unequivocally that the German right wing was marching in a generally south-easterly direction, away from Paris. All that was now needed for the counter-attack to take place was for 6th Army to reach full strength (IV Corps and the 55th and 56th Reserve Divisions were still to arrive), for Foch's detachment (soon to be renamed 9th Army) to be strengthened and for 5th Army to reach a suitable defensive position.

## 2 SEPTEMBER: THE GERMANS ATTEMPT TO CUT OFF THE FRENCH AT THE MARNE

Kluck's renewed attempt to catch up with the British ended in failure because they departed in the middle of the night rather than at dawn. As a result, the only action was against the French at Senlis where II Corps easily brushed aside part of the 56th Reserve Division which was covering the retreat of 6th Army. In the early afternoon Kluck was about to halt for the day when he received an important message from General von Quast, whose IX Corps was on the extreme left wing. According to this, a pilot had seen large enemy columns, approximately three corps strong (Lanrezac's left wing), retreating towards the Marne sector east of Château-Thierry and a long way short of the river. Quast said that his troops had been unable to catch up the British and so he had independently ordered the 18th Infantry Division to reach Château-Thierry and seize the Marne bridges in and to the east of the town before the French arrived. In addition, he had directly requested III Corps, which was on his right, to support the movement, and had asked Richthofen to delay the enemy's retreat by threatening their flank in the region between the Aisne and the Marne. Feeling that this was too good an opportunity to miss, Kluck confirmed Quast's decision and ordered the 18th Infantry Division and III Corps to continue with all available means to the Marne around Château-Thierry in order to arrive there before the French. On the right, IV Reserve Corps and II Corps were to overcome the remaining French forces in the neighbourhood of Senlis and IV Corps in the centre would

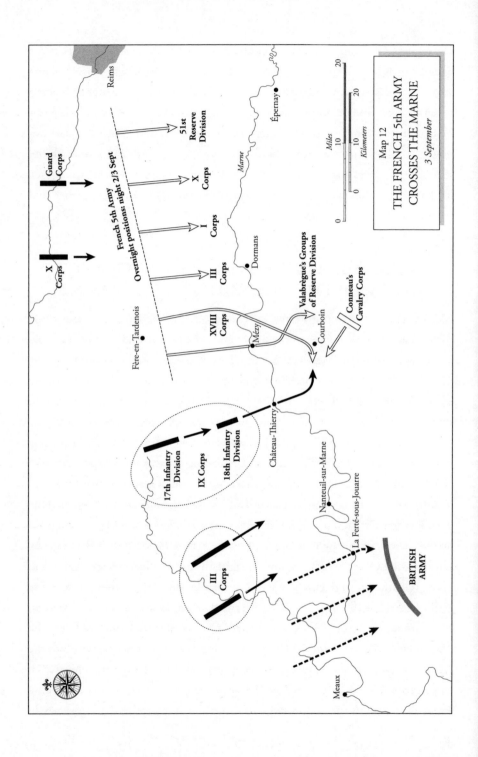

Map 12

THE FRENCH 5th ARMY
CROSSES THE MARNE

3 September

act as a link between the two wings. Although Marwitz's Cavalry Corps was in urgent need of rest, it was ordered to reconnoitre against the north and north-east fronts of Paris and either side of the Marne.

Once again, however, the task proved too much for the exhausted German infantry and despite long marches neither III Corps nor the 18th Infantry Division was able to reach the Marne by nightfall. Instead, the former went over to rest about 10 miles to the north-west of Château-Thierry and the latter reached the high ground to the north of the town and briefly bombarded it just as dusk was falling. According to Kluck's orders for the next day, Quast's troops were to capture Château-Thierry and occupy the bridges in and on either side of the town but not to cross the river. IV Reserve Corps and II Corps were to cover the right flank, linked to the left wing by IV Corps, which was to halt well before it had reached the Marne.

While 1st Army was zigzagging about in pursuit of first one enemy and then the other, 2nd Army had spent the last two days capturing the antiquated fortress of La Fère, much to the annoyance of Kluck and Kuhl who felt that they would have been far better employed in delaying Lanrezac's retreat. Although the French had escaped, the large amount of baggage, food and ammunition scattered along the roadside and in the neighbouring fields suggested to Bülow that they were disintegrating and would fall apart at the slightest blow. He therefore gave orders for a rapid pursuit the next day in the hope of catching up with them as they were crossing the Marne.

At OHL meanwhile, Moltke was in an ebullient mood after receiving reports that the enemy was retreating rapidly in front of 3rd, 4th and 5th Armies. Buoyed up by this news, and egged on by the elated Kaiser who was still in a state of euphoria after visiting his son's headquarters, he began to feel once more that victory was almost within his grasp, though not on the right wing, as he had previously believed, but in the centre.[19] Even so, niggling doubts remained about the situation of 1st Army from which there had been no news since Kluck's situation report for the 31st, which had reached OHL after a 30-hour delay. Furthermore, there was disturbing news that the French were transferring units from their right wing and centre to the region of Paris from where they would be able to strike 1st Army in the flank. According to Hausen, in the early morning a pilot had observed a large number of enemy troops embarking on his front and four long troop trains moving in a south-westerly direction. In an attempt to estimate the size of the enemy forces in the neighbourhood of the capital, Moltke asked Tappen to summarize all that was known about the French order of battle. According to the table that Tappen produced, the forces identified in the Paris region consisted of VII Corps, the 61st and 62nd Reserve Divisions, a number of Moroccan units, and several battalions of reserve Chasseurs Alpins. These might also be augmented soon by the French IV Corps, which had recently been withdrawn from the Lorraine front, and by some of the six reserve divisions, which they had been unable to locate.[20]

Moltke now had to decide how to make the right wing more secure without in any way diminishing the prospects of victory in the centre. If it continued to advance in a south-easterly direction it would be able to support the offensive in the centre but would expose Kluck's open flank to the enemy forces in the neighbourhood of Paris; on the other hand, if it reverted to a south-westerly course a dangerous gap would open up with the central armies at a critical point, just as they were about to achieve victory. In the end he decided to compromise by allowing the right wing to continue to the south-east but with 1st Army echeloned back on the right to cover the exposed flank. At 8.20pm the following radio message was sent out to 1st and 2nd Armies:

> The intention of the Supreme Army Command is to throw back the French in a south-easterly direction, cutting them off from Paris. 1st Army will follow the 2nd echeloned back and additionally will ensure flank cover for the armies.[21]

Besides, 6th Army was urged to attack the French forces in Lorraine at the earliest opportunity, to hinder the transfer of enemy units to the west and 5th Army was ordered to invest the eastern front of the fortress of Verdun to prevent the French from debouching from the far side of the Meuse in the direction of Toul–Nancy.

Moltke's decision was prescient, for at this very time Joffre was putting the finishing touches to his plans for the counter-attack. First of all, he ordered Lanrezac and Maunoury to accelerate their retreat, the former towards the Seine and the latter in the direction of Paris, so that gaps did not open up with the

British Army, which had unexpectedly fallen back during the night. Secondly, when he received confirmation that the Germans had transferred at least two army corps to the Eastern Front, he began to consider launching the counter-attack in the next few days. In the ensuing debate, Berthelot and several others argued forcefully for a delay until Lanrezac's troops were safely behind the Seine, while others, including several members of the Operations Bureau, wanted the offensive to take place as soon as possible. The clinching factor was the recent news that 4th Army and Foch's Detachment were about to be attacked by large masses of enemy troops from the direction of Rethel. Since 4th Army was still in a fragile state after the fighting in the Ardennes, and Foch's Detachment was still incomplete, Joffre decided to delay the offensive a little while longer. At 9.00pm, half an hour after Moltke sent the radio message to 1st Army telling Kluck to echelon back and act as flank guard, he issued an updated version of General Instruction No 4 which, for the first time, included provisions for the British to take part in the attack.

## 3 SEPTEMBER: KLUCK DISOBEYS HIS ORDERS AND PUSHES DEEPER INTO ENEMY TERRITORY

This was the day on which Kluck's intransigence tipped over into outright insubordination. Instead of obeying Moltke's order to echelon back behind 2nd Army, which had reached him in the early hours of the morning, he changed his mind about staying on the north side of the Marne and decided to push his left wing across the river to prevent the enemy from escaping. The French reserve divisions, which were several hours' march ahead of the rest of the army, reached the Marne at Mézy soon after dawn, at about the same time as Quast's troops were crossing the river at Château-Thierry a few miles to the west. When the ragged mass of reservists entered the narrow streets they became part of an enormous traffic jam, in which infantry, artillery, horsemen and wagons attempted to force their way through the heaving and tightly-packed crowd. By the time that the mess was sorted out, much valuable time had been lost and it was late morning before they reached the high ground to the south of the river. Originally they were then supposed to cover the left flank of the army while it crossed the river but on learning of their atrocious condition Lanrezac ordered them to change places with their immediate neighbours, XVIII Corps. When de Mas Latrie received the order he hurriedly pushed a brigade from the 36th Division on to the high ground at Courboin where it arrived just in time to oppose Quast's advance guard, which was ascending from the valley. Although the Germans brought up their heavy artillery, the French were soon reinforced by the rest of the division and by part of Conneau's Cavalry Corps, and prevented them from breaking out of their shallow bridgehead and taking the rest of the army in the flank. To the west, meanwhile, after a long forced march III Corps reached the valley of the Marne in the late evening as dusk was beginning to fall and went over to rest on the high ground to the north. The peaceful scene that greeted them as they came into view of the river was described by Hauptmann Bloem of the Brandenburg Grenadiers:

> The sun was beginning to set, when suddenly, spread out at our feet, was a picture of indescribable loveliness: the valley of the Marne. There was such a charm in its lazy atmosphere of serene unruffled peace that we greeted thankfully the order to halt, and we lay on the grass by the roadside struck dumb with the beauty of the scene... We marched on down and through the old country town of Nanteuil [-sur-Marne]. Not a soul in the streets but here and there a terror-stricken face peering through the shuttered windows. On the bridge were some of our cyclists: one of them, full of merriment, said to me: 'We had great fun, Sir! When we got to the bridge, people came up to us and asked "*Anglais?*" and as our lieutenant had told us always to say, "*oui, oui*", we said "*oui, oui, oui*". Then the people brought us a mass of stuff to eat and drink and put flowers in our buttonholes. But when our cavalry came up the people realized we were not English but Germans. They screamed and ran away in all directions, but it didn't matter; we'd got all we wanted.'
>
> And then we crossed the Marne. On the far side we halted, awaiting orders for billeting. Never shall I forget that evening. The firing to our left had ceased. The sun had sunk into a misty haze of deepest gold. The whole valley, steeped in the perfect stillness of a summer evening, shimmered in the golden light. Could this be war? Could anyone fight here? Impossible. It was peace on earth, the peace that passeth understanding.[22]

Although the French had narrowly escaped, Kluck decided to continue the pursuit the next day because of Bülow's claim that they were on the point of disintegration. With the exception of IV Reserve Corps and the 4th Cavalry Division, both of which would remain on the north bank to guard the right flank, the army was to cross the Marne and make another attempt to cut off the enemy's retreat despite the fact that this was in clear breach of Moltke's recent order.

At OHL, the unbridled optimism of the previous day had given way to increased concerns for the security of the right wing, firstly because the French were continuing to transfer troops to the Paris region and secondly with the realisation that 1st Army was at least a day's march *ahead* of 2nd Army and therefore not in a suitable position to guard against the threat. Given the increasing problems with signal communication (several messages had been delayed by more than 24 hours) they could not be certain that Kluck had received the order to echelon back behind 2nd Army. In his latest situation report Kluck had said that he was going to push his left wing as far as the Marne at Château-Thierry on 3 September; if the order had not yet reached him, he might even send his army across the river, making the situation even worse. With this in mind, Moltke, Tappen and the senior staff officers discussed whether they ought to send an officer by car to Kluck's headquarters, but decided that this was unnecessary since at the very latest the radio message would arrive before he issued his orders for the next day. Like his earlier decision to release 1st Army from Bülow's control, it was an omission which Moltke would soon very much come to regret.

In contrast to Moltke, who was becoming increasingly assailed by doubts, Joffre was more and more confident about the prospects for victory, to the extent that he considered launching the counter-attack before 5th Army reached the Seine. The latter would soon be behind the Marne, 4th Army was retiring in good order and Foch's Detachment, which filled the gap between them, was up to strength. On the left, 6th Army was falling back towards the entrenched camp of Paris, out of contact with the enemy, and would be complete when IV Corps had finished detraining. Last of all, he had received a personal letter from Sir John French in which the latter offered his full co-operation in the coming offensive.

Before unleashing the counter-attack there was one important piece of unfinished business to transact. He had already weeded out several incompetent generals including one army commander (Ruffey) and several corps commanders, replacing them with officers of worth such as Mangin and Pétain, each of whom had recently been put in charge of a division. With the battle approaching, he now decided that it was time to remove Lanrezac from the command of 5th Army and replace him with Franchet d'Esperey. Like several others at GQG, and a not inconsiderable number of officers at 5th Army Headquarters, Joffre felt that Lanrezac's reputation as a brilliant peacetime officer, his superbly analytical brain and comprehensive grasp of military theory, had not been matched by the ability to command troops in battle. By this stage in the campaign his heart no longer appeared to be in the struggle and his relationship with Sir John French had more or less reached rock bottom. There was no alternative; in the interests of the offensive, Lanrezac would have to go. In the early afternoon Joffre drove to Sézanne to carry out the painful deed. The dismissal was witnessed by Spears who watched the two men as they walked back and forth, deep in conversation, across the small playground of the school that housed Lanrezac's headquarters:

General Lanrezac was obviously dispirited and depressed. He talked a good deal and interrupted his walk now and then to make a point, but did not look at the Commander-in-Chief, and it was evident that the vigour he generally displayed in conversation was absent. His arms hung limp, he made no gestures except for an occasional movement of his hands.

General Joffre appeared to be talking a little more than was his habit, but even this unusual effort on his part did not amount to saying more than a few sentences. At first he seemed to be speaking emphatically, then, after long silences, to be remonstrating gently. One gathered he might be saying: 'No, it is not as bad as that.' How the news got about I do not know, but the whisper passed round: 'The Commander-in-Chief is dismissing the General.' For some time such a possibility had been in the air, and now the moment had come the atmosphere was electric.

The two big stout men, one fresh-coloured and calm, the other grey and haggard, continued to walk up and down, up and down. If the Commander-in-Chief was really dismissing Lanrezac, his manner appeared to be very soothing and fatherly now. I have no idea how long the scene lasted, it may have been short, but it appeared to be endless, every moment weighed down by the fate of the coming battle.

Suddenly the two Generals disappeared. Probably they walked out of the playground, but the picture left in my memory is that one moment they stood there and the next they were gone. I never saw General Lanrezac again.[23]

When Lanrezac had gone, Joffre stayed on for a while, walking alone in the playground until Franchet d'Esperey arrived to take over command, after which he drove back to GQG where he arrived in the middle of the evening. On his return, he found some extremely good news waiting for him. While he had been away, a message had arrived from British headquarters saying that according to aerial reconnaissance the German right wing, which had deviated the previous day to a southerly direction as it pursued them, had swung back to the south-east and was now marching rapidly towards the Marne section La Ferté-sous-Jouarre–Château-Thierry. This was the crucial information for which he had been waiting. Together with news from Maunoury that the Germans had vanished from the front of 6th Army, it confirmed that they had abandoned the French capital as their objective. Instead, they were advancing into the gap formed by the French left wing and exposing their flank to the counter-attack.

Joffre's final task before retiring to bed was to write to Galliéni, allaying his fears that Paris would be left undefended when the offensive began and requesting him to make preparations for 6th Army to advance. With confirmation that the German right wing was set on a south-easterly course, taking it away from Paris, most of the pieces of the jigsaw puzzle were now in place. Both the British Army and 5th Army were across the Marne, and 6th Army had been ordered to prepare to advance. All that was now needed for the attack to take place was news that 5th Army and 9th Army (previously Foch's Detachment) were both ready to take the offensive.

## 4 SEPTEMBER: THE GERMAN HIGH COMMAND SENSES THAT VICTORY IS SLIPPING FROM THEIR GRASP

After shaking off their pursuers without great difficulty, the French 5th Army ended the day level with Montmirail. Likewise, neither the British Army nor the French 6th Army saw any fighting; after an uneventful day, the former went over

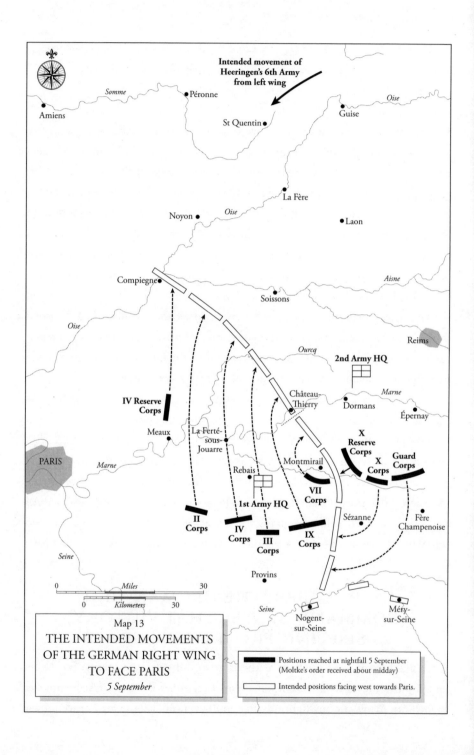

Intended movement of
Heeringen's 6th Army
from left wing

Somme

Péronne

Amiens

Oise

Guise

St Quentin

La Fère

Noyon

Oise

Laon

Compiegne

Oise

Soissons

Aisne

Reims

Ourcq

2nd Army HQ

Château-
Thierry

Marne

Dormans

Épernay

IV Reserve
Corps

Meaux

La Ferté-
sous-
Jouarre

PARIS

Marne

X
Reserve
Corps

X
Corps

Guard
Corps

Rebais

Montmirail

II
Corps

1st Army HQ

IV
Corps

III
Corps

VII
Corps

IX
Corps

Sézanne

Fère
Champenoise

Seine

Provins

Seine

Nogent-
sur-Seine

Méry-
sur-Seine

0        Miles        30

0      Kilometers     30

Map 13

THE INTENDED MOVEMENTS
OF THE GERMAN RIGHT WING
TO FACE PARIS

5 September

Positions reached at nightfall 5 September
(Moltke's order received about midday)

Intended positions facing west towards Paris.

to rest a short distance to the south of Meaux with its right wing resting on the Marne at La Ferté-sous-Jouarre and the latter reached the area around Dammartin, approximately 16 miles to the north-east of Paris.

During the late morning and early afternoon Kluck sent a long six-part radio message to OHL in which he complained of being kept in the dark about the situation of the other armies, claimed the praise which he felt was due for his own troops and justified his decision to disobey the order to echelon back and face Paris:

Can 1st Army be notified of the situation of the other armies, whose reports about decisive victory have repeatedly been followed by requests for support? Through continuous heavy fighting and incessant marching, 1st Army has reached the limit of its strength. It is only in this way that it has been able to open the passage of the Marne to the other armies and force the enemy to continue its retreat. In this case IX Corps has acquired greatest credit for the boldness of its operations. We still hope to exploit the success. Supreme Command's instruction prescribing 1st Army to follow 2nd Army echeloned back could not be followed in these conditions. The projected throwing back of the enemy to the south-east, cutting them off from Paris, can only be carried out if 1st Army advances. The necessary protection of the right flank must weaken the offensive force of the Army. It is instantly desirable that the right wing is soon reinforced by other units (III Reserve Corps and VII Reserve Corps). Given the ceaselessly changing situation, 1st Army will not be in a position to take important decisions unless it is permanently kept informed of the situation of the other armies which seem to be further back. Liaison with 2nd Army is assured in a constant manner.[24]

Late that evening, Kluck decided to continue the pursuit the next morning 'on the assumption that the Supreme Command still persisted in its resolution to force the enemy back from Paris in a south-easterly direction.'[25] The three left-wing corps were to advance across the Grand Morin, II Corps was to cross the Marne and cover the eastern side of Paris and IV Reserve Corps was to stay to the north of the Marne and advance towards Meaux to screen the city from the north-east. Marwitz's two remaining cavalry divisions (the 4th Cavalry Division had been transferred to IV Reserve Corps) were to make a wide sweep to the south-east and strike the flank of the French 5th Army as it approached the Seine.

At OHL, 4 September was a day of mounting apprehension as Moltke and Tappen became more and more anxious that serious trouble was brewing on the right wing and that victory, which had seemed almost certain a few days ago, was slipping from their grasp. The mood that evening was expressed by Helferrich, the Foreign Secretary, who was making a brief visit to the Kaiser's Military Headquarters:

> I found Generaloberst von Moltke by no means in a cheerful mood inspired by victory, he was serious and depressed. He confirmed that our advanced troops were only 45 kilometres from Paris, 'But' he added, 'we've hardly a horse in the army which can go faster than a walk.' After a short pause, he continued: 'We must not deceive ourselves. We have had successes, but we have not yet had victory. Victory means annihilation of the enemy's power of resistance. When armies of millions of men are opposed, the victor has prisoners. Where are ours? There were some 20,000 taken in the Lorraine fighting, another 10,000 here and perhaps another 10,000 there. Besides, the relatively small number of captured guns shows me that the French have withdrawn in good order and according to plan. The hardest work is still to be done.'[26]

Moltke had good cause to be worried about the situation on the right wing. Firstly, the latest intelligence bulletin confirmed the movement of up to five French corps in the direction of Paris. Secondly, according to an agent's report (which turned out to be false), British troops were disembarking at Ostend from where they would be able to disrupt the over-extended communications of the right wing. Thirdly, and most worrying of all, there was news that Kluck's left wing had crossed the Marne at Château-Thierry the previous day, leaving only the right wing on the north bank to cover against Paris. (This was contained in Kluck's radio message which was sent out during the afternoon of 3 September and which had taken about 24 hours to arrive.) Either Kluck had not yet received the order to echelon back behind 2nd Army or he had disobeyed it. Whatever the reason, the fact that he was still advancing was extremely worrying given the build-up of enemy troops near Paris.

During the afternoon Moltke and Tappen considered how to protect the right wing until victory was achieved in the centre. At 5.00pm, in the highly charged atmosphere of Moltke's office, the decision was taken to halt the march of the right wing and order it to face Paris to ward off the blow which they were convinced would come from that direction. In the evening the necessary orders were sent out to the armies, by radio to 1st, 2nd and 3rd Armies and by telephone to the others. Identical orders were received by 1st and 2nd Armies.

> 1st and 2nd Armies will remain facing Paris from the east. 1st Army between the Oise and the Marne, occupying the passages over the Marne to the west of Château-Thierry; 2nd Army between the Marne and the Seine, occupying the passages over the Seine between Nogent and Méry inclusive. 3rd Army has orders to march on Troyes.[27]

The Schlieffen plan was dead, killed off by the man to whom it had been bequeathed almost ten years ago. From now on all hopes of victory rested not on the right wing, which was relegated to a purely defensive role, but on the armies of the centre.

Moltke and Tappen were right to be concerned about the safety of the right wing since the French were making final preparations for the counter-attack. During the night of 3–4 September, Joffre had already sent messages to Galliéni and to Sir John French requesting them to prepare for an advance at some time in the next few days. When Galliéni became aware from aerial reconnaissance on the morning of the 4th that the German 1st Army had crossed the Marne, leaving only IV Reserve Corps on the north bank, he ordered Maunoury to prepare 6th Army for an advance the next day. Although this would take place in a generally eastern direction in order to strike IV Reserve Corps in the flank, the exact details depended on how far the British had retreated. If they ended up only a short distance to the south of the Marne, 6th Army would remain on the north side of the river and advance due east from the vicinity of Meaux. At the same time the British would advance in the parallel direction along the southern bank of the river. This so-called northern option (for 6th Army) would save time but would result in the two armies being separated from each other by the river. If, however, the British retreated further than this, 6th Army would cross to the south bank of the Marne and then advance eastwards, accompanied on their right by the British whose right wing would lean on the Seine. In this southern option, the two armies would remain in close contact with one another but the advance would have to be delayed by a day in order to give 6th Army sufficient time to cross the river.[28]

Before Galliéni drove off to GHQ at Melun to make the necessary arrangements with Sir John French, he sent a message to Joffre asking him which option he preferred. However, by the time that Joffre's reply returned saying that he favoured the southern option Galliéni had already left for Melun. When he arrived there in the middle of the afternoon he was dismayed to find Murray waiting for him and not Sir John French, who was visiting I Corps at the time. Galliéni explained that 6th Army would make preliminary moves during the afternoon, followed by an easterly advance on the 5th, and that providing they acted quickly they would be able to strike the flank of the German IV Reserve Corps, which was marching southwards in two columns in the direction of Trilport and Lizy-sur-Ourcq. If the British called an end to their retreat they would be in time to take part in the offensive the next day (the southern option). After three hours of discussions, the conference ended with a provisional agreement along these lines. A note was drawn up summarizing the plan and copies were given to Maunoury, Galliéni and to Lieutenant-Colonel Brécard who was to take it immediately to GQG for Joffre's approval.

If this had been all, the course of events would have run quite smoothly; there would have been one plan of attack, agreed to by Joffre (who had already chosen the southern option that morning) and by Sir John French (providing that he agreed with Murray). Unfortunately however, at the same time as the meeting at Melun was taking place, 30 miles away at Bray-sur-Seine different arrangements were being made between Franchet d'Esperey and Wilson. As Franchet d'Esperey waited with mounting impatience for the British contingent to arrive, a French staff car suddenly roared into the square, screeched to a halt and an officer jumped out and handed him an urgent telegram from Joffre. This read as follows:

> Circumstances are such that it may be to our advantage to deliver battle tomorrow
> or the day after against the German First or Second Armies with all the forces of

Fifth Army in conjunction with the British Army and the mobile elements of the Paris garrison. Please inform me whether you consider your army to be in condition to undertake this attack with chances of success.[29]

Before he had time to frame a reply, a Rolls Royce arrived carrying Wilson and Colonel Macdonogh, the Head of the Intelligence Section who went with him into the town hall, accompanied by a small group of staff officers, including Spears.

We all made our way from the sunny *Place* into the deserted *Mairie* and found a large empty room, the *Salle des Mariages*, on the first floor. I remember posting as sentry on the door the Highlander who acted as escort on the British car. Colonel Macdonogh then proceeded to open the doors of adjoining rooms and looked round them carefully to make sure there were no eavesdroppers, then lifted the green baize cloth covering the large table in the room where we stood in case somebody was hiding there. This quiet and methodical search so astonished the French General that it did much to calm him. It remained so firmly impressed on his mind that he could never evoke what was perhaps the most momentous event of his career without conjuring up a picture of Macdonogh peering under the table.[30]

After Macdonogh had summarized the latest intelligence on the enemy's movements and Wilson had outlined Sir John French's intentions for the next few days, Franchet d'Esperey proposed a combined offensive, beginning on 6 September and involving the British as well as the French 5th and 6th Armies. According to this, 6th Army would advance along the north bank of the Marne in the direction of Château-Thierry (the northern option) and his own army would halt when it reached the line Sézanne–Provins, turn about and attack the German 2nd Army. If the plan were to succeed, the British would have to fill the gap between the two armies and keep in step with them. He then showed them the telegram he had just received from Joffre and said that he was going to reply that his army was ready to take the offensive. After briefly discussing how the movements of the three armies could be co-ordinated and how 6th Army could strongly support the British left wing, the meeting ended and they returned to the sunlit square. Franchet d'Esperey then dictated a letter to Joffre outlining the plan, adding that his army could fight on the 6th although it would not be in a brilliant condition. This was given to Commandant Maurin to take to GQG without delay. By late afternoon, therefore, two provisional agreements had been drawn up for the offensive, neither of which was known to the two Commanders-in-Chief and which differed from one another both in extent (the Galliéni–Murray plan made no provision for 5th Army) and in the position of 6th Army (the southern option in the Galliéni–Murray plan and the northern option in the Franchet d'Esperey–Wilson plan).

While this was taking place, Joffre had spent the long, hot afternoon at his headquarters in the school at Bar-sur-Aube waiting patiently for Franchet d'Esperey to reply to his telegram. For hour after hour his massive, brooding figure remained lost in thought, undisturbed by his staff, alternately sitting in the school courtyard in the deep shade of a huge weeping ash tree or astride a chair in his spartan and barely furnished office, staring intently at the situation map on the wall.[31] As dusk began to fall and the searing heat slowly subsided, he recalled his senior staff officers in order to go over the ground once more. In response to Berthelot's persuasive argument in favour of a slight delay, and in the absence of news from Franchet d'Esperey, he decided to wait until the 7th to allow time for the troop movements to be completed and to make the necessary arrangements with the British. After Gamelin had left to begin drafting the preliminary orders, he retired to his private quarters in the Château Le Jard, a modest country house at the edge of the town, which had been loaned to the army by its proprietor, a Parisian lawyer, M Tassin. There, in the early evening, a little before his accustomed time, he sat down to dinner with his senior staff officers and with several guests including Major Clive (British liaison officer to GQG) and two visiting Japanese officers, neither of whom seemed to understand a word of French. Before long, the meal was interrupted by the sudden entrance of Commandant Maurin, who had arrived from Bray with Franchet d'Esperey's long-awaited reply.

Now that 5th Army was ready, the attack could take place almost immediately. However, the existence of this plan, which differed significantly from his own, placed Joffre in a difficult situation. Should he stick to the plan which Gamelin and his staff were drafting at that very moment (a start date of 7 September and the southern option for the movement of 6th Army) or should he replace it with

Franchet d'Esperey's version (a start date of the 6th and the northern option for 6th Army)? After a brief deliberation, he accepted both of Franchet d'Esperey's suggestions and told Gamelin to alter the plans accordingly. As soon as the meal was over he returned to his office where, together with Gamelin and Berthelot, he put the finishing touches to the orders they had drafted. Finally, at 10.00pm he signed General Order No 6, the order for the battle of the Marne. This was dispatched by means of cipher telegram to the armies involved and at the same time written confirmation was sent to them by staff officers in cars.[32]

# 8

# THE EVE OF BATTLE

## 5 SEPTEMBER

When General Instruction No 6 reached Franchet d'Esperey and Foch during the morning of the 5th, they immediately ordered their troops to halt and prepare for the offensive the next day. The news that the terrible fortnight-long retreat was at an end was received with great jubilation in the front line.

> The news brought by the cyclist immediately spread, and even before I had given an order or made a sign, everyone was in place, pack on back, ready to go. Their look was exhilarated; all the men, worn out with tiredness and lack of sleep, refound their ardour and we hurried towards our new outposts, despite the sun, which beat down stronger than ever. We didn't want the party to begin without us.[1]

Also, as the Chief Medical Officer of the 70e RI described, men who had previously claimed they were incapable of going a single step further because of illness or exhaustion suddenly and miraculously regained their strength and said that they were fit enough not only to march, but also to fight:

> I had just signed a leave ticket for Lieutenant Chevrinais who was unable to keep going any longer because of a serious liver problem. He took the ticket and put it in his pocket. 'I'll leave after the victory,' he told me; 'I command a company, everything in its time.' Next day he was killed by a bullet straight through his chest.[2]

Whereas 5th and 9th Armies saw no action at all on 5 September, 6th Army spent the afternoon and evening in violent combat after a chance encounter with the German IV Reserve Corps about 10 miles to the west of the River Ourcq. According to Maunoury's orders, they were to make a short approach march ending at Monthyon and Penchard, prior to crossing the Ourcq the next morning. De Lamaze's Group of Reserve Divisions (the 55th and 56th) were in the lead, flanked on the right by Ditte's Moroccan Brigade and on the left by Vauthier's VII Corps (14th Division and 63rd Reserve Division). The 45th (Algerian) Division was in reserve and Sordet's Cavalry Corps was invited to cover the army's left wing, cross the river and threaten the enemy's communications in the region of Château-Thierry. Ebener's Group of Reserve Divisions (the 61st and 62nd) and IV Corps were not yet available, the latter because its transport had been delayed and the former because it needed more time to refit after its defeat on the Somme bend several days earlier. When these forces arrived, 6th Army would be at full strength.

As we have seen, General von Gronau's IV Reserve Corps was given the task of screening the right wing from the north-east of Paris while the rest of the army crossed the Marne in pursuit of the French. Since the Germans were moving down the western side of the Ourcq at right angles to the French advance, their paths were about to intersect. At about noon the Germans crossed the River Thérouanne and halted for the day at Barcy (the 7th Reserve Infantry Division) and Chambry (the 22nd Reserve Infantry Division) to the north of Meaux. While his men settled down to a hot meal, as a precautionary measure Gronau sent mixed detachments of infantry and artillery to reinforce the cavalry, which were keeping watch to the west from where he expected to come under attack. A little later, however, he decided that instead of running the risk of being taken in the flank he would swing westwards and meet the threat head on. Accordingly, he gave the order to break camp and advance in the general direction of Dammartin; the 7th Reserve Infantry Division on the right towards Monthyon and the 22nd Reserve Infantry Division on the left towards Penchard, echeloned back to the south.

Meanwhile, de Lamaze's troops were making slow progress as they advanced towards the Ourcq. Unused to long marches, the reservists, many of whom were

Parisians, suffered badly from the exceptional heat and the hard and unyielding cobblestones which caused bad blisters and bloodied feet. In an attempt to raise their morale a little, several officers dismounted and marched alongside them and also loaded the packs of the weariest men on to their horses to give them a brief respite. As they passed through the villages, the few remaining inhabitants handed out water and even cider, dislocating the march and making it difficult for the officers to keep control. In the early afternoon, just as the Germans were breaking camp, the two divisions were approaching their objectives for the day, St Soupplets for the 56th Reserve Division and Monthyon for the 55th. At this point, the advance guard of the 56th Reserve Division was spotted by a German artillery officer in charge of one of the mixed detachments, who had gone forwards to reconnoitre from the high ground overlooking the village. He quickly dashed back to his batteries in the ancient chalk pits that dotted the crest and gave the order to open fire. It was approximately 1.00pm and these were the opening shots in the battle of the Marne.

When Gronau heard the sound of gunfire he ordered the 7th Reserve Infantry Division to swing right in its direction. The worst clash took place at Monthyon where the 14th Reserve Infantry Brigade became involved in a violent fire-fight with the head of the French 55th Reserve Division which had just reached Iverny, the next village to the west. Although neither side was able to cross the bare and open fields between the two villages, which were swept by continuous fire, the French batteries scored a tremendous success in the artillery duel which took place. Firing from concealed positions, they unleashed a devastating barrage on three German batteries that had misguidedly unlimbered in an exposed position at l'Hôpital Farm, at the base of Monthyon Hill. In less than an hour, all three batteries were wrecked, more than 70 horses killed and seven officers and over 100 men killed or wounded. At the same time, the nearby German infantry rushed forwards several hundred yards to escape the devastating fire and came to rest in a shallow valley halfway between Monthyon and Iverny where they remained for the rest of the day, pinned down and unable to move.

In the meantime, the 22nd Reserve Infantry Division was in action against the Moroccan Brigade at nearby Penchard. When General Riemann became aware that the 7th Division was under attack at Monthyon he ordered his men to come to their aid by turning northwards on to the main road when they reached Penchard. A little later, soon after the advance guard had left Penchard along the new route, Riemann and his artillery commander were appalled to see a mass of Moroccan infantry (identifiable from their khaki uniform) advancing towards the village from the south-west from where they could strike the division in the flank. Since the advance guard was by now beyond recall, he hastily ordered his other units to halt when they reached Penchard and hold on defensively until they could be reinforced. Fortunately, his order reached the next unit, RIR 82, just in time to prevent it from leaving in the wake of the advance guard, and in great haste they went through the village and climbed the steep slopes of the prominent wooded hill at its western edge. Having forced their way with considerable difficulty through the thick undergrowth, dense with brambles and other man-high bushes, they emerged on to the summit from where they looked out over the open plain. As they hurriedly dug shallow trenches along the path which skirted the edge of the hill, they saw numerous lines of khaki-clad troops crossing the open fields only 500 yards away and heading straight towards them.

Général Ditte had ordered Colonel Poeymirau's 2nd Regiment to advance directly towards Penchard, closely followed by the 1st Regiment. Commanded by Capitaine Richard d'Ivry, a legendary figure from the colonial wars, V Battalion was in reserve behind the centre. When I and II Battalions were halted by fire from the hilltop, Poeymirau ordered V Battalion to outflank the village from the east. While the former attempted to work forwards under heavy rifle and shellfire, Richard d'Ivry's men swept forwards at an accelerating pace towards the eastern side of Penchard, moving in extended order and in large bounds. The Germans, whose attention was firmly fixed on the situation in front of them, were taken completely by surprise as the Moroccans entered the almost undefended village at the charge. One company overwhelmed the combat train of the German field artillery group, while another captured the village after a brief hand-to-hand fight and then ascended the eastern side of the hill in order to take the Germans from behind. Threatened from both front and rear and with their artillery about to be overrun at any moment, the German position appeared to be on the point of collapse. However, at this critical moment, as the Moroccans were laboriously working their way up the steep slope, held back by the dense undergrowth and close-range rifle fire, they were reinforced by four battalions which entered the village from the north. Considerably outnumbered, and trapped between these new troops and those on the hilltop, the Moroccans were forced to retreat, leaving behind a large number of dead and wounded including their beloved commander, Richard d'Ivry, who insisted on remaining on horseback supported by two men after being wounded several times, and also the commander of the 9th Company, Lieutenant Hugot-Derville who, in spite of being badly wounded and trapped underneath the body of his horse, continued to hold off the enemy, revolver in hand, until he eventually succumbed to his injuries. During the evening the brigade fell back to a defensive position running through Villeroy where they spent the night bivouacked in the open fields.[3] When the fighting came to end, Gronau decided to fall back during the night to a stronger defensive position behind the river Thérouanne and wait for reinforcements to arrive. Although there were numerous problems (some units received the order very late and others not at all), they reached their new positions in the middle of the night and spent the next few hours entrenching in expectation that the French would renew their attack at dawn.

News of the fighting did not reach Kluck until late evening because 1st Army Headquarters were not in radio communication with Gronau and because aerial reconnaissance had not been carried out in this direction. Instead, his attention was firmly focused on events to the south of the Marne where he still hoped to catch up with and defeat the French 5th Army before it reached the Seine. Thus, when Moltke's order to fall back behind the Marne and face Paris reached him in the early morning, he did not immediately comply but allowed his three left wing corps, IX, III and IV, to cross the Grand Morin as planned during the late afternoon and early evening. Bülow, on the other hand, brought 2nd Army to an immediate standstill except for the Guard Corps which was allowed to advance a little further to facilitate the wheeling movement the next day. In addition, Kluck requested Moltke's permission to continue as far as the Seine before carrying out the order.

In compliance with the previous instructions of OHL 1st Army is advancing via Rebais–Montmirail against the Seine. On either side of the Marne, II Corps covering towards Paris. At Coulommiers there is contact with about three English divisions, at Montmirail with the west flank of the French. The latter are offering lively resistance with rearguards, and should suffer very considerably if pursuit is continued to the Seine. They have hitherto only been driven back frontally and are in no ways beaten out of the field. Their retreat is directed on Nogent-sur-Seine. If the investment of Paris, which has been ordered, is carried out, the enemy would be free to manoeuvre towards Troyes. The strong forces suspected in Paris are only in the act of assembly. Parts of the Field Army will no doubt be sent there, but this will require time. Consider breaking contact with the thoroughly battle-fit Field Army and shifting 1st and 2nd Armies is undesirable. I propose instead: pursuit to be continued to the Seine and then the investment of Paris.[4]

Kluck's request reached OHL at noon, followed soon afterwards by his situation report for 4 September and the long six-part message, both of which had been considerably delayed. The previous evening, Moltke was unaware if Kluck had received the order to echelon back behind 2nd Army; now, however, it was crystal clear that he had disregarded the order by crossing the Marne a day's march ahead of Bülow and moreover was intent on reaching the Seine. Rather than run the risk that another radio message would be greatly delayed, it was decided to send a staff officer by car to 1st Army Headquarters to make sure that Kluck immediately complied with the latest order. The choice fell on Hentsch, the Chief of the Intelligence Section, on the grounds that he was sufficiently senior, that he knew Kuhl extremely well, having served alongside him for several years in the General Staff in Berlin, and that, unlike Tappen and the other senior staff officers, he could be spared from his work. After a short briefing from Moltke, Hentsch set out on his mission to 1st Army Headquarters at Rebais in the early afternoon. If there were no delays, he would arrive in the late evening, in time to intervene before Kluck issued his orders for the next day.

In the meantime, there was a great deal more for Moltke to worry about. In addition to further intelligence about French troop movements towards Paris, an agent's report claimed that more British troops had recently arrived in Belgium and that they were about to be joined in the vicinity of Lille by a force of approximately 80,000 Russians which had landed in Ostend. Since Lepel's

Brigade had left Brussels to rejoin IV Reserve Corps, and VII Reserve Corps was still tied up at Maubeuge, the troops needed to secure communications in Belgium would have to be found elsewhere. Because victory now rested with the 3rd, 4th and 5th Armies in the centre, the necessary reinforcements would have to come from the two left wing armies, the Bavarian 6th Army in Lorraine and 7th Army in Alsace, which so far had played only a secondary role in the campaign. Two corps and a cavalry division were therefore requested from 7th Army and 6th Army was invited to nominate whatever units it could spare. However, the former insisted that they could afford to give up only one corps and the latter refused to release any units until they had captured Nancy. Moltke did not have the authority to overrule the Bavarian Crown Prince who commanded 6th Army; only the Kaiser could do this but he sided with the latter. As a result, Moltke was forced for the moment to scale down his plans to secure the situation in Belgium; instead, a new 7th Army would be formed under the command of General von Heeringen, which would consist of all the forces at present in Belgium together with XV Corps and the 7th Cavalry Division, withdrawn from the left wing. Assuming that 6th Army captured Nancy and made two corps available, the new army would consist of six corps, ie two from Antwerp, one from Maubeuge and three from the left wing.[5]

When Hentsch reached Rebais after a six-hour drive just as dusk was falling, his appearance came as a surprise to Kluck and Kuhl who were waiting impatiently for Moltke to reply to their request by radio. According to Kuhl, he began by painting a gloomy picture of the overall situation.

> The situation is bad (*misslich*). Our left wing is held up in front of Nancy–Epinal and isn't making a single step forward, despite heavy losses. Verdun is cut off. To the west of Verdun 4th and 5th Armies are carrying out an enveloping move to take in the flank the French, who are situated behind the front Verdun–Toul. There also, the advance is only slow. Transports appear to have taken place from the French right wing in the direction of Paris. They seem to be preparing something similar further north, probably in the region of Lille. Fresh English troops are in the course of disembarking, perhaps at Ostend. It is possible that they will reinforce Antwerp. An entirely new situation faces 1st Army. There is no longer any question

of our breaking through on the Upper Moselle as we had been counting. The French are in no way held up everywhere, important troop transfers are under way. The danger to our right flank is increasing, although an attack does not seem imminent. The proposal we had made in the morning to throw back the French beyond the Seine is now ruled out.[6]

There was no alternative; 1st Army must retreat behind the Marne and face Paris defensively. In reply, Kuhl said that it would be very difficult to reverse direction because the line of march would cross the baggage and combat trains and cause a great deal of confusion and delay. When questioned about the likely timing of the enemy's counter-attack, Hentsch replied that in OHL's opinion it was not imminent and that the retrograde movement could be carried out calmly and without haste. (As he was speaking, IV Reserve Corps was under attack.) Fortunately, provisional orders had already been prepared for this eventuality and they were hastily completed and issued at 10.00pm for the retreat to begin in the morning. The movement would begin in the west with II Corps and spread progressively eastwards with IV and III Corps departing later in the day. As it was furthest east IX Corps would be given a rest day on 6 September and would follow on the day after that. Advance guards were to be sent ahead to secure the crossings over the Marne, and Marwitz's Cavalry Corps was ordered to screen the movement from the direction of Paris and the lower Seine. During the night however, news arrived that IV Reserve Corps had been attacked by a superior force and urgently needed reinforcements. The departure of II Corps, which was the closest available unit, was therefore brought forwards from dawn to the early hours of the morning in the hope that it would arrive in time to stave off defeat.[7]

At GQG, Joffre spent the early morning waiting for news to arrive from the British. During the previous evening, when General Instruction No 6 was issued by cipher telegram to the armies, he had only been aware of the meeting at Bray between Franchet d'Esperey and Wilson. However, when Major de Galbert arrived later that night with news of the Galliéni–Murray meeting at Melun, he realized that the British would be confused by the presence of the two plans and uncertain as to which version would be carried out. At about 9.00am, however, a telephone call from Huguet set his mind at rest.

The Marshal is going to conform to the intentions expressed in Order No 6 of the GQG, but by reason of the withdrawal carried out last night with the object of leaving more room for 6th Army to debouch south of the Marne, it will probably not be possible to occupy exactly the position Changis–Coulommiers but a position a little to the rear of it. The details of the marches are being studied. As soon as they are fixed they will be telegraphed to GQG. To sum up, tomorrow morning the British Army will be in position facing east but a little to the rear of the line at first assigned to it.[8]

Joffre had worked unceasingly for over a fortnight at getting the British to co-operate in his plans; now that this had finally been achieved he decided to drive to Melun to thank his opposite number personally. The meeting began in the early afternoon and took place in the château of Vaux-le-Pénil where Sir John French had his private quarters. All the eyewitness accounts broadly agree that after Joffre had outlined the urgency of the situation, he made an emotional and very personal appeal for help to the British Commander-in-Chief.

No witness can forget the scene. As setting, a small Louis XV salon, emptied of furniture, entered through doors with decorated arches. Only a large trestle table of white wood separated the actors, on one side, his back to a window was General Joffre, surrounded by Colonel Huguet, Chief of the French Mission at British Headquarters … by Lieutenant-Colonel Serret, our last Military Attaché in Berlin, by Commandant Gamelin and by Capitaine Muller; on the other side stood Field Marshal French having at his side several of his staff officers, among whom were General Murray, General Wilson and Major Clive, responsible for liaison with our General Headquarters.

The Frenchman, very heavy in appearance, immediately began to speak with authority. He explained himself slowly, with simple phrases, punctuated by a short and repeated gesture with his forearms by which he appeared to throw his heart on the table, behind which, supporting his weight on his two hands, the Englishman listened with ardent and attentive ears. Smartly dressed in his sober khaki uniform, the Marshal appeared slim and, in spite of the grey colour of his hair and his moustache, astonishingly young. He didn't speak French but understood it sufficiently well not to lose a word of what was being said to him. There was no need for an interpreter, and when General Joffre, at the end of his eloquence and turning sharply, ended his discourse by invoking the honour of the English Army, the Marshal did not hide the emotion which gripped him. After a brief but very moving silence, he then gave his word that his army would do all that was possible for men to do… Far better than his words, the sound of his voice, the tears that one made out on the edge of his eyelids, gave the conviction that it was not only by means of the possible but also the impossible that our allies had decided to force victory. For the first time the heart of the two armies beat in unison.[9]

After this emotional exchange, the meeting ended in anticlimax when Murray pointed out that they would not be ready to advance until 9.00am the next day, three hours later than expected. Furthermore, because of the mix-up resulting from the two meetings, they would be starting from a point well to the rear of the one indicated by Joffre. The troops were too tired to retrace their steps today and so when the attack began they would be separated from 6th Army on their left by a small gap and from 5th Army on their right by a much larger one. None of this seemed however to affect Joffre unduly and he greeted the news with equanimity; all that mattered was French's promise that his men would do everything possible to make the attack a success. When the meeting ended they took tea together and then Joffre left for his new headquarters in the Convent of the Order of Cordeliers at Châtillon-sur-Seine from where he would direct the battle. Since his generals had already received their instructions and the troops were said to be moving in good order towards their positions for the attack, all that remained was to compose an inspiring order of the day. Seated in the austere surroundings of his office, a small sparsely furnished room with whitewashed walls which betrayed its origins as a monk's cell, Joffre penned a message which would leave them in no doubt of the gravity of the situation.

At the moment when the battle upon which hangs the fate of the country is about to begin, all must remember that the time for looking back is past; every effort must be concentrated on attacking and throwing the enemy back. Troops which can no longer advance must at all cost keep the ground that has been won, and must die where they stand rather than give way. Under present conditions no weakness can be tolerated.[10]

He had done everything possible to bring about victory; from now on all would depend on the energy, tenacity and bravery of the ordinary soldiers, increasingly exhausted and demoralized by their desperate fortnight-long retreat through their homeland.

# 9

# TAKEN BY SURPRISE

## 6 SEPTEMBER: THE GERMANS ARE TAKEN BY SURPRISE ALONG THE PETIT MORIN

After they had marched through the night, Henri Libermann's battalion of Chasseurs à pied reached Mont Août on the morning of 6 September as dawn was breaking. From here they had a panoramic view of the St Gond Marshes and the chalk uplands to the east where they, and the rest of Foch's 9th Army, were to spend the next four days in battle.

At the foot of Mont Août we halted and formed up behind the small woods that were dotted about on the slopes of the hill. Officers were called forwards to the commandant. All clustered around him and in a religious silence such as always precedes great events, his voice was raised, clear, distinct and resonant. 'Here, gentlemen, is the proclamation of our Commander-in-Chief, General Joffre.' He read it without making comment. I retain one phrase from it that above all was absolute and definitive: 'To die where they stand rather than give way.'

In the first light of dawn, from the summit of Mont Août, Mazurier [his superior officer] looked at the vast panorama extended in front of him. Mont Août, an outlier of the Allemant Massif, to which it is linked by a long undulating crest, completely dominating the region called the St Gond Marshes. This is a vast patch of marsh, bristling with treacherous greenery, covering fathomless pits and quaking fields that can be crossed only on narrow paths.

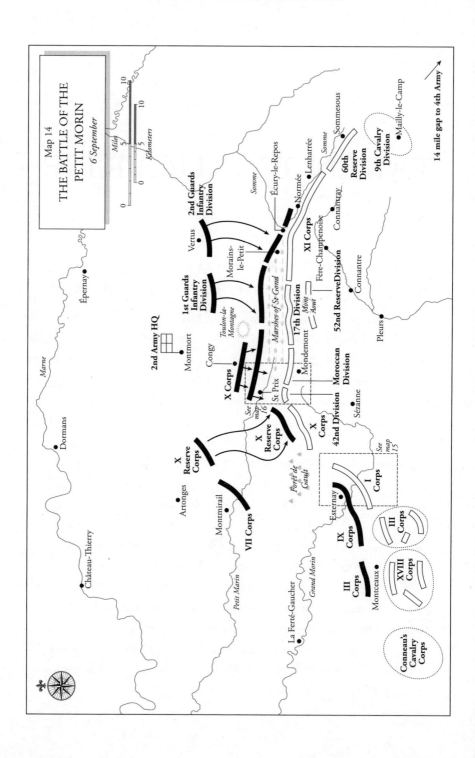

Map 14

THE BATTLE OF THE
PETIT MORIN

*6 September*

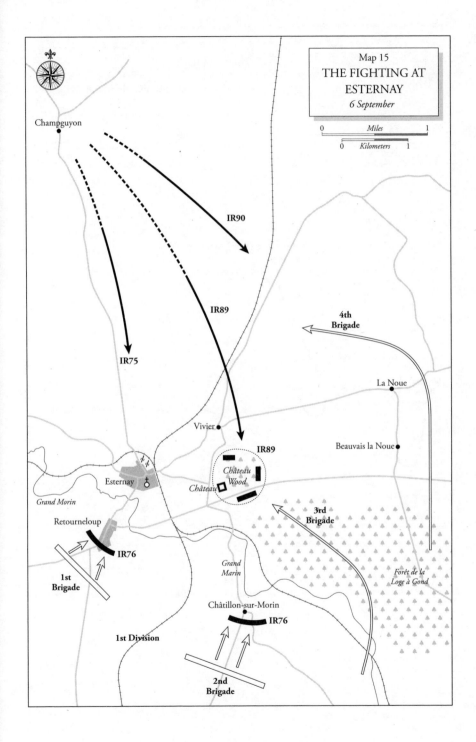

Map 15
THE FIGHTING AT
ESTERNAY
*6 September*

0        *Miles*        1

0        *Kilometers*        1

Champguyon

IR90

IR89

IR75

4th
Brigade

La Noue

Vivier

IR89

Beauvais la Noue

Château
Wood

Château

Esternay

*Grand Morin*

Retourneloup

3rd
Brigade

IR76

*Grand
Marin*

1st
Brigade

*Forêt de la
Loge à Gond*

Châtillon-sur-Morin

IR76

1st Division

2nd
Brigade

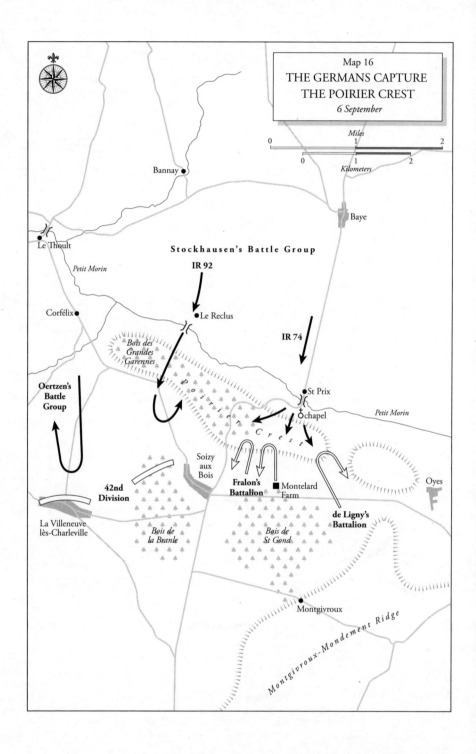

On the edge of the marsh there is a series of villages: to the south, Broussy-le-Petit, Broussy-le-Grand, le Mesnil-Broussy, Bannes, and at the extremity, Morains-le-Petit. On the north, no built-up area, but the terrain rises rapidly towards a line of high wooded hills where the villages of Coizard-Joches and Toulon-la-Montagne are buried among thick greenery. To the east, there extends an immense region covered with thick woods, which stretches as far as the camp of Mailly. The high church towers of Ecury-le-Repos, Fère-Champenoise, and further south, Connantre, rise above the pine trees.

While Mazurier was gazing out, the vast landscape was suddenly filled with intense life, disclosing the considerable forces that had built up in its confined spaces. From the woods close by, four long flashes shot out. The French battery opened fire and all along the line, from all of the patches of woodland, from behind the smallest hillocks, the cannonade began, furious, pressing, breathless. Two hundred steps to my right, an immense crater sprang up, its smoke thrown vertically up into the sky, then another and yet another. The noise of the bursts was deafening, ringing, terrible. The German artillery replied with all of its guns. There was nothing everywhere except immense jets of flame and of smoke escaping abruptly from the earth, or brief flashes which burst in the limpid morning air, in wreathes of green and white smoke … while the shrapnel watered the earth, escaping like rain with a plaintive wailing noise. The air became filled with a formidable noise. The thousands of cannon that spat out, ceaselessly sending death, raised their terrible voices, sounding without pity. From one end of the horizon to the other there was the endless clamour of an immense cannonade, of which the breath of flames exalted the imagination, made tangible to the warlike the grim reaper.[1]

That morning, two French armies were drawn up along a 50-mile front from Provins in the west to Sommesous (to the east of Fère-Champenoise) in the east. On the left, Franchet d'Esperey's 5th Army was to advance north-eastwards in the general direction of Montmirail, strongly echeloned back on the left to keep in touch with the British. With the exception of the deep-cut valley of the Petit Morin to the east of Montmirail and the Forests of Traconne and Gault to the west of Sézanne, there were few good defensive positions available to the Germans among the gently rolling uplands which formed the eastern extension of the great chalk massif of the Paris Basin. In comparison, the task of Foch's 9th Army was complicated by the difficult terrain and the weakness of several units. On their left, where the open country to the north of Sézanne favoured the offensive, the elite 42nd Division was to support the attack by the right wing of 5th Army. In the central sector, the St Gond Marshes and the hilly and heavily-wooded ground to the west were occupied by IX Corps (the Moroccan Division on the left and the 17th Division on the right). The marshes, which occupied a belt approximately 10 miles long and up to 2 miles wide between Oyes and Morains-le-Petit, formed a formidable defensive barrier whose treacherous surface was unable to bear the weight of a single soldier, let alone a gun carriage, even after the exceptionally hot, dry weather of the last few weeks. Moreover, they were crossed by only four narrow roads, which were completely devoid of cover and within artillery range from the high ground on both sides.

Similarly, the terrain immediately to the west of the marshes, between Oyes and Soizy-aux-Bois, also favoured the defence since it was covered to a great extent by dense woods traversed by only a few roads. At the point where the Petit Morin emerged from the marshes the area to the south of the river was completely dominated by a long, narrow and steep-sided ridge called the Poirier Crest, which was the strategic key to the sector and the scene of bitter fighting throughout the battle. In order to keep his options open Foch ordered the Moroccans and the 17th Division to remain initially on the defensive along the southern edge of the marshes while at the same time pushing strong advance guards on to the high ground which overlooked them from the north (Congy for the Moroccans and Toulon-la-Montagne for the 17th Division). If the attack by the 42nd Division was successful, both divisions would cross the marshes, join up with their respective advance guards, and take part in the general advance; if it failed, however, the advance guards would rejoin their main bodies, which would hold the southern exits against a German attack. On the far right, where the marshes gave way to the vast and monotonous Plain of Champagne, XI Corps was to remain on the defensive behind the upper reaches of the River Somme between Morains-le-Petit and Sommesous, and wait for the 18th Division to arrive from Lorraine. Unfortunately, not only was this corps very weak and lacking in officers but the river was narrow and easily fordable at many points

*Alfred von Schlieffen, Chief of the German General Staff and architect of the Schlieffen Plan. (Topfoto)*

Portrait of Generaloberst Alexander von Kluck. (Topfoto)

Generaloberst Karl von Bülow. (Topfoto/The Granger Collection)

Helmuth von Moltke the Younger, in a relaxed mood at his office desk. (Topfoto/Ullstein Bild)

*Field Marshal Sir John French, flanked by three aides-de-camp. (Topfoto / HIP)*

*General Joffre. Originally an engineer, Joffre's command of the French armies showed him to be a very competent officer. (Topfoto / The Granger Collection)*

*A French* soixante-quinze *Field Gun during the 1912 Manoeuvres. A formidable weapon in open country and a major factor in the French victory. (Bibliotèque Nationale de France)*

*Zouaves making the most of a break in the fighting to enjoy a meal. (Topfoto/Roger Viollet)*

*Mobilization. German soldier being adorned with flowers before setting out for the front at the start of the war. (Topfoto/Ullstein Bild)*

*A German infantry column from 3rd Army passing through the destroyed French town of Orchies at the end of August 1914. (Topfoto/Ullstein Bild)*

*German infantry passing through a Belgian village are offered water by a monk. (Topfoto/Ullstein Bild)*

*Belgian refugees flees from the German advance. (Bibliotèque nationale de France)*

*French infantry belonging to the 7th Division arrive at the Ourcq battlefield by Taxi.*
*(Topfoto / Roger Viollet)*

*French infantry attacking with bayonets fixed during the battle of the Marne. (Topfoto)*

*German corpses on the Ourcq Battlefield. (Topfoto/Roger Viollet)*

and their right flank was separated from 4th Army by a large and inadequately defended gap. If they came under strong pressure they were to swing back on their right, pivoting on the 17th Division, in order to avoid being rolled up.

Bülow did not have the slightest suspicion that he was about to be attacked; instead, as he explained to Richthofen early in the morning, he firmly believed that the French were intent on getting behind the Seine as fast as they could. In his opinion, 2nd Army would be able to carry out its wheeling movement towards Paris in an orderly fashion, undisturbed by the enemy, at the same time as 1st Army took up its new positions to the north of the Marne. During the night, at Kluck's urgent request, both II and IV Corps had left for the Ourcq battlefield several hours earlier than intended, leaving only III and IX Corps to the south of the Grand Morin, where they extended Bülow's right wing. As we have seen, III Corps was due to depart during the morning and IX Corps the following day; however, both corps were violently attacked soon after dawn which resulted in the former having to delay its departure for 24 hours and the latter having to fight for its life.

The day's events were dominated by the violent fighting that took place at Esternay (to the west of Sézanne) between the 17th Infantry Division from Quast's IX Corps and the French I Corps, which was commanded by Général Deligny following Franchet d'Esperey's recent promotion. When the Germans reached the area the previous evening, IR76 (the Hamburg Regiment) was pushed forwards to Esternay as advance guard while the rest of the division remained in and around Champguyon, about 4 miles to the rear. To the south of Esternay, the ground at first sloped gently down into the valley of the Grand Morin and then rose up sharply to the villages of Retourneloup and Châtillon-sur-Morin, which were separated by a narrow valley containing the railway line. About half a mile to the east of Esternay, the east-west high road was flanked on its northern side by the château of Esternay and its adjacent woods and on the south by the Forest of la Loge à Gond, a deep tract of woodland which stretched away to the south-east. When IR76 arrived at Esternay just before nightfall on 5 September, its commander, Oberst von der Goltz, placed strong outposts at Retourneloup while the rest of the regiment went into billets in the village itself. The troops were exhausted after covering more than 100 miles in the last five days but happy at the prospect of the long-hoped for rest day.

The French plan was bold and ambitious. While the 1st Division engaged the Germans frontally, fixing them in position and drawing in their reserves, the 2nd Division would sweep round to the right, taking advantage of the wooded terrain for concealment, and attack Esternay from the east. The outflanking movement was divided into two parts; the 3rd Brigade was to make a short right hook, passing through the forest until it reached the high road opposite the château from where it could take the Germans in the flank, and the 4th Brigade would make a wider movement by crossing the road further to the east and attacking them from the rear. Although they would be screened from the enemy by the dense woodland, the lack of roads meant that the going would be slow and that the artillery would have to be sent on a long detour, depriving them of its support for several hours.

Soon after dawn the French artillery opened fire on the enemy batteries in the fields to the north of Esternay, rudely awakening the Germans, most of whom were still fast asleep after their long march the previous day. Responding to the repeated bugle calls and the frantic shouts of their officers, they hurriedly assembled in the small village square, crammed into the spaces between the baggage wagons and horses where they waited apprehensively, afraid that they might be hit at any moment. As the first shells began to descend on the village they left the market place at the double and halted in the valley of the Grand Morin for a short while, after which one battalion was sent to Retourneloup, which was under heavy artillery fire, and another to Châtillon where patrols had signalled the approach of enemy infantry. For the moment, the remaining battalion remained in reserve in the dead ground along the valley. In order to secure his open left flank Goltz detached the 3rd Company and the Pioneer Company and sent them to reinforce the squadron of hussars already facing eastwards at the edge of the Château Wood.

When the II Battalion was level with Châtillon it came under rapid rifle fire and the men fixed bayonets, lay down in the fields of clover and returned fire:

> We went through Châtillon and remained to the right of the village in a firing line
> where we linked up with the other companies. We looked out ahead of us. We lay
> still and were surprised that we couldn't see the enemy. From half right we received

infantry fire and the enemy artillery fired with undiminished strength. It was a strange feeling lying in the green clover, seeing nothing but the tangle of herbs and grasses in front of us and the undulating land in the distance and yet being threatened from all sides... My neighbour in the firing line tore off the leaf of a plantain, showed me the fibrous strands which hung from the torn-off stalk and said with a laugh; 'Look at this, how many years do I still have left? One, two, three, four, five ... thirteen!'

We were staring apathetically across the shimmering field, when suddenly our attention was aroused as if by electricity. Here ... and there ... and there too ... in the woods ... behind the trees ... up on the hill ... behind that bend ... everywhere there was movement. Red and blue patches were visible in the far distance and then suddenly disappeared again in the green of the meadows. Our firing line came to life. 'Half left, rifles, sights at 700, fire!' '*Pfaff!*', the first shots hissed through the clover. The tension was broken. Shot after shot whistled over the meadow.

There. On the left! How close were the French. They rushed forwards in groups out of a small piece of woodland. We could see them running and then throwing themselves down on the grass. We could clearly distinguish their leaping legs, their rifles and the fixed bayonets. We could also see their faces as white patches under their dark caps. It was a picture that could have been taken from a toy box containing tin soldiers.

Which company was on our left, with the job of repelling the attack? We became more and more aware that there were no more German troops on our left. The word flank attack was heard.

The faces of the French were now becoming more distinct. We aimed and fired and didn't dare look to our left. I slowly laid my rifle butt against my cheek and took aim at one of the blue and red spots but again and again the pale surface of a French face appeared in front of my rifle barrel and I imagined that two dark black eyes were looking at me from it. I shut my eyes and aimed again, looking neither right nor left.

Gradually, the enemy shrapnel fire began to get stronger. I heard a groaning, then a whispering and then a cry. But I didn't look. In spite of this, I noticed shapes standing up in the firing line and that a few individuals were creeping or were being carried back. 'Fix bayonets!' The order ran along the line, one passing it on to another, and only now did we see the great gaps in the firing line. For a moment the bayonets were glinting in the sun! Then the rifles were lying on the grass again and the firing continued calmly. An ice-cold feeling had come over us as we saw the bayonets glinting; it was as if a bright light was hurrying across the sky like sheet lightning in broad daylight… Next to me lay a quiet man who had never before shown signs of aggression. As I looked over to him he hissed through his teeth; 'I'm going to get that chap there.' I was horrified by his remark since I knew him as a gentle, quiet man. I saw him put his head on to his left arm; the shot was fired. I wanted to laugh because it was far too high. His face was turned towards me but he didn't see me; his teeth were pressed together and his eyes were empty and cold. He was dead.[2]

It was now about 9.00am and Goltz's three battalions were spread out over a 2-mile front, isolated from one another and with no artillery support because the gun teams had broken loose and galloped away to the rear. After being forced to make a time-consuming detour to avoid the artillery fire, the first reinforcements (IR75 and the rest of the brigade artillery) began to arrive about two hours later and were immediately fed into the line in a piecemeal fashion wherever the need was greatest. Although this stabilized the situation at Retourneloup, the troops in Châtillon were coming under increasing pressure as more and more enemy troops infiltrated from the east down the valley of the Grand Morin. The critical situation was described by Max Tepp, who had been sent to Châtillon churchyard at the head of a small group of men with orders to report on the enemy's approach:

The sun burnt down and the air shimmered over the fields as if the earth was trembling with excitement. And it really was trembling for shells were tearing holes in the ground so that the sand was spraying around… Behind the churchyard we lay flattened against the wall and peered out at the hills on the far side and along the valley on the left. The enemy batteries beyond the high ground began to fire more briskly. The shots tore into the edge of the meadows. I looked over there and stared hard; I saw nothing. The shells hissed through the air and burst with a dull resonance. I stared across and saw nothing. The shells were now hissing over here. Then, crash! I couldn't breathe. I saw the beautiful blue sky and the shapes of the churchyard coming towards me. I lay there unconscious, for how long, I don't know. I woke as if from a dream, pulled myself together and remembered where I was and once more looked over there to the hills and the valley on our left, without realizing that something had happened.

Finally, it slowly dawned on me that there was a gap in my thoughts. I looked back. In place of the white cemetery walls, stood old decaying ruins. Were my comrades lying motionless behind it? Wounded? Dead? I now heard one of them groaning and another raised his head. I looked forwards once more and then crept back through the ruins to my comrades. One of them was already dead; the other three were badly wounded. The young one groaned, 'Take me to the first-aid post.' He had a gaping head wound. I was still occupied in helping my closest comrade who had a dangerous stomach wound when the youngster crept off on all fours towards the first-aid post. I was just bandaging up the last of my comrades when he came creeping back. He hadn't found the first aid post and had crawled round in a circle. He recognized us but thought that he had reached the first-aid post and said in a foolish voice, 'Well, you're great comrades, leaving me out there in the fire!' Then he lay down on the ground, stretched out a little and was quite still. Suddenly he sat bolt upright, supported himself with his hands behind him, looked ahead with a wild expression, with terribly beautiful eyes in his pale face, and then sank to the ground. He was dead.[3]

In the meantime, the French 3rd Brigade was moving through the woods to the east of Esternay, out of sight of the Germans. At about 1.00pm, the lead regiment was approaching the northern edge of the forest from where only 100 yards of open ground separated them from the high road and the Château Wood immediately beyond. At about the same time, the 4th Brigade had crossed the road further to the east and was moving northwards on its way to taking the Germans in the rear. If the two brigades had arrived half an hour earlier they would have swept away the weak flank guard and overrun the Germans from the east; by now, however, further reinforcements were starting to arrive in the shape of IR89 which was used to strengthen the left flank and IR90 which was ordered to secure the left rear where there was a large gap with X Corps.

When Oberstleutnant von Wangenheim, in command of IR89, arrived at Esternay Château ahead of his troops he found a chaotic situation; no one knew the whereabouts of the 33rd Brigade Command Post, units had been fed piecemeal into the front line leaving no unified command structure and there were strong rumours that the enemy was about to outflank them from the east. Having assessed the situation as best he could, he divided his force, sending II Battalion to the high road to the rear of Châtillon and I Battalion to the north-east corner of the Château Wood from where it could either intervene in the fighting at Châtillon or oppose a flank attack from the east. The III Battalion was held back in reserve behind the left flank. Although the II Battalion got off lightly as it worked its way forwards towards the low ground on the far side of the road, making skilful use of the folds in the terrain, the I Battalion was deluged by shellfire as soon as it entered the Château Wood. Trees were smashed like firewood, broken branches fell everywhere, and they were deafened by the continuous ear-splitting din and almost asphyxiated by the noxious fumes from the bursting shells. In spite of heavy losses they were forced to remain there for over an hour, waiting in vain for the order to advance. As one officer later said, 'I will never in my whole life forget the hours in this wood.'[4] Their ordeal finally came to an end at about 2.00pm, when Wangenheim ordered them to reinforce the troops in Châtillon after a sudden increase in the noise suggested that the French were about to capture the village. It was at this point, just as they were advancing, that the head of the French 3rd Brigade burst out of the woods opposite the château and hurled themselves across the open fields in their direction. What saved them from being overwhelmed were successive counter-attacks into the French flanks by Hauptmann Caspari's Company and Hauptmann Hamel's Pioneers. Despite this the French centre remained intact and when reinforcements arrived from the interior of the woods they began to force the German firing line back towards the château. Fortunately for the Germans, Wangenheim had by now tracked down his missing III Battalion (it had changed position to escape the shellfire) and ordered it to stem the tide. They then advanced over the shallow hill to the east of the château, swept down on the French centre and stopped them in their tracks, suffering heavy losses in the process.

In the 12th Company, the left hand section lay there as if mown down, 50 steps before the road. It looked as if they were a firing line in a battle. There was a distance

214

of two steps between each of the men, but all were dead, almost all shot in the head. Leutnant von Gruben, the adjutant, in the midst of the fiercest rifle fire, in attempting to bring the firing line to the correct front by standing and waving his outstretched arm as if on the parade ground, received a mortal head wound.[5]

In the middle of the afternoon, the French 3rd Brigade abandoned its attempt to outflank Esternay and the wider movement of the 4th Brigade also failed because IR 90 arrived just in time to stop them. When darkness fell the Germans abandoned Châtillon, leaving the French in possession of the burning ruins. Retourneloup remained in German hands, however, as did the area to the east of Esternay where the shattered remnants of IR 89 formed a thin defensive line along the road to the south of the Château Wood. Casualties on both sides were severe, especially among those units that had been involved in the fight for the Château Wood in the late afternoon. On the German side, III/89, which had carried out the counter-attack, lost 8 officers and 177 men and the I Battalion, which had endured a hellish bombardment before being hit by the French attack, lost more than 300 men. On the French side the two battalions of the 73e RI, which had spearheaded the attack, had suffered even more, losing approximately half of their strength.

The events at Esternay had important repercussions for the German III Corps on the right and X Reserve Corps on the left. The former had already been on the march north for about an hour when it was forced to return to its overnight positions because the rearguard, which had been left behind to cover the retreat, was under attack from the French XVIII Corps. For the next few hours, while the French infantry marked time 200 field guns and several batteries of heavy artillery remorselessly pounded the German positions in Montceaux and Sancy. In the late afternoon, the Germans were finally driven out of Montceaux, which by now was a burning and shattered wreck, but at nearby Sancy, where the bombardment was less intense, they clung on and when the firing came to an end at nightfall they were still in possession of the village. Meanwhile, to the north-east of Esternay, X Reserve Corps received orders in the late afternoon to swing to their right and come to Quast's aid. By this time the 19th Reserve Infantry Division was approaching the Forest of Gault which was impenetrable to large masses of troops, so General von Bahrfeldt ordered them to pass down its eastern side and then, once they were clear, to swing westwards in the direction of Esternay. However, when they were halfway down the narrow road that skirted the woods, they came under rifle and machine-gun fire from the villages of Jouy and Recoude and the nearby Château of Désire. (The French troops belonged to the 70e RI at the head of the 38th Brigade.) For the rest of the afternoon and into the early evening, the outnumbered French infantry put up strong resistance but were eventually driven back by the weight of numbers and the accurate fire of the German machine guns. When darkness fell they disengaged with difficulty and retreated, either down the road towards the hamlet of Clos-le-Roi, or into the safety of the forest. Their sister regiment, the 41e RI, was sent forward to give them support but in the absence of maps one battalion got lost in the woods and went into bivouac near the farm of La Godine, while the other two, along with the remnants of the 70e RI, spent the night to the south of the forest close to Guébarré Farm, a name which was to have a sinister significance for the Germans the next day.

On their left, the 2nd Guards Reserve Division became involved in an extremely disorganized and violent encounter battle on the plateau to the north of Charleville with the 2e RI at the head of X Corps. Although the French were taken by surprise and increasingly outnumbered, the Germans were unable to co-ordinate their attacks in the narrow strips of woodland that surmounted the plateau at this point, and ended up by firing at friend and foe alike. The unequal fight finally came to an end in the early evening by which time five French companies were holding off no fewer than six German battalions supported by two machine gun companies. Having suffered more than 60 per cent casualties, including their regimental commander, Colonel Perez, who was killed, the French gradually disengaged and fell back through the woods to Charleville where they rejoined the other companies. When dusk fell, the Germans retreated to the summit of the plateau where they spent an uneasy night in bivouacs in the open. They too had suffered badly in the fighting, especially the Jäger Battalion which had begun the fight and which lost almost 500 of its 700 men. Overall, the Division had suffered a bloody repulse, causing General von Susskind, the divisional commander, to end his situation report by saying that 'the division has been very sorely tried. Although it is still capable of facing up to an attack, it is no longer in a state to continue with the offensive.'[6]

Further east, where X Corps and the Guard Corps had a long march ahead of them on the left wing of the wheeling movement, the course of the fighting was determined by the presence of the St Gond Marshes. Since these were almost impassable, Bülow ordered the 20th Infantry Division and the 1st Guards Infantry Division to halt when they arrived at the northern edge and wait for their neighbours (the 19th Infantry Division and the 2nd Guards Infantry Division respectively) to advance down either side and open the way for them. As mentioned above, Foch had ordered the Moroccan Division and the 17th Division to push strong advance guards on to the high ground to the north of the marshes. However, by the time Sautel's Colonial Battalion advanced towards Congy late on the evening of 5 September, the village had already been occupied by the German 20th Infantry Division which opened fire on them, taking them completely by surprise (the Germans used powerful searchlights to illuminate them) and throwing them back across the marshes in disarray. Likewise, although the advance guard of the 17th Division had occupied the hilltop village of Toulon-la-Montagne without opposition the previous afternoon, they were attacked on the morning of the 6th by the 1st Guards Infantry Division and forced to fall back across the marshes to rejoin their main body in the villages along its southern edge. Even when they were safely across, panic still gripped the survivors, many of whom got as far as the slopes of Mont Août before they could be halted and reorganized.

Since it had proved impossible to maintain a bridgehead over the marshes, Foch decided instead to concentrate his efforts on the area to the immediate west, in the vicinity of Soizy-aux-Bois. At midday he ordered the 17th Division and the Moroccan right wing to defend the southern side of the marshes at all costs while the rest of the Moroccans side-stepped westwards, crossed the Poirier Crest and the woods around Soizy-aux-Bois and attacked the Germans along the Petit Morin in the neighbourhood of St Prix. As it happened, this put them on a collision course with IR74 at the head of the 19th Infantry Division, which had been ordered to capture the Poirier Crest prior to making a further advance. To begin with the Germans were pinned down by shellfire on the approaches to the Petit Morin, but they finally crossed the river at about noon and then sheltered for a while in the lee of the hill next to the ancient chapel of St Prix. Ahead of them, the dark mass of Botrait Wood rose steeply to the summit of the Poirier crest; on the right, the only road that crossed the ridge zigzagged up the hillside, cutting through the dense woods which could conceal an enemy machine gun post at each bend. In the woods themselves, the undergrowth was almost impenetrable because of the large number of enormous, ancient bramble bushes and the few paths which led to the summit were so narrow that they would have to be taken in single file. If they were attacked without warning, it would be impossible for the officers to maintain control among the trees and the dense undergrowth.

In the early afternoon the III Battalion advanced up the road and twice reached the summit only to be forced back, the first time by rifle and machine-gun fire from the deep undergrowth and the second time by shellfire from a French battery on the far side of St Gond Wood. Having suffered many casualties, and with no more reserves available, they prudently fell back to a position near the bottom of the hill and waited for nightfall. Meanwhile, the I Battalion had laboriously ascended the Poirier Crest. After a minor panic, the advance got under way again and about half an hour later the first troops emerged on to the open ground which covered the summit. They were not a moment too soon because ahead of them, at a distance of about 300 yards, a large mass of Moroccan infantry (Fralon's Battalion) was heading directly towards them from the direction of Montalard Farm at the base of the hill. When the Moroccans came under fire, they fixed bayonets, stormed up the slope and threw the Germans off the crest and into the woods on the reverse slope. Lieutenant Suffren, a section leader in the 3rd Company, described the scene:

> Behind the farm, we reorganized and then restarted our march towards our objective; the bullets persisted, they ricocheted in large numbers off the Oyes road and while our patrols filed ahead, we deployed in line, behind the road. We continued to advance, the 1st and 3rd sections concealed by the woods on the left, the 2nd and 4th in open country, in the clearing opposite the Poirier [Crest]; we were advancing towards the crest occupied by the enemy.
>
> The firing became very violent, our patrols no longer covered our front but we continued to make progress. I was in the woods on the extreme left, guiding the 1st Section; the fusillade redoubled in intensity and I gained the impression from the cries and the noise that the 2nd and 4th Sections were in contact with the enemy. Several machine guns now started up and their sinister tac-tac became

mixed up with the noise of the bullets. Immediately, I changed direction to the east to take the enemy in the flank. We charged out from the edge of the wood; the other two sections were there, with fixed bayonets, attempting to take the German position. At the moment when I charged, I cried out, '*En avant, à la baionette*', and as I pointed with my right arm to show the direction of attack to my Tirailleurs, I felt as if my right shoulder had been torn away. A bullet had passed through my chest. The violence of the blow knocked me down and I remained stretched out, unable to shift, but I followed the phases of the battle. Our Tirailleurs bravely faced up to the enemy, they advanced and after several minutes the Germans disappeared; on the crest I could only see about two sections' worth of men firing from a kneeling position. Some distance away, Tirailleur Malek, was standing, raising his rifle to his shoulder; I shouted to him to lie down but he replied, 'I'm a soldier, me; I'm not going to hide.' Several minutes later, he was killed by a bullet.[7]

This was far from the end of the fighting however. As the debris of the leading company recoiled down the hill towards Montalard Farm and the Germans sought safety in the woods, both sides deployed their reserves, three companies on the French side and one on the German side, and the desperate contest for the crest was renewed with heightened ferocity. Once again, the Germans were forced back off the summit; once again the Moroccans were decimated, this time by machine-gun fire from the woods on their flank, and the survivors retreated once more, allowing the Germans to claim possession.

Suddenly the fusillade broke out again and I heard Capitaine Grincourt, who had been firing in the middle of his Tirailleurs, cry out to his adjudant to take command of the company. Was he therefore also wounded? And what about the other officers? From movements that I glimpsed, I then understood that the Germans had reformed behind the crest and were about to encircle us. In vain, I tried to raise myself. Very soon the adjudant gathered together several unwounded Tirailleurs and fell back with them to Montalard Farm. This was all that remained of my brave men. If only Capitaine Grincourt, who is father of five children, isn't too seriously wounded. A great silence suddenly surrounded me. Time went by very slowly. But no, I hadn't been abandoned for here was

Messaoudine, my servant, who arrived full of anxiety, along with Caporal Crémant. But at the moment when they were lifting me up, the latter was killed by a bullet in his stomach. At the same time, I could hear the Germans approaching, I knew too well the frightful treatment which they dealt out to our valiant Tirailleurs and I gave Messaoudine a formal order to rejoin his comrades to avoid being massacred. He obeyed me reluctantly, the brave lad.[8]

The Germans were given no time in which to celebrate their success, however, because within minutes of driving off Fralon's Battalion, their left wing was threatened with envelopment by de Ligny's Battalion which attacked them from the south-east. Taking the Germans completely by surprise (their approach was concealed by a low hill to the west of Oyes), the French got to within 600 yards of the German line without being noticed, at which point they launched their attack. For a moment, it was touch and go for the Germans who fell back from the crest and into the woods on the northern slope but their reserve company arrived just in time to prevent the line from collapsing. As the attack lost momentum, the French were hit in the flank by machine-gun fire and fled towards the woods, pursued by shellfire that strewed the slopes with the bodies of dead and wounded Tirailleurs.

Although the fighting had lasted for little more than an hour, the casualties on both sides were extremely high. As night fell, IR74 pulled back from the crest, recrossed the river at St Prix and spent the night huddled together in the ditches alongside the St Prix–Soizy road. The regiment was reduced to approximately 1,200 men and in the I Battalion the survivors were so few that they were reorganized into two companies commanded by the adjutant. The melancholy scene as they retreated over the bridge was described by Hauptmann Stroedel, who had taken over command of the II Battalion:

As we moved back towards St Prix after 8.00pm, a deathly stillness reigned over the ridge of the broad hill; from among the broom bushes on its northern slopes however, there sounded the horrible groans of the wounded. From each bush and from every direction rang out heart-rending pleas for help. It wasn't possible for us to help individuals. The small consolation to our poor comrades and to ourselves was that we promised to send the medical orderlies here from the chapel at St Prix. In the chapel there was an icy silence; a great number of dead and badly wounded men were there, among whom were the best of our officers. Helmets off! A handshake to the living and for the dead a silent greeting and a silent oath of loyalty to be worthy of their sacrifice.[9]

As dusk began to fall, Fralon and de Ligny gathered together the survivors and established a defensive line along the edge of St Gond Wood, facing the clearing around Montalard Farm. Many of the wounded had to be left behind where they had fallen on the crest and on the slopes of the hill. Few of the rank and file survived, either because they died from their wounds or because they were put to death by the Germans. In contrast, the wounded officers were treated well, including Lieutenant Suffren who was discovered during the night by German stretcher-bearers:

Time went by; I could still hear several shots being fired. Always incapable of moving, I looked around me and saw that almost all of my Tirailleurs were dead; only one of them stirred, then sat down and remained inert. Night fell, there was more artillery fire, close by or far away; only the cries of the Germans from time to time broke the silence of the woods. When I fell, I had pulled down on me a branch of hawthorn whose sharp spines more and more stuck into my body. Well then, so this was going to be the end; I was spitting blood more and more often and a heavy weight seemed to be crushing my chest. A sharp noise sounded close by, like a branch that had been broken. I turned my head towards it; a German patrol was going over the battlefield and smashing the rifles which strewed the ground. Should I reveal myself to them? I was completely exhausted, without hope of rejoining our lines, paralysed as I was. I called out to them and they arrived and seeing my brilliant African uniform, said '*Offizier, Offizier!*' Very correct, they approached me and I intended speaking to them in German, but the words which came out were in Arabic! I began again. They immediately left and disappeared behind the crest; a little later, stretcher-bearers arrived led by a horseman. They cut off my equipment; a stretcher-bearer took my binoculars and used them to look at the stars. Then they put me on the stretcher and I crossed the enemy lines. Some officers whom I encountered came up to me and in excellent French said that

I would be taken to hospital. I arrived at a first aid post where I was put on board an ambulance. It was all very well organized.[10]

At the eastern end of the marshes, the 2nd Guards Infantry Division also failed to open up the crossings for its right hand neighbour, the 1st Guards Division. This was in spite of the fact that the French XI Corps which opposed it was weak, lacking in morale and exhausted after having marched almost without a break for the last 24 hours. (The 65e RI, for example, contained a large number of recently arrived reservists who had panicked and fled in disorder the first time they were bombarded.) The Germans were unable to overcome this feeble opposition partly because of the heavy shellfire and partly because they were worried that the enemy might penetrate the gap between themselves and 3rd Army. (No aerial reconnaissance was possible during the morning because of the thick cloud.) At Morains-le-Petit, the 4th Brigade (Regiments Franz and Augusta) waited all morning and into the early afternoon for greater artillery support, even though the village was held by only a single French regiment. The situation only changed in the middle of the afternoon when several junior officers in Regiment Franz became tired with waiting and ordered their men to assault the village, upon which the defenders immediately gave way and retreated to a new defensive line in the woods to the south. In the meantime, after wasting several hours in securing Clamanges on their left wing, which was mistakenly reported to be occupied by the enemy, the 3rd Brigade received orders to attack the sector Ecury–Normée, a short distance to the east of Morains-le-Petit. After they were held up for several hours by the heavy shellfire, resistance suddenly collapsed in the middle of the afternoon and the defenders fell back to a new line along the railway embankment a few miles to the south. Although several hours of daylight still remained, Plettenberg called off the offensive when he became aware that 32nd Infantry Division (the nearest 3rd Army unit) would not be able to reinforce him until the next morning at the earliest. Since his left flank would be exposed until they arrived, and since the first aerial reconnaissance of the day had detected a substantial number of enemy troops opposite his left wing (probably part of the 60th Reserve Division), he decided against resuming the attack, even though it meant that he would fall well short of his objectives for the day.

Despite the fact that his troops had been strongly attacked, Bülow saw no reason to abandon the wheeling movement, which had only just begun. In the evening, he therefore gave orders for the left wing and centre to resume the offensive next day to make enough space to swing round to the west. If Kluck withdrew III and IX Corps, the 13th Infantry Division would move forward from Montmirail (where it was in army reserve along with the 14th Division) and cover the army's right flank; if on the other hand he allowed them to remain where they were, it would slot into place between IX Corps and X Reserve Corps and take part in the offensive.

Later that evening, Hauptmann Bührmann returned from 1st Army Headquarters with the excellent news that the decision over the use of the two corps would be left to Bülow. If 2nd Army was attacked the next day they would temporarily come under his command and take part in the fight; if not, they would leave for the Ourcq as originally planned. In response, Bülow immediately drafted a reply for Bührmann to take back to Kluck. 'With the co-operation of 1st Army command, III and IX Corps will remain under my orders. Early on September 7th IX Corps will attack; III Corps will assume protection of the right flank of 2nd Army.'[11] However, Bülow's rejoicing was premature for at about midnight a staff officer returned from 1st Army Headquarters with the perplexing news that Kluck had changed his mind and decided after all to withdraw the two corps on the 7th. Kluck's decision followed news that powerful enemy forces had been seen on the march towards the exposed right wing of III Corps.[12] Since their withdrawal would weaken his right wing, Bülow modified his orders by restricting the offensive to the left wing and the centre and by going over to the defensive on the right. While X Corps in the centre and Guard Corps on the left renewed their attack, the right wing (13th Division and X Reserve Corps) would fall back to a defensive position along the Petit Morin, in order to protect the exposed flank and to keep in touch with IX Corps as it retreated to its new position to the north of the Marne. The 14th Division was to remain in army reserve and Richthofen's Cavalry Corps was instructed to protect the right wing as it swung back to its new position along the Petit Morin. Finally, a message was sent to Hausen in the early hours of the morning, explaining the situation and asking for his army to come to their help the next day with all available strength.

# 10

# BLOODY DAYS
# AT TROCY

## 6 SEPTEMBER: THE FRENCH 6TH ARMY ATTEMPTS TO CAPTURE THE TROCY PLATEAU AND BREAK THROUGH TO THE OURCQ

After IV Reserve Corps had retreated behind the river Thérouanne during the night, it occupied an approximately 8-mile front from the east of Brégy in the north to Varreddes in the south. Strong outposts were pushed forward to give advance warning of an enemy attack and the corps reserve was placed behind the right wing. Although the central sector was overlooked by the magnificent artillery position on the Trocy Plateau, there were obvious weaknesses on both flanks that could easily be exploited by the enemy. At the northern end of the line, the right wing of the 7th Reserve Infantry Division ended in open country, and it was inadequately protected by the weak 4th Cavalry Division, which was responsible for guarding the approaches to the Etavigny Plateau. At the southern end of the line it was imperative for the 22nd Reserve Infantry Division to secure the bridge over the Marne at Germigny to prevent the British from crossing the river and taking them in the rear.

The French had also retreated from the battlefield the previous evening and spent the night a few miles to the west, the Moroccans on the right facing Penchard, the 55th Reserve Division in the centre opposite Monthyon and the 56th Reserve Division on the left near St Soupplets. To the north, VII Corps

(14th Division and 63rd Reserve Division) was preparing to extend the left wing and to the south the 45th Division was expected to arrive in the afternoon, in time to take part in the fighting. In addition, the army would be brought up to strength in a few days' time by the arrival of IV Corps, which was detraining in Paris, and by Ebener's Reserve Divisions, reassembled with difficulty after their recent defeat.

To understand the course of events it is necessary to take a brief look at the terrain. Now that the Germans had relinquished the high ground at Monthyon and Penchard, the only obstacle that separated the French from the Ourcq Valley was the line of hills, parallel to the river. (From north to south, these were the Bargny, Etavigny and Trocy Plateaux.) However, in order to set foot on these heights, the French would have to make a long approach over completely bare terrain in full view of the German artillery and then cross the two rivers which ran diagonally across the axis of their advance, the Thérouanne, which gives access to the Trocy Plateau and the Gergogne which leads to the Plateau of Etavigny. Although the rivers themselves were quite narrow and fordable in places, their steep banks and thickly wooded slopes would be not be easy to traverse in the face of determined opposition, especially if the Germans fortified the villages of Acy and Etrepilly from where they could take them in the flank.

Maunoury's orders were for the 55th and 56th Reserve Divisions to capture the Trocy Plateau in the centre by means of a frontal attack, while VII Corps outflanked the German right wing and seized the Etavigny Plateau. After their losses the previous day, the Moroccans were replaced by the 45th Division, which would go straight into the battle when it arrived in the early afternoon. If the offensive succeeded, the Ourcq would be reached along the whole front and the bridges seized, ready for a general advance in the direction of Château-Thierry the next day.

In the early morning, the reserve divisions advanced towards the centre of the German line, supported on their right by the Moroccan Brigade. (The 45th Division had been delayed and was unlikely to reach the battlefield until very late in the day.) It was eerily quiet as they once again approached Monthyon and Penchard and saw the debris, human as well as material, from the previous day's fighting. At l'Hôpital Farm, at the entrance to Monthyon, they passed the shattered remains of the German batteries and saw the corpses of the gunners and the bodies of several horses lying where they had fallen beside the smashed guns

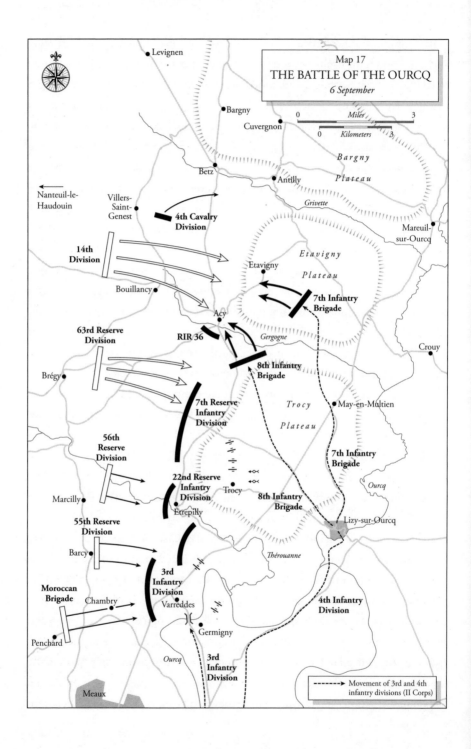

Map 17

THE BATTLE OF THE OURCQ

*6 September*

and artillery limbers and the farm pond, which was littered with abandoned shells. Other bodies, both French and German, were scattered about in large numbers in the fields on either side of the road leading into the village. It was here, in the late afternoon, that Henry d'Estre, a staff officer with the 45th Division, discovered the bodies of the famous poet Charles Péguy and his men, cut down as they attacked the village from the direction of Villeroy.

On the road an ammunition column had come to a halt. Its c/o, Commandant P… whom I knew, for his unit belonged to our division, was in a neighbouring field, a few hundred metres from us, leaning over a red spot which showed up against the fields. Intrigued by this, we moved closer and then made out not one, but eight, ten, twenty spots, ranged in a single line and regularly spaced. They were French infantry from the 276e Régiment. Death had taken them by surprise on the completely bare slopes that fell gently towards the Sorcières brook whose ditch separated the hills at Iverny–Villeroy from the heights of Monthyon-Neufmoutiers, which were held by the enemy. Without doubt, they had been mown down by machine guns aimed at this point, which they had been unable to cross. From far away, one could have taken them for poppies standing out from the greenness; from close by their attitudes were so natural that it seemed as if we were looking at soldiers who were fast asleep.

To all appearances, these brave men, struck down while facing the enemy, had passed without suffering into the great beyond. A soldier of athletic build still held his entrenching tool with which he had begun to scrape at the soil to find shelter. Next to this giant, his lieutenant, a man of about forty years, appeared quite small. [Charles Péguy.] He lay with his head supported by his left arm, which had been drawn back, the right extended. His face, which I saw in profile, was very calm and surrounded by a bushy beard that the dust had turned a greyish-yellow colour. On his features there were no traces of suffering. On his ring finger there was a wedding ring.[1]

Likewise, as the Moroccans passed through Penchard, they encountered the bodies of their comrades who had been killed in the epic action the previous afternoon. Fifty years afterwards, Maréchal Juin still remembered how, as a young Lieutenant in the 2nd Regiment, he and his men discovered the bodies of those who had been killed during their heroic assault on the village, including the famous commander of the V Battalion, Capitaine Richard d'Ivry:

> The next day, we found him in the field … from which he had directed the fighting of his battalion. At his side were the bodies of his staff officers. There were nine bullets in his body. We discovered the body of another hero, Capitaine Hugot-Derville, the commander of the 9th Company, on the summit of Penchard Wood. His horse had been shot down, and being wounded himself and unable to get out from under it, he had waited for the Germans, revolver in hand. It had ended with his death as he was hit by several bullets. Capitaine Rogerie and I took the trouble to remove the kid gloves that covered his hands, swollen by his wounds. Under one of them was a signet ring which we sent from the field to Monseigneur Marbot, the Bishop of Meaux, who was his relative.[2]

As the Moroccans were crossing the line Marcilly–Barcy–Chambry, they received the order to divert to the south-east to oppose the German II Corps, which after a seven-hour march, was approaching the Marne crossing at Germigny on their way to reinforcing Gronau's left wing. After II Corps Commander, General von Linsingen, had watched his men depart at 3.00am he went ahead by car to reconnoitre the position from the high ground to the south of the Marne bend at Trilport. From what he could see of the battlefield, and from the few reports that had reached him about the fighting, he took the unwelcome decision to split his force in two in order to give the maximum possible support to Gronau's hard-pressed troops. As a result, the 3rd Infantry Division, accompanied by the heavy howitzers of the corps artillery, would cross the Marne at Germigny and support the left wing while the 4th Division continued northwards and extended the right wing to prevent it from being outflanked.

At about 8.30am the artillery crossed the Marne at Germigny and forced their way through the narrow main street of Varreddes, which was crowded with vehicles and with wounded troops from the 22nd Reserve Division who gave them dire warnings about the warm reception waiting for them. The howitzers were sent to the valley between the Marne bend and the southern edge of the Trocy Plateau and the field artillery was split up, one regiment taking up position on the reverse slopes to the south of Etrepilly and the other in the low ground within the Marne bend at Germigny. When the first infantry units began to arrive about an hour later they relieved the troops which were guarding the southern end of the line, allowing them to rejoin the rest of the 22nd Reserve Infantry Division at Etrepilly. With no time to spare, the reinforcements passed through Varreddes at the double, crossed the canal and ascended the steep and heavily wooded slopes from where they emerged breathless on to the open ground at the edge of the plateau. The 5th Brigade was on the right, directly to the north of Varreddes and the 6th Brigade on the left where it faced Chambry, about a mile away across the open fields. As the lead unit (III/IR42) reached the crest and deployed, it came under violent shellfire and also rifle fire from the Moroccans who had just entered Chambry. In an attempt to escape from the fire, the German troops rushed forwards and became engaged in a costly fire-fight with the Moroccans and with parts of the 55th Reserve Division near Barcy. Since they had very little artillery support because of the poor observation (some observers were forced to climb the high poplars lining the roads in order to get a better view), and because their ammunition was running low, the wounded battalion commander, Major von Knobelsdorff, gave the order to retreat to the narrow poplar-lined track in the fields about 200 yards from the edge of the valley, where they excavated shallow trenches in the hard and stony ground. Casualties were also high on the French side, particularly among a Moroccan unit involved in a desperate fight at the cemetery at Chambry on the northern outskirts of the village.[3]

For the rest of the day there was stalemate between the German 6th Brigade along the edge of the plateau and the Moroccans at Chambry, with neither side able to advance in the face of the violent shellfire. The Germans suffered badly in their inadequate trenches from the devastatingly accurate fire of the French 75mm guns and the Moroccans were bombarded by the German heavy howitzers on the far side of the Marne, well out of range of the French guns. At about 1.00pm, fearing that the French were about to attack, Oberst Gräser ordered his last remaining reserve to enter the front line but when they left the woods they were struck by friendly fire from the batteries at Germigny, which mistook them for the enemy. In a desperate attempt to save the situation, the battalion adjutant, Leutnant

Lademacher, leapt on his horse, galloped headlong down the slope, swam the canal in full equipment and ran to the batteries to get them to cease firing. Unfortunately, the damage had already been done and the battalion was torn apart, as men fled in all directions to escape the shells. In the early afternoon the Germans suffered another crisis when a large mass of enemy troops (the newly arrived 45th Division) was seen advancing down the high road from Meaux directly towards their open left flank. Since Gräser had no reserves left he was forced to borrow a battalion from the 5th Brigade, which he placed astride the high road at the extreme left of his line. Although this was enough avert the crisis, the situation on the left wing had become so dire by the late afternoon that General von Trossel, the commander of the 3rd Division, asked Linsingen's permission to fall back to a new position. However, after a prolonged discussion they decided to remain where they were and wait for the arrival of II Corps' rearguard, which had left the Grand Morin at 10.00am, six hours after the main force.

Meanwhile, the 55th Reserve Division had failed to capture the Trocy Plateau by means of a costly frontal assault. At about 1.00pm the 110th Brigade moved out to the attack, the 246e RI in the lead, bayonets fixed and with all of the officers in the front line including Colonel Chaulet and his staff, accompanied by the regimental band. A short distance from Barcy, the buglers sounded the advance and the men set off over the bare and featureless ground towards the German line less than a mile away. Before long, they came under devastating fire not only from ahead (the German batteries at Trocy) but also at almost point-blank range from a battery that had been brought up behind the German firing line opposite Chambry on their right flank. With the enemy machine guns joining in at maximum range, and shells bursting all around them throwing up huge plumes of earth, large numbers were killed or wounded and the remainder went to ground to escape the fire, flattening themselves into the very slightest depression or huddling behind the inadequate cover of their packs. In a heroic attempt to restart the advance, Sous-Lieutenant Dumesnil seized the standard from the hands of the dying standard-bearer and rushed forwards with the cry 'En avant mes enfants, c'est pour la République.' Inspired by his example, the line rose up and followed him and the buglers sounded the charge once more. When he fell wounded, a sergeant took over from him but he was killed almost immediately, after which the standard disappeared from view under a heap of dead and wounded. More and more officers were hit, including Colonel Chaulet who, although badly wounded, his tunic torn off by a shell blast and with his shirt covered in blood, encouraged his men to attack until he finally collapsed.[4] By 3.00pm the fight was over and the survivors retreated to Barcy, leaving a large number of bodies strewn across the bare slopes leading up to the German positions. During the rest of the afternoon, several more attempts were made by units from the 110th and 109th Brigade and also from the 56th Reserve Division but all of them ended in failure, with huge loss of life.

On the German right wing meanwhile, the 4th Infantry Division arrived just in time to stave off a further crisis due to a mile-wide gap in the line at Vincy-Manoeuvre (to the south of Acy) where a battalion had broken and fled under the intense shellfire. Although they had been on the march for almost nine hours, Linsingen decided that they would have to go into battle as soon as they arrived. Furthermore, the situation was so critical that they would have to be split up, one brigade (the 8th) being used to plug the gap at Vincy-Manoeuvre while the other (the 7th) reinforced the right flank at Acy. They were also instructed to send the artillery ahead at the trot and Trossel was instructed to transfer II Corps' heavy howitzers to the right wing, even though they were desperately needed to defend the high ground around Varreddes.

The two hours spent waiting for the reinforcements to arrive were difficult ones for the German right wing. The French 27th Brigade (14th Division) reached Acy down the narrow valley of the Gergogne, concealed by the thick undergrowth, and became involved in a bitter street fight that continued into the evening without either side being able to get the upper hand. At the same time, the 4th Cavalry Division on the extreme right wing was shelled out of Villers-St Genest and forced to retreat as far as Betz, leaving the way open for the French 28th Brigade to bypass Acy to the north and get on to the Etavigny plateau unopposed. Fortunately for the Germans, by the middle of the afternoon the 4th Division infantry were beginning to arrive on the battlefield. However, when the commander of the 8th Brigade, which was at the head of the column, heard the sounds of heavy firing from Acy, he disobeyed Linsingen's orders to fill the gap at Vincy-Manoeuvre and instead ordered his men to head directly for the village. When they reached the valley of the Gergogne, they deployed and forced their way into Acy where they too became caught up in the street fight. Although this left the gap at Vincy unfilled, it led to an unintended piece of good fortune in that the 7th Brigade (at the tail) had to divert to the north, on to the plateau of Etavigny, where they were just in time to forestall the outflanking movement by the French. After deploying straight off the line of march, they advanced up the gentle slope and when they were near the top of the plateau met the French coming the other way. To begin with, the French resisted well but after the Germans had been reinforced by their machine gun company and several artillery batteries they were gradually forced to retreat until they came to rest at nightfall to the west of the Acy–Etavigny road.

As the battlefield fell silent, only the burning villages and farms testified to the severity of the combat that had raged along the whole front. On the German right wing, the 4th Cavalry Division went into bivouac about 6 miles to the north-east of Acy, after having taken almost no part in the fighting. In and around Acy, when darkness fell the two sides retreated to more secure positions, the French towards Chevreville and the Germans on to the high ground at the centre of the plateau. Between the Gergogne and the Thérouanne, where the 7th and 22nd Reserve Divisions had endured their second day of heavy and costly fighting, there were scenes of chaos; parts of the German line were either thinly held or not at all, many units had become inextricably mixed and the men were exhausted and hungry. Lastly, in the south the much depleted 6th Infantry Brigade still occupied the shallow trenches along the edge of the plateau opposite Chambry. The French too had suffered heavy losses, especially 55th and 56th Reserve Divisions, which had been repulsed when attempting to capture the Trocy Plateau in the late afternoon.

According to Joffre's General Instruction No 6, the British were to advance in a north-easterly direction towards Montmirail. Although the terrain was generally easy, with only the occasional village or the rare patch of forest to break up the monotony of the huge sweeping spaces, they would have to cross three rivers, the Grand Morin, the Petit Morin and the Marne, which were certain to be strongly defended. As we have seen, because of the confusion which had been caused by the two sets of plans, the one drawn up at Bray and the other at Melun, they began their advance from a position about 12 miles further back than Joffre had intended. Because of this, a large part of the morning was taken up with a preparatory movement, intended to bring them facing north-eastwards before the advance could begin. When they finally got going, the only action was between their cavalry, which was screening the advance, and units from Marwitz's 2nd Cavalry Corps, which quickly broke off the fight and retreated behind the Grand Morin, covered by the four attached Jäger battalions that guarded the bridges. Since the British were approaching the extensive Forest of Crécy, and since there was an 8-mile gap between his right wing and the French 5th Army, Sir John French decided to halt for the night to the south of the Grand Morin.

To begin with, Kluck did not show any great concern for the situation of IV Reserve Corps, even after Bergmann, his Deputy Chief of Staff, returned from a visit to Gronau's command post with news that the attack was more serious than had at first been thought. According to Bergmann, who found Gronau and his staff fast asleep in a roadside ditch, the situation appeared to be well under control. Similarly, the only message to arrive from Marwitz during the morning said that only minor skirmishes had taken place with the British cavalry, which, in his opinion, were still retreating. As the afternoon wore on, however, a series of reports indicated that the situation had deteriorated and that both wings were threatened with encirclement. In addition, it became clear that the enemy was not retreating (as Marwitz had claimed) but had in fact gone over to the offensive against both 1st and 2nd Armies. When Kluck became aware of this, he ordered IV Corps to march to La Ferté-sous-Jouarre from where they would be able to reach the Ourcq the following afternoon. In the late evening, however, he changed his mind and ordered them to march through the night so that they would reach the battlefield by dawn at the latest. In addition, III and IX Corps were to fall back at first light behind the Grand Morin, screened from the British forces to the west by the two cavalry corps.

# 11

# THE BARRIER OF THE MARSHES

## 7 SEPTEMBER: THE GERMANS ATTEMPT TO BYPASS THE ST GOND MARSHES

After a delay because of contradictory orders from Kluck and Bülow, III and IX Corps left their overnight positions adjacent to 2nd Army and departed for the Ourcq front. After a forced march, III Corps reached the Marne near La Ferté-sous-Jouarre at about midnight where they snatched a brief rest before leaving for the battlefield. Although IX Corps spent the whole morning at Esternay waiting for the confusion to be cleared up, it was not attacked even though its neighbours had long since retreated, leaving it in a very isolated position. When it reached the Grand Morin in late afternoon it was told by Kluck to continue to the north of the River Dolloir, which it reached at about midnight.

In order to protect his right flank after their departure, Bülow ordered X Reserve Corps to fall back behind the Petit Morin and establish contact with VII Corps, which was in reserve at Montmirail. With the exception of a battalion from RIR74 which was annihilated at Guébarré Farm on the south side of the Forest of Gault after it was trapped by a superior force, the Germans retreated without hindrance and were already digging trenches on the high ground to the north of the Petit Morin by the time the French noticed they were gone.[1] For the second day in a row X Corps became locked in a vicious contest with the Moroccan Division for possession of the Poirier Crest. During the previous

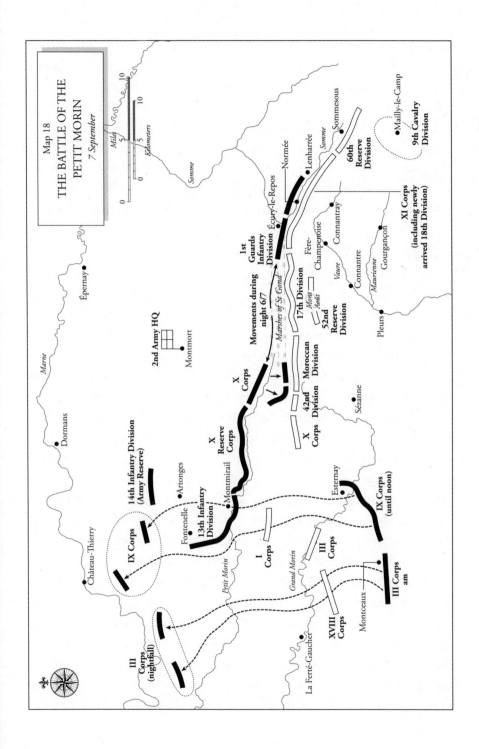

Map 18

THE BATTLE OF THE PETIT MORIN

7 September

evening, when Emmich discovered that the first attempt had failed he decided to repeat it in greater force and with fresh troops. Calculating that the French would stay on the defensive along the southern edge of the marshes, he ordered the 20th Infantry Division to side-step westwards during the night, leaving the northern exits guarded by only three infantry companies, albeit with strong artillery support. When they reached St Prix, they were to take over from the remnants of IR74, cross the Petit Morin and occupy the Poirier Crest. At the same time the 19th Infantry Division (less IR74) would renew the attack on Soizy-aux-Bois and then swing eastward to unhinge the French defence along the marshes. All preliminary movements were to be completed before dawn to avoid interference from the French artillery.

In the middle of the night the 20th Division set off in an enormously long single file along a field path that ran parallel to the marsh in the direction of St Prix. About three hours later, after a slow but uneventful journey, they crossed the bridge at St Prix and reached the base of the Poirier Crest where they prepared for the next stage in the advance. On the left, two battalions from IR164 marched down the country lane towards Oyes, in the centre III/IR79 began the awkward ascent of the Poirier Crest and on the right II/IR79, supported by the two machine gun sections, set off up the winding road which led across the wooded hill to Soizy-aux-Bois. IR77 was left behind at the chapel of St Prix as divisional reserve, accompanied by one battalion from each of the two assault regiments. After advancing cautiously for about half an hour through the early morning gloom, first contact was made just as dawn was breaking. On the extreme left, IR164 was met by a burst of rifle fire as it reached the outskirts of Oyes but rapidly deployed and forced their opponents, a battalion of Zouaves from Regiment Cros, out of the village. However, when the Germans set off in pursuit they were hit by a violent bombardment that forced them to dig in to the south of the village where they stayed, paralysed, for the rest of the day. On their right, after a stiff climb III/IR 79 reached the summit of the Poirier Crest where they found the terrible remains from the previous day's fighting. Patrols were sent out to establish the enemy's position and work was hurriedly begun digging trenches before the expected bombardment began. Meanwhile, the II Battalion advanced unopposed in the darkness along the winding road until they reached the southern edge of

Botrait Wood, only half a mile away from Soizy-aux-Bois. At this point, when the lead company emerged into the open it was overwhelmed by a sudden burst of rifle and machine-gun fire from close range and recoiled into the woods. Although the enemy outpost was rapidly overcome with the help of reinforcements, the French artillery also opened fire and the advance came to an abrupt halt. The four German battalions were now in a difficult situation, spread out along an extended 2-mile front, out of touch with one another and unable to bring up reinforcements because of the continuous and violent shellfire. In addition, their own artillery was powerless to help since the three groups to the north of the river were unable to locate the French batteries and the fourth, which had been laboriously manhandled all the way to the top of the Poirier Crest, was smashed by shellfire as soon as it reached the summit.

The situation appeared very different to the French, however. They had been forced out of Oyes, their numbers were greatly reduced and a German breakthrough appeared to be a distinct possibility, followed by the loss of the marshes. At about 8.00am, Humbert, the Moroccans' commander, sent an urgent appeal for help to Général Dubois at IX Corps Headquarters. In reply, Dubois promised to send him the 77e RI, which was in reserve for the 17th Division at Mont Août, together with a battalion from the 52nd Reserve Division and an artillery group. With their help, he was to go over to the offensive and force the Germans off the Poirier Crest and back across the river. (In the event, the 77e RI arrived too late to take part in the fighting and so Humbert was forced to postpone the attack until the morning.) In the middle of the afternoon, while the French batteries were moving to a new position from where they could protect the Mondement–Montgivroux ridge (where a last-ditch defensive line was being prepared), the Germans took advantage of the lull in the bombardment to reinforce their front line and resume their attack. A battalion from IR79 descended through the woods at the western end of the Poirier Crest and took the Moroccans by surprise, throwing them out of Montalard Farm and the adjacent pear orchards. They then poured flanking fire on to the French infantry in the northern edge of St Gond Wood, causing them to flee and allowing the III Battalion to leave their positions along the crest where they had been pinned down all morning. The two battalions then pursued the French as far as the east-west Soizy–Oyes road but were forced to halt in the late afternoon because of exhaustion and the renewed shellfire from the French batteries, which by now had found new emplacements.

A similar sequence of events took place opposite Soizy-aux-Bois, which was the objective of the 19th Infantry Division. Here too, the initial attack stalled under an intense bombardment but resumed in the early afternoon when the firing died down and it became possible for the first time to reinforce the front line. The village came under attack simultaneously from three sides and in spite of stubborn resistance from the French 42nd Division it fell to the Germans in the late afternoon. However, it was late evening by the time that they had completely cleared French stragglers out of the surrounding woods and there was no time to sort out the inextricably mixed units before the exhausted troops fell asleep wherever they happened to be.

The French had considerably more success on their right wing where for the second day in a row their artillery prevented the Guard Corps from making any headway at all. Like Emmich, Plettenberg had decided to concentrate all of his forces at the end of the marshes in the hope of achieving a decisive breakthrough, and so he ordered the 1st Guards Infantry Division to side-step to the east during the night, leaving only a small force to keep watch over the northern exits at Aulnay and Aulnizeux. When they arrived at the eastern end of the marshes they were to take over the sector Morains–Ecury from the 2nd Guards Infantry Division which would close up to the east to make room for them. (Since the 20th Infantry Division moved in the other direction at the same time, the whole of the marshes was now guarded by only a few isolated companies.) When the 1st Division reached their new positions a few hours before dawn there was very little time in which to dig trenches in the hard, unyielding ground before the French opened fire on them. Furthermore, most of the field kitchens got lost, making it impossible for the men to get a hot meal, patrols were unable to locate the enemy's positions and, worst of all, the unfamiliar terrain made it difficult for the artillery to find suitable covered positions.

Since Plettenberg was still worried about his open left flank, he decided to delay his attack until 7.00am, by which time the right wing of 3rd Army would be able to support him. However, the promised support failed to arrive on time;

the 23rd Infantry Division and 23rd Reserve Infantry Division ended the day well short of the Somme after they were pinned down by French shellfire, while the 32nd Infantry Division, which was the closest of the three, came under such an intense bombardment as it approached the river that Regiment Augusta had to be sent to its aid. Thus, after two days of combat against one of the weakest units in the whole of the French Army, all that the Guard Corps had achieved was the capture of Morains-le-Petit and Ecury and an advance of less than 3 miles.

Bülow was pleased with the situation when he reviewed the day's events that evening. Admittedly, the Guard Corps had been unexpectedly held back for the second day in a row, but the right wing had bent back successfully and there was a distinct possibility that X Corps might break through the French centre either tomorrow or the day after. However, this complacency was shattered a short while later by the arrival of news that a large enemy force had crossed the marshes after nightfall and had overwhelmed the weak German detachment that was guarding the village of Aulnizeux. (In reality, the attacking force was less than a battalion strong and was easily repelled after initial confusion in the darkness.) It now seemed to him that he had been wrong to allow the 20th Infantry Division and the 1st Guards Infantry Division to move apart, leaving the gap between them defended by a very weak force. If the attack on Aulnizeux heralded a major offensive, the French might break through in the centre and split his army in two, leading to immediate defeat. Without waiting for clarification, he immediately ordered the 14th Infantry Division, which was in army reserve, to fill the gap along the marshes and X Corps to abandon their hard-won positions at Soizy-aux-Bois and along the Poirier Crest and fall back behind the Petit Morin.

When the order to retreat reached X Corps Headquarters it was received with incomprehension by Emmich, who immediately sent his Chief of Staff to Army Headquarters to try and to Bülow to change his mind. By now the exhausted troops were fast asleep and the officers found it very difficult to wake them up and assemble them in the darkness, especially in the dense woods around Soizy-aux-Bois where the fighting had left many units intermingled and scattered over a wide area. For the second night in a row they were on the march, without food and sleep and having spent all day either in combat or pinned down helpless and immobile under a hail of shellfire.

At first we moved over the fields, one shell hole next to another; many unexploded shells lay round about. We had to avoid touching these. However, we couldn't always see what was smack in front of us and so we tripped over many of the duds without anything nasty happening. We noticed signs of fighting in the woods … in the meantime we lay apathetic in the road ditches despite the cold. 'Up! Further!'… On the road from Sézanne to St Prix the battle had raged terribly, the trees were smashed up. Between the branches and small mounds of earth lay the bodies of several brave men, with yellowish, dirty faces. We moved past them tediously, our exhaustion had robbed us of the last drop of sympathy. Mechanically we placed one foot in front of the other, without thinking and without speaking. Then suddenly there was a call to stop and rest! This was fortunate for the men. Although the sweat poured off our bodies, we threw ourselves down on the cold earth and immediately fell asleep.[2]

By dawn, the whole of X Corps was once more behind the Petit Morin. Meanwhile, the 14th Infantry Division had also been on the march all night and halted at Champaubert from where it was only a short distance to the marshes. When these measures to protect the centre were complete, Bülow turned his attention to the left wing. During the evening, a message arrived from Hausen saying that in order to neutralize the enemy's artillery he intended to launch a surprise attack during the night with his right wing, together with the Guard Corps, if Bülow gave his approval.

At about the same time, there was worrying news that the British were advancing into the gap between 1st and 2nd Armies. According to Richthofen, units of all arms had been seen approaching Rebais and La Ferté-Gaucher (from where they could threaten the right wing of 2nd Army) and had already crossed the Grand Morin. He added that he had fallen back behind the Petit Morin and that in the morning he would defend the sector La Ferté-sous-Jouarre–Villeneuve. Everything now depended on a speedy success on the left wing. If the night attack succeeded, there was still time to bring about victory; if it failed, however, the British might penetrate the gap and force both armies to break off the fight and beat a retreat. The stakes could not have been higher.

# 12

## STRUGGLE FOR THE HIGH GROUND

### 7 SEPTEMBER: THE GERMANS CLING ON TO THE HIGH GROUND TO THE WEST OF THE OURCQ WITH THE HELP OF REINFORCEMENTS

The first fighting of the day involved the attack on the German left and centre by the 45th Division. This was a two pronged affair: on the right, Général Trafford's brigade was to attack the German 3rd Division above Varreddes and throw it back into the valley of the Marne, while on the left Général Quiquandon's Brigade was to capture Etrepilly with the help of the 56th Reserve Division and then seize the Trocy Plateau. Unfortunately for Quiquandon, the already powerful German gun line on the Trocy heights had just been strengthened by several batteries from IV Corps' artillery, which opened fire on his men, bringing the attack to a halt when they were about half a mile from the German line. Attempts to close to within assault range were met by withering fire and they remained pinned down on the bare and featureless ground for the remainder of the day, suffering from the intense heat and a lack of water. It was a very different story further south, however, opposite Varreddes, where the ground was covered with man-high fields of maize that allowed Trafford's Brigade to approach the enemy's firing line without being seen. In addition, the French artillery took the end of the German line in enfilade and inflicted enormous damage, especially on the flank guard astride the road to Meaux at the extreme

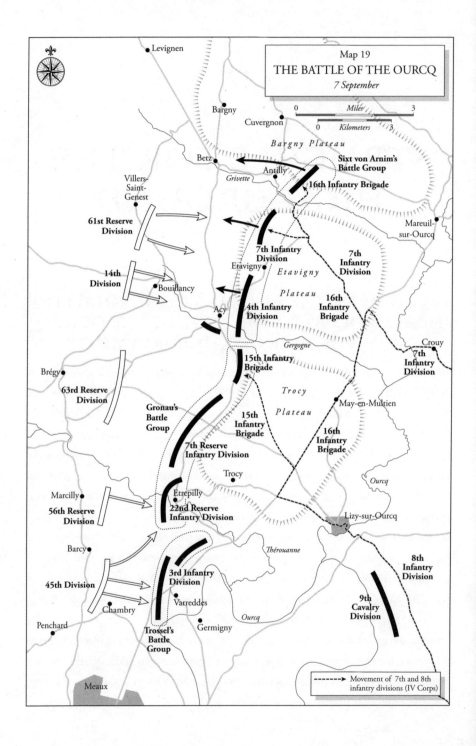

Map 19
THE BATTLE OF THE OURCQ
*7 September*

end of the line. In order to prevent a collapse, which would have exposed the vitally important bridge at Germigny, Trossel was forced to transfer a regiment from the 5th Brigade; in addition, two batteries of field guns were manhandled up the steep and winding road out of the valley and set up in exposed positions immediately behind the firing line, from where they shelled the French out of the maize fields and prevented the breakthrough which had seemed inevitable.

News of the precarious situation on the left wing reached 1st Army Headquarters at about noon, followed by a report that a pilot had seen large numbers of French infantry in the vicinity of Nanteuil-le-Haudouin (the 61st Reserve Division), opposite the right wing. Unless steps were taken to neutralize these twin threats the army might be defeated before III and IX Corps arrived the next day. A radio message was therefore sent to Marwitz, ordering him to send part of his artillery to Trilport, within the Marne bend to the south of Varreddes, so as to support the 3rd Division. Secondly, the commander of the Lines of Inspection troops was ordered to send as many men as possible to reinforce the right wing. Thirdly, in a measure that had a touch of desperation about it, Kluck placed his headquarters guard (an infantry battalion and a section of artillery), at Linsingen's disposal. Last of all, a message was sent to III and IX Corps ordering them to accelerate their march. Three of the four divisions (both divisions from IX Corps and one from III Corps) were to take the shortest route to Crouy, from where they could attack the French left wing while the other division from III Corps was to come to the aid of IV Reserve Corps in the centre. Fortunately for Kluck, IV Corps' infantry were now arriving after a gruelling forced march, which had begun at 9.00pm the previous evening and had continued almost non-stop during the night. This was described by Leutnant Lohrisch, an officer in IR27 from the 7th Infantry Division:

> I was already sinking into a state of unconsciousness when I was startled by the resounding noise of steps. They came through the yard and into the hall. 'Order from the Hauptmann. Alarm! The company must be at the crossroads at 9.30am etc, etc.' At half past nine the Hauptmann reported to the battalion commander that the company stood silently on the road, arranged in march-column. The light of the full moon lit up the faces of the rather sleepy men, not overjoyed at this

disturbance. And then began a night march such as we had never before experienced. Half asleep, the soldiers marched in silence. Each of them thought longingly of the beautiful straw mattresses that had been left behind. Where were we going? No one gave it any thought. One was used to being thrown here and there and getting the point of it only at the end or sometimes never. At one point a rumour ran through the column: 'The Reserve Corps has had its nose burned outside Paris. We're going to dig them out.'

On and on, further and further went the night march. All the time, other troop units joined us from places off to the side and extended our march-column. This functioned like a machine whose mechanical parts were running precisely but which was unaware that it was working. In that twilight state, only this much was clear to us: we were going backwards, here on this wooded riverbank where we had already been once before. It must have been the valley of the Petit Morin. However, how the region had been altered by the night! The moonlight wove a mysterious veil over all objects on the way. In the valley, a sea of white mist covered the river and all of the dark woods were obscured with thin veils of vapour … on and on and still further, the march continued. The legs moved more and more mechanically. If there was a hold-up or a short stop was made, the men fell down in sleep to the right and the left of the road, rifles in their arms. Apathetic and drunk with sleep, the column rolled forward at the call of our commander. Now and then we passed through places that lay dreaming and lifeless, wrapped in the dark cloak of the beautiful and mild autumn night. Doors and shutters were closed. Here and there, the moonlight picked out a white wall glaring out of the shadows. Like a vision, it all flew past a mind that was so drowsy. And the fact that we were then marching through the street of a fine looking town which took us over the Marne bridge and then climbed again on the other side, scarcely crossed the threshold of our conscious but lethargic minds.

Our half-closed eyes began to blink: it was starting to get light. And suddenly, the liberating call spread from company to company, 'An hour's halt. Receive coffee.' Shortly after, the columns were lying on the road. The greater part was too tired and indifferent and fell asleep straight away, the others crowded around the field kitchen, which in the meantime had gone ahead. Once these men had taken a cup full of the hot drink then they too also lay down and slept. And soon, the waning moon shone down on a peaceful idyll: to the right and left of the stacked rifles lay motionless grey shapes, heads resting on packs, here and there bedded down on straw or leaves which had been hastily bundled together but mostly on the bare, damp earth. And all around was silence: the only audible sound was the snoring from everywhere among the heap of men.

And suddenly, orders rang out again. A jolt went through the numbed mass of people. Here and there, a few were given a good shaking or a poke in the ribs to wake them up. And quickly, all were standing ready next to their rifles. 'Take your rifles! Slope arms! March!' And the march continued, always further, always further. After the rest we'd had, it was clear to all of us that there would be no more sleep. This knowledge, the new, clear light of day and the fresh morning air dispelled any sleepiness. One pulled oneself together and even if the legs only did their service sluggishly, the mind became more lively, the eyes brighter and one looked ahead with a sense of expectation. We could then distinctly hear the growling of the cannons. Where we came through villages we encountered troops. Red Cross flags fluttered in front of buildings that had been set up as field hospitals. We passed transports carrying wounded, going the other way. And finally we turned off the road on to a field path. The cannon fire was now ahead of us. To the right and left lay rearward troops from a corps that had arrived before us; among them, wounded were being bandaged. We knew that we had reached our destination and that it would soon be our turn. It was about ten o'clock in the morning and we had around 45 kilometres behind us.[1]

While his troops were on the march, their commander, General Sixt von Arnim, drove to Linsingen's headquarters to receive instructions. As they pored over the maps by the flickering light of a stable lantern, Linsingen's Chief of Staff explained the seriousness of the situation. At first they disagreed on how the reinforcements should be used; Linsingen insisted that both divisions must be employed defensively in the centre to shore up the badly damaged IV Reserve Corps whereas Sixt von Arnim preferred to use them on the right wing to carry out a decisive attack. Eventually they reached a compromise whereby the 7th Infantry Division would be used to reinforce the right wing while the 8th Infantry Division would be inserted in the centre to support IV Reserve Corps. When the

7th Infantry Division arrived in the late morning, it therefore occupied Boullarre on the far right opposite the Etavigny plateau and Montrolles Wood. However, Linsingen changed his mind about the 8th Division and split it in two, sending one part (the 15th Infantry Brigade) to fill the gap at Vincy-Manoeuvre, and the other (the 16th Brigade) to the extreme right wing where it extended the line of the newly arrived 7th Division to the north.

Since the command structure was fragmented after units had been inserted piecemeal into the line, Linsingen reorganized his force into three battle groups, a northern one commanded by Sixt von Arnim (16th Infantry Brigade, 7th Infantry Division and 4th Infantry Division), a central one commanded by Gronau (15th Infantry Brigade and IV Reserve Corps), and a southern one commanded by Trossel (3rd Infantry Division). In the late morning, by which time the reinforcements were all in place, Linsingen decided to go over to the offensive with the whole of Sixt von Arnim's Battle Group supported on the left by the 15th Infantry Brigade and the 7th Reserve Infantry Division from Gronau's Group. Meanwhile, the 22nd Reserve Infantry Division and the 3rd Infantry Division were to remain on the defensive at the southern end of the line. The intention was to cross the Etavigny plateau and envelop the French left wing, throwing it back on the centre and defeating it before the 61st Reserve Division could come to its aid. As it happened, however, the latter had finished detraining earlier than expected and was already advancing towards Montrolles Wood and the Etavigny Plateau, accompanied on their right by the 14th Division. Because of this the two sides collided at the western edge of the Etavigny Plateau, where an inconclusive fight took place. By early evening the whole of the German right wing, from Betz in the north to Acy in the south, had ground to a halt; units were mixed up, casualties were heavy and many of the men were almost at the end of their strength from the forced march, the hard fighting, the lack of food and drink and the pitiless scorching heat. A short while later the 4th Infantry Division abandoned Acy, which it had captured at great cost, and fell back to a more secure position on the plateau to the north-east of the village. Since this movement exposed the left flank of the 7th Infantry Division, General von Riedel also pulled his men back on to the plateau even though this meant relinquishing their hard-won gains. In the evening, not content with sending in the usual situation report, Sixt von Arnim sent his Chief of Staff to 1st Army Headquarters to warn them of the seriousness of the situation and to urge the rapid intervention of III and IX Corps.

The hardest fighting of the day took place at Etrepilly, which guarded the approaches to the Trocy Plateau. Remarkably, given its strategic significance, the Germans had abandoned the village the previous evening and had retreated to a defensive position on the forward slope of the plateau. During the morning the French mounted a pincer movement against the village involving the 2e Zouaves (on the left wing of the 45th Division), which advanced from the direction of Barcy to the south-west, and the 350e RI (from the 56th Reserve Division) which approached the village from the north-west along the valley of the Thérouanne. When General Mühlenfels, the commander of the 44th Reserve Infantry Brigade saw the enemy movements from his command post on the high ground in front of Trocy he immediately gave the order to occupy the village before they arrived. All four available battalions were urgently sent forward, two from RIR32 towards the village itself and two from RIR82 to the immediate north. The two sides reached the village at about the same time and became involved in a prolonged street fight, which was witnessed helplessly by several seriously wounded Germans who had been left behind in the care of their doctors after the previous day's fighting. After a while, several German batteries left their positions at Trocy and galloped down the steep hill to the outskirts of Etrepilly where they unlimbered and opened fire, bringing the fighting to a sudden end. By the early afternoon, the enemy had disappeared, leaving the Germans to form a defensive line along the north-south country road at the western edge of the village where they remained without interference until darkness.

In the late evening, however, the French repeated their attempt to capture the village, with the Zouaves once again coming from the direction of Barcy and the 350e RI advancing along the northern bank of the Thérouanne. The latter arrived first, appearing out of the pitch darkness and falling on the right wing of RIR82 along the sunken road on the northern outskirts of the village. Ignoring a standing order to use only their bayonets in the darkness, the defenders became involved in a frantic fire-fight in which it was impossible to tell friend from foe. For a while, the French were held at bay by the fire of two machine guns but these

HOME BEFORE THE LEAVES FALL

were soon captured and the defenders driven back to a second sunken road, parallel to the first, which ran past the village cemetery.

Meanwhile, the Zouaves had entered the village from the south-west across the bridge over the Thérouanne:

Night had fallen. Under cover of darkness the battalion assembled in columns of four, and took the direction towards the enemy, slanting to the west a little. We learned that we were going to attack Etrepilly. We advanced in silence and found ourselves at the entrance to the village. But the Germans were keeping a good look out. We were stopped by a resounding call of 'who goes there!' Adjudant Soulé from the 16th Company replied in a loud voice, 'France!' The immediate response was a burst of rifle fire, and it had an unfortunate effect. Colonel Dujubadoux, at the head of his regiment, was wounded in the forehead. However, the wound, which he said was light, did not prevent him from giving the signal to attack. Then, yelling at the tops of our voices, we rushed forwards into the streets, which sloped upwards quite steeply, and crossed the village without encountering resistance. But a machine gun, placed in a first floor room of one of the first houses, caused us considerable losses: it was rapidly silenced.

The main street bent round and became a road leading towards the end of the village. Until now we had made rapid progress but the Germans were dug in behind the cemetery and were putting up an energetic defence there. A temporary halt took place, but it only lasted a few seconds. An officer shouted, 'Sound the charge!' and suddenly, in the middle of the firing, we heard the stirring notes of the bugle. We fell furiously on to the defenders of this position and nailed them down.[2]

As the Zouaves rushed through the centre of the village, scattering the enemy as they went, they overran a German dressing station where the wounded from the earlier fighting were being treated. Fortunately, a French officer noticed the red cross on the building, just in time to prevent his men from killing the two doctors, several medical orderlies and the wounded whom they were tending. Other non-combatants were less fortunate, however, including a group of stretcher-bearers who were trapped at the western end of the village and summarily dispatched. (The most unfortunate Germans in Etrepilly that night belonged to a small group of men from a nearby Jäger battalion who had left their units and gone to the village in search of wine. Within moments of arriving they were rounded up by an officer who was brandishing a pistol, and made to take part in a counter-attack.)

Gradually, the fighting became concentrated around the cemetery. The confusion was absolute, except on the northern side of the combat zone, which was bathed in the bright light from a hay barn which the Germans had set on fire in order to provide illumination. Elsewhere, the only light came from the muzzle flashes as they fired at one another at almost point-blank range. Officers lost control of their men, repeated bugle calls sounded in the darkness and men became disorientated and headed in the wrong direction. With the help of several comrades, Bugler Meier was carrying his wounded company commander, Oberleutnant Wentrup, to safety across a ploughed field when they were overrun by a group of Zouaves. Having escaped by throwing themselves down into a deep furrow, a few minutes later they were appalled to see that the attack had failed and that the enemy was fleeing back in their direction. When they emerged unscathed from their hiding place, Wentrup was nowhere to be seen. Oberleutnant Hermann was leading a group of men to safety but they lost their bearings in the almost pitch darkness and were overwhelmed by a large number of Zouaves who were making for the cemetery where, before long, the fighting reached its highest intensity. A long thin rectangle in shape (the long north–south sides run parallel to the road), this was surrounded by high stone walls, which gave excellent protection against rifle fire. On the western side were the Germans, most of whom belonged to the two battalions of RIR82; on the eastern side, and separated from them by the cemetery enclosure, were the Zouaves, who had swung off to their right when they came under fire and had entered the village from the east. In the lee of the western wall, the three senior German officers, the brigade commander, Mühlenfels, and the two regimental commanders, Buttlar and Hering, attempted to assemble their men by means of bugle calls. However, when Hering left the safety of the wall at the head of a group of men he was immediately hit by a bullet and collapsed at Oberst von Buttlar's feet.

The night was very dark. Shots flashed out around us, only ten paces away. Some of our men were firing completely at random on all sides and I shouted at several

officers, including the brigade commander among others: 'Shut up.' When yet
another of the men claimed that here or there they had seen the enemy, I tried to
make them see sense again by always saying that it was our own shots they heard,
though I knew that this wasn't true. In addition to all of this, a haystack burst into
flames about a hundred paces in front of us, lighting us up as if it was daylight.
Although enemy bullets were still pouring in, I succeeded in making the
6th Company, which was closest to me on the road, form up in two lines. Then
Mühlenfels took two groups away from me and advanced with them in the
direction from where he had heard '*Attention, les Allemands*'. As he did this, a bullet
passed through his arm and the Adjutant was hit in the upper thigh. Meanwhile,
Wentscher (commander of the machine gun company) and I each took part of the
assembled men and went around the cemetery on the right and on the left, to force
back the enemy troops who from the rear were continually firing from the walls
down into the cemetery where our doctors and stretcher-bearers were working.[3]

Buttlar then returned to the western side of the cemetery and continued to rally
his men with bugle calls. While doing so, the soldier next to him was hit in the
chest, the bullet piercing his aorta, and he collided with Buttlar as he fell,
drenching his tunic with blood from the spouting wound. Soon afterwards,
Buttlar glimpsed a mass of dimly visible figures approaching them from their left
front and preparing to open fire. Were they enemy troops or German
reinforcements? There was only one way to find out. Taking his life in his hands,
one of the other officers dashed towards them, illuminated by the still fiercely
burning haystack, and discovered that they were indeed reinforcements. With
their help the Germans slowly began to take control of the area around the
cemetery and forced the enemy back into the village streets. The increasingly
precarious situation of the Moroccans, as they retreated step by step, was described
by one of their officers:

The cemetery, which overlooked the road, was solidly organized and occupied by
large forces. Once more, while we looked for shelter, we stopped for a while, which
could have been disastrous since the Germans made a turning movement towards
the right and attempted to encircle us. This movement forced us, under a rain of

fire, to momentarily return to the village by the only route that still remained open. Suddenly, the sound of shots came from this direction. Had they got round the back of us? The situation appeared critical, but we weren't about to give in. We were determined to defend ourselves, whatever the cost. However, by the light of the houses set on fire by the shells, we recognized the Tirailleurs who were coming to our aid. 'Cease fire!' our colonel shouted, as he rushed forwards towards them.

The enemy, well dug in, showered us with projectiles, and we were threatened with being enveloped by the Germans, who were continuing their movement towards the right. Colonel Dujubadoux, revolver in hand, led us on: '*A la baoonette, mes enfants!*' We hurled ourselves forwards frantically, electrified by his example. But the bullets took a terrible toll among us. The colonel fell, mortally wounded. There only remained a few men standing from my company. We were outflanked: there was no longer anything to do except fall back on Etrepilly to regroup and organize another attack, for, despite our losses and despite the obstacles, we had not abandoned our objective. We were dying of thirst and we searched for water with which to quench it. In a house I entered, two Germans were lying dead, nailed down to the wooden floor by blows of the bayonet through their chests. The village was full of Germans who had gone to ground during our vigorous advance, but who, during our retreat, took shots at us. They were discovered and massacred by the Tirailleurs. The latter searched the houses, forced them out of their hiding places, from under beds and from inside wardrobes and cut their throats.[4]

Demoralized by the loss of their colonel, and outnumbered despite being reinforced by the Tirailleurs, the Zouaves were gradually forced back from house to house and eventually out of the village altogether, leaving behind many dead and over a hundred prisoners, most of whom were badly wounded. Likewise, on the north-western side of the village, the 350e RI was forced to retreat after suffering heavy losses. The Germans also suffered many casualties, including not only Oberstleutnant von Hering but also the brigade commander, General Mühlenfels. When the exhausted troops began to pull out of the village in the early hours of the morning, they passed several groups of stretcher-bearers going the other way to gather up the dead and wounded. Doctors Strack and Zeuch, who had survived their terrifying ordeal unscathed, also stayed behind to tend to the many casualties.

It was almost first light when the survivors reached Trocy, among them a group from RIR32 who carried the body of their beloved commander, Oberstleutnant von Hering. When they reached the village the rest of the regiment halted and, as the carrying party passed along their ranks, they spontaneously removed their helmets in homage. Less than 24 hours after having set out, they went over to rest in the same trenches they had left with such high hopes the previous morning. Except for the dead and wounded and the stretcher-bearers going about their mournful duty, Etrepilly was completely unoccupied for the second day running.

The mood at Kluck's Headquarters during the evening was still optimistic even though the intervention of IV Corps had not led to the expected victory. Early next morning III and IX Corps would arrive to continue the offensive, followed the day after by Lepel's Brigade from Brussels and by the Lines of Communication troops commanded by Oberst von der Schulenburg. On the other hand, the British were advancing into the gap between 1st and 2nd Armies faster than had been expected and had to be prevented from reaching the Marne crossing at Germigny before the reinforcements arrived. Unfortunately, Marwitz had sent the whole of the 9th Cavalry Division to the Marne bend at Trilport (not just part of it as Kluck had indicated), leaving only the 2nd Cavalry Division and the four Jäger Battalions to cover the vitally important bridges in and around La Ferté-sous-Jouarre. As a precautionary measure in case the British succeeded in crossing the river, Trossel's Battle Group was ordered to fall back a short distance to the east the next morning to a position which was bent back at a sharp angle to the centre. When the reinforcements arrived, they would be used to extend the line of the army to the north; III Corps would come in on the right of the 16th Infantry Brigade to the north of Antilly and IX Corps on the extreme right flank opposite Cuvergnon. As soon as they were in place they would advance and envelop the French left wing.

Maunoury was also hoping to go over to the offensive the next day when the 7th Division reached the battlefield from the Argonne front. (The 8th Division had already arrived but at Joffre's insistence had been sent to support the British left wing.) On the right, the Moroccan Brigade and the 45th Division were to remain on the defensive and wait for the British to bring pressure to bear on the German left wing. In the centre, the 56th Reserve Division was to make yet another attempt to capture the Trocy Plateau, this time with the help of a massive artillery bombardment from its own guns, those of the 55th Reserve Division and two groups of heavy artillery taken from the Paris defences. The main effort, however, would involve an attack on the German right wing to the north of the Gergogne by the 7th Division, supported on the right by the 61st Reserve Division, which would once more try to capture Montrolles Wood. When the enemy's resistance had been broken, the two divisions would cross the Ourcq between Crouy and Mareuil, swing southwards and open up the line of the river to the rest of the army. On the extreme left, Sordet's three cavalry divisions were to advance at dawn on to the Plateau of Cuvergnon to the north of Betz, cross the Ourcq and disrupt the enemy's lines of communication. Général Boëlle, the commander of the 7th Division, was placed in overall control of the operation.

The 7th Division, which was to spearhead the attack, had arrived late in Paris after a punishing journey crammed into goods wagons, which at times slowed to a walking pace due to traffic congestion and a derailment. They completed their disembarkation in the early hours of 7 September, two days later than planned, and went into billets in the eastern suburbs of the city. Maunoury was now faced with the difficult problem of getting them to Nanteuil in time to take part in the fighting the next morning. A forced march of over 30 miles, followed by an immediate battle, would have tested the mettle of fresh troops, let alone these ones, exhausted by 12 days of heavy fighting followed by the difficult three-day-long journey, cooped up in cattle trucks.[5] Fortunately, Galliéni came up with an inspired piece of improvisation. As early as 1 September he had begun to requisition all motorized transport including the capital's taxicabs, holding them ready day and night for military purposes. So far they had only been used within the fortified camp of Paris for transporting food and other materials to the outlying suburbs, but from now on their civilian drivers would be called upon to leave the capital altogether and ferry front-line troops to the battlefield. On the evening of 6 September he ordered all available taxis to assemble on the esplanade of Les Invalides, ready to transport at least 600 men to a secret destination. By 10.00pm, approximately 350 taxis were drawn up ready to depart, 200 or so from the permanent reserve together with 150 which had been stopped by the police in the streets and forced to abandon their passengers before proceeding to the assembly point.

When the convoy was ready, it left the city to the north-east and drove as far as Villeneuve-sur-Dammartin, where they were told to stop and await further orders. When dawn broke on 7 September, the taxis were drawn up in a long column, protected from the sun by the ubiquitous poplar trees along the sides of the road. By now their drivers were getting restless; they had spent a sleepless night at the wheel driving down unknown roads with dimmed headlamps, constantly afraid of colliding with the vehicle in front or being hit from behind and they had not been given anything to eat or drink. Furthermore, no one seemed to know where they were going or when they would be allowed to return home. When the sounds of gunfire were heard in the distance some of them became rebellious and said that they intended to return to Paris, army or no army. However, the sight of two splendid cavalry squadrons which passed by on their way to the front reassured the faint-hearted, while at the same time their mutinous colleagues were threatened with having their vehicles taken away from them. Peace was finally restored in the afternoon when the Director of Transport arrived from the Paris Garrison at the head of a column of vehicles carrying food, drink, petrol, spare tyres and mechanics. At 5.00pm the convoy set off once more, this time to pick up two battalions of the 104e RI, which it transported during the evening and night to the south of Nanteuil. Here they were joined by their other battalion, which had arrived from Paris by rail. Similarly, all three battalions of 103e RI were transported by a second convoy of taxis, approximately 700 strong, which left Paris on the morning of the 7th and reached the area of Nanteuil in the early hours of the next day.

This strange procession was encountered during the night by Paul Lintier, a gunner with one of the batteries that were advancing down the high road in the direction of Nanteuil-le-Haudouin. Lintier evocatively described the day's events from the moment his battery left Paris for the front as dusk was falling on the 6th:

> Just as the battery was starting, two girls, the sister and the fiancée of one of
> the gunners, hurried up. For a moment or two they ran, flushed and panting, by
> the side of the horses, both speaking rapidly and at the same time. When they
> were quite out of breath they held out their hands, one after the other, to the
> gunner, who leant down from the saddle and kissed their fingertips.

We passed through the suburbs and then, by the Soissons road, approached the plain of Brie. Evening fell. The battery had been on the march for more than ten hours without halting. Far away in the background Montmartre reared its black silhouette against the western sky. The fields were lit up by the stars, which were exceptionally brilliant, but the road remained dark under the vault of tall trees planted in double rows on either side, between which floated a suffocating cloud of dust. A distant searchlight was sweeping the plain. The battery broke into a trot on the paved road, and the vehicles jolted and bumped so that it was veritable torture to sit on them. Sharp internal pains made us twist as we clutched on to the limber boxes; our aching backs seemed no longer capable of sustaining our shoulders, and the breaths came in gasps from our shaken chests. Our hearts thumped against our ribs, our heads swam and we perspired with pain. Should we never stop?

Hour after hour, we followed the same dark road, but the column had again slowed down to a walk. The bright headlights of an approaching automobile suddenly threw the trees into vertiginous perspectives like the columns of some cathedral, and showed up the teams and drivers, as they emerged from the gloom in a grotesque procession of fantastic shadows. The motor passed.

On our return [from watering the horses] we found the road crowded with horses. Other batteries had just arrived. An eddy in the stream had just pushed me up against the garden wall of a château when a motor, showing no lights, forced its way through the herd of horses, throwing against me a confused mass of men and animals whose weight crushed me against the stone. Another car followed, then another, hundreds of them, silently and interminably. By the light of the moon, which had now risen, I was able to recognize the oilskin caps usually worn by taxi drivers. Inside the cabs I caught a glimpse of soldiers sleeping, their heads thrown back.

'Wounded?' asked somebody. 'No', came the answer from a passing car. 'It's the 7th Division from Paris. They're off to the front.'[6]

Thanks to Galliéni's foresight, by dawn on 8 September the whole of the 7th Division was within striking distance of the battlefield, in sufficient time and in reasonably good shape to take part in the planned offensive. Of the 12 battalions that made up the division, five had been transported by taxis and the other seven by rail.[7]

# 13

# NIGHT ATTACK

## 8 SEPTEMBER: THE NIGHT ATTACK BY THE GERMAN 2ND AND 3RD ARMIES

Hausen's decision to attack the French right wing before dawn on the 8th was forced on him because of the paralysing effect of the enemy artillery. Thus, after the French infantry had been taken by surprise and overwhelmed it was vitally important to push on as quickly as possible and capture their batteries. It was however a very risky business as General von Winkler, the commander of the 2nd Guards Infantry Division, recognized when he received the order:

> I cannot deny that I passed on the orders with a heavy heart. I completely welcomed the resolute decision and the arrangements for the pre-dawn attack which was the only means of eliminating the very sensitive effect that the enemy artillery had had on us during 6 and 7 September. However it was very clear to me that this order could also signify the destruction of my division.[1]

As with all night attacks, a great many things could go wrong; officers would find it difficult to keep their men under control and units could easily become disorientated, lose touch with their neighbours and fire on one another. For this reason, standing orders were to advance with rifles unloaded and fixed bayonets until it was light enough to see clearly. Also navigation through the scattered pinewoods would have to take place by the compass and not (as practised in peacetime) by equipping the advance guards with lanterns open at the rear so that

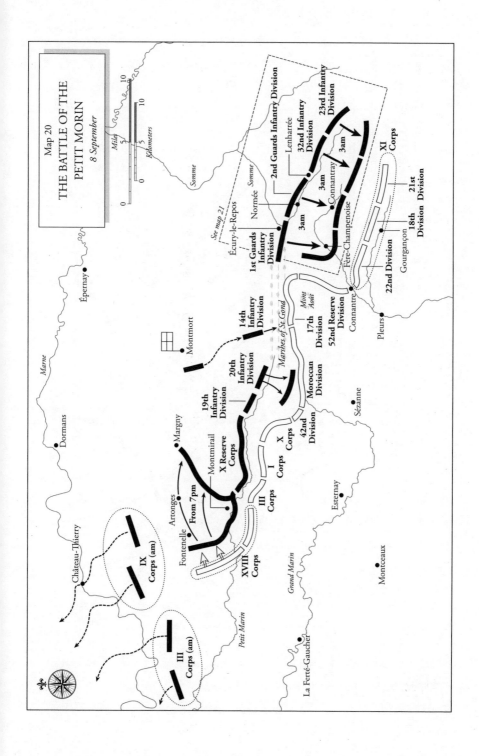

Map 20

THE BATTLE OF THE
PETIT MORIN
8 September

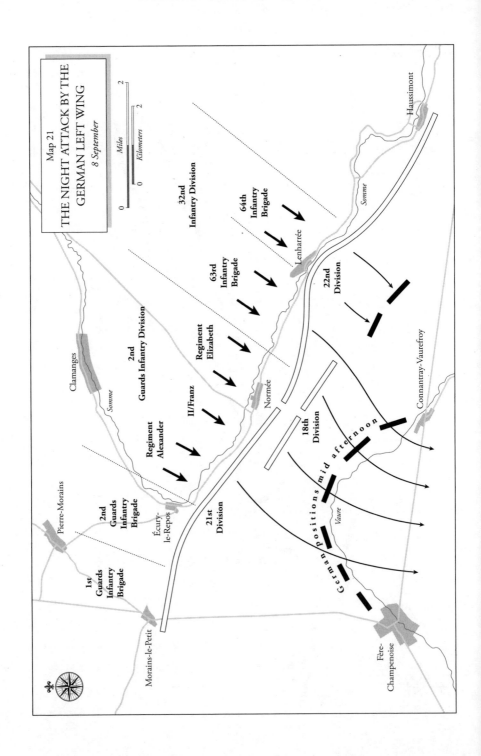

Map 21
THE NIGHT ATTACK BY THE
GERMAN LEFT WING
8 September

the main body could follow them. Furthermore, it was impossible to prepare properly for the attack because of the darkness and lack of time: several units received their orders at the last minute, headquarters could not always be found in the pitch darkness and in some cases messengers found all of the officers asleep and could only rouse them with great difficulty. Oberst von Roeder, for example, was fast asleep in a road ditch to the west of Normée, surrounded by his staff, when the order arrived.

> We were alone and lay down to sleep, wrapped in our capes among the sedge, when at approximately 3.30am we were woken up by a messenger from the 3rd Guards Infantry Brigade who had been fortunate in finding us in spite of the darkness. He brought the divisional order, a closely written carbon copy, smudged in many places, written down in a hurry and many sides in length. For illumination we had only a very feeble torch so deciphering it was hard work.[2]

Likewise, in another regiment, the adjutant was so exhausted that when the messenger left he immediately fell asleep again without having looked at the order. As a result, they only knew that the attack was taking place when they were woken by the noise of the neighbouring unit advancing towards the river.

These difficulties were of no consequence, however, because their opponents were in a shockingly poor condition and ill-prepared for the blow that was about to strike them. Morale in both the 21st and 22nd Divisions had plumbed new depths because of the continuing shortages of food and water and the prospect of being attacked for the third day in a row. Discipline was poor in many units, including the 65e RI, in which several of the men had left their bivouacs in the stiflingly hot pinewoods to the south of Morains the previous day and slipped away to the nearby town of Fère-Champenoise in search of water. Even the arrival of the 18th Division, which went into reserve at a point roughly midway behind the front line, did little to improve the situation. Firstly, it had only recently been cobbled together from different units (its two infantry brigades and both artillery groups were all from different divisions) and as a result communications between brigade and divisional staffs were poor. Secondly, several of the senior officers were of poor quality, including Général Jeannin, the commander of the 35th Brigade, who ordered his men to take up a position much too close to the front line. To make matters worse, he insisted that they must bivouac within the pinewoods even though this blocked their view and made them vulnerable to being taken by surprise. Amazingly, on the evening of the 7th the staffs of both the 21st and 22nd Divisions were unaware that they had been reinforced, even though Jeannin's Brigade had gone into bivouac within walking distance of them.

On the front of the 2nd Guards Infantry Division, the attack was carried out by Regiments Alexander and Elisabeth, supported by II/Franz. However, because of the numerous delays the only unit to advance on time was Regiment Alexander, which was on the extreme right of the division to the east of Ecury. At the given moment, the order was passed quietly down the line and they set off apprehensively up the gentle slopes leading to the first of the many strips of woodland to the south of the Ecury–Normée road, expecting at any moment to be hit by enemy fire. For a while all was quiet as they passed through one belt of woodland after another but as the dim light of dawn was starting to filter through the densely-planted trees they encountered the first French outposts and charged towards them with bugles blowing, drums beating and shouts of 'Hurrah'. Taken completely by surprise (their rifles were still stacked in pyramids), the French infantry leapt out of their trenches and fled for their lives. Oberleutnant von Viebahn described a scene that was repeated on numerous occasions during this initial phase of the attack:

> As we went over the moonlit hills, we expected artillery fire at any moment but all was still. I quietly whispered to the men what it was about. We entered the wood, a low, poorly growing pinewood; then a few shots rang out. Everything was still. And then suddenly there was a furious chattering sound with short pauses. The company ahead of us began to trot and we followed. 'Hurrah! Hurrah!' There were continuous shouts of 'Hurrah' on all sides. Furious rifle fire came from over there. That's the greatest thing you've ever experienced!
>
> Now we marched on and then once more broke into a trot, continuing to follow the 7th company in the darkness through the wood. Again and again we shouted 'Hurrah'; the drums were beating and the neighbouring companies also

roared 'Hurrah'. When they paused for a while we could hear in the distance the battle cry as two army corps attacked together, side by side. What a racket there was around us! Just past us and over us, infantry shots sang out, their cracks continuing to echo in the woods and the bullets smacking sharply into the trees. The light was becoming grey dawn light and the red glow of the morning. Forwards, again and again![3]

After pausing to load their rifles now that it was light enough to see clearly, the Germans rushed onwards and overran the French front line before they had time to respond to the cries of their outposts. Soon afterwards they reached the encampments of the second line where the enemy troops were leisurely preparing their morning coffee and overwhelmed them before they could react. When they reached the edge of the woods a short time later, they were presented with the unforgettable sight of thousands of French infantry streaming back in complete disorder across the open fields towards a railway embankment approximately half a mile away. At this point, as they emerged from the shelter of the woodland and set off in pursuit of the stricken troops, they came under fire from the French artillery and from stragglers who had concealed themselves in the dense undergrowth until the attack had passed by.

The shells were already falling so close to us that we didn't know which way to turn. The infantry bullets were smacking into the trees with a harsh sound and soon the first wounded were crying out. It was the bravery of our beloved company commander Hauptmann von Kalm and of Oberleutnant von Viebahn that kept up our spirits. As one, we all stormed forwards, through the zone of fire, in pursuit of the fleeing French. How our long coat-tails flew! Keep going at them; don't let them settle. We had to take the high ground in front of us. Very soon it was in our possession. However, in the valley below, we were presented with such a picture that I can remember it to this day. The tents had been put up and in them the French were still dreaming of *à Berlin* as our first bullets flew into their camp. They came out as if stung by a bee, ran to get their rifles, ran back into their tents again, came out once more, and were obviously stunned. Yes, indeed; how could we be so inconsiderate as to disturb their dreams?[4]

Despite coming under fire from several sides, and although units were badly intermingled after passing through the woodland in the darkness, the Germans pushed on and drove the completely demoralized French clean over the embankment and back towards Fère-Champenoise. In the space of less than two hours, Regiment Alexander had routed the enemy and had advanced approximately 3 miles, far more than had been achieved in the previous two days' fighting put together.

Approximately a quarter of an hour later than Regiment Alexander, II/Franz set off from its positions to the west of Normée with three companies in the front line, followed by the machine gun company whose guns had been muffled with cloths. By chance they struck the French 35th Brigade, which, as we have seen, had been foolishly pushed forwards until it was directly behind the 21st Division. Because of this, it did not have time to take defensive measures and was swept away at the same time as the front line.

The German advance was so rapid, and the surprise so complete, that there was considerable disruption to the French chain of command. Several headquarters staff had to flee to avoid capture (the commander of the 42nd Brigade escaped only by hiding in a culvert at the side of the road) and many messengers failed to return, having either been killed or carried away in the general rout. In the 18th Division the chaos was so great that its commander lost touch with both of his brigades and was forced to send out his Chief of Staff in one car, and a staff officer in another, to search for them! The former tracked down the 34th Brigade to the north of Connantray, but was then cut off and only made his way back after a nerve-racking detour which lasted several hours. The staff officer in the other car, Capitaine Zehrfuss, was not so fortunate, however, since when his car was part way along the Fère-Champenoise–Normée road, it came under fire from a German detachment belonging to Regiment Alexander and Zehrfuss, his driver and his two companions were all killed. One of the riflemen involved was Fusilier Amrhein of the 12th Company:

An enemy car, which had been under heavy fire from further to the left, was speeding along the road to Fère-Champenoise. We too fired at it. Suddenly it swerved off the road and into the field where it came to a halt next to a stream. Gefreiter Riemann and I charged towards it but came under heavy fire. We took up a position in the road ditch and fired on the occupants. Their firing soon stopped and so we went there. The driver was wounded. An officer was sitting in the car, apparently a general from his gold-embroidered képi, dead from several head wounds. Beside him was another officer, hit in the head and chest, likewise dead. Both of them had valuable maps and papers on them, which we removed and afterwards handed over to the staff of the 3rd Guards Infantry Brigade.[5]

The last unit to advance, an hour later than the rest, was Regiment Elisabeth which left its position at Normée and attacked the enemy outposts in the woods beyond the river. By this time, however, the French had been alerted by the noise of gunfire to the west and put up a brief resistance before they too were overwhelmed and forced to abandon their defensive lines in the woods and along the rail embankment to the south. Thus, by 9.00am, when the fighting died down and the exhausted German infantry came to a halt, the 2nd Guards Infantry Division had advanced as far as the river Vaure, which at this point describes a broad northerly arc between Fère-Champenoise in the west and Connantray in the east. On their right, the 1st Guards Division had advanced as far as the northern suburbs of Fère-Champenoise, which they captured later in the day.

Meanwhile, in the sector occupied by the 32nd Infantry Division (on the right wing of 3rd Army), the 64th Infantry Brigade had orders to capture Lenharrée while the 63rd Brigade bypassed the village to the west. After an initial delay while they crossed the river (in the absence of bridges they were forced to wade through with the water up to their chests), the 63rd Brigade advanced rapidly and forced the French to retreat to a new defensive position behind the rail embankment on the far side of the woods. On their left, however, the 64th Brigade was strongly opposed by four French battalions at Lenharrée, two in the village itself and two more at the southern exits where they guarded the bridge over the river. Although the defenders were considerably outnumbered, they had fortified the houses and outbuildings, barricaded the ends of the streets with farm carts and machinery and had turned the church, which was on a small rise at the centre of the village, into a strong point.

Hauptmann Kruspe of IR177 described the situation as the Germans approached the village in complete silence, hoping to take the French by surprise:

A solemn mood had seized the troops. In front of us, at a distance of about one and a half kilometres was the burning village of Lenharrée, above us the star-studded sky. Deathly quiet. It was 3.45am. March! The tempo, calm at first, accelerated more and more. Three quarters of the path must have been behind us when the first salvos chattered out on our right. A thousand-voiced hurrah immediately spread out among us. The tempo was getting faster and faster; we sprang over trenches whose occupants had ducked deeper into them after hearing the first shots and surprised by all these wild shouts of 'hurrah'.[6]

Alerted by the sound of firing from their outposts, the French battalions were ready and waiting when the Germans arrived in the northern suburbs and headed towards the area around the church. For the next one and a half hours the battle raged within the narrow village streets and in particular in the open space which surrounded the church. Most of the defenders remained hidden from view in the houses and in the church and directed their fire from windows and rooftops, while the more intrepid spirits climbed the tall poplar trees which lined the village streets and, balancing precariously among the branches, fired from there. Gradually, as more and more Germans entered the village (at the height of the battle it contained approximately 5,000 German and 2,000 French troops), they established fire supremacy and slowly drove the French back from the area around the church and the cemetery, where the fighting was at its most intense. The battle came to an end in the late afternoon when the Germans took control of this area and other units worked their way around the village, threatening to capture the bridge and trap the defenders in what was by now a complete ruin. After they had regrouped, the Germans advanced towards the rail embankment where the French were trying to establish a new firing line, causing them to abandon the attempt abruptly and retreat out of sight over the hills in the direction of Connantray. When an attempt to pursue them failed because of heavy shellfire, the brigade was ordered to halt and rest.

The German offensive gradually petered out in the early afternoon because of exhaustion and enemy shellfire. The French 21st Division, which had borne the brunt of the initial attack, had come off very badly including the loss of one of its brigadiers and two regimental commanders, and in the 18th Division the

35th Brigade had more or less been destroyed. However, although the Germans had taken the French completely by surprise and had advanced very quickly, they captured far fewer batteries than they had hoped, principally because the 18th Division had located its artillery well to the rear. During the afternoon the French fell back a little further to a more secure position on the high ground to the north of the River Maurienne, from Connantray in the west to Montepreux in the east. Their left wing was protected by the 52nd Reserve Division, which linked up with IX Corps at Mont Août, and their right by the 60th Reserve Division in the vicinity of Mailly. At Foch's insistence, an attack was made in the direction of Fère-Champenoise by the 52nd Reserve Division, but because of poor communications it began only as dusk was falling and after advancing very tentatively the troops immediately turned tail when they came under fire.

Elsewhere, events did not go as well for the Germans, particularly on the extreme right wing where the 13th Infantry Division was strongly attacked by the French XVIII Corps in the vicinity of Montmirail. Although the French 35th Division was prevented from capturing the town by the extremely powerful German heavy artillery, the 36th Division outflanked it from the west, crossed the Petit Morin unopposed, and by the middle of the afternoon had reached the enemy positions on the high ground between Marchais and Hill 207, close to the crossroads formed by the Paris and Château-Thierry high roads. The outnumbered Germans defended well for several hours, making full use of their machine guns and heavy artillery, but after a series of violent attacks and counter-attacks, the French captured the wooded crest which dominates Marchais from the west, forcing the German batteries to retreat in order to avoid capture. As the sun began to sink below the horizon and the thunderclouds gathered, first one infantry unit and then another broke and fled, leaving a gap in the centre of the line into which the French penetrated, setting in motion a general retreat. When General von dem Borne became aware of this, he gave orders to retreat during the night to a new position at Artonges and then further back still to Margny, approximately 8 miles to the north-east of Montmirail. As a result, their line was now bent back at an even sharper angle than before to X Reserve Corps, which had easily held on to the high ground to the north of the Petit Morin despite being heavily attacked by both I and III Corps.

Results were more mixed in the centre, where Bülow had ordered X Corps and the 14th Infantry Division to support the offensive by the Guard Corps. On the right, Emmich seized the opportunity to retake the territory he had been forced to abandon the previous evening and ordered the 20th Infantry Division once more to capture Soizy-aux-Bois and the Poirier Crest. Fortunately for them, the French offensive, which had been postponed from the previous evening, was called off at the last moment because the 77e RI was recalled to Mont Août where it was urgently needed to prevent a breakthrough on the right wing. The Moroccans made a last despairing attempt to retake the Poirier Crest but were once again thrown back with heavy losses and, as darkness fell, the survivors retreated to the high ground at Mondement-Montgivroux where a last-ditch defensive position had been prepared.

Further east, General von Fleck's 14th Infantry Division spent the whole day attempting in vain to cross the marshes. Since patrols had established that the crossing between Coizard and Bannes was opposed by a large enemy force, the only available road was the one which led southwards from Joches, crossed the first strip of marsh to a shallow rise (Hill 154), and then split in two before continuing across the main part of the marsh to Broussy-le-petit and Broussy-le-Grand. Their task was enormously difficult because the road would be swept by French shellfire, the marshes on either side were impassable and there was not the slightest bit of cover. The French had prepared for the attack by constructing a series of trenches terrace-wise in a shallow arc along the forward face of Hill 154, approximately half a mile to the south of Joches. For the next five hours, despite feeding unit after unit into what was an increasingly congested firing line, the Germans remained pinned down by a hail of shellfire and by machine-gun fire from the trenches, which were occupied by a single company of Zouaves. In the early afternoon, as the pressure of numbers finally began to tell, the Moroccans suddenly abandoned their trenches and retreated to new ones several hundred yards away and continued the fight. A few hours later, in a desperate attempt to break through before darkness fell, the Germans brought forward a field artillery group at the gallop down the narrow road from Joches, which unlimbered immediately behind the front line and opened fire, forcing the French to retreat. However, rather than pursuing them across the marshes

Fleck ordered his men to remain where they were, in the captured positions, because he was afraid that his flanks would be exposed if he advanced any further.

At nightfall, the Germans bivouacked where they were, at Soizy, Oyes, along the Poirier Crest and on Hill 154, while the Moroccans fell back towards the Mondement-Montgivroux ridge which they were ordered to hold on to whatever the cost. After three days of violent and almost unceasing combat Humbert's men were in an atrocious condition with more than 50 per cent casualties in most units. In Modelon's Battalion, for example, there were so few survivors that they were reformed into two companies and when the roll was called in de Ligny's battalion only 242 men out of the original 1,000 or so answered their names. From the company of Zouaves who had valiantly defended Hill 154 all day against the whole of the German 14th Infantry Division only 17 of them, under the command of Sergent Pendon, made it back unharmed to join the rest of the battalion.

Capitaine Canonge, who as one of Humbert's staff officers spent these days traversing the battlefield with orders, was an eloquent witness to the hardships endured by the Moroccan soldiers and NCOs and their French officers:

> Sometimes one saw scattered groups which no longer had the appearance of organized units. The bravest of the surviving officers took charge and once more led them into battle. I think of the Tirailleurs of Group Lucas-Bellini, which must have belonged to several companies and which formed itself around these two Lieutenants and continued fighting to the end. [There was] Blondlat with his Colonials and Zouaves, Lagrue, in rags, with his képi ripped by a bullet, Fellert, who failed to return, Colonel Ducrot and his artillerymen. And one can recall a word, a look, a moment, a critical instant and a confidence, or a silence or a vigorous sortie, in response to the transmission of a message or an order.[7]

For reasons which are no longer clear, in the early evening Bülow received a report which erroneously stated that the inner wings of X Corps and X Reserve Corps had been forced apart, opening up a gap into which the enemy could penetrate and split the army in two. Instead of waiting for the news to be confirmed, the somewhat shaken army commander impetuously rushed off to the front line to see what was happening. According to General von Einem:

There were serious faces at army headquarters, everyone was deeply alarmed. The enemy seemed to have broken through on the front of X Corps... Bülow asked me to accompany him to Champaubert. [When we got there] Bülow went forward with some of his men, leaving me behind. Very soon he returned, laughing and in the best possible mood, there had been no breakthrough, the enemy had been bloodily forced back and all was glorious![8]

With his confidence fully restored, Bülow returned to his headquarters in the magnificent Renaissance Château of Montmort in a thoroughly ebullient mood. Much to his surprise, he was met by Hentsch, who had just arrived from Luxembourg accompanied by two staff officers, Hauptmann König and Hauptmann Koeppen. To understand the reasons for this visit we must briefly look back at events at OHL during the previous two days. The first news that the right wing had been attacked was contained in Kluck's and Bülow's situation reports for 6 September, which reached OHL the following day. In neither case did there appear to be serious cause for concern. According to Bülow, 2nd Army was in indecisive combat with enemy forces advancing from the direction of Esternay, Sézanne and Fère-Champenoise; support from 3rd Army was weak and reinforcements would be needed to achieve a decisive outcome. Kluck said that 'II and IV Reserve Corps are in hard combat to the south-west of Crouy against a strong enemy coming from the direction of Paris. Tomorrow IV Active Corps will intervene here. To the west of Montmirail III and IX Corps cover the flank of 2nd Army.'[9] However, the next morning, 8 September, several reports arrived which indicated that the situation on the right wing was far more serious than they had previously believed. Firstly, in his situation report for the 7th, Bülow claimed that because of losses during the campaign the strength of 2nd Army was now equivalent to that of only three corps! On the face of it, Kluck's report was more positive:

Combat of II and IV Reserve Corps has made progress through the intervention of IV Corps on the right wing towards the line Nanteuil–Meaux. III and IX Corps are on the march towards the battlefield. The attack will be continued tomorrow with the prospect of success. The Cavalry Corps covers the region of Coulommiers where no important enemy forces are advancing.[10]

However, if the prospects for victory were so good, why were III and IX Corps so urgently needed? Could it be that the fighting was not going as well as Kluck was making out? In addition, their withdrawal would not only uncover Bülow's right wing but would also increase the already sizeable gap between the two armies, which was protected only by the two cavalry corps. As Moltke was considering this, his worst fears were confirmed by the arrival of an interrupted radio message from Richthofen to Bülow saying that the British had crossed the Petit Morin and that he had therefore been forced to fall back behind the River Dolloir. Kluck's assurances that the British had not yet reached the area of Coulommiers were now superfluous; further east, they were across the Petit Morin and only the line of the Marne now stood between them and the rear of the two German armies.

Towards the end of the morning, Moltke had a meeting with Tappen, Dommes and Hentsch to decide what could be done to protect the right wing until it was reinforced by Heeringen's new 7th Army. Opinions were divided from the start. Whereas Moltke and Hentsch firmly believed that the situation of 1st and 2nd Armies was untenable, given the fact that they were outnumbered and that the gap between them was very wide and inadequately protected, Dommes and Tappen took a much more positive view, basing their arguments on Kluck's confident tone and his expectations of victory. Admittedly, the gap was large but the British had not yet crossed the Marne, which would prove a formidable obstacle if well defended by the two cavalry corps. If Kluck was successful, the French would be thrown back towards Paris and the British would also be forced to retreat, allowing 1st and 2nd Armies to move together and close the gap between them. What was needed at this critical juncture was unshakable confidence in the morale and fighting power of the troops; to deny this would lead to victory being thrown away at the last moment. Swayed by their arguments, Moltke agreed to wait and see how events developed before taking a definite decision. In the meantime, in order to make his views known to Kluck and Bülow, and to get a clearer picture of the situation on the right wing, Hentsch would go and see them without delay.[11]

In mid-morning Hentsch set out on his fateful journey, accompanied by König and Koeppen. In case they broke down on the way they took two cars, Hentsch and König in one and Koeppen in the other. König later recollected that his fellow passenger was in good physical shape during the journey and seemed to show no after-effects from the gall bladder trouble which had affected him only a few weeks before (and whose recurrence in 1918 led to his death, following an operation). On the other hand he appeared to be in low spirits throughout the journey and said that the task should have been given to a more senior colleague such as Dommes or Stein, or failing that at least to someone from the Operations Department who was more familiar with the situation. On several occasions he lamented the lack of written orders and said that if there were misunderstandings and things turned out badly he would be blamed. In addition, he did not share the rosy view held by Tappen and Dommes. 'Oberstleutnant Hentsch himself considered the position of the German armies to be serious and was of the opinion that it would be necessary for the right wing to retreat.'[12]

On their way to the right wing they stopped successively at the headquarters of 5th, 4th and 3rd Armies to check on the latest turn of events. The situation on the fronts of 5th and 4th Armies was very favourable; both were in the middle of an offensive which was going well and which seemed likely to end in victory in the next few days. Likewise, when they arrived at 3rd Army Headquarters in the late afternoon, they were told by Hausen's Chief of Staff that the attack was making excellent progress but that the right wing of 2nd Army had got into difficulties and was threatened with envelopment. Before he left, Hentsch made a very brief addition to 3rd Army's situation report, merely saying that the situation and view of 3rd Army was thoroughly favourable.

When they arrived at 2nd Army Headquarters at Montmort in the early evening they were disconcerted to find that Bülow was absent and that the headquarters staff were frantically packing up because, so they said, enemy units had broken through in the centre and were advancing in their direction! Not long afterwards, however, an order arrived countermanding the move and this was followed shortly afterwards by the arrival of Bülow himself, with news that the breakthrough had been an illusion. Hentsch explained his presence by saying that 'he had been sent from the Supreme Command to become acquainted with the situation from the Army's High Command and to bring their further steps into agreement with the views of the Supreme Command.'[13] After a short conversation, during which Hentsch and his two companions received a very favourable impression of Bülow, the latter gave his apologies and retired to his quarters for a while, leaving them with his Chief of Staff, General von Lauenstein and with Oberstleutnant Matthes, his other senior staff officer. While Matthes got on with some work in an outer room, Lauenstein took Hentsch into his office and rapidly brought him up to date with the latest situation. When Lauenstein returned to the workroom, he told Matthes that:

> he had just learnt from Hentsch that the situation of 1st Army was much more serious than they had previously been led to believe and that according to Hentsch it might not be able to turn away the French advance from the direction of Paris nor to prevent the enemy from penetrating into the gap between 1st and 2nd Armies. In the opinion of the Supreme Command circumstances might arise which would mean taking into account the possibility of having to retreat behind the Marne… In reply, Oberstleutnant Hentsch said that if the enemy broke through in strength between 1st and 2nd Armies then no other course of action remained. He added that the Supreme Command held the view that a punctual and voluntary retreat of the right wing of the armies would be not nearly as fatal as the enemy breaking through, taking 1st Army in the rear and completely wiping it out. If this were to happen, then naturally all of the other armies would be forced to retreat.[14]

After Lauenstein had briefly acquainted Bülow with what had been said, a meeting took place in the Chief of Staff's office involving Hentsch, Bülow, Lauenstein, Matthes, König and Koeppen.[15] Bülow began by giving them a pessimistic view of 2nd Army's condition. The campaign, he said, had taken a heavy toll on his men and as a result the army's strength was greatly diminished. He then followed this up with the exaggerated claim that it had been burnt almost to a cinder. He remained confident in the morale of his troops and in their fighting capabilities but in his opinion the army was no longer strong enough to bring about a resounding victory.[16] Moving on, he painted a detailed picture of the latest situation, according to which the right wing was under pressure but holding fast in a defensive position in the area of Montmirail, and the left wing was making good progress in the offensive which had begun before dawn. Casting aside professional etiquette, he then launched into an attack on the recent decisions that had been taken by Kluck and Kuhl. In his view 1st Army was in an untenable situation, for which they had only themselves to blame. They should never have been drawn into fighting a battle in front of Paris in the first place since the French could use their extensive rail network to bring up reinforcements rapidly and, if defeated, could retreat into the fortified camp around the city. In addition, the decision to withdraw III and IX Corps from 2nd Army control had not only placed his own right wing in a dangerous situation but had increased the gap between the two armies just as the British were advancing towards it. He added that four large enemy columns, each approximately a division in strength, had been seen on the march directly towards the gap and there could be no guarantee that the two cavalry corps were strong enough to turn them away.

Next, Hentsch voiced Moltke's concerns about the situation on the right wing, and added that he had been granted full powers by the latter to order a retreat should this prove necessary. In reply, Bülow observed that although the danger of an enemy breakthrough was certainly present, it had not yet happened. Instead of both armies retreating, as Hentsch seemed to think was necessary, he proposed that 2nd Army should stay where it was for the moment, and continue to attack with its left wing, while 1st Army disengaged and moved towards them, thereby filling the gap. Since the British were advancing quite slowly into the gap this was achievable, providing that it took place without delay. To lend greater weight to his suggestion, Bülow went over to a large-scale map that was hanging on the wall and repeatedly pointed with his finger to the line La Ferté Milon–Château-Thierry (ie the defensive line facing Paris, which Kluck had been told to occupy in Moltke's order of 5 September.) Hentsch, however, was not impressed by this argument. He questioned whether 1st Army would be able to complete the movement before the British crossed the Marne and attacked them in the flank or rear. If 1st Army was in serious difficulties, as all of the participants agreed, then surely the safest option would be for *both* armies to disengage and retreat along convergent lines so as to eliminate the gap. He reminded Bülow that he was as much at risk as Kluck since if the British penetrated the gap they could easily swing eastwards and take 2nd Army in the rear rather than turning westwards against 1st Army. He said that in the opinion of OHL, the only way to avoid this catastrophe was for a voluntary retreat before it was too late. Once more, he suggested that the best option was for both armies to disengage immediately and retreat towards the north-east in such a way as bring together their inner wings. He repeated that Moltke had granted him full powers to order a retreat if it appeared necessary.

Having reached an impasse, the two sides finally agreed on a compromise. As long as the British had not crossed the Marne, 2nd Army would remain where it was and continue to attack with the left wing in the hope of achieving victory. However, if the British crossed the river in force, they would immediately disengage and fall back in the direction of Fismes where they would make contact with 1st Army. In the meantime, Hentsch would drive to 1st Army Headquarters and then send Koeppen back to Montmort with the latest news. When the meeting came to an end Hentsch sent off the following radio message to OHL: 'Situation of 2nd Army is serious but not without hope.' And that was all. No attempt was made to give a detailed picture of the situation or even the briefest outline of what had been decided.

During the subsequent meal, Hentsch appeared dejected by the seriousness of the situation and seems to have cast a pall of gloom over his fellow diners. According to Prince August Wilhelm of Prussia, 'he made a very serious, almost gloomy impression which undoubtedly had a strong influence on the usually cheerful character of the army commander. There was a generally depressed mood at the table.'[17] In the opinion of Matthes, Hentsch 'was mentally speaking, suffering very badly from the task which he had been given'.[18] At the end of the meal, Hentsch said farewell to Bülow, whom he would not see again before he departed for Kluck's headquarters later that evening.

Foch spent the day at his command post at Pleurs, from where he could hear the sounds of gunfire all along the front. In the evening, after he had returned to his headquarters, he sent off a surprisingly optimistic account of the situation to GQG in which he said that his army had withstood the principal shock for the second day running and that 'the general situation is therefore excellent, the attack directed against 9th Army appears to be the means by which the Germans can assure the retreat of their right wing'.[19] However much he may have dressed up the events of the day for consumption at GQG, the truth of the matter was that his army was in a desperate situation. Firstly, XI Corps was certain to be attacked again the next morning and would have to swing back to the south, pivoting on their left wing, to avoid envelopment. Worse still, if the Germans launched an attack from Fère-Champenoise, which they had captured the previous day, they might sever the link between IX and XI Corps, cutting off the latter from the rest of the army and bringing about its destruction. The attempt to recapture the town the previous evening had failed miserably and would have to be repeated the next day if a crisis was to be overcome. Secondly, in the centre, after three days of violent combat, the Moroccan Division had finally lost control of the Poirier Crest and the marshes and had fallen back to a last line of defence along the Mondement–Allemant Crest. If, in their exhausted and weakened state, they were forced off the high ground, the enemy would split the army in two, bringing about a general retreat.

What was needed was a substantial mobile reserve that could shore up whichever part of the front came under the greatest pressure, either on the right or in the centre. Initially, Foch chose the 18th Division for this task but changed his mind when he discovered that what was left of Jeannin's Brigade was no longer battle-worthy after its rough treatment earlier that day. Since he had no substantial reserves of his own with which to carry out this task, he telephoned Franchet d'Esperey and asked for his support. Without hesitation, and without seeking Joffre's permission, the latter immediately placed the 19th and 20th Divisions at Foch's disposal together with X Corps Artillery. (The remaining division in X Corps, the 51st Reserve Division, would be temporarily transferred to I Corps.) The idea was for the two divisions to extend their line to the east and relieve the 42nd Division in the sector opposite Villeneuve and Soizy-aux-Bois, leaving the latter free to act as Foch's mobile reserve. When the handover was complete, it would march eastwards, behind the Montgivroux-Mondement–Allemant Crest, and go into reserve behind the army's centre. If the 21st Division could hold on to Fère-Champenoise with their support for the next few days, and if the Moroccans could prevent the enemy from breaking through in the centre along the ridge, there would be time for 5th Army to achieve victory against the German right wing; if instead, the Germans broke through in the centre, the French line would be split in two and they would probably be defeated.

# 14

# STALEMATE ON THE OURCQ

## 8 SEPTEMBER

From Acy in the north to Etrepilly in the south, the German centre was the scene of an enormous artillery duel that lasted all morning and well into the afternoon. On the French side the massed batteries of the 55th and 56th Reserve Divisions, together with several heavy-calibre cannon from the Paris garrison, fired from well-concealed positions to the north of Marcilly; on the German side, the batteries of IV Reserve Corps and IV Corps were in a long gun line just behind the crest of the Trocy Plateau, supported by II Corps heavy artillery in the low-lying area within the Marne bend to the east of Varreddes. Apart from the fact that the French were handicapped by a lack of forward artillery observers, the two sides were reasonably well matched and neither was able to land a knockout blow. At about 7.00am Trossel gave the order for his 3rd Infantry Division to fall back about 3 miles to a new a position to the north of Congis, which meant that from now on the German left wing would face to the south-west, bent back at a sharp angle to the centre to which it was connected at Etrepilly. At nightfall, following news that the British were approaching Germigny, he ordered the bridges in his sector to be destroyed and the right hand brigade to move a little closer to the river so that if necessary it could bring the opposite bank under fire.

In the middle of the morning the bombardment increased in intensity, especially on the front of the 44th Reserve Infantry Brigade, which had not

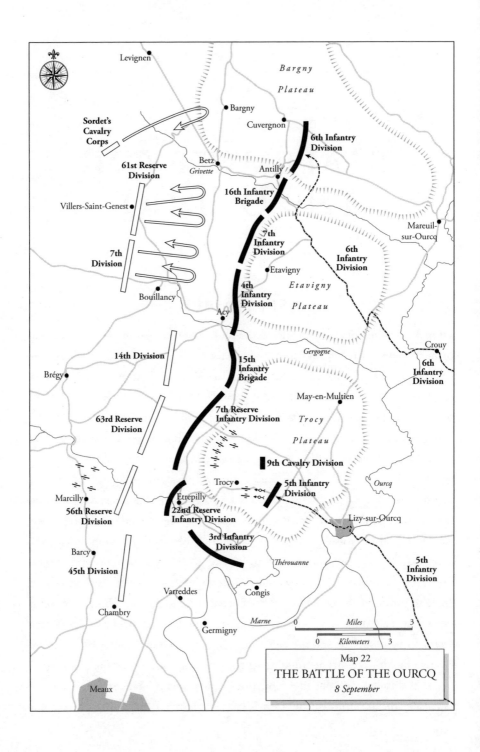

Map 22

THE BATTLE OF THE OURCQ

*8 September*

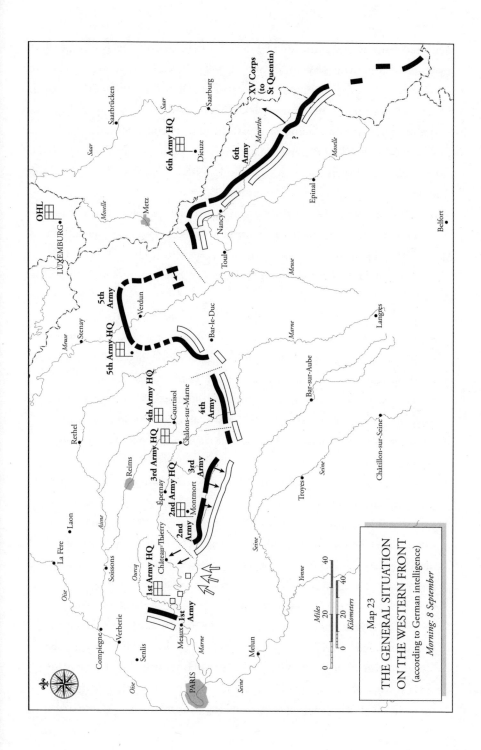

Map 23

THE GENERAL SITUATION
ON THE WESTERN FRONT
(according to German intelligence)
*Morning: 8 September*

recovered from its ordeal in Etrepilly during the night and which was guarding the sensitive point where the road from the village ascended to the Trocy Plateau. As they fixed bayonets in anticipation of an attack, behind them Trocy was in flames and swarming with panic-stricken figures rushing this way and that to escape the shells and the falling masonry. An officer who was searching for the headquarters of the 22nd Reserve Infantry Division found General von Riemann and his staff standing behind a haystack only a hundred yards or so behind the front line, carrying rifles with bayonets fixed![1]

The German batteries on the nearby plateau also suffered badly from the bombardment. The worst damage occurred to the 4th Battery of the 75th Field Artillery Regiment, which lost five out of its six guns to enemy fire. Leutnant Richter described the situation from the moment when he took over command of the 6th Battery:

Hurriedly, I proceeded to the barn, reported to the major and went off with the rangefinder NCO behind the observation wagon, which, disguised with straw, nestled up against the right hand end of the barn. We had scarcely reached it before the familiar whining and whistling began as the enemy's morning greeting exploded over our heads, close to my battery. Since I could only observe the landmarks to the right of the road through the rangefinder, while our actual target was the area to its left around Etrepilly, we left our protective cover and were about to move behind one of the two haystacks which were still standing, just as another salvo burst right in front of the barn, churning up the ground very close to us with large searing shell splinters. Now it was a matter of waiting for the right moment to reach the haystack from the barn. We rushed back, crossed the path where lay the 5th battery signallers whose telephone lines had already been shot through: one quick and mighty leap and we were behind the haystack, but in the next moment a shell burst over the path which we had just left. There was a terrible roaring and calls of 'just kill me' rang out on the path to our left. We peeped out from behind the haystack and saw how one of the gunners had had the whole of his behind torn off by the first shell burst. We turned away, horrified, waiting for the next group of the black devils to arrive and, as we had convinced ourselves that the terrain on the left could not be observed any better from behind or next to the haystack, we leapt back to the barn. We had scarcely reached it when four more shells burst above us. It seemed to be getting even worse than yesterday!

... A few minutes later the first shells from our 6th battery burst over the houses of Etrepilly. The 5th Battery and also the 4th targeted enemy artillery which they thought they had spotted to the left of the village. Over us there buzzed shells from the batteries of the 22nd Reserve Artillery Regiment and close by on our right there was the long drawn out whistling noise of the shots from our heavy artillery. I had just discovered troop movements on the road which led from Etrepilly towards Trocy, when howling shells flew over us on our left, causing us to duck our heads involuntarily. And there, at the left end of the 4th Battery, there was a mixture of smoke, metal, parts of human bodies and screaming. We were seized with horror. As the smoke cleared, we saw the wreckage of both of the left wing guns and behind them a tangled ball of writhing human bodies. Horrible cries split the air. Then all was silent. And soon afterwards the telephone reported that all of the officers and men belonging to the two guns were either dead or seriously wounded and that the cannons themselves had been badly damaged. What an amazing stroke of fate! If I hadn't been given command of the 6th Battery early this morning, only a few hours ago, I too would have been a casualty, with no hope of survival.[2]

For the rest of the day, the three batteries remained in their firing positions adjacent to Trocy, trading shots with the French artillery and helping to prevent an attack from the direction of Marcilly by the 56th Reserve Division. In the early evening, as Richter was returning from taking a message to the brigade commander in Trocy, the 4th Battery was hit once more, knocking out two of the four remaining guns and killing and wounding several men. Not long afterwards, as dusk was falling, a further gun was destroyed leaving only one intact from the original six.

During the morning, Linsingen was preoccupied with how to prevent the French from breaking through in the centre before III and IX Corps arrived to take part in the offensive on the right wing. A request for help to Trossel and to Sixt von Arnim met with a mixed response; the former replied that he was under attack himself and did not have a man to spare, whereas the latter promised to send two battalions from the relatively quiet sector at Betz but added that it would take them at least four hours to get there. Next, Linsingen ordered Marwitz to move the 9th Cavalry Division to Lizy-sur-Ourcq from where, if the situation deteriorated any further, it could cross the river and come to Gronau's aid. Thirdly, a message was sent to 1st Army Headquarters with news of the perilous situation and asking for reinforcements. (The phrase 'Help urgently necessary through Lizy' was underlined twice.) Unknown to Linsingen, however, Kluck had already taken measure to strengthen the centre by ordering the 5th Infantry Division, which had crossed the Marne at La Ferté-sous-Jouarre at dawn, to divert to Lizy-sur-Ourcq from where it was only a short distance to the battlefield. The 6th Infantry Division, which was the right hand march-column, was to continue northwards as planned and go into action on the right wing at Antilly the moment it arrived. In the meantime, the 9th Cavalry Division had crossed the river at Lizy-sur-Ourcq and had advanced as far as the ravine on the eastern outskirts of Trocy from where it was prepared, if necessary, to charge any enemy units which set foot on the plateau, allowing Gronau's infantry to disengage and escape over the Ourcq.

In the event, it was not their cavalry which got the Germans out of trouble but the timely arrival of III Corps Artillery, which reached Trocy about 9.00am just as the French were about to attack. Throwing up a whirling dust cloud, the howitzers arrived at the trot and rapidly unlimbered, surrounded by burning farm carts and ammunition wagons belonging to neighbouring field artillery batteries. Within moments, they were given the enemy positions by an observation officer from one of these batteries, lent extra telephone wires by another, and shortly afterwards opened fire on the French artillery to the north of Marcilly. In addition to their own observation, they were helped to locate the French batteries by two spotter planes, which flew from a temporary airstrip adjacent to Linsingen's headquarters. (According to accounts written at the time, in addition to dropping written messages the observers used flash lamps to signal over and under to the gunners and the pilots moved their planes from side to side to indicate lateral corrections.) Indeed, so effective was this co-operation between the two sets of observers, those on the ground and the others in the air, that within less than an hour the French batteries were forced to cease fire and fall back out of range, bringing the attack to an end.

At approximately the same time, the head of the 5th Infantry Division reached the high ground to the east of the Ourcq valley from where they could hear the noise of the battle ahead of them.

[The report of the fighting] was confirmed by the rumbling thunder of battle that was getting louder and louder ahead of us. Forwards, then! On, on into it! Once again the tired-out bones, the aching feet, and worn-out boots had to give all that was left of them.

The fusiliers in front had already crossed the top of the hill that separated us from the Ourcq valley and one of them, Hauptmann von Freyhold, rode back to me, the leading company. 'Look out Bloem, when you get to the top! You'll see something!' In the foreground was a deep valley, the further slope rising up to a rolling plateau covered with small woods and villages. At the back was a long ridge of hills that rose up like the wall of a gigantic fortress, and along the whole length of this horizon lay a thick, motionless layer of mist several miles in length. Sudden flashes, like lightning, and columns of white smoke continually shot up through and beyond it. 'Some artillery position, eh?' said Freyhold, who had come up with me.

Our artillery began to arrive, rattling and clattering past us. First the light field guns and then the heavies, their great horses pounding on streaming with sweat, their muscles standing out like cords of steel. And we continued our march down into the valley of the Ourcq, and through the town of Lizy. A crowd of wounded and prisoners streamed past without end. We were now close to the battlefield, the noise of it drowning all other sound, and began to ascend the further slope of the valley. Here we deployed and halted, awaiting the final order for the advance.[3]

After four days of remorseless combat, Gronau's troops had reached the limit of their physical and mental strength. In addition to suffering from lack of sleep, they were hungry and extremely thirsty. Once the immediate threat of an attack was over some units received a little water and a few of the more resourceful men managed to scrounge some food, although in most cases there was only enough for a small morsel each. (In one battalion there were only four loaves of bread for each company, hardly sufficient for one bite per man, while in another company one soldier said that at nightfall someone appeared with half a loaf of bread, which they shared between the 14 of them.) When darkness fell, the 5th Infantry Division was sent forward to relieve the worst affected units. Hauptmann Bloem described the awful scene which awaited them as they entered Trocy on the way to replacing the 44th Reserve Infantry Brigade:

> As darkness drew on the roar of battle suddenly ceased after a final mad burst of firing, a usual custom apparently, and soon afterwards we were ordered forward to relieve the remnants of the 44th Reserve Brigade (the 32nd and 82nd Regiments) in the front line. We marched on across the hollow, and then up the hill into the village, which was now gradually crumbling away and burning into a heap of rubble. Dead men lay in the road, shadowy forms passed by our equally shadowy forms, voices asked 'What regiment? Where are you going?' A [Hauptmann], wandering aimlessly and alone, spoke to me: his speech was confused, and the light of my torch showed a haggard face with the restless shifting eyes of a madman. 'I once had a company. I'm all that's left of it.' On all sides was the tramping of troops, the clatter of horses, the rattle of guns on the march, and the shouting or moaning of human beings. 'Where is the staff of the 44th Reserve Brigade?' 'A Company, where's A Company?' 'Stretcher-bearers wanted! Stretcher-bearers!' 'Friends, do give us a hand; don't let me lie here, I'm dying.' And all in pitch darkness, no moon, no stars, and the flames from the burning houses had died down to a smouldering glow.[4]

Similarly, a short distance to the north, a regiment was sent ahead to reinforce the 14th Reserve Infantry Brigade. On arrival, their commander found General von Wienkowski and several of his staff fast asleep in a shepherd's hut. When he woke him up he received very short shrift indeed:

> I don't know the situation. Go and see it for yourself in the trenches. You'll find mostly corpses there. We've been burnt to cinders. All of the officers in this regiment, down to the last one, are dead, wounded or incapable of fighting.[5]

In the northern part of the battlefield the first few hours of the morning were relatively peaceful because both sides were waiting for reinforcements to arrive before they renewed the offensive. As we have seen, Maunoury had ordered the 7th Division to advance across the Etavigny Plateau while the 61st Reserve Division captured Montrolles Wood in order to cover their flank. After a delay of about three hours because the former was not ready, by late morning the two divisions had reached the high ground to the west of the wood where they came into view of the German right wing. Having had ample warning of the attack from aerial reconnaissance, the Germans had strengthened the front line by deploying their reserves, repairing some of the damage to their firing positions and bringing up extra ammunition. In addition, the newly arrived batteries from the 6th Infantry Division were hurriedly found emplacements and, in an attempt to boost morale, word was passed round that their infantry were expected to arrive at any moment. (By late morning they were approaching Crouy, about two hours' march from the battlefield. They had covered 33 miles the previous day and another 20 miles that morning after having crossed the Marne before dawn.)

As it happened, the reinforcements were not needed, since the attack by the French 7th Division broke down completely in the face of rifle and machine-gun fire from the well-entrenched German infantry, and in particular because of the heavy shellfire from the newly arrived batteries. At the same time, the 61st Reserve Division was unable to capture Montrolles Wood because they were forced to change front to avoid being outflanked from the direction of Betz. Although they eventually succeeded in taking the village, it was too late to resume the advance and so Boëlle gave the order for both divisions to dig in for the night where they were. Likewise, Sordet's cavalry also failed to pass round the enemy's open flank via the Bargny Plateau. The three divisions left their bivouacs around Nanteuil-le-Haudouin at dawn and were approaching Lévignen when they received the unexpected news that Sordet had been replaced by Général Bridoux, the commander of the 5th Cavalry Division. The 1st and 3rd Divisions then resumed their advance but were halted by shellfire from the newly arrived German artillery and from Schulenburg's Lines of Communication Detachment, which had just left the forested area to the north. At dusk, both divisions gave up the half-hearted attempt to carry out their orders and returned to Nanteuil to feed and water their horses.[6]

Thus ended the fourth day of the battle, a day in which once again neither side had been able to gain an advantage. With the exception of the German left wing, which was now bent back at a sharp angle, the front line was more or less where it had been on the morning of 6 September, albeit considerably extended to the north by the arrival of reinforcements on both sides. During the evening Maunoury reluctantly decided to go over to the defensive and wait for the British to arrive and strike the Germans in the rear. Admittedly, he still had at his disposal the 62nd Reserve Division and the 8th Division (which Joffre had released from its task of supporting the British), but their fighting abilities were highly suspect after they had been roughly handled earlier in the campaign, the former on the Somme bend near Péronne and the latter in the Ardennes where they had suffered heavy casualties and had lost several guns. In addition, the German right wing was about to be reinforced by their IX Corps whose movements had been tracked by aerial reconnaissance, and possibly within the next few days by units released from the siege of Maubeuge. He therefore gave orders for the left wing to fall back gradually if it was strongly attacked the next day, trading space for time, and wait for the British to arrive. As a precaution, with the help of the engineers the 62nd Reserve Division was to prepare a system of earthworks to serve, if necessary, as a line of last resort.

In contrast, Kluck remained confident that he could achieve victory the next day when IX Corps and Lepel's Brigade arrived. After an almost superhuman forced march lasting two days, the 17th and 18th Infantry Divisions spent the night at La Ferté-Milon and Mareuil respectively, less than 6 miles away from the battlefield. When they arrived next morning they would be joined by Schulenburg's Detachment, which had reached the edge of the forest not far from Betz, and by Lepel's Brigade, which had reached Verberie from where it would be able to threaten the French rear. When IX Corps arrived, a new command structure would come into effect. The right wing, commanded by Quast (4th Cavalry Division, IX Corps and 6th Infantry Division) would carry out the offensive, the central group, under Sixt von Arnim (16th Infantry Brigade and 7th and 4th Infantry Divisions), would if possible support the attack while the left wing, commanded by Linsingen (15th Infantry Brigade, IV Reserve Corps and 3rd Infantry Division), would stay on the defensive. Schulenburg's Detachment would join the attack, linking up with the extreme right wing, while Lepel's Brigade, supported by the artillery of the 10th Landwehr Brigade, would take the enemy in the rear, advancing from the area to the north of Nanteuil-le-Haudouin. Army Headquarters would move to Mareuil in order to be closer to the decisive action on the right wing and from where it would be linked by telephone to divisional commands.

However, all of this planning would be worthless if the two cavalry corps were unable to prevent the British from penetrating the large gap between the two armies. By the evening of the 7th, the only remaining obstacles to the British advance were the Marne to the west, and its tributary the Petit Morin to the east, which were guarded by Marwitz's and Richthofen's Cavalry Corps respectively. The story of the day along the eastern sector, where the Guard Cavalry Division and 5th Cavalry Division were defending the Petit Morin against the British I Corps, was one of German failure. Since the steep-sided and heavily wooded valley was entirely unsuitable for cavalry, both divisional commanders pushed their attached rifle battalions, machine gun companies and pioneer detachments into the valley bottom in order to defend the river crossings, leaving the cavalry on the high ground to the north. When the British advance guards arrived at the river in the early morning, the Germans hung on valiantly, making full use of their skilfully concealed positions among the orchards and farms. Some units artfully constructed dummy trenches, which they adorned at intervals with helmets. However, there were too many bridges to defend and at noon, by which time a large number of British troops had crossed the river and infiltrated their positions, Richthofen gave the order to disengage and fall back to a defensive position behind the river Dolloir. Although the cavalry had no difficulty in getting away, the other units suffered horrendous casualties as they attempted to escape from the valley under heavy fire from the British batteries on the high ground to the south. The Guard Rifle Battalion was annihilated at Orly after it failed to receive the order to retreat and at Boitron the two machine gun companies attached to the Guard Jäger Battalion were also more or less wiped out.[7] By early evening, the Guard Cavalry Division had come to a halt behind the Dolloir but the commander of the 5th Cavalry Division, General von Ilsemann, seems to have lost his nerve and continued to retreat, only stopping when they were well to the north of the Marne and out of touch with Richthofen's headquarters.

In comparison with this unmitigated disaster, there was a more mixed picture along the Marne in and to the east of La Ferté-sous-Jouarre. In the early morning,

Marwitz ordered his 2nd Cavalry Division and the Jäger Battalions to fall back to the Marne where they occupied the town and formed a defensive line a short distance to the rear. When Kluck got to know that the British were not far from the river (III Corps towards La Ferté-sous-Jouarre and I and II Corps between the town and the confluence with the Petit Morin), he ordered Marwitz to hold the position unconditionally and instructed Quast, whose IX Corps was on the march towards the Ourcq, to detach two mixed brigades and send them to Montreuil-aux-Lions, from where they could guard the crossing points to the east of La Ferté-sous-Jouarre. If the British approached the river in force, all of the bridges in his sector were to be destroyed.

Although Marwitz's force prevented the British from crossing the river at La Ferté-sous-Jouarre (the bridge was blown up in the early afternoon, after which the town was tenaciously defended by one of the Jäger Battalions), events at Montreuil-aux-Lions did not go to plan. First of all, Quast once more acted independently and instead of detaching two brigades as instructed (which would have halved his force), he left behind only two infantry regiments (one from each division) together with two field artillery groups and a pioneer company, amounting in all to one reinforced brigade commanded by General Kraewel. Quast also told Kraewel that three cavalry divisions (ie both of Richthofen's Divisions and the 2nd Cavalry Division from Marwitz's Corps) would be made available to him. When Kraewel arrived at Montreuil-aux-Lions at about 6.00pm he was faced with an extremely difficult situation; darkness was drawing in, the terrain to the south was broken and heavily wooded, obscuring the river from view, and he only possessed two maps of the region, neither of which was of any use. (One of them was on an impossibly large scale and the other was a poor sketch map in a newspaper cutting which had been obtained by one of his officers!) Worse still, he did not know the whereabouts of either the enemy or the three cavalry divisions which were supposed to be helping him and the pioneer detachment which was meant to blow up the Marne bridges was nowhere to be seen. Without them he lacked the large amount of explosives needed to do the job.[8]

Faced with these difficulties, and aware that his troops were exhausted after the long marches of the previous two days (one battalion had covered 40 miles in the last 36 hours with hardly a break), Kraewel decided to concentrate his force in the immediate vicinity of Montreuil-aux-Lions, even though this meant leaving the bridges undefended. One part was concentrated in and around the village itself, another part was situated on the high ground to the south (Hill 189) and security detachments were pushed out in several directions, including westward towards La Ferté-sous-Jouarre from where there were sounds of a violent cannonade. Although Kluck's order had stated that the line of the Marne must be held at all cost, by nightfall the sector between Chamigny to the west and Nogent to the east was undefended and its seven bridges intact and unguarded.[9] Of the three cavalry divisions that Kluck was expecting to help guard the river, only one was in place and Kraewel's Detachment was half the size of what it should have been.

# 15

# THE BEGINNING
# OF THE END

## 9 SEPTEMBER: THE GERMAN 2ND ARMY BREAKS OFF THE FIGHT ALONG THE ST GOND MARSHES AND RETREATS

Having gained Hentsch's reluctant approval the previous evening, Bülow ordered the Guard Corps to renew its attack on the morning of the 9th, while the right wing remained on the defensive. Although the 13th Infantry Division was in a difficult position, bent back at a sharp angle to its neighbour, X Reserve Corps, it was able to fend off an offensive by the whole of the French I Corps with the aid of its numerous batteries of heavy artillery. In the centre, the 19th Infantry Division was unable to capture the Mondement-Montgivroux Ridge at dawn, as ordered, because the men were widely dispersed and intermingled in the woods where the fighting had ended the previous evening. Although the situation was more favourable on the left where the 39th Infantry Brigade occupied the more open terrain in the neighbourhood of Oyes, one regiment (IR79) was exhausted after an abortive attempt to capture the ridge during the night and the other (IR164) received the order very late, by which time the French artillery had opened a tremendous bombardment. As a result, the attack was only carried out by a battalion from IR164 whose commander, Hauptmann Purgold, decided to advance while the French artillery was blinded by the extremely dense early morning mist. Although they easily captured the village

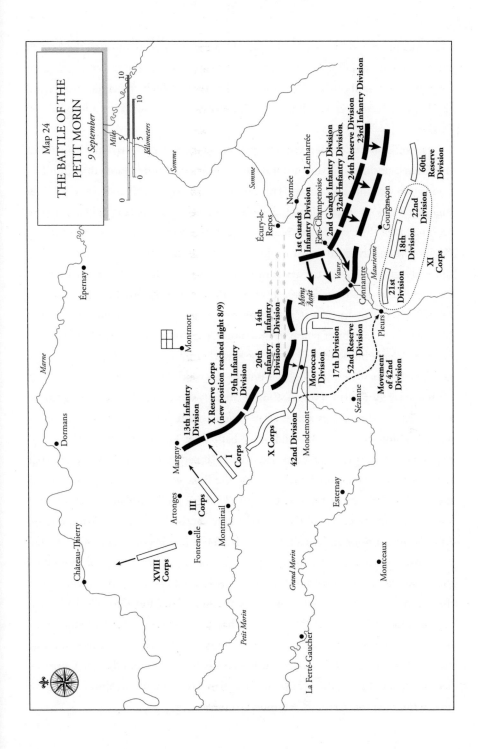

Map 24

THE BATTLE OF THE
PETIT MORIN

*9 September*

of Mondement and the nearby château, the attempt to break through the French line was bound to fail since they received no support from the rest of the brigade or from the neighbouring 14th Infantry Division, which remained inactive all day because Fleck was afraid that his wings might be exposed if he advanced any further.[1]

The offensive by the left wing began at dawn with a massive bombardment of the French positions on and around Mont Août. After three hours of hellish fire, huddled in trenches dug terrace-fashion into the hillside, firstly individual soldiers, then small groups and finally whole units drifted back to the rear, oblivious to the commands of their officers to remain where they were. The 1st Guards Infantry Division then advanced towards the hill, which they took almost unopposed in the early afternoon. In the meantime, on their left the 2nd Guards Infantry Division, supported once more by three divisions from 3rd Army, caused the French XI Corps to retreat in disorder to a new position behind the River Maurienne. After a brief pause to reorganize, the Germans renewed their attack but were swiftly brought to a halt by the French artillery which by now had found new emplacements on the high ground to the south of the river.

Fortunately for the French, the Germans were too exhausted to continue with the fight and so they were left in peace to wait for the arrival of Grossetti's 42nd Division from the other end of the battlefield. However, the latter had been relieved by X Corps several hours later than planned and so was only approaching the area at about 6.00pm, by which time the light was beginning to fade. When they arrived, the three regiments in the lead adopted combat formation and advanced in the direction of Connantre to the south-west of Fère-Champenoise. After about an hour and a half, by which time it had become so dark that they were forced to navigate by the compass, there was still no sign of the enemy, so their commander suggested to Grossetti that it would be prudent to halt where they were and continue with the attack the next day. After Grossetti had gone forwards to see for himself (he ordered a haystack to be set on fire to guide him back to his command post), he ordered them to fall back a short distance and bivouac for the night. Likewise, the other attack divisions found that the Germans had disappeared from the whole of XI Corps front, leaving behind only a few men who were too seriously wounded to move.

Indeed, not only the 1st Guards Infantry Division had been ordered to retreat but also the whole of 2nd Army. As we have seen, Bülow had agreed with Hentsch the previous evening that he would break off the fight and retreat if the British crossed the Marne in force. When the first news arrived at Montmort in the early morning it was not good; according to a captured radio message from Marwitz to Kluck, strong British columns were moving in an easterly direction from La Ferté-sous-Jouarre. An hour later, he received a detailed aerial reconnaissance report which stated that five enemy columns were on the march northwards, along a line La Ferté-sous-Jouarre–Montmirail and that at 8.15am their heads were approaching the river. This was soon followed by another captured radio message, which said that the British were across the Marne in force. ('Strong infantry columns are advancing in a northerly direction through Charly and Nanteuil; the Cavalry Corps has been given the order to attack.'[2]) Although the situation of 1st Army would remain unclear until Kluck got in touch by radio or Koeppen returned from their headquarters, Bülow reluctantly decided that the time had come to retreat.

In the late morning, therefore, provisional orders were drawn up for the general retreat; this would begin immediately on the right wing but the centre and the left wing would be allowed to continue for a little longer with their offensive to shoulder away the enemy so as to make disengagement easier. At the same time, a radio message was sent to Kluck, passing on the contents of the aerial reconnaissance report, and letting him know that 2nd Army's right wing was about to retreat in the direction of Damery [sic: it should have read Dormans] and urgently requesting news of 1st Army's situation. After an hour had gone by without a reply, Bülow decided that he could wait no longer and gave the order for the retreat to begin at noon. After four days of ferocious combat, the battle of the Petit Morin had finally come to an end.[3]

# 16

# THE LAST RETREAT

## 9 SEPTEMBER: HENTSCH ORDERS 1st ARMY TO RETREAT AND THE BATTLE COMES TO AN END

At dawn, the situation along the Marne was as follows. In the west, Marwitz's 2nd and 9th Cavalry Divisions and the Jäger Battalions held the sector between Tancrou (close to the confluence of the Ourcq and the Marne) and the Marne bend upstream of La Ferté-sous-Jouarre. Although the British III Corps had reached La Ferté-sous-Jouarre the previous day it had been unable to cross the river because the Germans had blown up all the bridges except for the two rail viaducts to the east of the town. The central sector between La Ferté and Nogent, towards which the British I and II Corps were advancing, was only weakly held by Kraewel's Detachment at Montreuil-aux-Lions, which was unable to carry out Kluck's express order to blow up the bridges. Thirdly, the eastern sector from Nogent to Château-Thierry, which was in the path of Conneau's Cavalry Corps and the right wing of Haig's I Corps, had been left completely open with its bridges intact and unoccupied following the disorderly flight of Ilsemann's Cavalry Division the previous afternoon.

In order to co-ordinate the defence of the river, Kluck placed Marwitz in command of all the forces in the area, including not only Kraewel's Detachment but also Ilsemann's 5th Cavalry Division which was transferred for this purpose from Richthofen's Corps. In the early morning, Marwitz learnt that Kraewel had not destroyed the bridges in his sector and that Ilsemann was unable to give his support because his division was under attack. (This was untrue because there

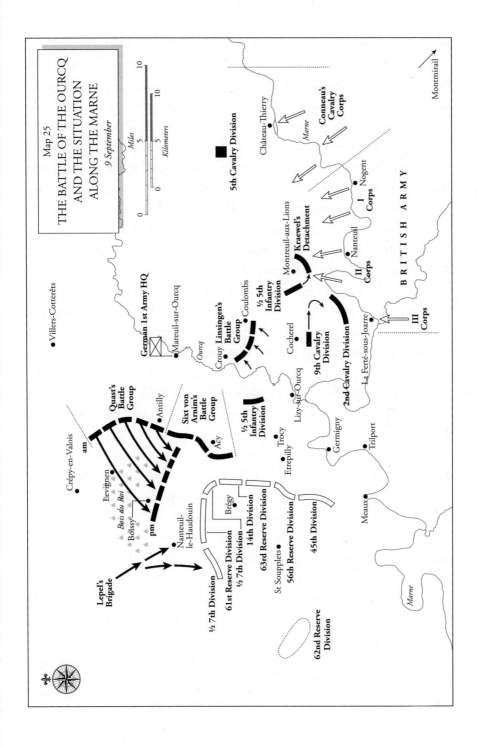

Map 25

THE BATTLE OF THE OURCQ
AND THE SITUATION
ALONG THE MARNE

*9 September*

were no French troops in the area at the time!) Since Ilsemann refused to co-operate, and since the British at La Ferté-sous-Jouarre were showing no signs of aggression, Marwitz ordered his two divisions to leave their positions near the town and move eastwards to the high ground at Cocherel (midway between Lizy-sur-Ourcq and Montreuil-aux-Lions) from where they had extensive views and could easily intervene in whatever direction was necessary. In a calculated gamble, the only forces which were left behind to keep watch on the British III Corps were a company of cyclists in the Marne bend at Changis, a section of Jäger at the bridge at Chamigny and the IV Jäger Battalion, which remained dug in among the ruins of La Ferté-sous-Jouarre where they had so far prevented the British from constructing a pontoon bridge or crossing the river in boats.

In the early morning, the British advance guards began to cross the Marne unopposed in the central sector, I Corps on the right at Nogent and Charly and II Corps at Saâcy-sur-Marne and Nanteuil-sur-Marne. About an hour later, news of this disaster reached 1st Army Headquarters in the form of three brief radio messages, which arrived like hammer blows in rapid succession. At 9.28am from the Guard Cavalry Division: 'Strong enemy infantry and artillery on the march over the Marne bridge at Charly.' At 9.30am from II Cavalry Corps: 'Strong enemy infantry are advancing via Charly and Nanteuil. 5th Cavalry Division and [the 2nd Cavalry Division] have been ordered to attack.' At 10.11am, also from II Cavalry Corps: the message of 9.30am repeated, but before anything further could be added it ended abruptly with the words, 'I must march off very quickly.'[1]

Events had now reached crisis point. The Marne had been the last obstacle in the way of the British and with this gone there was now very little to prevent them from falling on the flank or rear of 1st Army at the very moment when its right wing was about to begin the offensive. Since they were less than 12 miles from the army's centre at Lizy-sur-Ourcq immediate action was needed to avert a catastrophe. In order to decide what should be done, a meeting was called between Kuhl, Bergmann and several other senior staff officers. Surprisingly, given the seriousness of the situation, Kluck himself was not present. According to Kuhl, they agreed that it was unthinkable to retreat when victory was in their grasp. Instead, while IX Corps attacked as planned as soon as it reached the battlefield, part of the 5th Infantry Division would be removed from Trocy, where it was in reserve, and sent to reinforce Kraewel's Detachment. At the same time, Linsingen's Battle Group on the left wing would cross to the east bank of the Ourcq, swing back and occupy an east-west line, facing south, from where it could hold off the British. Sixt von Arnim's Battle Group, which was in the centre, would act as the pivot for this movement while at the same time supporting the attack by Quast's Battle Group on the right. These decisions were approved by Kluck and issued as an army order at 11.00am. Quast's attack was described as a thrust – *Vorstoss* – in the direction of Nanteuil-le-Haudouin.[2]

Meanwhile, Maunoury had taken measures to protect his left wing from the anticipated German offensive. While the right wing and the centre remained where they were, the left wing swung back, pivoting on Acy, so that it faced north and north-east in the direction of the expected attack. On the left, the 61st Reserve Division moved back a short distance and then turned through 90 degrees to face north along a shallow arc through the villages of Boissy and Fresnoy. Ahead of them, bare fields gently descended towards the dark mass of the King's Wood approximately 500 yards away, while on the left their flank rested on the high road to Paris, on the far side of which was Nanteuil-le-Haudouin. The 7th Division, which was on the right, faced north-eastwards along a line from Villers-St Genest in the west to the outskirts of Acy in the east; in front of them there was the heavily wooded valley of the Grivette which the Germans would have to cross during their attack. Rather than place the majority of his troops in the front line, Boëlle prudently pushed forward only two battalions, one facing Betz and the other at the boundary with the 14th Division. The other ten battalions were concentrated to the north-east of Sennevières from where they could act as a mass of manoeuvre, quickly reaching any sector which was under threat. On the far left, Bridoux's two cavalry divisions received orders to cover the left flank or, if this turned out to be unnecessary, to destroy the Soissons–Montdidier railway line in order to stop German reinforcements arriving from Maubeuge. Lastly, a line of earthworks was dug about 3 miles to the rear by troops from the 62nd Reserve Division with help and advice from the engineers and using materials taken from the front line divisions.

During the morning the Germans were untroubled by the French artillery, which kept up a desultory bombardment of their positions. Some of them were sent out to collect the dead and wounded while the remainder repaired their trenches, which had been battered by the almost continuous shellfire. Towards the end of the morning, Linsingen's Battle Group on the left wing slipped away from their trenches, descended the valley and crossed the river on two pontoon bridges that had been constructed by the pioneers the previous afternoon. Their condition after several days of relentless combat was evocatively described by Hauptmann Wirth of RIR66, who by chance encountered several friends from his former battalion:

> From the firing line came parts of my former battalion. They marched clumsily and with difficulty. They came to a halt not far from us under some trees, laid down their packs and stretched out to rest on the grass. I hurried across to them and found two dear comrades, who had earlier looked so cheerful and had been able to speak so amusingly. Their eyes were sunken into their sockets, with dark rims. Deadly serious, they looked directly ahead of them into an unknown distance and out of their lips there came but a few scarce words of greeting. Their uniforms were covered with grime and torn, their faces plastered with dust and sweat, and in one of them by splashes of blood. I took out what supplies I still had in my pack and gave them to the latter. He seized them greedily. After a long silence they began to answer my questions, however their words only painfully and haltingly escaped from their lips, as if something was closing up their throat, something horrible and terrible that seemed to be continuously visible to them… I only saw my comrades fleetingly in the next few days so this was our last get-together and our final farewell. Both of them met their heroic death on the Aisne. I was able to decorate the grave of one of them with ivy, however where the other one was laid to rest, no one knows.[3]

Rather surprisingly, their retreat took place without interference from the French, who kept up a half-hearted bombardment of their empty trenches long after they had gone. It was only in the middle of the afternoon, after patrols had been sent out to see why the German artillery had been silent for some time, that they discovered the Germans had disappeared, leaving their trenches full of debris but empty of life except for a few men who were too seriously wounded to be moved. The situation in the late afternoon was described in a report sent to Kuhl by Hauptmann von Schütz, 1st Army liaison officer at Linsingen's headquarters. After he had spent several hours at the crossroads at Beauvoir-ou-Beauval (where the road from Lizy-sur-Oucq to Trocy crosses the high road which runs parallel to the Ourcq along its western side) watching the troops file past on their way to the river, Schütz stayed on, helping to round up stragglers and send them on their way. In the late afternoon, puzzled by the enemy's absence, he decided to get a better view of the battlefield from the tower of the nearby church.

> I went to May-en-Multien and climbed to the top of the very high church tower. In the clear evening sky the Eiffel Tower was visible to the south-west. The French artillery fire had completely stopped. Despite the excellent view over the whole area, it was free of enemy; there were also no cavalry patrols at all visible. Towards evening, [our] columns reached the line Fussy–Coulombs. There was still no enemy to be seen on the west bank of the Ourcq. General von Linsingen was firmly convinced that the threat from the English had been taken into account by bending back the left wing and that the right wing offensive, moving forwards well, must lead to a victory for the army.[4]

By the time the left wing was crossing the river, the offensive by Quast's Battle Group had been in progress for several hours. At about 7.00am, after a short approach march from their overnight positions, the 17th and 18th Infantry Divisions reached their jumping-off points at the western edge of the Forest of Villers-Cotterêts. From Antilly, where they linked up on their left with the 6th Infantry Division, their line formed a shallow south-west-facing arc that extended northwards as far as Gondreville, where their open flank was covered by the 4th Cavalry Division. In order to reach Nanteuil-le-Haudouin and envelop the enemy's left wing they would have to cross the Bargny–Lévignen Plateau, traverse either the King's Wood or the valley of the Grivette, and finally cross a second plateau dominated by Boissy and Fresnoy. When the attack was under way they would be supported on the left by the 6th Infantry Division and on the right by Schulenburg's Detachment, which had bivouacked in the forest overnight.

Since Quast was uncertain of the enemy's position, and because the view to the south-west was blocked by the woods, he decided on a methodical advance in which the infantry and artillery moved forwards alternately, one step at a time, to provide mutual support. By mid-morning, the advance guards of both divisions had reached the centre of the first plateau, from where a patchwork of golden wheat and dark green fields of sugar beet descended towards the dark mass of the King's Wood. A short distance away to the right, the clustered houses of Lévignen nestled among the trees and orchards and surrounded the church whose massive tower was a viewpoint for miles around. No sounds of gunfire disturbed this peaceful scene, nor was there a single enemy to be seen. The next two hours were spent patiently consolidating their position and moving the artillery forwards to prepare for the next stage in the advance. It was about 10.30am by the time that they got going again and there was still no sign of the enemy, except for a cavalry squadron that briefly debouched on to the plateau at Lévignen but instantly turned around and disappeared into the woods when they came under fire.

At the same time as Quast's troops were approaching Nanteuil-le-Haudouin from the north-east, Lepel's Brigade was preparing to attack the town from the high ground to the north-west. Earlier that morning they had been reinforced by two Landwehr batteries which had been trailing them by half a day's march and which now arrived at the trot as they were approaching the town. After they had easily driven off a small force of French cavalry, the two batteries unlimbered and prepared to open fire. From where they stood, they had a panoramic view of the French rear; in the near distance, just over a mile away, stood the parallel lines of the railway and the poplar-lined high road, on their right was Nanteuil itself (the location of Boëlle's headquarters) and directly ahead of them, in the far distance, they could see Boissy and Fresnoy where the troops of the 61st Reserve Division were guarding the French left flank. When the batteries opened fire on the crowded baggage trains along the high road, Lepel ordered his brigade to advance towards Nanteuil.

Meanwhile, Quast's troops had left the Bargny Plateau and resumed their advance. Although there was no sign of the French infantry, the going was very slow, especially on the right where the 17th Infantry Division found it difficult to cross the woods, which contained only one good road and a few inadequate narrow paths that restricted movement to a single file. As a result, by the early afternoon, six battalions of infantry and nine field artillery batteries had come to a standstill in a huge traffic jam backed up along the road that ran through the woods towards Nanteuil-le-Haudouin. Similarly, on the left, the 6th Infantry Division encountered difficulties in crossing the valley of the Grivette in the face of strong artillery fire. By the middle of the afternoon, however, the obstacles had all been overcome and the 23 battalions that formed Quast's main body were strung out on a shallow curve running along the southern edge of the woods and along the valley of the Grivette. After having spent more than seven hours on their slow and painstaking advance, they were finally within striking distance of the enemy's front line, on the top of the second plateau.

The French left wing was now in a desperate situation, under attack from the north-west where Lepel's Brigade was about to capture Nanteuil-le-Haudouin and from the north-east by Quast's Battle Group. In order to meet these twin threats, Boëlle was forced to alter his dispositions. Firstly, he ordered the two artillery groups that were targeting the German 18th Infantry Division as it crossed the Grivette to move westwards to the high ground overlooking Nanteuil from where they could direct their fire on Lepel's Brigade. Secondly, the mass of manoeuvre at Sennevières was moved westwards and split up, one brigade being used to reinforce the 61st Reserve Division at Boissy and Fresnoy while the other took up a position further west where it faced Lepel's Brigade. As a result of these changes the French line was now bent back in a huge semi-circle from Acy in the east to the south of Nanteuil-le-Haudouin in the west. With the battle about to begin, Boëlle gave the order for the position to be held to the last man.

Once again, as on so many occasions during the last four days, it was the superb French gunnery that came to their rescue. Lepel's attack was the first to collapse under the onslaught of the French shellfire. For a while, as the Germans closed in on the railway line and the adjacent high road, seizing the railway station from where they shelled the traffic along the road, it looked as if they were about to capture the town. However, the picture changed abruptly when the newly arrived French batteries opened fire, causing Lepel's troops to flee and putting the two antiquated Landsturm batteries out of action within moments. Paul Lintier, who served in one of the French batteries, described the devastating effect of their fire on the German infantry:

Orders came for us to go and take up positions between Sennevières and Nanteuil-le-Haudouin. There could be no doubt about it. The enemy was turning our lines. We were seized with a fit of wild rage. Would they manage to pass us and get to Paris? To Paris … to our homes … to kill, sack, rape? 'Ah,' growled Hutin, 'what wouldn't I give to murder some of those savages!' We took up position with our guns pointing north-east. Behind us the sun, already low in the western sky, lit up the railway line and the road from Nanteuil to Paris, flanked with tall trees. Sections of infantry began to fall back. 'You see?' repeated Millon. 'They can't stick it, the beasts! Haven't they read the Army Order then?' Suddenly, almost behind us, rifle fire broke out. We had been outflanked. On the main road to Paris, and between the road and the railway, dense masses of infantry were debouching from behind Nanteuil. We were encircled by a huge hostile horseshoe, and it now seemed as if the only means of retreat open to the IV Army Corps was the narrow road running south-east between Sennevières and Silly. An officer wearing an aviator's cap arrived in a motor car and hurried up to the observation post. Shortly afterwards, the major ordered us to turn our guns right round. At any moment we might be caught between two fires, for, to the north-west of Nanteuil, on the hills commanding the road, there could be no doubt that the enemy's artillery was taking up position in order to support the infantry attack.

Our batteries opened fire. The same wild frenzy immediately gained possession of men and guns. The latter became roaring monsters and raging dragons, which from their gaping mouths belched fire at the sun as it sank to rest in the soft summer twilight. Piles of smoking cartridge cases mounted up behind the guns. In the stricken zone in front of us we could see men waver, turn tail, run and fall in heaps. From the heights above Nanteuil, from which our guns could have been counted, came no answering roar of artillery.[5]

At about the same time, Quast's troops were advancing against the French positions at Boissy and Fresnoy. At approximately 4.00pm, under cover of an artillery bombardment, the two divisions began to ascend the slopes leading to the two villages. On the left, the 18th Division came under concentrated fire from French batteries to the east of Sennevières and before long a series of salvoes struck their left hand regiment, causing many of them to rush back in panic. In contrast, the 17th Infantry Division advanced in one long rush to within assault distance of Boissy, almost unopposed because the French had prudently withdrawn from the village leaving behind only a weak rearguard. Attacked simultaneously from both sides, the place was quickly captured after a brief period of hand-to-hand fighting after which the defenders retired over the bare ground to the rear followed by a destructive pursuit fire. Now that the villages were in German hands, General von Bauer called a temporary halt to allow the divisional artillery to change position prior to the next stage in the advance. While this was taking place, the infantry and the machine gun companies halted on the south sides of the two villages where they impatiently awaited orders to resume their offensive against what in their opinion was a demoralized and defeated enemy. Suddenly, however, as they were taking this well-earned rest, a hail of shellfire descended on their positions, on the two villages and on the area adjacent to the woods where the German batteries were seeking new emplacements. Within moments, the whole scene was one of chaos; buildings were set on fire, several haystacks burst into flame and the Germans ran back towards the woods several hundred metres to the rear. Only the intervention of Bauer and his staff made it possible to halt the reflux and put some order into the mass of frightened men, many of whom had undoubtedly still not recovered from their terrifying experiences in the recent fighting at Esternay.

When evening fell and the French artillery ceased firing, the Germans dug trenches at the edge of the woods and, as searchlights played over the night sky from the forts of Paris, they went over to rest shortly before midnight. Likewise, on their left neither the 18th Division nor the 6th Division had been able to advance any further because of the French shellfire, and ended the day on the southern edge of the King's Wood and along the valley of the Grivette respectively. The envelopment of the French left flank, which had begun in a mood of great confidence that morning, had failed at all points along the line.

If Kluck's expectations of a decisive victory on the right wing proved unfounded, so too were his fears that the British would break out of their bridgehead across the Marne and savage the army's rear. Although Kraewel's small force was hugely outnumbered to begin with (two British corps supported by cavalry versus one mixed brigade), they held on tenaciously to Hill 189 thanks to the difficult, heavily-wooded terrain, some inaccurate aerial reconnaissance and because of unwarranted caution by Haig and French. The British I Corps could easily have outflanked Montreuil-aux-Lions from the east and opened the way for II Corps, which was facing stiff opposition as it ascended the steep and heavily wooded slopes leading to the hill. However, Haig halted them soon after they had crossed the river because of a report that pilots had observed a large mass of enemy troops in the vicinity of Château-Thierry from where they could threaten his exposed right flank. (This was probably part of Ilsemann's Cavalry Division and not IX Corps as Haig believed at the time.) At about midday, by which time they had been stationary for four hours, he gave the order to resume the advance, but they had not got very far when Sir John French arrived and told them to halt for the day when they reached the Château-Thierry–Montreuil-aux-Lions high road. As a result, they had advanced a mere 5 miles beyond the river and had squandered a golden opportunity to envelop and destroy Kraewel's Detachment.

In the middle of the morning, Marwitz decided to go over to the offensive. Advancing from the west, the 9th Cavalry Division and the three Jäger battalions would take the British II Corps in the flank before it reached Hill 189, while the 5th Infantry Division skirted round the village to the north and headed off I Corps. The 2nd Cavalry Division was to cover the attack from the south (in case more British troops attempted to cross the river immediately to the east of La Ferte-sous-Jouarre) and the 5th Cavalry Division was asked to hold off Conneau's Cavalry Corps, which was in the neighbourhood of Château-Thierry. The counter-attack had only limited success, however, because Marwitz found it difficult to co-ordinate the actions of the widely dispersed groups and because not all of the promised reinforcements arrived. (Needless to say, Ilsemann's cavalry was nowhere to be seen and the 5th Infantry Division was only able to spare a reinforced brigade.) The only success was at Montreuil-aux-Lions, where the latter was diverted to Hill 189. It arrived just in time to prevent the 1st Duke of Cornwall's Light Infantry from capturing the crest and threw them back into the valley with heavy losses. In the late afternoon Marwitz's cavalry also advanced towards Montreuil-aux-Lions but was forced to withdraw when units from the British III Corps crossed the Marne to the east of La Ferté-sous-Jouarre and threatened his right flank.

If Kluck had been given a free hand he might have continued with the offensive the next day in the hope of bringing about a last-minute victory. However, Hentsch's intervention put paid to this once and for all. After a brief early morning discussion in the park at Montmort with Lauenstein and Matthes (he had changed his mind and spent the night there in case any last-minute news arrived), Hentsch and his two companions left for 1st Army Headquarters at Mareuil-sur-Ourcq. Under normal circumstances the 50-mile journey could easily have been covered in about two hours, but it took them almost three times as long because they were forced to make several time-consuming detours to avoid roads clogged with baggage trains and wounded troops. In the report he wrote a week later, Hentsch described the difficulties they encountered and the effect this had on him:

The impression that I gained on my drive to 1st Army Headquarters was not at all favourable. Everywhere I encountered the trains and baggage wagons of the cavalry division retreating in wild haste; all of them taking the route to Fère-en-Tardenois. Wounded troops were streaming back in the same direction; they were afraid that they might already have been cut off. In Neuilly-St Front everything was blocked because of the columns; an attack by an enemy aeroplane had caused complete panic. Repeatedly, I had to descend from my car and force a way through. In front of Neuilly I turned off to the south to reach Mareuil by way of Crouy. At Brumetz I was forced to turn around since English cavalry were already in the vicinity. It was approaching midday when we reached Mareuil via Chézy... On the way, I heard that the enemy had driven our cavalry away from the Marne and had already crossed the river.[6]

What he saw on the drive powerfully reinforced his view that Kluck should break off the fight without delay and retreat to a position from where he could make contact with 2nd Army. When they arrived at Mareuil just before noon they were met in the street by Kuhl, who briefly acquainted them with the general situation before taking them inside. Despite the fact that only an hour had gone by since the left wing had been pulled back to avoid envelopment and reinforcements had been urgently sent to Kraewel, 1st Army Chief of Staff appeared in remarkably confident spirits. Showing no signs of tension and nervousness at this time of crisis, he explained that the measures which had been taken to support the left wing were already having an effect and that the attack by the right wing was going well. When they were inside, he took Hentsch into his office for a more detailed discussion, while König and Koeppen remained behind in an adjacent room where several staff officers were hard at work. When König and Koeppen questioned them about the situation, opinions were divided; some were optimistic and thought that the right wing would achieve victory; others, however, were concerned that the British had crossed the Marne and could prevent the Army from escaping. Meanwhile, after their short tête-à-tête Hentsch and Kuhl were joined in the latter's office by Bergmann, the Deputy Chief of Staff, and they got down to serious business. Kuhl opened the conversation by giving a detailed appreciation of the situation. On the right wing, IX Corps, together with the 6th Division and Lepel's Brigade, were in the process of enveloping the French right wing in an attack which promised to bring success by the end of the day. The left wing, it was true, had been forced to swing back to protect its open flank, but the British were advancing only slowly into the gap between the two armies and with the help of the reinforcements could be delayed until victory had been achieved on the right wing.

This positive reading of the situation appears to have taken Hentsch by surprise. According to Bergmann, 'The surprise was plain to see on his face. I remember clearly that he appeared flabbergasted as his preconceived opinions were contradicted by this depiction.'[7] Hentsch asked if 1st Army would be able to come to the aid of 2nd Army the next day, assuming that Kuhl was correct and that the right wing was victorious. He went on to explain that 2nd Army was in a very serious situation and would be forced to retreat unless it received immediate support from 1st Army. On the right wing, VII Corps had been forced back (*zurückgeworfen*) instead of pulled back (*zurückgegangen*) and would, if necessary, retreat in the direction of Epernay. If the British penetrated the gap between the two armies, 1st Army would also have to retreat in order to make contact with Bülow's right wing, either in the region Soissons–Fismes or possibly further back in the vicinity of Laon–La Fère. The new army that was being formed at St Quentin would stabilize the situation and allow offensive operations to resume. In order to leave no doubt as to his meaning Hentsch drew the new positions in charcoal on Kuhl's large scale situation map.

The mention of retreat did not go down at all well with Kuhl and Bergmann, who strongly argued against it. For the last four days the army had been involved in a costly and indecisive struggle for supremacy. Why should they call off the offensive when at any moment now it would end in victory? To halt the troops in the middle of the attack and then retreat would lead to chaos, given their exhausted condition and the difficulties of disengaging. Furthermore, many of the baggage trains were only just arriving after the hurried retreat to the Ourcq and there was also the strong possibility that enemy cavalry could cut off the retreat by penetrating the heavily wooded area that separated them from the Aisne. If a retreat were necessary, it would be far better to do so after they had defeated the enemy when they could more easily disengage. If the French fell back in the direction of Paris, the British would be forced to retreat alongside them and contact with the right wing of 2nd Army could then be made at leisure, after which the armies of the right wing would be free to advance once more.

All of this fell on deaf ears, however. Hentsch explained that Bülow had agreed that 2nd Army would retreat if the British crossed the Marne in force. From what he had just seen on the drive to Mareuil this could be only a matter of time and might already have begun. To leave 1st Army where it was would be to court disaster. When Kuhl expressed astonishment at Bülow's decision, Hentsch explained that the latter had been very reluctant but felt that it was unavoidable because, according to him, 2nd Army had been burnt to a cinder by several days of continuous heavy fighting. According to Kuhl, it was this news that struck a mortal blow to his hopes of avoiding retreat:

> These words remain firmly fixed in my memory; a mistake was impossible … as far as I was concerned, it was decisive. If 2nd Army had been defeated, and 'burnt to a cinder' and their retreat already taking place, then 1st Army could no longer remain standing in isolation where it was. It could only complete the battle on the Ourcq if 2nd Army remained in place.[8]

With Kuhl and Bergmann now wavering, Hentsch delivered the final blow by explaining that he had been granted full powers by Moltke to order a retreat if he believed that this was necessary. Since it would take too long to get in touch with

OHL and with 2nd Army, they needed to act immediately, before it was too late. At the earliest possible opportunity, 1st Army must break off the fight and begin to retreat, starting with the left wing, which would fall back in the direction of Soissons. No further discussion was possible. After a brief delay while Kuhl went off to get Kluck's agreement, Hentsch and König set off for Luxembourg via 3rd Army Headquarters, while Koeppen returned as promised to Montmort to let Bülow know what had happened. ('The business with 1st Army is now in order; I have spoken about everything with Kuhl; complete agreement now prevails with 2nd Army.'[9]) According to his driver, Landrat von Marx, Hentsch appeared to be mentally shattered during the drive back to OHL as he reflected on the gravity of events and his responsibility for the decisions that had been taken. Likewise, König said:

> The necessity and correctness of the decisions that had been taken pervaded his thoughts, nevertheless, he was not in any doubt about the consequences. He repeatedly stressed that because of a lack of written instruction, he would from many sides be made the scapegoat for the unfortunate outcome of the operations.[10]

Not long after they had gone, a message arrived from Bülow confirming that the British had crossed the Marne in force and that 2nd Army had already begun to retreat. Preparatory orders were first of all sent to the 4th Cavalry Division, which was to secure the Aisne crossings between Soissons and Attichy and cover the left wing against enemy cavalry in the area of Soissons, and to Marwitz's Cavalry Corps and the attached 5th Infantry Division, which were to cover the retreat. Soon afterwards the general retreat order was sent out to corps commanders by telephone and also by staff officers. It was to begin that day and was to continue until the army was across the Marne on both sides of Epernay. The movement was to start on the left, followed by the centre and last of all on the right where 'the offensive movement of the group of General von Quast will not be carried further than is necessary to shake clear of the enemy, and in such a way that connection with the movement of the rest of the army is possible.'[11]

The order reached the right wing in the middle of the afternoon, just as Quast's troops were preparing to assault the French position at Boissy and Fresnoy. When Hauptmann Bührmann, who had been attached to IX Corps for the day, was told of the decision over the telephone he found it so inexplicable that he immediately telephoned Kuhl to seek confirmation. Meanwhile, a written copy of the order had reached Quast's headquarters and had been passed down to the two divisions. When it reached General von Kluge, the commander of the 18th Infantry Division, whose troops were just about to attack Villers-St Genest and Fresnoy, he immediately telephoned Quast's Chief of Staff and said that he refused to carry it out because the enemy was in full retreat. After Quast himself had also bitterly complained to Bührmann that they were throwing victory away, the latter telephoned Army Headquarters once again in an attempt to get the order annulled. At his insistence he spoke briefly with Kluck, but the latter refused to go into details and passed him back to Kuhl who repeated that the retreat was absolutely necessary because of the difficult situation of 2nd Army.[12] In the event, Quast took full advantage of the licence given him in Kluck's orders and continued with the attack on Boissy and Fresnoy although, as we have seen, this ended in failure. By the time that the fighting came to an end it was nightfall and too late to begin the retreat. As a result, they bivouacked for the night on the battlefield and set out the next morning, undisturbed by the enemy.

The campaign, which had begun with so much promise just over three weeks ago when Liège had fallen and Kluck's troops had set out across the Belgian plain in the direction of Brussels, had ended in defeat. During that time 1st Army had covered more than 300 miles without a single rest day and after their encounters with the British at Mons and Le Cateau they had fought a bitter, five-day battle to prevent the French from crossing the Ourcq. Their feelings as they retreated from the battlefield leaving behind the bodies of so many of their fallen comrades can easily be imagined. Let us give the last word to Hermann Richter, battery commander in the 75th Field Artillery Regiment, whom we saw in action the previous day on the Trocy Plateau. When the order to retreat reached them in the late afternoon, they believed at first that it was only a tactical withdrawal and that before very long they would renew the fight from new positions a short distance to the rear. However, as the hours passed by without respite, and as more and more troops joined them on the march, the awful truth gradually dawned on them.

Together, we travelled northwards. Where we were going, no one knew. The news arrived that we were only falling back a few kilometres in order to prevent our left wing from being enveloped. All the officers whom we marched past were surprised and horrified and asked us where we [were] heading. The fact that the enemy still continued to fire on the emplacements which we had left … as much as three or four hours earlier, not having noticed our changed positions, greatly reassured us and indicated thereby that we had not in any way been defeated.

We retreated over the area to the rear of Trocy to Vincy where there was the field hospital belonging to our army corps. Our hearts were pierced by the sight of our wounded. What was going to happen to all these poor souls now that we were giving up the village? Our path took us further northwards, past the batteries of the 74th and 40th Regiments, which were covering the march. On the road leading towards Le Plessis-Placy we saw numerous columns, amalgamated infantry regiments in three march-columns moving north. In the neighbouring fields several units were still assembled in which many men were resting or feeding their horses. On all of the faces, however, one could see the exhaustion after the five-day-long, violent and bloody struggle and also the questions about the direction of the march.

Next to us there marched an infantry regiment belonging to IV Reserve Corps, at the head of which was an Oberst, an Oberstleutnant and a Major, all on foot. They told us that their horses had been killed and I offered them a place on my guns. They accepted with gratitude. Since our drivers had gone ahead on foot to spare the horses, I asked the Oberst to take the place of the first driver, the Oberstleutnant to take the place of the second and the Major to climb on board one of the limbers. Since the drivers were keeping an eye on the road they didn't know about this.

Just before Le Plessis-Placy the road went downhill. Since no one applied the brakes, one of the riders turned round and shouted 'you fucking arsehole, brake properly!' at the Oberst [who didn't know what to do]. 'Are you all asleep there at the back?' His coarse language was too much for the Oberst after all the efforts of the last few days and so together with the Oberstleutnant and the Major he jumped down and returned to his regiment.

As [we] were approaching Le Plessis-Placy we received an order to go into emplacement. We remained there for one to two hours, making use of a large haystack as an observation post. Unceasingly to our left one battery after another, infantry columns and baggage trains, streamed past us along the road. As the sun was beginning to sink, a car belonging to the High Command carrying a general staff officer drove past us. Our major dashed forward and asked him what the actual situation was. 'No cause for concern! Following an order at the highest level, we are changing fronts for strategic reasons by moving our flank. I don't know anything more than this.'

Soon afterwards we received the order to limber up. At the edge of Le Plessis-Placy we marched off in closed column. Most of the men were calm because of the news; only a few pessimists believed that we were fleeing. Still, no rest beckoned. With a couple of swigs of red wine we once more strengthened our worn-out nerves and then it was time to march again.

It was now completely dark. We carried on northwards. Apparently we were trying to join up with another army. One rumour after another spread among us as the hours passed by in uninterrupted march. It was moonlight and the night was cold. Cars buzzed past us. Would none of them bring the order to go over to rest? The horses were tired and stumbled forwards. The men slept on the guns and on the limbers, nestling up close to one another and our eyes fell shut. From time to time, some of the battery staff fell asleep on horseback, allowing their horses to wander, and had to be got back into place by means of shouts.

At about two o' clock in the morning we reached Villers-Cotterêts and encountered troops belonging to IX Army Corps. They were furious at having to retreat. They had taken 10,000 prisoners and had captured 50 cannon. The order to retreat made no sense if it was a flank movement carried out on strategic grounds. Here also there was no rest for us. Onwards, through night and fog, without food or sleep! We had marched on unswervingly for ten hours. The riders grumbled and groaned because their arms and legs hurt but it was to no avail. The morning gradually dawned. We still marched. A veil of mist lay cold and foggy over the fields of northern France.

At about five in the morning we finally came to a halt on the road leading to Soissons. An hour's rest. We fell off our horses and using the small, sharp-edged cobblestones as our pillows we lay down in the road ditches, and in restless, exhausted half-sleep once more dreamt of the marvellous advance on Paris and of the bloody days at Trocy. A new battlefield, new fights and new deeds beckoned us.[13]

The battle of the Marne had ended in defeat, the campaign was over and German hopes of bringing the war to a speedy and victorious conclusion were in ruins.

# 17

# ANALYSIS

On the face of it, the German strategy bore all the hallmarks of success; it was audacious and meticulously planned, it took the French completely by surprise having been a closely guarded secret for more than a decade, and it led to overwhelming numerical superiority at the point where it mattered, on the right wing. Why then, having begun the campaign with these enormous advantages, did the Germans lose? To the members of the 'Schlieffen School', a group of the great man's disciples of whom Ludendorff and Groener were the best known and most vociferous, there was no doubt whatsoever. At the centre of the myth they wove around Schlieffen's name was the allegation that Moltke was principally to blame for having watered down the perfect recipe for a rapid and decisive victory and then bungling its execution. According to them, he ignored Schlieffen's repeated warnings to make the right wing as strong as possible, did not keep the army commanders on a tight rein and instead of aiming for victory on the right wing he sought a decision wherever the enemy's main body happened to be.

Let us begin by looking at the assertion that Moltke failed to do everything in his power to strengthen the right wing. The list of items on the charge sheet was certainly impressive: before the war he strengthened the left wing at the expense of the right (thereby reducing the strength ratio from 7:1 in the Schlieffen Plan to 3:1 in the 1914 Deployment Plan); on the outbreak of war he used the newly-raised *ersatz* divisions to reinforce the left wing and not the right; after the successful counter-attacks in Lorraine in the third week of August he did not transfer two corps to the right wing as Schlieffen would have done and lastly, he unnecessarily sent two corps to East Prussia at a time when they were desperately needed in the West. Admittedly, a lack of numbers on the right wing was a major factor in the German defeat. By the third week in August gaps had begun to open up between the right wing armies as the front expanded after the battles of the Frontiers and as a result of the new march directions in the 27 August Directive. As we have seen, the problem became particularly acute for 3rd Army, which lost contact with Bülow's left wing between 25 August, when Hausen swung south-eastwards to support 4th Army, and 8 September, when his right wing took part in the night attack against the French XI Corps. Likewise, in order to keep in touch with 1st Army as it pursued the British over the Somme and the Crozat Canal, Bülow dangerously extended his right wing to the south-west of St Quentin on 28 August, thus exposing it to attack during the battle of Guise. Also, if the German right wing had been covered by several reserve corps (as in the Schlieffen Plan) Joffre's counter-attack might have failed and 1st Army would not have needed to march back to the Ourcq with great haste, thereby opening up the fateful gap with 2nd Army. However, as Moltke's critics must have been aware when they levelled this particular criticism at him, the Schlieffen Plan was intended for a war with France alone and not, as in 1914, for a war on two fronts. Moltke omitted the covering force not because he thought that it was unnecessary but because the troops were needed as part of 8th Army on the Eastern Front. If instead we compare the 1914 Deployment Plan with the 1906 *Aufmarsch II* (*West und Ost*) for a war on two fronts (the last plan for which Schlieffen was responsible), we find that in both cases the right wing (Brussels–Givet) was 32 infantry divisions strong.[1] Secondly, Moltke's decision to send the *ersatz* divisions to Lorraine was governed by logistics and not by a wish to downplay the importance of the right wing. In the Great Memorandum Schlieffen had concentrated almost exclusively on strategy and had glossed over the problems involved in supplying the million or so troops on the right wing during their long march through Belgium and northern France. In the final version all that he had to say about this was as follows:

> If success is to be achieved, the right wing must make very great exertions. But the roads to be used are on the whole very good. Quartering, too, should be

satisfactory in many localities, unless the right wing corps are forced to march in such close order that even the densest population is not enough [to provide quartering]. On the other hand, there can hardly be a shortage of provisions. The rich land of Belgium and northern France can furnish much, and if they lack anything they will produce it – under suitable pressure – from outside.[2]

The only discussion of the Belgian rail network, which was vital for supplying the troops with food and ammunition, occurs in draft IV, where he briefly mentioned that the right wing would be dependent on the railways to the north and west of the Meuse.

> The Belgian railways west of the Meuse will have to be the principal lines of communication for the German Army. Reliance should not be placed on the railways in the Meuse valley, which is blocked by the two fortresses of Givet and Mézières and can be obstructed by demolition of its many tunnels. East of the Meuse, a number of inefficient but adequate Belgian railways run near the river but not across it ... lines of communication must therefore be sought to the north of the Meuse.[3]

Concerned by this rather cavalier approach to what was after all a fundamentally important problem, Moltke began to consider the logistics of the plan in more detail within months of taking office. In the western staff ride he conducted in the spring of 1906 he investigated what would happen to the right wing if the Belgians partially destroyed their rail network before German deployment was complete. Although the notional demolitions had less of an effect than had been expected (principally because of some adept staff work which enabled detraining points to be changed at the last moment), the advance was delayed by four days. Since this did nothing to allay his concerns, in the autumn of that year he instructed Groener to prepare a memorandum on the difficulties of supplying the right wing. In his report Groener concluded that the problems involved in maintaining a rapid advance were serious but not intractable. On the one hand, requisitioning foodstuffs as they went along would be time-consuming and would probably slow the march; on the other, supplying the troops by rail was likely to suffer from damage to the network, especially since only a few main lines ran in the appropriate direction west of the Meuse. (As a minimum, each army required one double-tracked line for its supply.) If any of these were destroyed, or if any of the numerous tunnels were blocked, the distance between the railheads and the marching columns might increase to the point where the horse-drawn supply trains that connected them would be unable to keep up and the advance would grind to a halt because of inadequate supplies of food and ammunition.

As anticipated, when war broke out both the Belgians and the French carried out the planned destruction of their rail networks ahead of the invading Germans.[4] As far as the Belgians were concerned, the speed and direction of the German advance took them by surprise, leaving them with insufficient time to carry out serious demolitions before they were compelled to withdraw to Antwerp. In particular, by advancing so rapidly from the border at Aachen the Germans were able to prevent them from wrecking the vitally important line leading to Liège, on which all three right wing armies would depend for their supplies. The line was extremely vulnerable to strategic demolitions since the 30-mile stretch between Aachen and Liège contained more than 20 tunnels, one viaduct and 15 bridges. Likewise, the Belgians did little damage to the rail network to the west of the Meuse, including the important double-tracked Liège–Brussels line, because they had not anticipated that the Germans would come this way. On the other hand they carried out considerable destruction to the east of the Meuse, where most of the major river crossings and several tunnels had been prepared for demolition in the weeks leading up to the war. Thus, by the time that the German 2nd Army was approaching the major rail junction of Namur most of the rail bridges across the Sambre and the Meuse had been blown up, as had the nearby tunnel at Seilles, thereby completely severing all the lines which entered the city from the east.

Within France there were two areas of concern; *le système Nord* towards which the German 1st Army was advancing and *le système Est*, which was in the path of 2nd Army. Since the French had not anticipated that the Germans would make a wide sweep through Belgium, preparations for demolition had been given low priority in *le système Nord* and the destruction was therefore on a very limited scale. In comparison, *le système Est* had been given a higher priority, with the result that several bridges over the Sambre, the Aisne and the Crozat Canal were blown up when the war began and two major tunnels were completely destroyed on the main line leading to Charleville and Sedan.

When the German advance guards crossed the border into Belgium and Luxembourg they were closely followed by the 66 specialised railway construction companies (approximately 20,000 men) whose task was to repair the damage as they advanced behind the front line. In Belgium west of the Meuse and in *le système Nord* in France they made good progress, since the damage was limited to torn-up track and the destruction of telephone and telegraph wires, signal boxes and water towers. A few tunnels had been blocked at the last moment by running locomotives into one another at high speed but these were also cleared without a great deal of delay. As a result, the double-tracked line that served 1st Army was opened up to traffic to Louvain on 24 August, Brussels on the 26th and Cambrai on the 30th. On 5 September, the eve of the battle of the Marne, the main railhead had reached Chaulnes (a short distance to the south of Péronne and about 80 miles from the front line at Montceaux–Esternay) with a spur leading from Cambrai to St Quentin. In contrast, progress was much slower to the east of the Meuse where many viaducts had been destroyed and several tunnels had been blown up. Thus, until 2 September when the bridge over the Sambre at Namur was reconstructed, all of 2nd Army's rail traffic had to bypass the city by travelling down the main Liège–Brussels line as far as Landen (to the west of Huy) where it branched off along a single-track line leading to Charleroi. From Charleroi, which was reached on 20 August, the route followed a further single-track line to Chimay from where on 2 September it reached the railhead at Fourmies, approximately 85 miles from the front line at the start of the battle of the Marne. Likewise, the destruction of the bridges over the Meuse in and to the south of Namur caused 3rd Army huge problems. Until the way was clear as far as Charleroi, the railheads stopped at the Meuse; once Charleroi was cleared, however, the main supply line passed through the town and then swung southwards along a single-track line which ended at Couvin, about 60 miles from the front line when the fighting began.

In spite of the considerable damage to the network east of the Meuse, the supply of food and ammunition to the three right wing armies did not break down during the campaign. However, the system was stretched to breaking point, especially on the line to the west of Liège, which had to carry traffic for both 1st and 2nd Armies and at Liège itself, where the railway station handled the traffic for all three right wing armies. (A few well-placed bombs in the station buildings or the marshalling yards could easily have paralysed the German right wing for several days.) In addition, the horse-drawn heavy transport columns which connected the railheads to the corps and regimental supply columns unexpectedly proved too slow to keep up with the advance and had to be replaced by the motor lorries of the motor transport companies. Since both the repaired rail network and the supply columns were working flat out, it is therefore highly probable that if the *ersatz* divisions had been sent to the right wing instead of Lorraine they could not have been supplied with the necessary quantities of food and ammunition.

Similarly, as Tappen stated, the damage to the rail networks and the slow pace of reconstruction prevented troops from being transferred from the left wing to the right in the days immediately following the victory in Lorraine.

> From 20 to 23 August, 6th and 7th Armies reported a great victory in Lorraine … OHL had then to decide how the results of this victory should be exploited. Should they continue to pursue the enemy with 6th and 7th Armies or ultimately transfer to the right wing those forces that had become available? At that moment the right wing of our armies was in a fully victorious advance. Further to the left, 4th and 5th Armies had also just announced a great success. It was however impossible to carry out the transports from the left wing to the right wing because the Belgians had almost completely destroyed their railways, so that we had to wait, and those sections which had been provisionally repaired were used to bring IX Reserve Corps [from Schleswig-Holstein] to the right wing. If at that time we had withdrawn troops from 6th and 7th Armies to bring them by stages to the right wing, they would have been paralysed for a long time, not to speak of the difficulties of supplying them, and they would in all likelihood have arrived too late to have taken part in the decisive combat on the right wing.[5]

The first units to be transferred from the left wing to the right belonged to Heeringen's new 7th Army, which was formed to fill the gap between 1st and

2nd Armies as they fell back towards the Aisne after the battle of the Marne. Despite the fact that a great deal of reconstruction work had been carried out since 27 August when IX Reserve Corps had completed its movement, it took XV Corps over a week to reach St Quentin (via Aachen–Liège–Brussels) from where it got to the front just in time to take part in the fighting on the Aisne. In theory, if Moltke had transferred units to the right wing from Lorraine on 24 August, immediately after the French defeat, they could have arrived just in time to take part in the battle of the Marne. In practice, however, because the reconstruction work was then less advanced, the journey would almost certainly have taken much longer than that of XV Corps and they would also have had a longer march from the railheads to the battlefield. In addition, the large number of troop trains involved would have temporarily cut off supplies to the right wing armies just as they were entering French territory. (According to the German official history of the war, the movement of XV Corps was achieved only by ruthlessly stopping the movement of supplies to the right wing.)

Whereas Moltke's decision not to strengthen the right wing makes good sense, his decision to send the Guard Reserve and XI Corps to the Eastern Front is open to debate. Although with hindsight they would have been better employed in the West, we should not forget the situation at the Kaiser's Military Headquarters following Prittwitz's warning that he would be forced to retreat across the East Prussian border if he did not receive urgent reinforcements. According to Plessen, the news that German territory was threatened with invasion caused near panic and threw everyone into a great depression. 'But East Prussia! Gumbinnen and Allenstein occupied by the enemy! The Russians are burning and pillaging everything! We must make haste to finish in the West as quickly as possible in order to come to the rescue of the East.'[6] As mentioned above, a series of highly favourable reports from several army commanders, including Kluck and Bülow, not unreasonably led Moltke to conclude that the war on the Western Front had more or less been won. Under these circumstances it is unfair to take him to task for his initial decision to withdraw several corps from the West and use them to reinforce 8th Army. However, when Moltke and Tappen reviewed the situation two days later, on 27 August, the situation was less clear-cut and there was a case to be made for retaining them in the West. Since they had not yet reached their embarkation points (Aachen for the Guard Reserve Corps and Malmédy-St Vith for XI Corps), there was still time to rescind the order. Moltke decided against doing so, partly it appears because the situation in the East was still not completely clear (the news of the great victory at Tannenberg did not arrive until the next day) and partly because of an aversion to countermanding orders. In any case, as Dommes said, if they had been sent back they would probably have arrived too late to take part in the battle of the Marne:

> The next day's report let it be known that a considerable victory had indeed been achieved [in the West] but that a major decision had not yet been reached. Accordingly, it was necessary to examine whether or not to halt the Guard Reserve and XI Army Corps and return them to the right wing. Generaloberst von Moltke wrestled heavily with this decision. The consideration that both corps would arrive too late to take part in the next pursuit battle and the aversion for countermanding orders, which could have an adverse effect on trust in the leadership, seems to have been the decisive factor. I remember that in connection with these considerations, Generaloberst von Moltke said, 'order, counter order, disorder'.[7]

A further accusation was that Moltke allowed the army commanders, Kluck and Bülow in particular, too much freedom of action and therefore lost control over events in the crucial period before the battle of the Marne. Admittedly, his failure to keep Kluck firmly under control at this vital time contributed significantly to the defeat, but this was primarily due to a disastrous breakdown in signal communications and not because he was unwilling to face up to his independent-minded and strong-willed subordinate. This breakdown, which began on about 20 August just as the first battles were about to take place, originated in a decision which was taken by the General Staff four years earlier, in 1910. At that time there were three means of long distance communication, two of which, telephone and telegraph, involved the use of fixed wires, and the third of which, radio telegraphy, did not. Towards the end of the 19th century the use of wire telegraphy for military communication had become well-established in all the major European armies and had proved its worth to the British in the Boer War. However, in 1910, acting on reports from the Russo–Japan War that the

Japanese Army had encountered serious problems (partly, it seems through lack of trained operators) the German General Staff made the fatal mistake of rejecting wire telegraphy for military purposes, despite the fact that it had been tested in manoeuvres by their own Signal Corps and found eminently suitable. It used well-established and reliable apparatus capable of sending and receiving many messages per hour (from about 15 per hour for a simple key-operated instrument to several hundred for a large telegraph printer), it could operate effectively over large distances (several hundred miles using simple portable relay apparatus) and could potentially make use of existing telephone and telegraph wires in occupied territories. In addition, the Hughes apparatus, which was favoured by the German Signal Corps up to 1910, was also used extensively throughout Germany by the civilian Imperial Post and Telegraph Service.

Instead, the General Staff decided that all military communications would henceforth take place by means of fixed wire telephony. In theory this was much superior to telegraphy since it allowed direct speech: in practice, however, the system broke down irretrievably during the third week of August, just as the German right wing was about take part in the battles of Mons and Charleroi. This happened because the Germans were unable to use the wire networks in the occupied territories, partly because of extensive destruction, and partly because the Signal Corps lacked the expertise needed to understand the complexities of the foreign circuitry. (Ironically, this knowledge was present within the Imperial Post and Telegraph Service but through an astonishing oversight most of its 80,000 members were drafted into front line units on the outbreak of the war rather than into the Signal Corps.) As a result, the Signal Corps was forced to construct its own wire network as it followed the advancing armies into Belgium and northern France. If they had been able to construct and wire up new telephone poles at the same rate as the right wing armies were advancing there would have been no problem, since well-built permanent pole lines are capable of transmitting messages over a distance of several hundred miles. However, the number of men allocated to the Signal Corps when hostilities began (approximately 800 officers and 2,500 men) proved insufficient and so the rate of construction fell short of what was required, leaving a gap between Army Headquarters and the end of the permanent pole lines. In consequence, this gap had to be filled by ground-laid wires, which were easily damaged by the movement of vehicles or sabotaged by the civilian population and which, moreover, had a limited transmission range of approximately 20 to 25 miles. In the early stages of the campaign, the field wires that linked the headquarters of 1st, 2nd and 3rd Armies to the permanent network were relatively short and so Kluck, Bülow and Hausen were able to remain in direct touch with OHL. (The last telephone conversation between OHL and 1st Army Headquarters seems to have taken place on 22 August, when Kuhl complained about Bülow's recent decisions and asked for 1st Army to be given its independence. Kluck's headquarters at the time were at Louvain, where they remained for two days.) However, from the end of August, when 1st and 2nd Armies crossed the border with France and the advance gathered pace, the pole construction teams fell further and further behind and the point was soon reached when the field wires exceeded the maximum transmission distance, ruling out long distance calls altogether.

In the absence of a viable telephone network, and with the distance too great to send messages by car on a regular basis, the only way for OHL to keep in touch with the headquarters of the three right wing armies was by means of the fledging technology of radio telegraphy. (The other four armies were able to communicate with OHL by telephone throughout the campaign because they advanced relatively slowly.) Each army headquarters was provided with two large radio receiver/transmitter sets with a range of up to about 170 miles for communication with OHL and the cavalry corps and a smaller short-range set for keeping in touch with neighbouring armies. On the other hand, individual corps were not provided with sets and so were forced to communicate with one another and with army headquarters by using relays of staff officers in the traditional way.

There were two reasons why radio telegraphy was inadequate, one technical and one to do with organization. Firstly, by the beginning of September the distance between OHL and the headquarters of the right wing armies was at the very limits of radio transmission. As a result, reception was poor and messages were difficult to read because of the high level of background noise and interference from the powerful French transmitter on the Eiffel Tower. This also meant that messages had to be kept very short because the misreading of a single letter or group of letters in the double transposition code rendered the whole content illegible. (Longer messages such as the one from Kluck to Moltke on 4 September were divided into several parts, each of which was transmitted separately so that errors would cause only the loss of the affected part and not the whole message.) Secondly, the system became grossly overloaded because it was originally intended only to provide short-term backup if the telephone system suffered from temporary problems. For this reason OHL possessed only a single large Telefunken set and the number of operators and cipher clerks was completely inadequate to deal with the unexpectedly large volume of traffic. Furthermore, the system handled not only military traffic but also messages to and from other parts of the Kaiser's Military Headquarters, some of which were of a trivial and personal nature. (A message from the mother of Prince Frederick Charles of Prussia to her children describing how their father had received the Iron Cross first class from the Kaiser was approximately twice as long as Kluck's daily situation reports.[8]) Since there was no system in place for prioritising traffic, urgent military communications were often held up for a considerable time in the queue for transmission or deciphering.

If Moltke's headquarters had been closer to the front than first Koblenz and then Luxembourg, as several officers suggested, there would have been fewer problems with reception. Namur and Rethel were proposed as possible locations but appear to have been ruled out by Moltke because he would be unable to guarantee the Kaiser's safety on French soil. The alternative approach of separating OHL from the Kaiser's Military Headquarters and transferring it to a forward base much closer to the front line seems to have been rejected by Moltke on the grounds that he needed to be in close touch with the Emperor in order to obtain his signature for important orders.[9] In addition to greatly improving radio reception, a forward location for OHL would have allowed Moltke to make regular visits to the front line. As it was, the distance between OHL and the headquarters of both Kluck and Bülow never fell below 120 miles, a distance which took several hours by car. Possibly because of this, Moltke did not visit the front until 11 September, two days after the battle of the Marne, when the enemy was threatening to break through between 2nd and 3rd Armies and even then he complained that it was difficult to take important decisions in the Kaiser's absence. The contrast with Joffre, whose headquarters were never more than 60 miles from the front line, is very instructive. Despite being in constant touch with all of his army commanders by both telephone and telegraph, Joffre visited their headquarters on numerous occasions even though he was obliged to be absent from GQG for many hours at a time. Given that he was extremely corpulent, that the weather was ferociously hot and that cars at that time were badly sprung and the roads poor, one must hugely admire his energy and his determination to keep in touch with events at the front. In the ten days preceding the battle of the Marne, he visited Lanrezac four times, Sir John French three times and Ruffy and de Langle de Cary once each. On 29 August, after spending the morning at Lanrezac's headquarters seeing how he conducted the battle of Guise, he drove to Compiègne for a meeting with Sir John French before returning to Vitry-le-François in the late evening after an exhausting round trip of over 220 miles.

The most serious consequence of the breakdown in communications was that it gave Kluck the scope to disobey Moltke's orders and push 1st Army across the Marne, thereby exposing his open flank to attack from the direction of Paris. Aged 68 when the war broke out, Alexander von Kluck was one of Germany's most experienced officers; as a young man he had seen service in the Wars of Unification, he became a general in 1906 and soon afterwards was promoted to one of the prestigious corps commands. His selection for the command of 1st Army, which would be in the vanguard of the great wheeling movement through Belgium and northern France, was appropriate in the light of his reputation as a dynamic and aggressive general who believed wholeheartedly in Schlieffen's doctrine of envelopment. (This strategy brought him excellent results in the annual pre-war manoeuvres.) At the same time, however, he was known to be vain, egotistical and a risk-taker, capable of making rash decisions and impatient of authority and so at the start of the campaign Moltke placed him under Bülow's control in an attempt to curb his more aggressive instincts. Tall and strongly built, with a close-cropped bullet head, he appears in photographs as the archetypal Prussian officer of popular imagination. One of the best descriptions of him at this time, albeit highly coloured by the fact that the writer was French and that his house was about to be requisitioned, came from Albert Fabre, a prominent citizen in the village of Lassigny, near Noyon. Having heard the sounds of firing in the early morning of 1 September, M Fabre saw large numbers of Germans entering the village where they immediately began to ransack the houses that had been abandoned by their owners several days earlier. A short while later, a group of staff officers arrived at his house and demanded accommodation for 28 officers and for a table to be laid with luxurious settings for a meal for the same number. When the preparations were ready, one of them insisted that M Fabre accompany him to the gate of the property to watch the march past of a German regiment. Before long a staff car arrived containing the 1st Army Commander himself.

Suddenly, a movement took place among the officers who were drawn up around the gate. A car had stopped there. An officer of impressive and arrogant bearing got out. He advanced alone as far as the middle of the courtyard. He was large, majestic, with a clean-shaven and ravaged face, hard features and a frightening look. In his right hand he held a rifle, his left hand rested on the butt of a revolver. He turned around several times and striking the ground with the butt of his rifle adopted a theatrical pose. No one seemed to dare approach him. He had a truly terrible air. I had a vision of Attila. It was the famous General von Kluck.

A group of high-ranking officers including generals had remained at the entrance to the street. Kluck gestured to them; one of the generals came forwards, stopped a short distance in front of him, held himself bolt upright, gave a military salute and received an order. Kluck demanded a garden table and a chair. I suggested to the general that 'his Excellency', as he was addressed, would be better on the terrace of the villa. I thus hoped to remove him from our view. He replied, 'It's true. But his Excellency has given an order and I can't discuss it. He would not tolerate it if I attempted to make a suggestion of this nature.' My servant carried a table and a garden chair to the spot he had indicated. Kluck sat down, spread out his map and examined it attentively. My servant waited nearby for his orders. There then took place an extraordinary and unbelievable scene. I felt a blow on my shoulder and having turned round saw someone dressed in black wearing a bowler hat on his head. He said to me, 'Is that your servant over there?' I replied, 'Yes'. 'Call him back at once. This man is terrible; you don't know him. He's very fierce. If he thinks that your servant was trying to see what he was doing, he would shoot him with his revolver as if he were a dog.' I immediately called my servant back and I said to this extraordinary German who spoke our language admirably, 'but who are you to express yourself so in this way?' He replied 'I am the police officer charged with watching over his Excellency's security'... When Kluck had consulted his map and had dined ... I saw his Chief of Staff descending the external staircase of the house. He called me over to him and as on the previous occasion a few hours earlier [when the Germans had first arrived] I was forced to hear a speech on the subject of the annihilation of France in general and the destruction of Paris, a speech which must certainly have reflected the thoughts of his master.[10]

Kluck's disobedience was gradual. For the first few days after 27 August, when Moltke inadvisably caved in to his repeated requests for independence, he readily conformed to the latter's strategy. For example, the decision which he took on 30 August to swing inwards to the south-east was undoubtedly a short-term tactical manoeuvre aimed at enveloping Lanrezac's left wing and did not contravene the 27 August General Directive, which specified a south-westerly path for 1st Army, taking it around Paris. Likewise, on the evening of 1 September, when he decided that he could no longer catch up with the French, he very properly informed Moltke and added that he was waiting for further instructions. Only a few hours later, however, after learning that the British would after all be within striking distance he decided to renew the pursuit the following morning, even though this would take them ahead of 2nd Army, which had marked time for the last two days while it besieged La Fère. The next day, 2 September, he slipped into outright insubordination by pushing his left wing across the Marne instead of carrying out Moltke's order to echelon back behind 2nd Army and cover in the direction of Paris. By nightfall on the 4th three out of his five corps were across the Marne and one more was preparing to join them the next day, leaving only an inadequate force (IV Reserve Corps and the very weak 4th Cavalry Division) to cover against Paris. Finally, when he received the order on the morning of the 5th to fall back to a position between the Ourcq and the Marne and face Paris, he not only allowed the advance to continue but also requested permission to continue as far as the Seine. By the time that Hentsch arrived later that day to insist that Moltke's orders were carried out, it was too late and IV Reserve Corps was already under attack.

On its own, Kluck's decision to continue the pursuit would probably not have had fatal consequences and indeed could have led to victory if he had succeeded in cutting off the French retreat and enveloping their left wing.[11] His real mistake was to discount the threat to his exposed right flank from the direction of Paris, based on his belief that both the British Army and the French 6th Army were spent forces after their defeats at Le Cateau and on the Somme bend respectively.[12] On 28 August, two days after the battle, he firmly believed that the British were intent on escaping to the coast and claimed that they no longer posed a credible threat. 'The left wing of the main French forces [ie the French 5th Army] is retreating in a southerly and south-westerly direction in front of the victorious Second and Third Armies. It appears to be of decisive importance to find the flank of this force … and force it away from Paris and outflank it. Compared with this new objective, the attempt to force the British Army away from the coast is of minor importance.'[13] Likewise, he was convinced that after the drubbing they had received, the French forces that had been encountered on the Somme bend were highly unlikely to cause him any further trouble. This was a view he continued to hold right up to the battle of the Ourcq, in spite of warning signs from about 2 September that the French were in fact assembling a new force in the Paris region. For example, on the evening of 2 September Linsingen reported that the 3rd Infantry Division had been in action near Senlis against a large enemy force of about one infantry division supported by strong cavalry and which was not British as expected, but surprisingly French. ('At the same time [Linsingen] reported that his II Corps had been opposed the previous day [at Verberie] not only by British cavalry but also by French troops, among them reserve Alpinejäger, which led one to conclude that some of the French troops that had been defeated at Amiens–Moreuil had since then joined up with the British.'[14])

If Kluck had carried out detailed reconnaissance in the Paris area in the first week of September he would have observed the gradual build-up of the French 6th Army and would have had plenty of time to take counter-measures. However, his attention was so firmly concentrated on the pursuit of Lanrezac's troops that he neglected to do so and allowed Maunoury to assemble his force almost completely unnoticed. In any case, IV Reserve Corps did not possess any aeroplanes of its own and was therefore completely dependent for aerial reconnaissance on its closest neighbour, II Corps. Unfortunately, during the first few days of September when the French build-up in front of Paris was in full swing, the normal practice of copying the results of II Corps' aerial reconnaissance to both IV Reserve Corps and to 1st Army Headquarters appears to have broken down. The last report to reach Kluck, which arrived on the evening of 30 August, said that the French had given up Amiens and were retreating in great disorder behind the Avre. On 2 September, however, in a report which does not seem to have reached him, pilots said that they had seen large bodies of enemy troops estimated at approximately two and a half corps and one and a half cavalry divisions in the area Chantilly–Senlis–Dammartin. The next day, 3 September, II Corps Headquarters received a further report, according to which there was an enemy division to the south-west of Dammartin and artillery on the march towards the town. 'Like a number of other reports from 2 September, this report does not appear in the records of 1st Army or in the records of IV Reserve Corps.'[15] Although this breakdown in communications can hardly be laid at Kluck's door, it is remarkable that he neither complained about the lack of information nor ordered aerial reconnaissance to the north-east of Paris. On the contrary, on 4 September he ordered II Corps to direct all of its flights to the south, in the direction of Château-Thierry and beyond, and none in the direction of the city.

Nor was there any significant reconnaissance in the latter direction by the German cavalry, which was in a lamentable condition because of the unexpectedly long marches, the remorseless hot weather and the lack of fodder and horseshoes. To make matters worse, during the first few days of September they were all ordered south, ahead of 1st and 2nd Armies, in order to sever the enemy's communications with the rear and to cut off their retreat. On the evening of 31 August Marwitz's Cavalry Corps was instructed to cut off the British force, which were reported to be marching south from Soissons and Vic-sur-Aisne. After he ordered a ruthless pursuit, the three divisions left behind all unnecessary impedimenta including bridging trains, spare horses and telegraph wagons and rode through the night with scarcely a pause for rest. Having passed through the Forest of Compiègne they spent the early hours of the next morning resting in march-column along the high road in darkness and steady rain. They took part in the action at Verberie on 1 September and on the next day were ordered to advance rapidly, 'without consideration for man or horse' in a further attempt to outflank the British. As a result of these exertions, on 3 September, when the need for reconnaissance in the Paris area was of critical importance, all three divisions were given a rest day in order to allow the horses to recuperate and to receive badly-needed new horseshoes. The next day, the 4th Cavalry Division, which was extremely weak after the disastrous action at Néry, was assigned to IV Reserve Corps while the 2nd and 9th Divisions, together with the Jäger Battalions, were ordered to reconnoitre ahead of the main mass of the army in the direction of the Marne at La Ferté-sous-Jouarre. If Kluck had concentrated more of his cavalry on the right wing and had been less obsessed with the situation on the far side of the Marne he might possibly have detected the appearance of new enemy forces in front of Paris. As it was, the 4th Cavalry Division was too weak for the job and was easily turned away from the sensitive area by the French cavalry.

Another factor that contributed to the German defeat was inadequate co-ordination between the three right wing armies, which resulted from poor communications and from professional differences between their commanders, Kluck and Bülow in particular. Early on in the campaign their headquarters were reliably connected by telephone but the system broke down after about 20 August because they were on the move all the time, and because the under-strength Signal Corps could not spare the men needed to construct the necessary lateral lines. (Ironically, a direct connection between 1st and 2nd Armies was re-established on 9 September, just one hour after the orders were issued for the retreat.[16]) Unable to keep in touch with one another by telephone, Kluck, Bülow and Hausen were forced to fall back on radio telegraphy, but the paucity of sets and the inadequate number of trained cipher clerks meant that messages were often considerably delayed and had therefore also to be sent by staff officers.

In addition to these technical difficulties, professional animosity bedevilled the relationship between Kluck and Bülow and prevented them from co-operating fully with one another. Superficially they had a great deal in common: they were approximately the same age, had both taken part in the wars with Austria and France and had effortlessly risen to the top via one of the much sought after corps commands, followed by an army inspectorship. However, their personalities could not have been more different. Whereas Kluck was egotistical and impatient, ready to run risks in order to achieve rapid and decisive victory, Bülow generally erred on the side of caution and preferred the carefully prepared frontal assault to seizing the enemy's flanks. Kluck believed that minor fortresses such as La Fère posed no threat and could be easily masked by weak forces; Bülow, on the contrary, insisted that they should be besieged even if it meant delaying the advance by several days. Whereas Kluck acted independently and disregarded Moltke's orders, firstly to echelon back behind 2nd Army and secondly to retreat and face Paris, Bülow scrupulously did as he was told the moment his orders arrived. In addition, unlike Kluck whose aggressive attitude was at least constant, Bülow was subject to quite sudden mood swings, coloured by events at the front and probably exacerbated by the heart and circulatory problems that were to lead to a stroke in April 1915 and his death six years later. As a result, he was easily rattled and was prone to making hasty and unjustified decisions on the spur of the moment. For example, the mauling of the 2nd Guards Reserve Division at Gozée and Marbaix on 23 August affected him to such an extent that he made an urgent and unnecessary appeal for help from Hausen the next day. Likewise, on the evening of 7 September he misguidedly ordered X Corps to abandon the Poirier Crest and Soizy-aux-Bois and the 14th Infantry Division to cover the gap opposite the St Gond Marshes because of unfounded rumours that the enemy was about to break through at this point. In particular, it was his greatly exaggerated report of victory after the battle of Charleroi which suggested to Moltke that the war on the Western Front was as good as won and that it was safe to withdraw several corps and send them to the East.[17]

There were two occasions when better co-operation between Bülow and Kluck could have had a decisive outcome. The first of these was in the period before the battles of Mons and Charleroi when Bülow was responsible for co-ordinating the movements of the three right wing armies in order to trap the French within the Sambre–Meuse Salient. Whereas Kluck wanted to push 1st Army out to the west to envelop the British, Bülow insisted that it should swing inwards to support his right wing as it crossed the Sambre. As far as Kluck was concerned, Bülow was to blame for missing a golden opportunity for defeating not only the British but also the French:

The proposal of the 1st Army Commander to keep his Army out on the western flank away from 2nd Army was thus refused, and this at a time when the fateful crisis on the western wing of the German armies was approaching. Had 1st Army been free and untrammelled, it would probably have been in a position to outflank and crush the British Army by coming in against it from the west, and, investing Maubeuge, to force it back on the French 5th Army, and then take them both in the rear.[18]

Kluck's claim does have some substance. The fighting at Mons took place along the Mons–Condé Canal to the west of the town between the British II Corps and the German IX, III and IV Corps, which were wheeling round to the south prior to crossing the border with France. Neither the British I Corps, which was bent back at an acute angle to the east of the town, nor the German II Corps, which was strongly echeloned back on the right to cover the open flank, took part in the battle. If 1st Army had been pushed out further to the west the day before the battle, as Kluck requested, it might have overlapped the western end of the British line, leaving his IV Corps free to envelop their open flank. If this had happened, and both the British and the French 5th Army had been defeated, there would have been little to prevent the Germans from rolling up the French left wing, thus bringing the war in the west to a victorious conclusion.[19]

One week later relationships between them worsened when Bülow gave 2nd Army two successive rest days while they prepared for the siege of the antiquated fortress of La Fère. Already, the two army commanders had clashed over the use of IX Corps to besiege Maubeuge and in Kluck's eyes Bülow was now making an even bigger mistake when his troops should have been in rapid pursuit of the defeated enemy:

In the evening [of 30 August] Hauptmann Bührmann arrived at Péronne from 2nd Army Headquarters and announced that on the 31st 2nd Army would remain where it was and 'rest'. According to Bülow, after the long marches and heavy combat which they had experienced, the state of his troops unfortunately did not allow them to undertake the pursuit with all their forces. Well, on our part we had definitely been counting on this pursuit. In future, it seemed impossible to us to push 1st Army on its own in a markedly southern direction. The gap that separated us from 2nd Army would become too great and we would be in the air.[20]

When 2nd Army resumed its pursuit, Bülow was convinced from the amount of debris on the roads and in the adjacent fields that the French were in a desperate condition and announced that he was hard on their heels. To Kluck, whose troops had spent the last few days going flat out to catch up with the enemy, first at the Aisne and now as they were approaching the Marne, this call to arms must have sounded rather hollow. No wonder that the long six-part radio message to Moltke on 4 September opened with the pointed phrase 'Can 1st Army be notified of the situation of the other armies, whose reports about decisive victory have repeatedly been followed by requests for support.' As at Mons, one week earlier, an opportunity to envelop the French left wing had been lost because of Bülow's poor judgment and unwillingness to take risks.

For various reasons including the loss of surprise, escalating supply problems and fewer and more exhausted troops, the chances of a German victory declined the longer the campaign lasted. The myth that the German 1st Army would have triumphed on 9 September had it not been for Hentsch's unfortunate interference and Bülow's unnecessary order for 2nd Army to retreat was sedulously propagated and widely believed in Germany after the war. Not only did most of the former High Command subscribe to this warped version of events but so also did the normally reliable German official history, which went into great detail on the matter. However, a mere glance at the facts shows that this was a myth and nothing more. Whether or not Hentsch exceeded his powers in forcing 1st Army to retreat, or Bülow misinterpreted Kluck's message that his left wing was falling back, is immaterial; the fact of the matter was that the British had crossed the Marne in force and that Quast's Battle Group had failed to envelop the French left wing, which had merely bent back before them. In all probability Kluck and Kuhl knew that the game was up well before Hentsch arrived at Mareuil. This would explain why Quast's attack was merely referred to as a push – *Vorstoss* – and also perhaps why, unlike Bülow, Kluck avoided meeting Hentsch. As Hentsch had feared, he became the scapegoat which allowed the German High Command to rid itself of blame for losing the battle.

The best chance of a German victory was at the battle of Charleroi, where they had the advantages of superior numbers and almost total surprise. It was not until 22 August, by which time the battle was in full swing, that the French belatedly realized the German right wing was wheeling round to the south, and even then they considerably underestimated the scale of the threat. In reality, excluding units which were screening Antwerp, Maubeuge and Namur, or which were more than one day's march to the rear, the total strength of the three right wing German armies was 20 divisions, compared to a total of 15 divisions for the French 5th Army and the British combined, and therefore more than sufficient to overwhelm them. Once the French had escaped from the trap and the British had successfully retreated from the battle of Mons, the scales progressively tipped against the Germans to such an extent that even if they had won the battle of the Marne they would almost certainly have been forced to come to a halt soon afterwards. Firstly, as the campaign progressed it became increasingly difficult to supply the fast-moving right wing with adequate supplies of food and ammunition. To begin with, the lorries that had replaced the horse-drawn heavy transport columns were able to keep up with the front line, but they soon began to break down in large numbers because of the poor roads and non-stop use. In the absence of sufficient spare parts and new tyres their numbers steadily diminished, and by the time of the battle of the Marne only 60 per cent were still in a useable condition.[21] Furthermore, because the rail reconstruction companies fell progressively behind, the crucially important distance between the railheads and the front line increased from about 35 miles on 22 August to more than double that when the battle of the Marne began (as Groener had feared might happen). If the campaign had not taken place at a favourable time of year, when many crops had just been harvested and were stored in barns and depots or still lying in the fields where they had been cut, it is likely that many units would have run out of food well before the battle.

Secondly, combat effectiveness remorselessly declined due to a combination of battlefield losses, long marches and the absence of rest days.[22] Many units had already suffered severe losses by the time the battle of the Marne took place. During the battle of Charleroi for example, RIR15 from the 2nd Guards Reserve Division lost 28 officers and 640 men in the disastrous action at Gozée on

23 August, and during the battle of Guise the 1st Guards Regiment suffered terribly at Colonfay, as did both IR77 and IR78 on the long slope to the north of La Désolation Farm. Needless to say, the battle of the Marne also took a tremendous toll on many units, including (once again) RIR15 which after its catastrophic action against the French 2e RI on the plateau to the north of Charleville was reduced to approximately one third of its strength at deployment. Similarly, IR73 suffered an enormous number of casualties in the violent contest for the possession of Soizy-aux-Bois and the Poirier Crest and on the evening of 8 September could muster only 671 rifles. (The war strength of an infantry regiment was about 3,300 men and 70 officers.) In several cases, large units were almost as badly affected as individual regiments. For instance, IV Reserve Corps, which had hung on grimly during the whole five days of the Ourcq battle, sustained approximately 40 per cent casualties, a figure which was matched only by IX Corps after the fighting at Esternay and at Boissy and Fresnoy.

As far as fatigue was concerned we can look at the experience of IR76 (the Hamburg Regiment), which belonged to the 17th Infantry Division in IX Corps. In the three weeks between 17 August, when the advance began, and 6 September, at the start of the battle of the Marne, they covered more than 350 miles at an average pace of approximately 15 miles a day. Between 1 September and 5 September, in an attempt to catch up with the French, they stepped up their pace to an average of 22 miles a day (33 miles on 2 September). Having fought at Esternay on the 6th (where they suffered almost 40 per cent casualties in the desperate fighting at Châtillon), the next day they departed for the Ourcq battlefield, which they reached on the early morning of the 9th after two successive forced marches, each of 33 miles. With hardly any time in which to rest, they then took part in the offensive against the French left wing, which came to an end at nightfall. All in all they had marched for more than three weeks without a single rest day, had covered almost 400 miles and had fought in two major battles. Little wonder, therefore, that IX Corps was singled out for praise by many commentators including Kluck, and received special mention in the official German history of the war.[23]

Thirdly, the inability of the Germans to catch up with the British and with the French 5th Army after the opening battles gave Joffre the necessary breathing space to put his new strategy in place, and to increase efficiency by weeding out incompetent generals and improving tactics. The first units to be transferred to the left wing entrained between 25 and 27 August, and appeared in the Amiens region approximately three to four days later. Therefore, the Germans needed to win the campaign by the end of August at the latest, when 6th Army was incomplete and posed no threat to their exposed flank. At the same time as Joffre began to formulate his new strategy, he began a ruthless cull of incompetent generals. Greatly to the astonishment of those who had been taken in by his placid temperament, he turned out to be an excellent butcher: in the first two months he dismissed two of the six army commanders, 10 of the 25 corps commanders and more than half of the 80 divisional commanders. As a result of this brutal but wholly necessary surgery, 5th Army in particular was transformed in the two weeks that separated the battle of Charleroi from the battle of the Marne. In addition to the weary and defeatist Lanrezac, out went III Corps Commander Sauret, who had proved his incompetence during the battle of Charleroi, together with the commander of XVIII Corps, de Mas Latrie, who had shown a lamentable lack of drive during the battle of Guise. The dynamic and forceful Franchet d'Esperey was promoted to the army command and several inspirational junior officers, such as Pétain and Mangin, were given divisions. In comparison, the only German generals to lose their posts did so as a result of illness or enemy action, such as the commander of X Reserve Corps, General von Kirchbach, who was badly wounded by fire from French stragglers towards the end of the battle of Guise. Although the overall quality of the German generals at the start of the campaign was much higher than that of their French counterparts (and any deficiencies were usually compensated for by their highly competent chiefs of staff), candidates for dismissal were not lacking. Indeed, it is hard to believe that Joffre would have tolerated Kluck's intransigence for very long if he had been in Moltke's shoes, nor would he have been satisfied with Plettenberg's lack of drive or with the performance of divisional commanders such as Schmundt, whose incompetence led to the decimation of IR 77 during the battle of Guise.[24]

In addition to remoulding the high command, Joffre also began to remedy some of the more glaring faults in tactics that had been distressingly exposed in the opening battles, when attacks had been launched with little or no artillery support and with troops bunched together, making them easy targets for the German riflemen and machine gunners. In a note sent to all army commanders on 24 August, he gave detailed instructions on tactics in the light of the lessons that had been learnt in the first weeks of the campaign. In particular, he emphasized the need to improve the effectiveness of the artillery and to get them to co-operate more fully with the infantry when preparing for an attack.

> Army commanders will once more and in the most emphatic way possible call the attention of the troops under their orders to the *absolute necessity* of ensuring complete co-operation between infantry and artillery. Up to the present this has not been achieved in all cases. The one has attacked in too much of a hurry; the other is often engaged after much delay, hesitatingly and sparingly. It is to this capital error that the greater part of the losses sustained by the infantry is imputable.
>
> Furthermore, the work of the batteries is inadequately co-ordinated. The impression is often given that the batteries are engaged singly, depending for their action on the initiative of their captains. The use made by several corps of 75mm guns, firing at a maximum range, with the trail dug in, should be more general. Finally, we must copy our adversaries in using aeroplanes to prepare artillery attacks.[25]

As a result, at neither the battle of Guise nor the battle of the Marne does there seem to have been the needless losses that took place during the battle of Charleroi, when assaults were launched with inadequate artillery support. In cases where losses were heavy, as with Néraud's Brigade at Cornet d'Or during the battle of Guise or the 55th and 56th Reserve Divisions at the Ourcq, the deciding factor was the overwhelming fire power of the German artillery, especially the heavy guns which easily outranged the French 75mm guns, rather than a lack of co-operation between the French infantry and artillery. Whereas the French artillery had a negligable effect on the outcome of the fighting during the battle of Charleroi, by the time of the battle of the Marne only a fortnight later it had become perhaps the single most important factor in the French victory. It led, for example, to Hausen's decision to carry out the potentially hazardous night attack against Foch's right wing.

Of all the individuals in this drama, the one who came out of it with an enhanced reputation was Joffre. Without his tenacity and cool-headedness it could have ended very differently, whatever the failings on the German side. Many of the charges which were later levelled against him possess at least a grain of truth: he failed to make use of all of his reserve units many of which were left behind in their garrisons on the outbreak of the war; despite evidence to the contrary he was unwilling to accept that the Germans would use reserve formations in the front line; he never suspected that they would advance west of the Meuse and he compromised his own war plan by attacking prematurely in Lorraine before he knew how they were deploying. On 24 August, when he became aware of the full magnitude of the disaster and realized that his carefully-wrought plans had come to nothing, he could easily have broken down under the strain as Moltke was to do on 10 September after the battle of the Marne.[26] Instead, he kept his nerve and energetically got to grips with the new situation, taking steps to remedy the worst deficiencies in the army and devising the strategy that led to victory two weeks later. The path towards the final battle was not an easy one, however, and had it not been for his steadfastness and will-power he could easily have been blown off course on several occasions. When the first attempt to assemble the new 6th Army on the Somme in the vicinity of Amiens failed because of the rapid German advance, he did not despair but arranged for the battle to take place further south in the area of the Seine. He was indefatigable in maintaining good relations with the volatile and unreliable Sir John French, doing what he could to boost his *amour-propre*, to heal the rift with Lanrezac and to keep the British Army in the line, ready to take part in the planned offensive. Individuals such as Galliéni and Millerand, who had the authority to interfere with his plans, were neutralized with smooth efficiency and great tact so that he got his way.[27] Rather than communicate by telegraph or telephone, he was in the habit of visiting army headquarters to talk to his generals, encouraging some and taking others to task, in order to keep in close touch with what was happening at the front. Incompetent and untrustworthy generals were sacked, promising ones were promoted in their place and the army's tactical doctrines were overhauled in preparation for the decisive battle. He was, it is true, ably served by several outstanding officers, most notably Foch and Franchet d'Esperey, but without his unflappability and consistent sense of purpose during a time of great national crisis it is difficult to see how the French Army could have survived the campaign. In the summer of 1911 he had become Commander-in-Chief only because Galliéni had turned down the post and because Pau had proved unacceptable. When Messimy selected him because of his easy manner with politicians and not because of his military accomplishments, of which there was little evidence, little did he think that his choice had fallen on a man who would in three year's time save the nation from defeat.

If Joffre came out of the campaign well, the same cannot be said of Sir John French. Although essentially a generous and warm-hearted man (as was apparent in his final meeting with Joffre on the day before the battle of the Marne), his excitable temperament, uncertain judgment based on rumour and personal experience and his tendency to over-exaggerate problems did not suit him to be in command of the army. At best, his more questionable decisions led to a lack of support for his ally at critical moments in the campaign; at worst, they threatened to wreck completely Joffre's carefully laid plans for the counter-offensive. On 30 August, for example, within a few hours of indicating that he would support 5th Army by delaying his retreat, he performed a complete about-turn and insisted that he needed to pull the whole of the army out of the line for a considerable time in order to rest and refit. On at least two occasions he countermanded Haig's orders for I Corps without a great deal of justification. On 29 August he prevented them from taking part in the battle of Guise, thus forcing Lanrezac to use Valabrègue's Reserve Divisions instead. (If Haig's men had advanced down the road from La Fère as intended they might well have overwhelmed the German troops at Essigny-le-Grand and brought about the collapse of the 19th Reserve Infantry Division.) Likewise, at Montreuil-aux-Lions on 9 September, he stopped I Corps from advancing any further, and so prevented them from taking Kraewel's Detachment in the flank. After the skirmish at Landrecies he more or less gave up I Corps as lost and, worse still, his conviction that II Corps was no longer battle-worthy after the action at Le Cateau was based more on one brief encounter rather than on a dispassionate appraisal of the evidence. In the days after the battle of Guise, the British Army was approximately half to one day's march ahead of Lanrezac's right wing, leaving a gap into which

Kluck's troops almost penetrated with potentially disastrous consequences, firstly at Vauxaillon on 31 August, and secondly at Château-Thierry on 3 September; conversely, although the British advance into the gap between the German 1st and 2nd Armies triggered their retreat, it took place without any great sense of urgency because of French's continuing concerns for the safety of his flanks. Without Joffre's sensitive and emollient handling, and at the critical moment the almost brutal intervention of Lord Kitchener, it is unlikely that he would ever have given his full co-operation and that as a result Joffre's plans would have been fatally compromised.

Whatever French's failings, his troops fought well both at Mons, where they gave the Germans a nasty shock, and in particular at Le Cateau where, despite being greatly outnumbered and in an extremely dangerous situation, II Corps fought tenaciously and with great courage against increasing odds and then withdrew from the battlefield intact and in good order. However, although Le Cateau was a great achievement it owed as much to the lack of urgency on the German side as it did to the bravery and tenacity of Smith-Dorrien's men. What really saved the British during the retreat was Kluck's inability to catch up with them after the battle of Mons, because of his unfounded opinion that they were retreating along their lines of communication towards the coast. Indeed, following Mons he seems to have believed that they were a spent force, a view that was greatly strengthened by the results of the battle of Le Cateau, when several guns were captured and some British regiments were overwhelmed after they failed to receive the order to retreat. From this point onwards, he appears to have removed the British from his calculations and as late as 8 September, when they were advancing into the gap with 2nd Army, he still was convinced that they posed no real threat.

Let us end, where we began, with Moltke. From what has been said, it should be clear by now that most of the charges laid against him by his critics were unfounded. Neither the logistics problem, which limited the size of the right wing and made large scale troop transfers almost impossible, nor the breakdown of signal communications which prevented him from keeping close control over events at the front, was of his making. Instead, as we have seen, they were inevitable consequences of Schlieffen's strategy. With hindsight, Moltke's greatest mistake by far was to accept the broad outlines of this strategy and the premises on which it was based, namely the overriding need for a rapid and decisive victory. Perhaps deep within his brain, he harboured lingering doubts about this. (His remark about not invading Holland so that the country could serve as 'a windpipe which will enable us to breathe' seems to suggest that he had not completely ruled out the possibility of a long war.) However, if this was so, it was not enough to cause him to break with the almost universal consensus and develop a radically new plan at a time when war was on the horizon. Far better, he believed, to accept the framework of Schlieffen's plan and merely tinker about with it at the margins in the hope of achieving a little more flexibility instead of risking all on one throw of the die as his predecessor had done.

It is instructive to briefly compare the Schlieffen Plan with two famous and successful campaigns, the capture of Ulm by Napoleon's Grande Armée in the autumn of 1805 and *Sichelschnitt* (the Reapers' Cut), which brought about the fall of France in the spring of 1940. Given that all three were boldly conceived, meticulously prepared and took the enemy completely by surprise, we need to ask why the Schlieffen Plan was the only one to end in failure. Unlike the German armies in 1914 which needed an enormous quantity of supplies, the Grande Armée travelled very light as it carried out the great wheeling movement which cut off the Austrian retreat and trapped them in Ulm. Not only did Napoleon's troops live off the country, requisitioning food from the local inhabitants, but they also needed very few supply trains, because their expenditure of ammunition was several orders of magnitude less than in 1914. Secondly, because armies at the start of the 19th century were much smaller than 100 years later, and battlefields more compact, communication was much less of a problem to Napoleon than it was to Moltke. For example, at the start of Napoleon's advance the average distance between neighbouring corps was about 25 miles, but because the front progressively narrowed as they approached the Danube it fell to about 10 miles, a distance which could easily be covered in an hour or so on horseback. Likewise, the fact that Napoleon's headquarters advanced behind the front line meant that he could keep in close touch with events at the front through a constant flow of staff officers.

By 1940, the extent of the battlefield matched, and in some cases exceeded, that in 1914. By this time, however, the problem of how to communicate reliably and securely over long distances had been solved by advances in radio telegraphy and the development of the Enigma machine. In addition to efficient signals communications, the German High Command in 1940 had one other great advantage over Moltke. In 1914, Kluck's and Bülow's infantry foot-slogged their way through northern France in a vain attempt to catch up with and defeat the enemy, wearing themselves out in the process; in 1940, however, after they crossed the Meuse at Sedan, it took Guderian's Panzer Divisions less than a fortnight to reach the coast at Abbeville, cutting off the bulk of the allied forces in Belgium and leading to French capitulation. If Panzer Divisions had been available to Moltke in 1914, he would undoubtedly have concentrated them on the right wing (the *Schwerpunkt* in Second World War parlance) and would have enveloped the British and 5th Army and rolled up their line from the west before Joffre could transfer troops from the right wing and centre. Essentially, the German High Command in 1940, and Napoleon in 1805, succeeded not only because of the unexpected direction of their attack but also because they were able to advance at a pace that had a paralysing effect on the enemy, throwing them off balance, destroying their morale and leaving them with insufficient time to organize an effective response. In the absence of motorized infantry, the German right wing in 1914 was fated never to catch up with the retreating enemy despite making almost superhuman efforts. Schlieffen's tragedy was to have been born at the wrong time; if he had lived either 100 years earlier or 30 years later, his strategy might well have led to victory for the reasons outlined above; as it was, it failed in 1914 primarily because Moltke did not have the means at his disposal to carry it through to a successful conclusion. Far from being an infallible recipe for victory, as Schlieffen's disciples claimed after the war, his strategy contained the seeds of its own destruction. His military legacy, the plan that Moltke accepted with few reservations, proved toxic, and condemned his countrymen to four years of bloody conflict and the loss of innumerable lives.

# POSTSCRIPT

When the campaign came to an end, almost three quarters of a million French, German and British soldiers were dead, missing or wounded. Among those who were killed in action was Commandant Georges Michon who was mortally wounded on the evening of 21 August when he led his battalion in the attack on the hamlet of Haut-Batys during the battle of Charleroi. Under normal circumstances his wife would have known very little about his death apart from what could be gleaned from the usual formulaic letter of condolence from his colonel. And there the matter would have rested, at least until after the war when she would perhaps have discovered a few more details, including where he was buried. However, in February of the following year she received a remarkable letter, which reached her through neutral Italy.

Berlin Tempelhof
Hohenzollencorso 67
18 February, 1915

Very dear Madame,

In the hope that these lines reach you without too much delay, it is with my great regret that I have to bring you some bad news. It gives me great pain to have to inform you of the death of your husband, bravely fallen on the field of battle near to Auvelais–Arsimont on the Sambre. After the battle, my husband, Oberst von Dassel, happened to be near to a very badly wounded French soldier. To the best of his abilities my husband bandaged his wounds and gave him something to drink from his flask. Your husband, feeling that his end was near, gave my husband a brown case, which contained his watch, an amulet and three letters. My husband promised him he would make sure that these objects were returned to you as soon as possible, and in return he asked my husband to give you his love for the last time. A short time later, when my husband returned, he had breathed his last and was delivered from his great suffering. Our soldiers, to whom my husband gave the order to bury the dead, buried your beloved husband at the same time as our officers and soldiers. Now, I wish to explain why this sad news has reached you so late. After the fighting on 21 August, our troops made many long marches and had to endure great fatigue, and my husband was so greatly occupied that he was unable to carry out his promise to your husband to send these objects to you, but he took good care of them and kept them in his trunk.

My dear husband was in his turn wounded on 8 September, and having rejoined me in Berlin on 13 September he died in the same month. He had told me of the sad events concerning your husband but since the objects were in the bottom of his trunk, which was still on the way back to me, and I did not have your address, I was obliged to wait for the arrival of my husband's effects, which only reached me at the end of January.

Since I am concerned that these objects, which are very precious to you, might go missing in this period of war, I will look after them carefully and will in due course send them to you by secure means.

I would like once more to give you my profound and sincere sympathy on the occasion of your great bereavement and say that although we have been enemies from a political viewpoint, as human beings and as women we are overwhelmed by the same grief and by the same suffering since, as I have been able to make out from your letter to your husband, you were waiting to give birth. Perhaps your child has now been born and finds himself without a father like my dear little girl born on the 18 December. Since my husband rendered a last service and honour to yours, I feel able to overcome the normal boundaries that would separate us and so as women enduring the same suffering, I feel able to clasp your hand and ask God to console you.

Perhaps using the same means which I have employed, you would be able, Madame, to let me know if my lines have reached you. My address is:

Frau von Dassel, care of Signora de Liguoro,

45 via nuovo Pizzofalcone,

Naples,

Italy.

I reiterate my expressions of deepest sympathy.

Charlotte von Dassel[1]

Did her husband's effects safely reach Madame Michon when the war was over, I wonder. Did they perhaps meet to console each other and to share their joy in their new children? We will probably never know. Before very long, one hundred years will have gone by since Wilfried von Dassel gave what help he could to Georges Michon as he breathed his last that evening on the hills overlooking the Sambre valley, and since Oberst von Dassel was himself mortally wounded during the battle of the Ourcq approximately two weeks later. By the middle of September, well over 100,000 men were dead, all of whom, like these two, left behind families to grieve for them silently.

*In Memoriam (Easter, 1915)*

> *The Flowers left thick at nightfall in the wood*
> *This Eastertide call into mind the men,*
> *Now far from home, who, with their sweethearts, should,*
> *Have gathered them and will do never again.*

Edward Thomas

# APPENDICES

## APPENDIX 1

### COMPOSITION AND ORDER OF BATTLE OF THE FRENCH 5TH, 6TH AND 9TH ARMIES

| | |
|---|---|
| Commander-in-Chief: | Général Joffre |
| Chief of Staff: | Général Belin |
| Deputy Chiefs of Staff: | Général Berthelot and Colonel Pellé |

#### 5TH ARMY

| | |
|---|---|
| Commander: | Général Lanrezac until 3 September, then Général Franchet d'Esperey |
| Chief of Staff: | Général Hély d'Oissel |
| Deputy Chief of Staff: | Lieutenant-Colonel Daydrein |
| **I Corps (Lille):** | **Général Franchet d'Esperey until 3 September, then Général Deligny** |
| 1st Infantry Division: | Général Gallet |
| 1st Infantry Brigade: | Colonel de Fonclare |
| 43e RI; 127e RI | |
| 2nd Infantry Brigade: | Général Sauret |
| 1er RI; 84e RI | |
| 2nd Infantry Division: | Général Deligny until 3 September, then Général Duplessis |
| 3rd Infantry Brigade: | Colonel Bernard |
| 33e RI; 73e RI | |

| | |
|---|---|
| 4th Infantry Brigade: | Colonel Doyen |
| 8e RI; 110e RI | |
| Unattached units | |
| 201e RI; 284e RI; 384e Reserve RM | |

| | |
|---|---|
| **III Corps (Rouen):** | **Général Sauret until 25 August, then Général Hache** |
| 5th Infantry Division: | Général Bloch until 31 August, then Général Mangin |
| 9th Infantry Brigade: | Général Tassin |
| 39e RI; 74e RI | |
| 10th Infantry Brigade: | Général Lautier |
| 36e RI; 129e RI | |
| 6th Infantry Division: | Général Verrier until 31 August, then Général Pétain |
| 11th Infantry Brigade: | Colonel Hériot |
| 24e RI; 28e RI | |
| 12th Infantry Brigade: | Général Lavisse |
| 5e RI; 119e RI | |
| 37th Infantry Division: | Général Comby |
| 73rd Infantry Brigade: | Colonel Degot |
| 2e Zouaves RM | |
| 2e Tirailleurs RM | |
| 6e Tirailleurs RM | |
| 74th Infantry Brigade: | Colonel Le Bouhélec |
| 3e Zouaves RM | |
| 5e Tirailleurs RM | |
| 7e Tirailleurs RM | |
| Unattached units | |
| 239e RI; 274e RI | |

| | |
|---|---|
| **X Corps (Rennes):** | **Général Desforges** |
| 19th Infantry Division: | Général Bonnier until 5 September, then Général Bailly |
| 37th Infantry Brigade: | Colonel Pierson |
| 48e RI; 71e RI | |
| 38th Infantry Brigade: | Lieutenant-Colonel Passaga |
| 41e RI; 70e RI | |

| | |
|---|---|
| 20th Infantry Division: | Général Boë until 22 August, then Général Menissier, followed on 5 September by Général Rogerie |
| 39th Infantry Brigade: | Général Menissier |
| 25e RI; 136e RI | |
| 40th Infantry Brigade: | Général de Cadoudal |
| 2e RI; 47e RI | |
| 51st Reserve Division: | Général Boutegourd |
| 101st Infantry Brigade: | Général Petit |
| 233e RI; 243e RI; 327e RI | |
| 102nd Infantry Brigade: | Général Leleu |
| 208e RI; 273e RI; 310e RI | |
| Unattached Units | |
| 241e RI; 270e RI | |

| | |
|---|---|
| **XVIII Corps (Bordeaux):** | **Général de Mas Latrie until 4 September, then Général de Maud'huy** |
| 35th Infantry Division: | Général Excelmans until 4 September, then Général Marjoulet |
| 69th Infantry Brigade: | Général Durand |
| 6e RI, 123e RI | |
| 70th Infantry Brigade: | Général Pierron |
| 57e RI; 144e RI | |
| 36th Infantry Division: | Général Jouannic |
| 71st Infantry Brigade: | Général Simon Bertin |
| 34e RI, 49e RI | |
| 72nd Infantry Brigade: | Général Trinité-Schilmans, then Colonel de Sèze |
| 12e RI; 18e RI | |
| 38th Infantry Division: | Général Muteau, then Général Schwartz |
| 75th Infantry Brigade: | Général Colonel Vuillemin |
| 1er RZ | |
| 1er RT | |
| 76th Infantry Brigade: | Général Bertin until 6 September, then Colonel Pichon |
| 4e RZ | |
| 4e RT | |
| 8e RT | |

Unattached units
218e RI; 249e RI

**4th Group of Reserve Divisions:** — Général Valabrègue

53rd Reserve Division: — Général Perruchon until 7 September, then Général Journée

105th Infantry Brigade: — Général Montangon
205e RI; 236e RI; 319e RI

106th Infantry Brigade: — Lieutenant-Colonel Masson
224e RI; 228e RI; 329e RI

69th Reserve Division: — Général Le Gros until 9 September, then Général Néraud

137th Infantry Brigade: — Général Rousseau
287e RI; 306e RI; 332e RI

138th Infantry Brigade: — Lieutenant-Colonel Piguet until 8 September, then Colonel Cadoux

251e RI; 254e RI; 267e RI

**Conneau's Cavalry Corps:** — Général Conneau
4th Cavalry Division: — Général Abonneau
4th Light Brigade: — Général Requichot
2e RH; 4e RH

4th Dragoons Brigade: — Général Dodelier
28e RD; 30e RD

3rd Cuirassiers Brigade: — Général Sabry de Monpoly
3e RC; 6e RC

8th Cavalry Division: — Général Mazel, then Général Baratier
8th Light Brigade: — Colonel Peillard
12e RH; 14e RH

4th Dragoons Brigade: — Général Gendron until 8 September, then Colonel Guéneau de Montbeillard

11e RD; 18e RD

10th Cavalry Division: — Général Grellet
2nd Light Brigade: — Général Contades-Gizeux
17e RCh; 18e RCh

10th Dragoons Brigade: — Général Chêne
15e RD; 20e RD

15th Dragoons Brigade: — Colonel Sauzy
10e RD; 19e RD

## 6TH ARMY

Until 8 September, subordinate to Général Galliéni, Military Governor of Paris

| | |
|---|---|
| Commander: | Général Maunoury |
| Chief of Staff: | Général Guillemin |

| | |
|---|---|
| **IV Corps (Le Mans):** | **Général Boëlle, from 7 September** |
| 7th Infantry Division: | Général de Trentinian |
| 13th Infantry Brigade: | Colonel de Favrot |
| 101e RI; 102e RI | |
| 14th Infantry Brigade: | Général Félineau |
| 103e RI; 104e RI | |
| 8th Infantry Division: | Général Lartigue |
| 15th Infantry Brigade: | Colonel Fropo |
| 124e RI; 130e RI | |
| 16th Infantry Brigade: | Colonel Desvaux |
| 115e RI; 117e RI | |
| Unattached units | |
| 315e RI; 317e RI | |

| | |
|---|---|
| **VII Corps (Besançon):** | **Général Vauthier** |
| 14th Infantry Division: | Général de Villaret |
| 27th Infantry Brigade: | Colonel Bourquin |
| 44e RI; 60e RI | |
| 28th Infantry Brigade: | Général Faès |
| 35e RI; 42e RI | |
| 63rd Reserve Division: | Général Lombard |
| 125th Infantry Brigade: | Général Dolot |
| 216e RI; 238e RI; 298e RI | |
| 126th Infantry Brigade: | Général Guillin |
| 292e RI; 305e RI; 321e RI | |
| Unattached units | |
| 352e RI; 45e BCP; 47e BCA; 55e BCP; 63e BCA; 64e BCA; 67e BCA | |

| | |
|---|---|
| **5th Group of Reserve Divisions:** | **Général de Lamaze** |
| 55th Reserve Division: | Général Leguay |
| 109th Infantry Brigade: | Général Arrivet |
| 204e RI; 282e RI; 289e RI | |

| | |
|---|---|
| 110th Infantry Brigade: | Général de Mainbray |
| 231e RI; 246e RI; 298e RI | |
| 56th Reserve Division: | Général de Dartein |
| 111th Infantry Brigade: | Lieutenant-Colonel Bonne |
| 294e RI; 354e RI; 355e RI | |
| 112th Infantry Brigade: | Général Cornille |
| 350e RI; 361e RI; 65e BCP; 66e BCP; 69e BCP | |
| **6th Group of Reserve Divisions:** | **Général Ebener** |
| 61st Reserve Division: | Général Desprez |
| (transferred to VII Corps, 7 September) | |
| 121st Infantry Brigade: | Général Delarue |
| 264e RI; 265e RI; 276e RI | |
| 122nd Infantry Brigade: | Lieutenant-Colonel Tesson |
| 219e RI; 262e RI; 318e RI | |
| 62nd Reserve Division: | Général Ganeval |
| (Transferred to Army Reserve, 8 September) | |
| 123rd Infantry Brigade: | Colonel Peyriaque |
| 263e RI; 278e RI; 338e RI | |
| 124th Infantry Brigade: | Général Ninous |
| 250e RI; 30e RI; 308e RI | |
| **45th Infantry Division:** | **Général Drude** |
| 89th Infantry Brigade: | Colonel Castaing |
| 1er Zouaves RM | |
| 3rd Zouaves RM | |
| 90th Infantry Brigade: | Général Passard |
| 2e Zouaves RM | |
| 2e Tirailleurs RM | |
| **Moroccan Brigade:** | **Général Ditte** |
| 1er Régiment de Chasseurs Indigenes | |
| 2e Régiment de Chasseurs Indigenes | |
| **Sordet's Cavalry Corps:** | **Général Sordet until 8 September, then Général Bridoux** |
| 1st Cavalry Division: | Général Buisson |
| 5th Dragoons Brigade: | Général Silvestre |
| 6e RD; 23e RD | |

| | |
|---|---|
| 2nd Cuirassiers Brigade:<br>1er RC; 2e RC | Général Louvat |
| 11th Dragoons Brigade:<br>27e RD; 32e RD | Général Corvisart |
| 3rd Cavalry Division: | Général de Lastours |
| 3rd Light Brigade:<br>3e RH; 8e RH | Général de la Villestreux |
| 13th Dragoons Brigade:<br>5e RD; 21e RD | Général Leorat |
| 4th Cuirassiers Brigade:<br>4e RC; 9e RC | Général Gouzil |
| 5th Cavalry Division: | Général Bridoux until 8 September, then Général Lallemand du Marais |
| 5th Light Brigade:<br>5e RCh; 15e RCh | Général Cornulier-Lucinière |
| 3rd Dragoons Brigade:<br><br>13e RD; 22e RD | Général Lallemand du Marais, until 8th September |
| 7th Dragoons Brigade:<br>9e RD; 29e RD | Général de Marcieux |

## 9TH ARMY

(Army Detachment Foch until 6 September)

| | |
|---|---|
| Commander: | Général Foch |
| Chief of Staff: | Lieutenant-Colonel Weygand |
| **IX Corps (Tours):** | **Général Dubois** |
| Moroccan Division: | Général Humbert |
| 1st Brigade:<br>Zouaves RM<br>Colonial RM | Général Blondlat |
| 2nd Brigade:<br>1er Tirailleurs RM<br>2e Tirailleur RM | Lieutenant-Colonel Cros |
| 17th Infantry Division: | Général Moussy |
| 33rd Infantry Brigade<br>68e RI; 90e RI | Colonel Simon |

| | |
|---|---|
| 36th Infantry Brigade: | Colonel Eon |
|    77e RI; 135e RI | |
| 52nd Reserve Division: | Général Battesti |
| 103rd Infantry Brigade: | Colonel Doursout, then Lieutenant-Colonel Lévy |
|    291e RI; 347e RI; 348e RI | |
| 104th Infantry Brigade: | Lieutenant-Colonel Claudon |
|    245e RI; 320e RI; 49e BCP; 5e BCP | |
| 18th Infantry Division: | Général Lefèvre |
| (transferred to XI Corps, 8 September) | |
| 34th Infantry Brigade: | Général Guignabaudet |
|    114e RI; 125e RI | |
| 35th Infantry Brigade: | Colonel Janin |
|    32e RI; 66e RI | |
| Unattached units | |
|    268e RI; 290e RI | |
| | |
| **XI Corps (Nantes):** | **Général Eydoux** |
| 21st Infantry Division: | Général Radiguet |
| 41st Infantry Brigade: | Colonel de Teyssière |
|    64e RI; 65e RI | |
| 42nd Infantry Brigade: | Colonel Lamy until 8 September, then Colonel Bouyssou |
|    93e RI; 137e RI | |
| 22nd Infantry Division: | Général Pambet |
| 43rd Infantry Brigade: | Général Costebonel |
|    62e RI; 116e RI | |
| 44th Infantry Brigade: | Général Chaplain |
|    19e RI; 118e RI | |
| 60th Reserve Division: | Général Joppé |
| 119th Infantry Brigade: | Général Reveilhac |
|    247e RI; 248e RI; 271e RI | |
| 120th Infantry Brigade: | Général Margueron |
|    202e RI; 225e RI; 336e RI | |
| 42nd Infantry Division: | Général Grossetti |
| 83rd Infantry Brigade: | Général Krien |
|    94e RI: 8e BCP; 19e BCP | |

| | |
|---|---|
| 84th Infantry Brigade: | Colonel Trouchard |
| 151e RI; 162e RI | |

**XXI Corps:** **Général Maistre**
13th Infantry Division: Général Bacquet
25th Infantry Brigade: Colonel Griache
  17e RI; 17e BCP; 20e BCP; 31e BCP
26th Infantry Brigade: Lieutenant-Colonel Schmidt
  21e RI; 109e RI
43rd Infantry Division: Général Lanquetot
85th Infantry Brigade: Colonel Menvielle
  149e RI; 158e RI
86th Infantry Brigade: Colonel Olleris
  1er BCP; 3e BCP; 20e BCP; 31e BCP

**9th Cavalry Division:** **Général de Lespée**
9th Dragoons Brigade: Général Sailly
  1er RD; 3e RD
16th Dragoons Brigade: Général Gombaud
  24e RD; 25e RD
4th Cuirassiers Brigade: Colonel Cugnac
  5e RC; 8e RC

**Key to abbreviations**

| | | | |
|---|---|---|---|
| BCA | Battalion of Chasseurs d'Afrique | BCP | Battalions of Chasseurs à pied |
| RC | Cuirassiers Regiment | RCh | Regiment of Chasseurs à cheval |
| RD | Dragoons Regiment | RH | Hussars Regiment |
| RI | Infantry Regiment | RM | March Regiment |
| RT | Tirailleurs Regiment | RZ | Zouaves Regiment |

## COMPOSITION OF THE PRINCIPAL FRENCH UNITS

**Infantry Division (15,000 all ranks, 36 guns and 24 machine guns)**

1 infantry division = 2 infantry brigades, 1 cavalry squadron, 3 field artillery groups, 1 engineer company

1 infantry brigade = 2 regiments

1 infantry regiment = 3 battalions plus HQ company

1 battalion = 4 companies and 1 machine gun section (22 officers and 1,030 other ranks)

## Cavalry Division (4,500 all ranks and 8 guns)

1 cavalry division = 3 cavalry brigades, 1 horse artillery brigade (each with 2 4–gun batteries), cyclist group (4 officers and 320 other ranks), telegraph detachment etc

1 cavalry brigade = 2 regiments and machine gun section

1 cavalry regiment = 4 squadrons (total of 32 officers, 651 all ranks and 687 horses)

1 cavalry squadron = 5 officers, 145 other ranks, 143 horses

## Artillery

Field artillery

1 regiment of divisional field artillery = 3 groups, 1 regiment of corps artillery = 4 groups

1 group = 3 batteries

1 battery = 4 guns, 12 wagons etc

Heavy artillery (allotted to armies and corps)

1 regiment – strength variable eg in 5th Army = 6 120mm batteries and 7 144mm batteries

1 battery = 4 guns, 8 wagons, observation wagon etc

## Reserve Division

1 division = 2 brigades, 1 cavalry squadron, 3 field artillery groups

1 reserve brigade = 3 regiments and 1 chasseur battalion

1 reserve regiment = 2 battalions

# COMPOSITION AND ORDER OF BATTLE OF THE GERMAN 1ST, 2ND AND 3RD ARMIES

Note: The following units are not included because they played a very minor part in the campaign.

III Reserve Corps (1st Army): Responsible for the siege of Antwerp.

IX Reserve Corps (1st Army): At first held back to oppose a possible landing in Schleswig-Holstein, then involved in the siege of Antwerp.

VII Reserve Corps (2nd Army): Involved in the siege of Maubeuge.

Guard Reserve Corps (2nd Army) and XI Corps (3rd Army): Involved in the siege of Namur from 20–26 August, when they departed for the Eastern Front.

Chief of the General Staff: Generaloberst von Moltke

Deputy Chief of the General Staff: General von Stein

Chief of the Operations Section: Oberst Tappen

Chief of the Intelligence Section: Oberstleutnant Hentsch

Chief of the Political Section: Oberst von Dommes

## 1st Army

| Commander: | Generaloberst von Kluck |
| Chief of Staff: | Generalmajor von Kuhl |
| Deputy Chief of Staff: | Oberst Bergmann |

**II Corps (Stettin):** — **General von Linsingen**
3rd Infantry Division: — Generalleutnant von Trossel
5th Infantry Brigade: — Generalmajor Freiherr Treusch von Buttlar-Brandenfels

Gren.R2; Gren.R9
6th Infantry Brigade: — Oberst Gräser ·
Füs.R34; IR42
4th Infantry Division: — Generalleutnant von Pannewitz
7th Infantry Brigade: — Generalmajor von Runckel
IR14; IR149
8th Infantry Brigade: — Oberst Jennrich
IR49; IR140

**III Corps (Berlin):** — **General von Lochow**
5th Infantry Division: — Generalleutnant Wichura ·
9th Infantry Brigade: — Generalmajor von Doemming
Leib-Grenadier 8; IR48
10th Infantry Brigade: — Generalmajor Sontag
Gren.R12; IR52
6th Infantry Division: — Generalmajor von Rohden
11th Infantry Brigade: — Generalmajor von Wachter
IR20; Füs.R35
12th Infantry Brigade: — Generalmajor von Sabain
IR24; IR64

**IV Corps (Magdeburg):** — **Generalleutnant Sixt von Arnim**
7th Infantry Division: — Generalleutnant Riedel
13th Infantry Brigade: — Generalmajor von Schüssler
IR26; IR66
14th Infantry Brigade: — Generalmajor von Oven
IR27; IR165
8th Infantry Division: — Generalleutnant Hildebrandt

| | |
|---|---|
| 15th Infantry Brigade: | Generalmajor Reichenau |
| Füs.R36; IR93 | |
| 16th Infantry Brigade: | Generalmajor von Jarotsky |
| IR72; IR153 | |

**IX Corps (Altona):**            **General von Quast**

| | |
|---|---|
| 17th Infantry Division: | Generalleutnant von Bauer |
| 33rd Infantry Brigade: | Generalmajor von Lewinski |
| IR75; IR76 | |
| 34th Infantry Brigade: | Generalmajor von Kraewel |
| Gren.R89; Füs.R90 | |
| 18th Infantry Division: | Generalleutnant von Kluge |
| 35th Infantry Brigade: | Oberst von Obernitz |
| IR84; Füs.R86 | |
| 36th Infantry Brigade: | Generalmajor Freiherr von Troschke |
| IR31; IR85 | |

**IV Reserve Corps (Magdeburg):**    **General von Gronau**

| | |
|---|---|
| 7th Reserve Infantry Division: | Generalleutnant Graf von Schwerin |
| 13th Reserve Infantry Brigade: | Generalmajor von Dresler und Scharfenstein |
| RIR27; RIR36 | |
| 14th Reserve Infantry Brigade: | Generalmajor von Wienskowski |
| RIR66; RIR72; Reserve Jäger Battalion IV | |
| 22nd Reserve Infantry Division: | Generalleutnant Riemann |
| 43rd Reserve Infantry Brigade: | Generalmajor von Lepel |
| RIR71; RIR94; Reserve Jäger Battalion XI | |
| 44th Reserve Infantry Brigade: | Generalmajor von Mühlenfels |
| RIR32; RIR82 | |

**II Cavalry Corps:**             **General von der Marwitz**

| | |
|---|---|
| 2nd Cavalry Division: | Generalmajor Freiherr von Krane |
| 5th Cavalry Brigade: | Oberst von Arnim |
| Drag.R2; Ul.R3 | |
| 8th Cavalry Brigade: | Generalmajor Freiherr Thumb von Neuberg |
| Kür.R7; Hus.R12 | |

| | |
|---|---|
| 4th Cavalry Division: | Generalleutnant von Garnier |
| 3rd Cavalry Brigade: | Oberst Graf von der Goltz |
| Kür.R2; Ul.R9 | |
| 17th Cavalry Brigade: | Generalmajor von Schimmelmann |
| Drag.R17; Drag.R18 | |
| 18th Cavalry Brigade: | Oberst von Printz |
| Hus.R15; Hus.R16 | |
| 9th Cavalry Division: | Generalmajor Graf von Schmettow |
| 13th Cavalry Brigade: | Oberst Seifert |
| Kür.R4; Hus.R8 | |
| 14th Cavalry Brigade: | Oberst von Heuduck |
| Hus.R11; Ul.R5 | |
| 19th Cavalry Brigade: | Oberstleutnant von Preinitzer |
| Drag.R19; Ul.R13 | |
| Jäger Battalions III, IV, IX and X | |

## 2ND ARMY

| | |
|---|---|
| Commander: | Generaloberst von Bülow |
| Chief of Staff: | Generalleutnant von Lauenstein |
| **Guard Corps:** | **General Freiherr von Plettenberg** |
| 1st Guards Infantry Division: | Generalleutnant von Hutier |
| 1st Guards Infantry Brigade: | Generalmajor von Kleist |
| 1st Guards Foot Regiment; 3rd Guards Foot Regiment | |
| 2nd Guards Infantry Brigade: | Generalmajor Schach von Wittenau until 6 September, then Oberst von dem Busch |
| 2nd Guards Foot Regiment; 4th Guards Foot Regiment | |
| 2nd Guards Infantry Division: | Generalleutnant von Winckler |
| 3rd Guards Infantry Brigade: | Generalmajor von Petersdorff |
| Guard-Gren.R1; (Kaiser Alexander): Guard-Gren.R3 (Königin Elizabeth) | |
| 4th Guards Infantry Brigade: | Generalmajor von Gontard |
| Guard-Gren.R2 Kaiser Franz); Guard-Gren.R4 (Königin Augusta) | |
| **VII Corps (Münster):** | **Generalleutnant von Einem** |
| 13th Infantry Division: | Generalleutnant von dem Borne |
| 25th Infantry Brigade: | Generalmajor von Unruh |
| IR13; IR158 | |

26th Infantry Brigade

14th Infantry Division:     Generalleutnant Fleck

27th Infantry Brigade:     Oberst von Massow
    IR16; IR53

79th Infantry Brigade:     Generalmajor Schwarte
    IR56; IR57

**X Corps (Hanover):**     **General von Emmich**

19th Infantry Division:     Generalleutnant Hofmann

37th Infantry Brigade:     Oberst Freiherr von Gregory
    IR78; IR91

38th Infantry Brigade:     Oberst von Oertzen
    IR73; IR74

20th Infantry Division:     Generalleutnant Schmundt

39th Infantry Brigade:     Generalmajor von L'Estocq
    IR79; IR164

40th Infantry Brigade:     Oberst Graf zu Rantzau
    IR77; IR92

**X Reserve Corps (Hannover):**     **Generalleutnant von Kirchbach until 29 August, then Generalleutnant von Eben**

19th Reserve Infantry Division:     Generalleutnant von Bahrfeldt

37th Reserve Infantry Brigade:     Oberst von Winterfeldt
    RIR73; RIR78

39th Reserve Infantry Brigade:     Generalmajor von Wright
    RIR74; RIR 92

2nd Guards Reserve Division:     General Freiherr von Süsskind

26th Reserve Infantry Brigade:     Oberstleutnant Cotta
    RIR15; RIR77

38th Reserve Infantry Brigade:     Oberstleutnant Wünsche
    RIR77; RIR91

**I Cavalry Corps:**     **Generalleutnant Freiherr von Richthofen**

5th Cavalry Division:     Generalmajor von Ilsemann

9th Cavalry Brigade:     Generalmajor Rusche
    Drag.R4; Ul.R10

11th Cavalry Brigade:     Oberst von Wentzky

Leib–Kür.R1; Drag.R8

12th Cavalry Brigade:            Generalmajor von Pfeil

Hus.R4; Hus.R6

Guard Cavalry Division:          Generalleutnant von Storch

1st Guard Cavalry Brigade:      Oberst von Barensprung

Guard–Kür.R

Gardes du Corps Regiment

2nd Guard Cavalry Brigade:     Generalmajor Graf von Rothkirch und Trach

Guard–Ul.R1

Guar–Ul.R3

3rd Guard Cavalry Brigade:     Oberst Freiherr von Senden)

Guar–Drag.R1

Guard–Drag.R2

Guard Jäger Battalion

Guard Rifle Battalion

## 3RD ARMY

Commander:                   Generaloberst Freiherr von Hausen

Chief of Staff:              Generalmajor von Hoeppner

**XII Corps (Dresden):**         **Generalleutnant von d'Elsa**

23rd Infantry Division:         Generalleutnant Freiherr von Lindenau

45th Infantry Brigade:          Generalmajor Lucius

Leib–Gren.R100; Gren.R101

46th Infantry Brigade:          Generalmajor von Watzdorff

Füs.R108; IR182

32nd Infantry Division:        Generalleutnant Edler von der Planitz

63rd Infantry Brigade:         Generalmajor von Gersdorff

IR102; IR103; Reserve Jäger Battalion XII

64th Infantry Brigade:         Generalmajor Morgenstern-Döring

IR177; IR178

**XIX Corps:**                    **Generalleutnant von Laffert**

24th Infantry Division

47th Infantry Brigade

IR139; IR179

48th Infantry Brigade
  IR106; IR107
40th Infantry Division
88th Infantry Brigade
  IR104; IR181
89th Infantry Brigade
  IR133; IR134

**XII Reserve Corps:**                  **General von Kirchbach**
23rd Reserve Infantry Division:         Generalleutnant von Larisch
45th Reserve Infantry Brigade:          Generalleutnant von Suckow
  Reserve Gren.R100; RIR101; Reserve Jäger Battalion XII
46th Reserve Infantry Brigade:          Generalleutnant Hempel
  RIR102; RIR103
24th Reserve Infantry Division:         Generalleutnant von Ehrenthal
47th Reserve Infantry Brigade:          Generalleutnant Ullrich
  RIR104; RIR106; Reserve Jäger Batalion XIII
48th Reserve Infantry Brigade:          Generalleutnant Wilhelm
  RIR107; RIR133

**Key to abbreviations**
Füs.R   Fusilier Regiment            Gren.R  Grenadier Regiment
Hus.R   Hussar Regiment              IR      Infantry Regiment
Kür.R   Cuirassier Regiment          RIR     Reserve Infantry Regiment
Ul.R    Uhlan Regiment

## COMPOSITION OF THE PRINCIPAL GERMAN UNITS

**Infantry Division (17,500 all ranks, 4,000 horses, 72 guns, 24 machine guns)**
1 infantry division = 2 infantry brigades, 1 field artillery brigade (72 guns), 1 cavalry regiment, 1 or 2 pioneer companies, (3 per corps), 1 divisional bridging train, 1 telephone detachment
1 infantry brigade = 2 regiments
1 infantry regiment = 3 battalions and a machine gun company (6 guns)
1 battalion = 4 companies (26 officers and 1,050 other ranks)

**Cavalry Division (5,200 all ranks, 5,600 horses, 12 guns, 6 machine guns)**
1 cavalry division = 3 cavalry brigades, 1 horse artillery detachment (three 4–gun batteries), between 1 and 3 Jäger battalions (each with a machine gun company

with 6 guns), 1+machine gun battery (mounted), 1 pioneer detachment, motor transport column, heavy and light wireless stations

1 cavalry brigade = 2 regiments

1 cavalry regiment = 4 squadrons (36 officers, 686 other ranks, 765 horses)

1 squadron = 6 officers, 163 other ranks, 178 horses

**Artillery**

Field artillery

1 field artillery brigade = 2 regiments (72 guns)

1 regiment = 2 detachments

1 detachment = 3 batteries, 1 light ammunition column

1 battery = 6 guns, 6 ammunition wagons, 1 observation wagon

Foot (heavy artillery) of the field army

1 regiment = 2 battalions

1 battalion = 4 batteries of 15cm howitzers

1 battery= 4 guns

**Reserve Divisions**

The same as an active division except that they had 6 field artillery batteries instead of 12 and lacked aeroplanes.

# COMPOSITION AND ORDER OF BATTLE OF THE BRITISH EXPEDITIONARY FORCE

| | |
|---|---|
| Commander-in-Chief: | Field Marshal Sir John French |
| Chief of Staff: | Lieutenant-General Sir Archibald Murray |
| Deputy Chief of Staff: | Major-General Sir Henry Wilson |
| | |
| **I Corps:** | **Lieutenant-General Sir Douglas Haig** |
| 1st Division: | Major-General Lomax |
| 1st (Guards) Brigade: | Brigadier-General Maxse |

1st Coldstream Guards

1st Scots Guards

1st Black Watch

1st Cameron Highlanders

2nd Infantry Brigade:                         Brigadier-General Bulfin

2nd Royal Sussex Regiment

1st Loyal North Lancashire Regiment

1st Northamptonshire Regiment
2nd King's Royal Rifle Corps
3rd Infantry Brigade:             Brigadier-General Landon
    1st Queen's Regiment
    1st South Wales Borderers
    1st Gloucestershire Regiment
    2nd Welsh Regiment
2nd Division:             Major-General Monro
4th (Guards) Brigade:             Brigadier-General Scott-Kerr
    2nd Grenadier Guards
    2nd Coldstream Guards
    3rd Coldstream Guards
    1st Irish Guards
5th Infantry Brigade:             Brigadier-General Haking
    2nd Worcester Regiment
    2nd Oxford and Bucks Light Infantry
    2nd Highland Light Infantry
    2nd Connaught Rangers
6th Infantry Brigade:             Brigadier-General Davies
    1st King's (Liverpool) Regiment
    2nd South Staffordshire Regiment
    1st Royal Berkshire Regiment
    1st King's Royal Rifle Corps

**II Corps:**             **General Sir Horace Smith-Dorrien**
3rd Division:             Major-General Hamilton
7th Infantry Brigade:             Brigadier-General McCracken
    3rd Worcestershire Regiment
    2nd South Lancashire Regiment
    1st Wiltshire Regiment
    2nd Royal Irish Rifles
8th Infantry Brigade:             Brigadier-General Doran
    2nd Royal Scots Regiment
    2nd Royal Irish Regiment
    4th Middlesex Regiment
    1st Gordon Highlanders

9th Infantry Brigade:                      Brigadier-General Shaw
- 1st Northumberland Fusiliers
- 4th Royal Fusiliers
- 1st Lincolnshire Regiment
- 1st Royal Scots Fusiliers

5th Division:                             Major-General Sir Charles Ferguson

13th Infantry Brigade:              Brigadier-General Cuthbert
- 2nd King's Own Scottish Borderers
- 2nd Duke of Wellington's (West Riding) Regiment
- 1st Royal West Kent Regiment
- 2nd King's Own Yorkshire Light Infantry

14th Infantry Brigade:              Brigadier-General Rolt
- 2nd Suffolk Regiment
- 1st East Surrey Regiment
- 1st Duke of Cornwall's Light Infantry
- 2nd Manchester Regiment

15th Infantry Brigade:              Brigadier-General Count Gleichen
- 1st Norfolk Regiment
- 1st Bedfordshire Regiment
- 1st Cheshire Regiment
- 1st Dorsetshire Regiment

**III Corps (formed in France, 31 August): Major-General Pulteney**

4th Division:                             Major-General Snow
(landed in France night 22/23 August)

10th Infantry Brigade:             Brigadier-General Haldane
- 1st Royal Warwickshire Regiment
- 2nd Seaforth Highlanders
- 1st Royal Irish Fusiliers
- 2nd Royal Dublin Fusiliers

11th Infantry Brigade:             Brigadier-General Hunter-Weston
- 1st Somerset Light Infantry
- 1st East Lancashire Regiment
- 1st Hampshire Regiment
- 1st Rifle Brigade

12th Infantry Brigade:                      Brigadier-General Wilson
   1st King's Own Regiment
   2nd Lancashire Fusiliers
   2nd Royal Inniskilling Fusiliers
   2nd Essex Regiment
Unattached units
19th Infantry Brigade:                     Major-General Drummond
(formed at Valenciennes on 22 August)
   2nd Royal Welsh Fusiliers
   1st Cameronians
   1st Middlesex Regiment
   2nd Argyll and Sutherland Highlanders

**The Cavalry Division:**             **Major-General Allenby**
1st Cavalry Brigade:                     Brigadier-General Briggs
   2nd Dragoon Guards
   5th Dragoon Guards
   11th Hussars
2nd Cavalry Brigade:                    Brigadier-General de Lisle
   4th Dragoon Guards
   9th Lancers
   18th Hussars
3rd Cavalry Brigade:                    Brigadier-General Gough
   4th Hussars
   5th Lancers
   16th Lancers
4th Cavalry Brigade:                    Brigadier-General Bingham
Composite Regiment of Household Cavalry
   6th Dragoon Guards
   3rd Hussars
5th Cavalry Brigade:                    Brigadier-General Chetwode
   2nd Dragoons
   12th Lancers
   20th Hussars

## COMPOSITION OF THE PRINCIPAL BRITISH UNITS

**Infantry Divisions (18,073 all ranks, 5,592 horses, 76 guns)**

1 infantry division = 3 infantry brigades and divisional troops

1 infantry brigade = 12 battalions

1 battalion = 4 companies (possessing 2 machine guns)

**Cavalry Division (9,269 all ranks, 9,815 horses, 24 guns, 24 machine guns)**

1 cavalry division = 4 cavalry brigades and divisional troops

1 cavalry brigade = 3 cavalry regiments

1 regiment = 3 squadrons

Note: The total ration strength of the BEF in 1914 was approximately 110,000, of which the rifle strength was 66,000.

# APPENDIX 2

## TABLE OF EQUIVALENT RANKS

| French | British | German |
|---|---|---|
| Sous-Lieutenant | Sub-Lieutenant | Leutnant |
| Lieutenant or Adjudant | Lieutenant | Oberleutnant |
| Capitaine | Captain | Hauptmann |
| Lieutenant-Colonel or Commandant | Lieutenant-Colonel | Oberstleutnant or Major |
| Colonel | Colonel | Oberst or Major |
| Général (de Brigade) | Major-General | Generalmajor |
| Général (de Division) | Lieutenant-General | Generalleutnant |
| Général (de Corps d'Armée) | General | General (der Infanterie etc) |
| Général (d'Armée) | Field Marshal | Generaloberst |

# APPENDIX 3

## DIRECTIVE OF 27 AUGUST

### General Directions for the 1st to the 7th Armies for the Further Conduct of Operations

It is most important by a rapid march of the German forces on Paris to prevent the French Army from coming to rest, to stop the assembly of fresh bodies of troops and to take from the country as much as possible of its means of defence. Belgium is placed under a German Governor-General and a German administration. It is to serve as the hinterland for supply of the First, Second and Third Armies and thus shorten the lines of communication of the German right wing.

His Majesty orders the advance of the German forces in the direction of Paris. The First Army, with the II Cavalry Corps attached, will march west of the Oise towards the lower Seine. It must be prepared to co-operate in the fighting of the Second Army. It will also be responsible for the protection of the right flank of the forces and will take steps to prevent the enemy from assembling fresh bodies of troops in its zone of operations. The detachments (III Reserve and IX Reserve Corps) which have been left behind for the investment of Antwerp are placed immediately under OHL. The IV Reserve Corps is again put at the disposal of the First Army.

The Second Army, with the I Cavalry Corps attached, will advance via the line La Fère–Laon on Paris. It will also invest and capture Maubeuge, and later La Fère; also Laon in co-operation with the Third Army. The I Cavalry Corps will reconnoitre on the fronts of both the Second and Third Armies, and will send any information obtained to the Third Army.

The Third Army will continue its march via the line Laon–Guignicourt, west of Neufchâtel, on Château-Thierry. Hirson will be captured, also Laon with Fort Condé in co-operation with the Second Army. The I Cavalry Corps, on the front of the Second and Third Armies, will provide the Third Army with information.

The Fourth Army will march via Rheims on Epernay. The IV Cavalry Corps, attached to the Fifth Army, will also send reports to the Fourth Army. Any siege material required for the capture of Rheims will be provided. The VI Corps is transferred to the Fifth Army.

The Fifth Army, to which the VI Corps is transferred, will advance against the line Châlons sur Marne–Vitry le François. It will be responsible for the flank protection of the forces by echeloning back its left wing until the Sixth Army can take over this task west of the Meuse. The IV Cavalry Corps remains attached to the Fifth Army but will reconnoitre on the fronts of the Fourth and Fifth Armies and send reports to the Fourth Army. Verdun will be invested. Besides the five Landwehr brigades from the Nied position [the fortified area in the region of Metz], the 10th and 8th Ersatz Divisions are also assigned to it as soon as they can be spared by the Sixth Army.

The Sixth Army, with the Seventh Army and the III Cavalry Corps, in touch with Metz, has first to prevent an advance of the enemy into Lorraine and Upper Alsace. The fortress of Metz is placed under the Sixth Army. If the enemy retires, the Sixth Army, with the III Cavalry Corps, will cross the Moselle between Toul and Epinal and take the general direction of Neufchâteau. This Army will then be responsible for the protection of the left flank of the forces. Nancy and Toul are to be invested; Epinal is to be masked with sufficient troops. In this case, the Sixth Army will be reinforced by portions of the Seventh Army (XIV and XV Corps and one Ersatz Division) but the 10th and 8th Ersatz Divisions will be handed over to the Fifth Army. The Seventh Army will then become independent.

The Seventh Army will at first remain under the Sixth Army. If the latter crosses the Moselle, the Seventh Army will become independent. The fortress of Strasbourg and the Upper Rhine fortifications, with the troops in them, will remain under it. The Seventh Army will prevent an enemy breakthrough between Epinal and the Swiss frontier. It is recommended that strong defences should be constructed opposite Epinal, and from there to the mountains, also in the Rhine valley in connection with Neubreisach, and that the main strength should be kept behind the right wing. The XIV and XV Corps, as well as one of the Ersatz divisions, will then be transferred to the Sixth Army.

All armies will mutually co-operate with one another and support each other in fighting for the various lines which are to be gained. The strong resistance which may be expected on the Aisne, and later, on the Marne, may necessitate a wheel of the Armies from a south-westerly to a southerly direction.

A rapid advance is urgently desirable in order to leave the French with no time to reorganise and offer serious resistance. The Armies will therefore report when they begin the advance. The Armies on the wings are recommended to attach infantry, in addition to the Jäger Battalions, to their cavalry divisions as required, in order to break the resistance of francs-tireurs and civilian inhabitants as quickly as possible. Only by severe measures against the population can a national uprising be nipped in the blood.

Reichsarchiv (ed.), *Der Weltkrieg 1914 bis 1918,* Volume 3, pp.7–10

# APPENDIX 4

## JOFFRE'S ORDER FOR THE BATTLE OF THE MARNE

Instruction No 6

GQG 4 September 1914. 22 hours.

1.  The time has come to profit by the adventurous position of the German First Army and concentrate against that Army all the efforts of the Allied Armies of the extreme left. All dispositions will be made during 5 September for beginning the attack on the 6th.

2.  The following will be the positions to be attained by the evening of the 5th:

    a.  All available forces of 6th Army north-east of Meaux ready to cross the Ourcq between Lizy-sur-Ourcq and May-en-Multien in the general direction of Château-Thierry. The available portions of I Cavalry Corps which are at hand will be placed under the orders of Général Maunoury for this operation.

    b.  The British Army, established on the front Changis–Coulommiers, ready to attack in the general direction of Montmirail, II Cavalry Corps ensuring liaison between the British Army and 5th Army.

    c.  Fifth Army, closing slightly to the left, will be established on the general front Courtacon–Esternay–Sézanne, ready to attack in a general north-south direction.

    d.  Ninth Army, (Général Foch) will cover the right of 5th Army, holding the southern exits of the St Gond Marshes and sending a part of its forces on the plateau to the north of Sézanne.

3.  These various Armies will take the offensive on the morning of 6 September.

Edmonds, *Military Operations, France and Belgium 1914,* Appendix 30, p.543

# NOTES

## INTRODUCTION

1   In IR 76 (the Hamburg Regiment), for example, the 6th Company left their barracks in the city on 7 August 1914 with 5 officers and 261 other ranks. At the end of the war, only 13 of them were still serving with the company. Even allowing for transfers to other units, the losses in dead and wounded were clearly enormous. See Nau, Appendix 3, p.79.

2   Anon., *Das Totenfeld zwischen Marne und Ourcq*, in Duvernoy, pp.201–204.

## 1: THE SCHLIEFFEN-MOLTKE PLAN

1   For the evolution of Germany's war plans, see Ritter pp.17–68, Mombauer 2001, pp.41–105 and Holmes. The recently discovered annual deployment plans from 1906 to 1914 and the associated maps are given in Ehlert, pp.401–484. In 1999 Terence Zuber claimed that the Schlieffen Plan was not intended for use if war broke out but was aimed at getting the Minister for War to sanction a large increase in the size of the Army. Although this thesis has been discredited, it led to a valuable critical debate on the subject. For excellent summaries, see Mombauer 2005 and Gross 2008.

2   This parsimonious attitude came to end as a result of the war scare brought about by the second Moroccan crisis. However, the subsequent army bill of 1912 contained provision for the creation of only two new army corps, much less than Moltke the Younger had demanded.

3   For a description of the Great General Staff in the years leading up to the war, see Bucholz, pp.137–145, and Mombauer 2001, pp.34–41.

4   For a general account of the staff rides, see Bucholz, pp.142–145. Detailed descriptions of individual rides are given in Foley, Robert T., (ed.) *Alfred von Schlieffen's Military Writings*, pp.3–71 and Zuber 2004, pp.133–165.

5   In a memorandum of August 1892. See Zuber 2004, pp.51–52.

6   Quoted in Foley, Robert T., (ed.) *Alfred von Schlieffen's Military Writings*, p.149.

7   Zuber 2004, p.74.

8   Ibid, p.95.

9   There is a map showing the deployment of the six armies in Ehlert et al, p.400.

10  Zoellner, pp.42–43. For a discussion of the 1904 staff ride, including Schlieffen's exercise critique, see Zoellner, pp.42–45, and Zuber 2004, pp.155–165.

11  The 1905 western staff ride is discussed in Zoellner, pp.47–52, and Holmes, pp.220–222.

12 Zoellner does not specify how many troops were detached from the right wing for this purpose, only saying that they were 'considerable' (*erheblich*). They cannot however have been very numerous since the right wing was still strong enough to overcome the French offensive to the west of Metz easily.

13 For a brief description of the different drafts, see Ritter, pp.131–133. The text of the plan is given in Ritter, pp.134–148, and Holmes, pp.163–174.

14 In the margin of the text of the 1906 *Aufmarsch I (West)* there is a handwritten note saying that this 'coincides with Schlieffen's Memorandum of December 1905'. See Ehlert 2006, p.409. In addition, the numbering of the corps corresponds closely to that in the maps that accompany the Great Memorandum.

15 Ritter, pp.134–135.

16 Ibid, p.136.

17 Ibid, p.157. This statement comes from Draft IV. It also appears in a more conditional form in Draft I, where he says 'the intention, if possible, is to force the enemy's left wing southwards and thus away from Paris, but at the same time also to outflank the rear position Rheims–La Fère with the right wing.'

18 Ibid, p.145.

19 Ibid, p.141.

20 Ibid, pp.142–143. Army service was subdivided into service with the standing army and its reserve and with the Landwehr. From the age of 20 all infantry recruits served two years full-time in the standing army, followed by a further five years on the reserve, during which time they had to carry out up to 16 weeks of training each year. On the outbreak of war the reservists were used either to bring the active units up to strength or to form additional units. Service continued between the ages of 27 and 39 in the Landwehr, which was used in time of war to support the standing army, either by the formation of independent units or, if necessary, to fill up the ranks in active units. The duties of the Landsturm, which consisted of men aged 17 to 20 and 39 to 45, was to take part in the defence of the country in wartime.

21 Ritter, p.151.

22 Quoted in Mombauer 2001, p.50.

23 Ibid, p.52.

24 Moltke, *Erinnerungen*, p.306, quoted in Mombauer 2001, p.56.

25 Ritter, p.165.

26 Quoted in Mombauer 2001, p.94.

27 Ibid.

28 Ritter, p.166.

29 This was not, however, the last change he made to the war plans. In 1913, he made one final alteration, which although ultimately without military significance, had a harmful effect on his morale and his relationship with the Kaiser. Until then, the General Staff had prepared plans for a war with France alone (*Aufmarsch West*), for a war with Russia alone (*Aufmarsch Ost*) and for a war on two fronts (*Aufmarsch West und Ost*). However, in that year Moltke decided (apparently without consulting the politicians) that it was no longer necessary to plan for a war against Russia alone because the recent strengthening of the Franco–Russian alliance ruled this out. The non-existence of an *Aufmarsch Ost* gave rise to short-lived crisis on the afternoon of 1 August 1914 when, shortly after the Kaiser had signed the general mobilization order, it seemed that Britain and France might both remain neutral. For an account of this crisis and the effect it had on Moltke, see Mombauer 2001, pp.216–226.

## 2: PLAN XVII

1 See Porch 1981, Chapters 5, 6 and 7, pp.73–133.

2 Perhaps the most serious consequence of these frequent changes was the failure to develop heavy artillery in the years immediately before the war. See Porch 1981, Chapter 12, pp.232–245.

3 For French war plans between c.1900 and 1911, see Marchand, pp.145–197, and Williamson, *French Strategy in Transition, 1905–1911.*

4 See Snyder, pp.81–85, and Tanenbaum, pp.150–156. The Deuxième Bureau's assessment of Schlieffen, made at this time, said that he was 'basically irresolute in nature, afraid to make any decisions whatsoever, is old and tired… He is the sleeping Uhlan.'

5 Quoted in Snyder, p.89.

6 For details of Michel's plan see Ministère de la Guerre, *Les Armées Françaises dans la Grande Guerre,* Tome I, Volume 1, Annexe No 3, pp.7–11. There are also accounts in Percin, pp.42–49, and Selliers de Moranville, pp.38–42. Given the strength of the French left wing (which at least equalled that of the German right wing) and the fact that it extended almost to the coast, it is quite likely that a German offensive at this time would have failed.

7 In the first years of the 20th century, Morocco was the only North African state not to have come under the control of a European power. In May 1911, the French sent troops to the city of Fez, ostensibly to protect French nationals during a local uprising but in reality to increase their influence and eventually turn the country into a protectorate. In a show of strength which was designed to minimize French influence and force concessions (by allowing them a free hand in the south of the country), the Germans sent the gunboat *Panther* which docked in the harbour of Agadir on 1 July. Unfortunately for the Germans, rather than driving a wedge between France and its allies (Britain in particular), it strengthened them and they were left diplomatically isolated and in a weak bargaining position. After a very difficult period when it looked as if war was about to break out, negotiations took place in which the humiliated Germans agreed to the establishment of a French protectorate in Morocco in return for an insignificant part of the French-controlled Congo.

8 Percin, pp.37–57 and 179–191, describes the meeting of the Supreme War Council and subsequent events.

9 Porch 2006, p.124.

10 Joffre, p.24.

11 Ibid, pp.67–68.

12 Ibid, pp.34–35.

13 Quoted in Doughty, p.433.

14 Ibid, pp.434–435.

15 Troisième Bureau Memorandum, *Concentration des armées allemandes* (late 1911 or early 1912), in Tanenbaum, p.165.

16 Joffre, pp.50–51.

17 For a description of Plan XVII, see Ministère de la Guerre, *Les Armées Françaises dans la Grande Guerre,* Tome I, Volume 1, pp.18–67. The text of the general directive and of the specific instructions for each army (*directives particulières*) are given in Tome I, Volume 1, Annexe No 8, pp.21–35.

18 Ministère de la Guerre, *Les Armées Françaises dans la Grande Guerre,* Tome I, Volume 1, p.39.

19 Ibid, p.40.

20 Ibid, p.40.

21 Ibid, p.22.

22 Ibid, Volume 1, Annexe, p.21.

23 Lanrezac, pp.60–61.

## 3: OPENING MOVES

1  Spears, pp.105–107.

2  Lieutenant Charles de Gaulle, in the 33e RI, was wounded in the arm during the attack on the German-held bridge.

3  Ministère de la Guerre, *Les Armées Françaises dans la Grande Guerre*, Tome I, Volume 1, Annexe No 450, pp.424–425.

4  For the map that accompanied the intelligence summary, see Reichsarchiv, *Der Weltkrieg 1914 bis 1918,* Volume 1, sketch 3, before p.347.

5  None of Kluck's pilots flew far enough south to detect the British and Richthofen's 1st Cavalry Corps, which was his only other means of reconnaissance, had not yet reached the right wing.

6  See Reichsarchiv, *Der Weltkrieg 1914 bis 1918,* Volume 1, p.260.

## 4: THE BATTLE OF CHARLEROI

1  From the memoirs of Général Daydrein, former Deputy Chief of Staff of 5th Army. Quoted in Gay, p.129.

2  First contact was made at dawn on 22 August when a section from the 4th Dragoon Guards drove away a German outpost on the road between Mons and Soignies. As far as the British were concerned, these were the opening shots in the war.

3  For a description of the events at Tamines on 21 August, including the use of human shields by the Germans, see Schmitz and Nieuwland 1920, pp.79–95. The troops involved belonged to IR77.

4  For a French account of the fighting around Arsimont on 21 August, see Gay, pp.142–157, and Valarché 1926, pp.36–58. For the German side see Gontard, Rieben, pp.38–56 and von Bose, *Das Kaiser Alexander Garde-Grenadier-Regiment Nr 1 im Weltkrieg*, pp.24–28.

5  Hauptmann von Rieben, 4th Company Regiment Franz, quoted in Rieben, p.48.

6  Ibid, pp.50–51.

7  Ibid, pp.49–50.

8  Gontard, p.40. The French dead were later buried in a military cemetery on the outskirts of Auvelais, near Fosse No 2. Since most of them came from Brittany, the memorial was given the form of a typical Breton lighthouse.

9  Spears, pp.132–133.

10 In von Bose, *Das Kaiser Alexander Garde-Grenadier-Regiment Nr 1 im Weltkrieg*, p.27.

11 Lieutenant Denolle, quoted in Valarché 1926, pp.85–86. About 30 minutes before the Zouaves arrived, the Germans had abandoned the bridgehead and begun to recross the river, because aerial reconnaissance indicated (erroneously) that more than three French divisions were approaching the battlefield. However, the order was quickly cancelled and they returned to their positions just in time to meet the attack. See Gontard, pp.37–39.

12 For the fighting on the front of the 5th Division, see Gay, pp.183–205 and d'Argenlieu, pp.5–42.

13 From the memoirs of Général Dutheil, quoted in d'Argenlieu, p.30.

14 Gay, pp.198–204.

15 Spears, p.145.

16 As on the previous day, Kluck complained bitterly that his task was to find and defeat the British, not to support 2nd Army. Once again, a staff officer was sent to 2nd Army Headquarters to remonstrate, but to no avail. Likewise, he sent a radio message to OHL asking to be released from Bülow's control but was refused.

17  See Reichsarchiv, *Der Weltkrieg 1914 bis 1918,* Volume 1, p.377.

18  State Prosecutor Tschoffen, quoted in Horne and Kramer, p.48. For an account of the various massacres that took place in Dinant, see Horne and Kramer, pp.42–53.

19  Quoted in Schmitz and Nieuwland 1922, pp.155–164.

20  Ibid, p.159.

21  Ibid, pp.159–160.

22  Ibid, p.162.

23  Ibid, p.163.

24  As it happened, 4th Army had been defeated the previous day in the battles of Virton and the Semoy and were retreating.

25  Spears, pp.153–154.

26  For details of Franchet d'Esperey's audacious plan, and the complicated manoeuvre which it entailed, see de Lardemelle, pp.146–166.

27  There are numerous accounts of the battle of Mons including Edmonds 1966, pp.71–95 and Holmes, *Army Battlefield Guide; Belgium and Northern France*, Ministry of Defence, London, 1995, pp.64–69.

## 5: THE RETREAT BEGINS

1  For an account of events on the front of 3rd Army on 24 August, see Baumgarten-Crusius 1919, pp.33–44.

2  Reichsarchiv, *Der Weltkrieg 1914 bis 1918,* Volume 1, p.398. The message was premature since 3rd Army was nowhere near Philippeville, the proposed junction between the inner wings of the two armies, and the French 5th Army was still intact, albeit greatly weakened by the fighting.

3  Spears, p.202.

4  Telegram to the Minister for War, 9.35am.

5  Joffre, p.183. Lanrezac had other ideas, however. He decided early on not to make use of Maubeuge as a point of support but to retreat as far as the line Hirson–Mézières before contemplating an attack.

6  Edmonds 1966, p.135.

7  Ibid, p.136.

8  Ibid, p.142.

9  Ministère de la Guerre, *Les Armées Françaises dans la Grande Guerre,* Tome I, Volume 2, p.21.

10  Reichsarchiv, *Der Weltkrieg 1914 bis 1918,* Volume 1, p.440.

11  Ibid, pp.339–342 for the reports from 4th and 5th Armies.

12  Ibid, pp.405–406. In a letter written on the evening of the 25th, Lauenstein, the Chief of Staff of 2nd Army, expressed the mood of victory at Army Headquarters. See also Reichsarchiv, *Der Weltkrieg 1914 bis 1918,* Volume 1, p.508.

13  Tappen, pp.110–111. This was also Plessen's view.

14  Quoted by Spears, p.226.

15  Joffre, p.196.

16  For an account of Le Cateau from the British side, see Edmonds 1996, pp.152–200. For a German account, see Reichsarchiv, *Der Weltkrieg 1914 bis 1918,* Volume 1, pp.521–528.

17  Kluck, pp.68–69.

18  Quoted in Spears, p.235. According to Edmonds 1996, p.201, on the evening of 26 August 'GHQ seems to have given up II Corps for lost.'

19  Edmonds 1996, Appendix 17, p.521.

20  Ministère de la Guerre, *Les Armées Françaises dans la Grande Guerre*, Tome I, Volume 2, p.51.

21  Spears, p.242.

22  See Ministère de la Guerre, *Les Armées Françaises dans la Grande Guerre*, Tome I, Volume 2, pp.56–57 and Joffre, pp.200–203.

23  For this quarrel, see Lanrezac, pp.218–219. Although Lanrezac wrote his book while still an extremely embittered man, so his words cannot always be trusted, his account of this meeting is supported by Spears, who was present at the time. See Spears, p.249.

24  See Reichsarchiv, *Der Weltkrieg 1914 bis 1918*, Volume 1, p.531.

25  Ibid, p.566.

26  Ibid, pp.608–609.

27  Tappen, p.109.

28  See Appendix 3. The translation is from Edmonds 1996, pp.234–236.

29  Ibid.

30  For a map of this situation, see Koeltz, *Le GQG Allemand et la bataille de la Marne,* after p.16.

31  Emmich, commander of X Corps, failed to keep Bülow fully informed of their lack of progress. In his late evening situation report he optimistically claimed that they would go over to rest on a line Origny-Ste-Benoite–Courjumelles–Landifay, only 6 miles short of their objectives for the day.

32  For events concerning 6th Army between 27 August and 1 September, see Ministère de la Guerre, *Les Armées Françaises dans la Grande Guerre*, Tome I, Volume 2, pp.115–165.

# 6: THE BATTLE OF GUISE

1.  For a detailed account of the battle from the German side, see Heydemann 1924 and 1928, and from the French side Valarché 1928 and Larcher. There are also descriptions of the *Battle in Reichsarchiv, Der Weltkrieg 1914 bis 1918*, Volume 3, pp.141–179 and in Ministère de la Guerre, Les Armées Françaises dans la Grande Guerre, Tome I, Volume 2, pp.51–86.

2   Unteroffizier Vorwerk, quoted in Heydemann 1928, p.150.

3   Sergent Pincemin, 9th company, 48e RI, quoted in Valarché 1928, pp.80–81. The 48e RI had already suffered badly in the fighting at Arsimont on 22 August where it lost 19 out of its 45 officers and approximately a quarter of its rank and file.

4   Heydemann 1928, p.145. The dead were buried in a cemetery where the western end of the ridge is crossed by the road to Le Sourd. Alongside their bodies is that of Oberst von Bismarck, who was mortally wounded during the battle of the Somme and who asked to be buried at Colonfay with his former comrades.

5   Leutnant der Reserve Trierenberg, 1st Company, 2nd Regiment of Foot Guards. Quoted in Heydemann 1928, pp.162–163. Hauptmann von Oesterreich was awarded his country's highest decoration, the *Pour le Mérite*, for his leadership in this action.

6   General Freiherr von Süsskind, the commander of the 2nd Guards Reserve Division, had received Kirchbach's order to come to the aid of Riebensahm's force at Essigny-le-Grand at about 11.00am, soon after his troops had begun to cross the Crozat Canal at St Simon.

7   See Palat, *La Retraite sur la Seine*, pp.198–203 and Heydemann 1928, pp.195–196.

8   Although his headquarters was less than 2 miles away from Clanlieu, Schmundt spent all day unaware that the village had been captured by IR92 early that morning.

9   Hauptmann Graf von Büdingen, quoted in Heydemann 1928, pp.108–109.

10  Capitaine Nachin, Machine Gun Company of the 43e RI. Quoted in Larcher, pp.116–117.

11  An anonymous soldier of the 7th company, IR77. Quoted in Heydemann 1928, pp.206–207.

12  Georges Cavrois, private in the 110e RI. Quoted in Bourget, pp.165–167.

13  Kutscher, pp.68–69.

14  Spears, p.268. For Lanrezac's account of the day, including his inconclusive telephone call to GQG that evening, see Lanrezac, pp.235–242.

15  Joffre, pp.213–214.

## 7: THE RETREAT CONTINUES

1   Spears, p.286.

2   This had been formed to fill the gap between 4th and 5th Armies. When it was complete, it became 9th Army.

3   Spears, pp.288–289.

4   French, p.91. In reality, their condition was nowhere near as bad as he claimed. In the period up to and including 27 August, excluding missing soldiers many of whom subsequently found their way back to their units, I Corps had lost approximately 1,700 men and II Corps about 12,700, See Edmonds 1966, p.238.

5   Quoted in Spears, p.290.

6   Reichsarchiv, *Der Weltkrieg 1914 bis 1918,* Volume 3, p.177.

7   Ibid, p.187.

8   Bloem, pp.113–114.

9   Bourget, pp.176–179.

10  Spears, pp.313–314.

11  Koeltz, *Le GQG Allemand et la Bataille de la Marne*, p.46.

12  Spears, p.320.

13  Bourget, pp.194–195.

14  For the action at Néry, see Edmonds 1996, pp.256–258. Garnier was forced to borrow four guns from the other two cavalry divisions.

15  Spears, Appendix XXXI, pp.536–537, gives the texts of the different versions.

16  See Ministère de la Guerre, *Les Armées Françaises dans la Grande Guerre,* Tome I, Volume 2, p.530.

17  Edmonds 1996, p.264.

18  Ibid.

19  Not everyone at the Kaiser's Military Headquarters was carried away by the rising tide of optimism. In response to one particularly extravagant outpouring, for example, Falkenhayn (the Prussian Minister for War and later Moltke's successor as Chief of the General Staff) retorted that the enemy was making a methodical retreat and asked them to show him their trophies and prisoners.

20  The table is given in Koeltz, *Le GQG Allemand et la Bataille de la Marne,* pp.34–38.

21  Reichsarchiv, *Der Weltkrieg 1914 bis 1918,* Volume 3, p.232.

22  Bloem, pp.123–124.

23  Spears, pp.366–367. See also Joffre, p.238 and Lanrezac, pp.276–279.

24  Reichsarchiv, *Der Weltkrieg 1914 bis 1918,* Volume 3, pp.248–249. The reference in the first paragraph to armies which report decisive victories followed by repeated pleas for help appears to be a barbed, though fair, comment about Bülow.

25  Kluck, p.102.

26  Reichsarchiv, *Der Weltkrieg 1914 bis 1918,* Volume 3, pp.17–18.

27  Ibid, pp.311–312.

28  For maps illustrating the two options, see Spears, pp.392–393.

29  Joffre, p.246. The same message was sent to Foch asking if 9th Army was ready to take part in the battle.

30  Spears, p.388.

31  For an eyewitness account of the events at GQG that day, see Muller, pp.83–96.

32  Ministère de la Guerre, *Les Armées Françaises dans la Grande Guerre,* Tome I, Volume 2, p.785, Appendix 4.

## 8: THE EVE OF BATTLE

1  Commandant Grobert, III Battalion, 41e RI, quoted in Valarché 1929, p.9.

2  Médecin-Major Montagne, 70e RI, quoted in Valarché 1929, p.9.

3  For the fighting at Penchard, see Juin, pp.67–84 and Dahlmann, pp.25–31.

4  Reichsarchiv, *Der Weltkrieg 1914 bis 1918,* Volume 4, p.26. For the genesis of the message, see Kuhl, 1930, pp.179–180. There is no evidence that Moltke was making preparations for the siege of Paris.

5  Koeltz, *Le GQG Allemand et la Bataille de la Marne*, pp.124–127.

6  Kuhl 1930, pp.186–187. Kuhl claimed that his account was based on notes he made during the meeting.

7  The complex logistical problems caused by the retreat to the north of the Marne are outlined in Kuhl and Bergmann, pp.26–30.

8  Spears, p.411.

9  Muller, pp.106–107. See also Joffre, pp.253–254 and Spears, pp.417–418.

10  Spears, p.427.

## 9: TAKEN BY SURPRISE

1  Libermann, pp.147–152.

2  Tepp, pp.71–73.

3  Ibid, pp.74–77.

4  Leutnant von Schach, 1st Company IR89, quoted in Bose, *Schlachten des Weltkrieges, Band 22,* p.70.

5  Hauptmann von Thielau, commander I/89, quoted ibid, p.76.

6  Koeltz, 1930, p.73. The division had already suffered very badly at Gozée and Marbaix during the battle of Charleroi and in the heavy fighting at Ribemont on 30 August.

7  Quoted in Ginisty and Gagneur, pp.265–266.

8  Ibid, pp.266–267.

9  Bose, *Schlachten des Weltkrieges, Band 22,* p.178.

10  Ginisty and Gagneur, pp.267–268.

11  In order to avoid any mistake in this vitally important matter, Bührmann copied down Kuhl's instructions in his notebook.

12  Bührmann and Brinckmann had arranged to meet that night on the way back to their respective headquarters. When they did so, they immediately realized the potential for confusion because of the conflicting orders from Kluck and Bülow.

## 10: BLOODY DAYS AT TROCY

1 D'Estre, pp.83–85.

2 Juin, p.80. There is a memorial to Hugot-Derville in the place where he died on the slopes of the hill.

3 IR42 lost almost 1,000 men during the battle. They were buried in a mass grave in a cemetery at the point where the Varreddes–Chambry road leaves the valley and crosses the track along which they built their trenches.

4 For an account of this and related attacks, see Michel pp.134–142. Remarkably, Colonel Chaulet survived his wounds and returned to active service. He was killed in January 1915 near Ypres.

## 11: THE BARRIER OF THE MARSHES

1 The battalion involved, III/RIR74, was trapped in a shallow trench and suffered over 600 dead and more than 150 seriously wounded, most of whom died from their injuries. When the firing came to an end only six officers and 87 men were able to walk to the French lines and almost all of them had been wounded at least once. See Bose, *Schlachten des Weltkrieges, Band 23*, pp.22–27 and Valarché 1929, pp.76–83.

2 Leutnant Gehring, 3rd Company, IR164, quoted in von Bose, *Schlachten des Weltkrieges, Band 23*, p.82.

## 12: STRUGGLE FOR THE HIGH GROUND

1 Lohrisch, pp.139–143. There is another account of the march in Bircher 1922, pp.125–126.

2 Sergent Gadal, 2e Zouaves. Quoted in Ginisty and Gagneur, pp.232–233.

3 Oberst von Buttlar in a letter home, written soon after the fighting, quoted in Dahlmann, p.161.

4 Ginisty and Gagneur, pp.232–234. Colonel Dujubadoux's body was found next day when the French reoccupied the village. There is a plaque on the cemetery wall at the spot where he fell.

5 Their commander was so convinced they were unfit for immediate combat that he pleaded for them to be given at least two days' rest. Some units had lost almost one third of their strength in the fighting in the Ardennes.

6 Lintier, pp.209–212.

7 A great deal was made of the 'Taxis of the Marne' after the war, with claims that they had saved the day at a crucial point in the battle. In actual fact, the achievement was of no consequence since the 7th Division's attack failed completely and had no influence on the subsequent withdrawal by the Germans.

## 13: NIGHT ATTACK

1 Quoted in Bose, *Schlachten des Weltkrieges, Band 24, 1928*, p.139.

2 Ibid, p.142.

3 Leutnant von Viebahn, 5th Company, Regiment Alexander, quoted in Bose, *Schlachten des Weltkrieges, Band 24, 1928*, p.146.

4 Feldwebel Kindermann, quoted ibid, p.148.

5 Ibid, pp.150–151. For the identification of the car as the one sent out from 18th Division Headquarters, see Villate 1933, p.164. There is a simple monument to the two dead officers on the roadside near the spot where they were killed.

6 Ibid, p.229.

7 Quoted in Grasset, 1936, pp.230–231.

8  From the diary of General von Einem. Reichsarchiv, *Der Weltkrieg 1914 bis 1918,* Volume 4, p.186.

9  Ibid, p.215.

10  Ibid, pp.220–221.

11  Ibid, p.224. Hentsch was given only verbal instructions for his mission. For the enormous controversy surrounding this matter, see Reichsarchiv, *Der Weltkrieg 1914 bis 1918,* Volume 4, pp.220–245, Muller-Loebnitz, and Edmonds 1921. With the exception of Hentsch, all those who took part in the meeting later agreed that his powers were limited to giving Kluck and Bülow instructions if they had already decided to retreat.

12  Reichsarchiv, *Der Weltkrieg 1914 bis 1918,* Volume 4, p.231.

13  Oberstleutnant Matthes, Chief of 2nd Army Operations Section. Quoted in Reichsarchiv, *Der Weltkrieg 1914 bis 1918,* Volume 4, p.233.

14  Ibid, p.234.

15  Neither Bülow, in his book about the campaign, nor his Chief of Staff, Lauenstein, left an account of the meeting. What was said at the time is therefore based on the evidence of Hentsch, Matthes, Koeppen and König, all of whom testified to the enquiry into Hentsch's mission, which was carried out by Ludendorff in the spring of 1917. (Bülow was seriously ill by then and Lauenstein was dead.)

16  The German word used was *Schlacke,* which translates literally as 'slag'. His use of the term was important because, as we shall see, Hentsch repeated it to Kuhl and Bergmann as part of his argument to get 1st Army to retreat.

17  Reichsarchiv, *Der Weltkrieg 1914 bis 1918,* Volume 4, p.242.

18  Ibid, p.242.

19  Villate 1933, pp.206–207.

# 14: STALEMATE ON THE OURCQ

1  Diary of Leutnant Förster of the 5th company IR24, quoted in Koeltz, *Armée von Kluck à la Bataille de la Marne,* p.158.

2  Richter, pp.121–124.

3  Bloem, pp.157–158.

4  Ibid, p.160.

5  Dahlmann, p.227.

6  In complete contrast, the 5th Cavalry Division spent the next two days on a daring long-distance raid behind the German lines, which almost led to the capture of Kluck and his staff at 1st Army Headquarters at Vendrest! See Héthay, pp.137–138.

7  For an account of the capture of the Petit Morin by the British I Corps see Pugens, pp.80–99 and Edmonds 1966, pp.318–326. There is also a remarkable eyewitness account of the destruction of the 3rd Company, German Guard Rifle Battalion at Orly in Duvernoy, pp.142–144.

8  For reasons unknown, the pioneer company in question, (1/Pionier 9 from the 17th Division) does not seem to have received the order to join up with Kraewel's Detachment. In the early morning of 9 September, their commanding officer received an order to go to La Ferté-sous-Jouarre and blow up the bridges there, only to find on his arrival that they had already been destroyed. Reinhardt Biernatzki, an officer in 1/Pionier 9, makes no mention of any order to move to Montreuil-aux-Lions in his account of the retreat to the Ourcq battlefield. See Biernatzki, pp.46–47.

9  There is a useful table in Pugens, p.131, showing the state of the various Marne bridges on the night of 8/9 September.

## 15: THE BEGINNING OF THE END

1   The action at Mondement was later given an almost mythical status by the French who chose the spot as the site for the national memorial to the battle of the Marne. For accounts of the fighting see Chamard 1934 and 1939, Grasset, *Marais de St-Gond*, pp.251–257 and pp.280–285 and von Bose, *Schlachten des Weltkrieges, Band 25, Das Marnedrama 1914, 1. Abschnitt des 3 Teiles, Der Ausgang der Schlacht*, pp.26–39 and pp.154–156.

2   Reichsarchiv, *Der Weltkrieg 1914 bis 1918*, Volume 4, pp.268–269.

3   Not long after Bülow had given the order to retreat, a message arrived from Kluck saying that his left wing had pulled back from the line Crouy–Coulombs to Montigny–Gandelu. Bülow mistakenly interpreted this to mean that the whole of 1st Army was retreating, thus confirming his own decision. In the end it made no difference since the British were across the Marne in strength and 1st Army would have been forced to retreat sooner or later.

## 16: THE LAST RETREAT

1   Reichsarchiv, *Der Weltkrieg 1914 bis 1918*, Volume 4, p.207.

2   Ibid, pp.208–209.

3   Wirth, pp.54–55.

4   Reichsarchiv, *Der Weltkrieg 1914 bis 1918*, Volume 4, pp.214–215. Surprisingly, the French did not make any aerial reconnaissance over the German left wing at the time.

5   Lintier, pp.226–228. For an account of the fighting as seen from the German side, see Dahlmann, pp.276–279 and pp.309–313. The latter is highly misleading since it falsely claims that Lepel's men were on the point of victory when their advance (and that of Quast) was called off.

6   Reichsarchiv, *Der Weltkrieg 1914 bis 1918*, Volume 4, p.256. Writing after the war, Koeppen suggested that Hentsch had over-reacted to the confusion behind the front line and that the actual situation was not as bad as he believed at the time.

7   Ibid, Volume 4, p.260.

8   Ibid, Volume 4, p.264. For Kuhl's account of Hentsch's visit, which must be treated with caution, see Kuhl 1930, pp.296–300.

9   Kluck later made the highly improbable claim that he was unaware of Hentsch's visit, despite the fact that Kuhl must have sought his approval for the decision to retreat. See Kluck, p.137.

10  Reichsarchiv, *Der Weltkrieg 1914 bis 1918*, Volume 4, p.266.

11  Edmonds 1996, pp.352–253.

12  For the reception of the retreat order on the right wing, see Reichsarchiv, *Der Weltkrieg 1914 bis 1918*, Volume 4, pp.274–274 and Kuhl 1930, pp.301–302. A final, despairing attempt was made to get the order rescinded, this time by the Grand Duke of Mecklenburg–Schwerin, who was attached to IX Corps Headquarters.

13  Richter, pp.135–139.

## 17: ANALYSIS

1   For the 1906 plan, see Ehlert et al, pp.410–411.

2   Ritter, pp.145–146.

3   Ibid, pp.156–157.

4   For what follows, see Van Creveld, pp.128–134, Kuhl and Bergmann, pp.61–64 and Reichsarchiv, *Der Weltkrieg 1914 bis 1918*, Volume 3, pp.334–339.

5   Tappen, pp.104–105. However, Müller-Loebnitz, who was one of Moltke's critics, later claimed that Groener, the Head of the Railways Department in the General Staff and

therefore well placed to know, believed that it could have been done without causing too much disruption. See Mombauer 2001, p.243.

6   Plessen's diary entry for 24 August, quoted in Mombauer 2001, p.247.

7   Reichsarchiv, *Der Weltkrieg 1914 bis 1918,* Volume 1, pp.608–609.

8   See Koeltz, *Le GQG Allemand et la Bataille de la Marne,* p.297.

9   In theory the Kaiser's presence at OHL was necessary because of his constitutional role of Supreme War Lord and Commander-in-Chief of the German Armies. In reality, however, he was a mere figurehead and there was no practical reason preventing OHL from separating from his Military Headquarters and moving to an advanced location closer to the front line.

10   Quoted in Hanotaux, *Histoire Illustrée de la Guerre de 1914,* Volume 8, pp.157–158.

11   The German Army had a long tradition of *Auftragstaktik* (mission command) according to which officers at all level were allowed considerable freedom of action in achieving the tactical goals that they were given. Kluck's attempts to outflank the enemy and cut off their retreat should be seen in this light.

12   Reichsarchiv, *Der Weltkrieg 1914 bis 1918,* Volume 1, pp.531–532.

13   Kluck, p.75. Whatever Sir John French might have intended, at this time the British were still in the line and were not heading towards the Channel coast.

14   Reichsarchiv, *Der Weltkrieg 1914 bis 1918,* Volume 3, p. 212.

15   Ibid, Volume 3, p.212 and p.239.

16   A way round the problem would have been to amalgamate the three right wing armies into an army group such as the one used for the invasion of France in 1940. The group commander's headquarters could have been a short distance to the rear of the three armies, keeping step with them as they advanced and linked to them via the wire network.

17   The differences between Kluck and Bülow might not have mattered quite so much if their respective Chiefs of Staff had possessed contrasting temperaments. However, 1st Army Chief of Staff, Kuhl, was just as aggressive and willing to take risks as was Kluck whereas 2nd Army Chief of Staff, Lauenstein, was ill, like Bülow, in his case suffering from a long-standing thyroid defect and associated heart problems which led to his death in the autumn of 1916.

18   Kluck, pp.41–42.

19   For criticism that Bülow's appeal for help to Hausen on 24 September prevented 3rd Army from reaching Fumet in time to cut off the French retreat, see Baumgarten-Crusius 1919, pp.38–44. Given the very difficult terrain down the eastern side of the Meuse, this would in any case have been a very difficult task.

20   Kuhl, p.149.

21   See van Creveld, p.126.

22   For casualties see Villate 1926 and also Dahlmann, pp.347–350, who gives the losses of those regiments which fought at the Ourcq together with their strengths at the end of the battle. The first replacement drafts did not arrive at the front until October.

23   For a table giving march distances and overnight locations, see Nau, pp.75–78. In an accompanying table on p.79, Nau also gives the casualties in his company for each day of the campaign, up to and including the fighting at Esternay. Of the 124 losses, 97 took place at Esternay.

24   Muller, p.111, gives a summary of the generals whom Joffre dismissed in the first few weeks of the war. Schmundt was also personally responsible for the disaster which engulfed the 10th Field Artillery Regiment at Flavigny-le-Grand on 28 August, the day before the battle of Guise. After they had unlimbered in an exposed position, according to his direct orders, they were hit by a tremendous barrage and lost more than half of their guns.

25   From *Notes by GQG on the Employment of Artillery.* Quoted in Spears, p.518.

26  For a vivid eyewitness account of Moltke's fragile state of mind at this time, see Mombauer 2001, p.265.

27  In his memoirs, Galliéni claimed that he, and not Joffre, was responsible for the 'Manoeuvre of the Marne', which led to the French victory. (Until 8 September, as Military Governor of Paris, charged with the defence of the city, he was in control of 6th Army and Joffre's orders to Maunoury had to pass through him.) From what has been said above, it should be clear that this claim was absolute nonsense. For an excellent analysis which convincingly refutes Galliéni's claims, see Lyet.

# POSTSCRIPT

1  From Valarché, Le Combat d'Arsimont, pp.96–97. Charlotte von Dassel was half German, half English. Her father, Walther von Richthofen, was the uncle of the famous German air ace, Manfred von Richthofen, known as the 'Red Baron', and also a relative of Generalleutnant von Richthofen who commanded I Cavalry Corps during the Marne campaign. Her mother, Jane Oakley, came from Forest Hill in south London. Charlotte was born in Denver, Colorado, after her parents had emigrated there in the 1870s, and died in Wehrheim, Germany, in 1982, aged 100. Her husband, Oberst Wilfried von Dassel probably served with Regiment Kaiser Franz at the time of the battle and cannot have been in command of Regiment Alexander as Valarché indicated. He is probably identifiable with the Oberst von Dassel who was later the commander of IR165, which belonged to the 7th Infantry Division in Sixt von Arnim's IV Corps. If this is the case, he would have been mortally wounded on 8 September in the battle of the Ourcq. This information comes from the entry on Walter von Richthofen by Trygve Has-Ellison on the website h-net.msu.edu (accessed 1 June 2011).

# BIBLIOGRAPHY

Anon., *Un Fantassin Français à Charleroi*, Amitiés Français de Charleroi, 1979

Argenlieu, Commandant Thierry d', *Le Troisième Corps d'Armée de la Sambre à la Marne*, École supérieure de Guerre, Cours d'Histoire Militaire, 1931–1932

Bartillat, Christian de, *La Marne, Bataille de Multien, 5–10 Séptembre 1914. Une tragédie en 5 jours*, Etrepilly, 1994

Baumgarten-Crusius, Artur, *Die Marneschlacht 1914, insbesondere auf der Front der deutschen dritten Armee*, Leipzig, 1919

Baumgarten-Crusius, Artur, *Le Haut Commandement allemand pendant la Campagne de la Marne*, Paris, 1924

Beau, Georges and Léopold Gaubusseau, *En Août 1914 Lanzerac a-t-il sauvé la France?* Paris, 1964

Belmont, Ferdinand, *A Crusader of France, Lettres d'un Officier de Chasseurs Alpins*, London, 1917

Bircher, Eugen, *Beiträge zur Erforschung der Schlacht an der Marne, Heft 1, Die Schlacht am Ourcq*, Bern, 1922

Bircher, Eugen, *Die Krisis in der Marneschlacht, Kämpfe der II and III deutschen Armee gegen die 5. and 9. französische Armee in den Marais de Saint Gond*, Frauenfeld, 1926

Biernatzki, Reinhart, *Als Pioneer in Frankreich*, Bielefeld and Leipzig, 1915

Bloem, Walter, *The Advance from Mons*, London, 1930

Bose, Thilo von, *Das Kaiser Alexander Garde-Grenadier-Regiment Nr. 1 im Weltkrieg*, Zeulenroda, n.d.

Bose, Thilo von, *Schlachten des Weltkrieges, Band 22, Das Marnedrama 1914, 1. Teil*, Oldenburg/Berlin, 1928

Bose, Thilo von, *Schlachten des Weltkrieges, Band 23, Das Marnedrama 1914, 2. Teil*, Oldenburg/Berlin, 1928

Bose, Thilo von, *Schlachten des Weltkrieges, Volume 24, Das Marnedrama 1914, 1. Abschnitt des 3 Teiles, Die Kämpfe des Gardekorps und des rechten Flügels der 3. Armee vom 5. bis 8. September*, Oldenburg/Berlin, 1928

Bose, Thilo von, *Schlachten des Weltkrieges, Band 25, Das Marnedrama 1914, 2. Abschnitt des 3 Teiles, Der Ausgang der Schlacht*, Oldenburg/Berlin, 1928

Boudon, Victor, *Avec Charles Péguy de Lorraine à la Marne*, Paris, 1916

Bourget, Pierre, *Fantassins de 14, de Pétain au Poilu*, Paris, 1964

Bucholz, Arden, *Moltke, Schlieffen and Prussian War Planning*, Oxford, 1991

Bujac, Colonel E., *Le XVIII Corps Français sur la Sambre 22–23–24 Août 1914*, Rochefort-Sur-Mer, 1924

Caix de Saint-Aymour, Comte de, *La Marche sur Paris de l'Aile droite Allemande*, Paris, 1916

# BIBLIOGRAPHY

Chamard, Elie, *La Bataille de Mondement,* Paris, 1939

Dahlmann, Rheinhold and Alfred Stenger, *Schlachten des Weltkrieges Band 26, Die Schlacht vor Paris, Das Marnedrama 1914, 4.Teil,* Oldenburg/Berlin, 1928

D'Estre, Henry, *D'Oran à Arras, Impressions de Guerre d'un Officier d'Afrique,* Paris, 1916

Dupont, Marcel, *En Campagne, Impressions d'un Officier de Légère,* Paris, 1916

Duvernoy, Max von (ed.), *Der deutsche Krieg in Feldpostbriefen, Band 5, der Marsch auf Paris,* Munich, 1916

Echevarria, Antonio J., *After Clausewitz, German Military Thinkers Before the Great War,* Kansas University Press, 2000

Edmonds, Brigadier-General J.E., (compiled), *Military Operations, France and Belgium 1914,* third revised edition, London, 1996

Ehlert, Hans; Michael Epkenhans and Gerhard, P. Gross (eds), *Der Schlieffenplan, Analysen und Dokumente,* Paderborn, 2006

Engerand, Fernand, *La Bataille de la Frontière (Août 1914) Briey,* Paris, 1920

Engerand, Fernand, *Le Secret de la Frontière, Charleroi,* Paris, 1918

Foley, Robert T., *Alfred von Schlieffen's Military Writings,* London, 2003

French, Field Marshal Viscount, *1914,* Boston and New York, 1919

Galliéni, Général, *Mémoires du Général Galliéni, Défense de Paris,* Paris, 1920

Gay, Georges, *La Bataille de Charleroi: Août 1914,* Paris, 1937

Ginsty, Paul and Capitaine Maurice Gagneur, *Histoire de la Guerre par les Combattants,* Paris, 1917

Le Goffic, Charles, *General Foch at the Marne,* London, 1918

Le Goffic, Charles, *Les Marais de Saint Gond (Histoire de l'Armeé Foch),* Paris, 1916

Grandmaison, Commandant de, *Dressage de l'Infanterie en Vue de Combat Offensif,* Paris, 1908

Grandmaison, Commandant de, *Deux Conferences. La Notion de Sureté et l'Engagement des Grandes Unités,* Paris, 1911

Grasset, Colonel A., *La Bataille des Deux Morins,* Paris, 1934

Grasset, Colonel A., *Les Marais de Saint Gond,* Paris, 1936

Hanotaux, Gabriel, *Histoire Illustrée de la Guerre, Volumes 1–11,* Paris, 1915–1920

Hanotaux, Gabriel, *L'Enigme de Charleroi,* Paris, 1917

Hanotaux, Gabriel, *La Bataille de la Marne,* Volumes 1 and 2, Paris, 1922

Hausen Colonel- Général Baron von, *Souvenirs de la Campagne de la Marne en 1914,* Paris, 1922

Herr, Général F.G., *L'Artillerie,* Paris, 1923

Héthay, J., *Le Rôle de la Cavalerie Française à l'Aile gauche de la Première Bataille de la Marne,* Paris, 1919

Heydemann, Kurt, *Schlachten des Weltkrieges, Band 7a, Die Schlacht bei St. Quentin 1914, 1st part, Der rechte Flügel der deutschen 2. Armee am 29 und 30 August,* Oldenburg/Berlin, 1924

Heydemann, Kurt, *Schlachten des Weltkrieges, Band 7b, Die Schlacht bei St. Quentin 1914, 2nd part, Garde und Hannoveraner vom 28. bis 30. August,* Oldenburg/Berlin, 1928

Horne, John and Alan Kramer, *German Atrocities 1914, a History of Denial,* Yale, 2001

Hurault de Ligny, Colonel, *La Division du Maroc aux Marais de Saint Gond,* Paris, 1933

Jacobson, Wojcieck, *En Marche sur Paris avec l'Armée prussienne du Général von Kluck,* Brussels, 1937

Joffre, Maréchal, *The Memoirs of Marshall Joffre* (translated by T. Bentley Mott), Volume 1, London, 1932

Juin, Maréchal, *La Brigade Marocaine à la Bataille de la Marne,* Paris, 1964

Kluck, General Alexander von, *The March on Paris and the Battle of the Marne 1914,* London, 1920

Koeltz, Louis, *D'Esternay aux Marais de Saint Gond,* Paris, 1930

Koeltz, Louis, *L'Armée von Kluck à la Bataille de la Marne,* Paris, 1931

Koeltz, Louis, *La Garde Allemande à la Bataille de Guise,* Paris, 1928

Koeltz, Louis, *Le GQG Allemand et la Bataille de la Marne,* Paris, 1931

Kuhl, General Hermann von, *La Campagne de la Marne en 1914* (translated by Commandant L. Koeltz), Paris, 1930

Kuhl, General Hermann von and General von Bergmann, *Movement and Supply of the German First Army during August and September 1914,* The Command and General Staff School Press, Fort Leavenworth, Kansas, 1929

Kutscher, Artur, *Kriegstagebuch*, Munich, 1915

Lanzerac, Général, *Le Plan de Campagne Français et le Premier Mois de la Guerre,* Paris, 1920

Larcher, Lieutenant-Colonel L, *Le 1er Corps à Dinant, Charleroi, Guise.* Paris, 1932

Lardemelle, Général de, *1914, le Redressement Initial,* Paris, 1935

Libermann, Henri, *Ce Qu'a Vu un Officier de Chasseurs à Pied,* Paris, 1916

Lintier, Paul, *My '75, Reminiscences of a Gunner of a 75mm Battery in 1914,* London, 1917

Lohrisch, Hermann, *Im Siegessturm von Lüttich an die Marne,* Leipzig, 1917

Lucas, Colonel, *Le 10e Corps à la Bataille de Charleroi,* Paris, 1930

Lyet, Capitaine, *Joffre et Galliéni à la Marne,* Paris, 1938

Marchand, A., *Plans de Concentration de 1871 à 1914,* Paris, 1926

Michel, Commandant R., *Un Combat de Rencontre, Monthyon, le 5 et 6 Séptembre à la 55e D.R.,* Paris, 1931

Ministère de la Guerre, Etat-Major de l'Armée-Service Historique, (ed.), *Les Armées Françaises dans la Grande Guerre, Tome 1, Volumes 1, 2 and 3, annexes to Volumes 1, 2 and 3,* Paris, 1932

Mombauer, Annika, *Helmuth von Moltke and the Origins of the First World War,* Cambridge, 2001

Muller, Commandant, *Joffre et la Marne,* Paris, 1931

Nau, Oberleutnant W., *Beiträge zur Geschichte des Regiments Hamburg, I, Der Marsch auf Paris,* Hamburg, 1924

Noce, Major Daniel, *Strategic Demolitions in Front of the German Right Wing, August-September, 1914,* US Army Engineer School, occasional papers No.72, The Command and General Staff College, Fort Leavenworth, Kansas, 1940

Palat, Général, *La Retraite sur la Seine,* Paris, 1920

Palat, Général, *La Victoire de la Marne,* Paris, 1920

Palat, Général, *Le Part de Foch dans la Victoire,* Paris, 1930

Percin, Général, *1914 Les Erreurs du Haut Commandement,* Paris, 1920

Porch, Douglas, *The March to the Marne. The French Army 1871–1914*, Cambridge, 1981

Poseck, von M., *Die deutsche Kavallerie in Belgien und Frankreich 1914,* Berlin, 1921

Pugens, Lieutenant-Colonel, *Deux Corps de Cavalerie l'Armée à la Bataille de la Marne,* Paris, 1934

Reichsarchiv (ed.), *Der Weltkrieg 1914 bis 1918,* Volumes 1 to 4, Berlin, 1925–1926.

Richter, Hermann, *Unter Kluck bis vor Paris und vor Soissons, Kriegserlebnisse eines Feldartilleristen,* Berlin, n.d.

Rieben, Dr von, *Kaiser Franz Garde-Grenadier-Regiment Nr.2,* Oldenburg/Berlin, 1929

Ritter, Gerhard, *The Schlieffen Plan, Critique of a Myth,* New York, 1958

Rouquerol, Gabriel, *Charleroi, Août 1914,* Paris, 1932

Rouquerol, Gabriel, *La Bataille de Guise,* Paris, n.d.

Rouquerol, Gabriel, *Le 3e Corps d'Armée de Charleroi à la Marne, essai de Psychologie militaire,* Paris, 1934

Roussel-Lépine, Josèphe, *Les Champs de l'Ourcq,* Etrepilly, 1982

Schlieffen, Alfred von, *Alfred von Schlieffen's Military Writings* (ed. and translated by Robert T. Foley), London, 2003

Selliers de Moranville, Lieutenant-Général de, *Du Haut de la Tour du Babel, Commentaire sur la Préparation à la Guerre et la Situation stratégique de la Belgique en 1914,* Paris, 1925

Schmitz, Chanoine Jean and Dom Norbert Nieuwland, *L'Invasion allemande dans les Provinces de Namur et de Luxembourg, Volume 3, Tamines et la Bataille de la Sambre,* Brussels, 1920

Schmitz, Chanoine Jean and Dom Norbert Nieuwland, *L'Invasion allemande dans les Provinces de Namur et de Luxembourg, Volume 4, Le Combat de Dinant, II, Le Sac de la Ville,* Brussels, 1922

Snyder, Jack, *The Ideology of the Offensive, Military Decision making and the Disasters of 1914,* Ithaca, 1984

Spears, Major General Sir Edward, *Liaison 1914, a Narrative of the Great Retreat,* London, 1930

Tardieu, André, *Avec Foch, Août–Novembre 1914,* Paris, 1939

Tepp, Max, *Im Siegessturm bis vor Paris! Bilder aus dem Vormarsch des Regiments Hamburg, August bis September 1914,* Köln, n.d.

Valarché, Colonel E., *La Bataille des Frontières,* Paris, 1932

Valarché, Colonel E., *La Bataille de Guise, les 28, 29 et 30 Août au 10e Corps d'Armée,* Paris, 1928

Valarché, Colonel E., *Le Combat d'Arsimont, les 21 et 22 Août à la 19e Division,* Paris, 1926

Valarché, Colonel E., *Le Combat du Petit Morin du 6 au 9 Séptembre au 10e Corps d'Armée,* Paris, 1929

Veaux, Georges, *En Suivant nos Soldats de l'Ouest,* Rennes, 1917

Villate, Capitaine Robert, *Foch à la Marne,* Paris, 1933

Vogel, Hofprediger Dr., *3000 Kilometer mit der Garde-Kavallerie,* Bielefeld and Leipzig, 1916

War Office, *Battle of the Marne 8th to 10th September 1914, Tour of the Battlefield,* London, 1935

Wirth, Alfred, *Von der Saale zur Aisne, Kriegstageblätter,* Leipzig, n.d.

Zuber, Terence, *Inventing the Schlieffen Plan,* Oxford, 2002

Zuber, Terence, *German War Planning 1891–1914, Sources and Interpretations,* Woodbridge Suffolk, 2004

# JOURNALS

Bülow, Karl von, 'Mon Rapport sur la Bataille de la Marne', *Documents Allemands sur la Bataille de la Marne* (translated by L Koeltz), Paris, 1930

Chamard, Elie, 'Le Combat de Mondement, Récit d'un Témoin', *Revue des deux Mondes,* Volume 22, 1934, pp.172–198

Doughty, Robert A., 'French Strategy in 1914: Joffre's Own', *The Journal of Military History,* Volume 67, April 2003, pp.427–454

Edmonds, Brigadier-General J.E., 'The Scapegoat of the Battle of the Marne, 1914. Lieut-Colonel Hentsch and the order for the German Retreat', *Army Quarterly,* Volume 1, No.2, January 1921, pp.346–358

Evans, Paul W., 'Strategic Signal Communications: a Study of Signal Communications as Applied to Large Field Forces, Based on the Operations of the German Signal Corps during the March on Paris in 1914', *Signal Corps Bulletin,* 82, (1935): pp.24–58

Foley, Robert T., 'The Origins of the Schlieffen Plan', *War in History,* Volume 10 (2), 2003, pp.222–232

Foley, Robert T., 'The Real Schlieffen Plan', *War in History,* Volume 13 (1), 2006, pp.91–115

Gontard, Generalleutnant von, 'Das Gefecht bei Auvelais am 21. und 22. August 1914', *Das Ehrenbuch der Garde; Die preussische Garde im Weltkrieg,* Eisenhart Rothe, E. von and, Dr Martin Lezius (ed), Volume 1, Berlin, n.d.

Gross, Gerhard, P., 'There was a Schlieffen Plan: New Sources on the History of German Military Planning', *War in History,* Volume 15 (4), 2008, pp.389–431

Holmes, Terence M., 'The Reluctant March on Paris: a Reply to Terence Zuber's "The Schlieffen Plan Reconsidered"', *War in History,* Volume 8 (2), 2001, pp.208–232.

House, Jonathan M., 'The Decisive Attack: a New Look at French Infantry Tactics on the Eve of World War I', *Military Affairs,* December 1976

Howard, Michael, 'Men against Fire: the Doctrine of the Offensive in 1914', Paret, Peter (ed.), *Makers of Modern Strategy, from Machiavelli to the Nuclear Age,* Princeton New Jersey, 1986

Mombauer, Annika, 'Of War Plans and War Guilt: The Debate Surrounding the Schlieffen Plan', *The Journal of Strategic Studies,* Volume 28, No.5, October 2005, pp.857–885

Muller-Loebnitz, Wilhelm, 'La Mission de Lieutenant-Colonel Hentsch du 8 au 10 Séptembre 1914, *Documents Allemands sur la Bataille de la Marne* (translated by L. Koeltz), Paris, 1930

Porch, Douglas, 'French War plans, 1914: The Balance of Power Paradox', *The Journal of Strategic Studies,* Volume 29, No.1, February 2006, pp.117–144

Tanenbaum, Jan Karl, 'French Estimates of Germany's Operational War Plans', *Knowing One's Enemies, Intelligence Assessment Before the Two World Wars,* (ed. Ernest R. May) Princeton, New Jersey, 1986

Tappen, Gerhard, 'Jusqu'à la Marne en 1914' *Documents Allemands sur la Bataille de la Marne* (translated by L Koeltz), Paris, 1930

Van Creveld, Martin, 'The Wheel that broke', *Supplying War, Logistics from Wallenstein to Patton,* Cambridge, 1977

Van Evera, Stephen, 'The Cult of the Offensive and the Origins of the First World war', *Military Strategy and the Origins of the First World War* (Steven Miller et al ed.), Princeton New Jersey, 1991

Villate, Capitaine Robert, 'L'Etat material des Armées allemandes en Août et Séptembre 1914' *Revue d'Histoire de la Guerre Mondiale,* (4) October 1926, pp.310–326

Williamson, Samuel R., 'French Strategy in Transition, 1905–1911', in *The Politics of Grand Strategy, Britain and France prepare for War,* London, 1990, pp.115–130

Williamson, Samuel R., 'Joffre Reshapes French Strategy', *The Politics of Grand Strategy, Britain and France prepare for War,* London, 1990, pp.205–226

Zoellner, Generalleutnant von, 'Schlieffens Vermächtnis', *Militärwissenschaftliche Rundschau, Sonderheft,* January 1938

Zuber, Terence, 'The Schlieffen Plan Reconsidered', *War in History,* Volume 6 (3), 1999, pp.262–305

# INDEX

# INDEX